Interpreting Company Reports For Dummies

CW00468940

Key Parts of an Annual Report

Annual reports can be daunting, and you may be relieved to know you don't actually need to scour every page of one. The following parts best serve to give you the big picture:

- **Chairman's statement:** A report from the chairman about progress during the preceding year and prospects for the future.
- **Operating review:** Sometimes called the *Operating and Financial Review* (or OFR), this is a report by the key directors of the main divisions of the company giving management's view on progress.
- **Directors' report and directors' remuneration report:** These reports give information required by the Companies Act and the Stock exchange.
- **Auditors' report:** A statement by the auditors regarding the findings of their audit of the company's books.
- **Financial statements:** These include the balance sheet, income statement, and the statement of cash flows.

Profitability Ratios

You can test a company's stock market reputation and money-making prowess using the following important formulas:

- *Price/earnings ratio* compares the price of a share to earnings per share. A ratio of 10 means that for every £1 in company earnings per share, people are willing to pay £10 per share to buy shares in the company.

  Price/earnings ratio = Share price ÷ Earnings per share

- *Dividend cover* shows the number of times profits 'cover' the dividend. So, if profits were 100 and the dividend payment was 25 then dividend cover would be 4 times. Use it to determine whether a company is paying out earnings as opposed to retaining them in the business to fund growth. You can also see how likely it is that the company will be able to maintain its dividend strategy in the future.

  Dividend cover = Earnings per share ÷ Annual dividends per share

- *Return on sales* tests how efficiently a company is running its operations by measuring the profit produced per pound of sales.

  Return on sales = Profit before taxation ÷ sales

- *Return on assets* shows you how well a company uses its assets. A high return on assets usually means the company is managing its assets well.

  Return on assets = Profit for the year ÷ Total assets

- *Return on equity* measures how well a company earned money for its investors.

  Return on equity = Profit for the year ÷ Shareholders' equity

- The *gross margin* gives you a picture of how much revenue is left after all the direct costs of producing and selling the product have been subtracted.

  Gross margin = Gross profit ÷ Sales or revenues

- The *operating margin* looks at how well a company controls costs, factoring in any expenses not directly related to the production and sales of a particular product.

  Operating margin = Operating profit ÷ Sales or revenues

Interpreting Company Reports For Dummies®

Cheat Sheet

Liquidity Ratios

If a company doesn't have cash on hand to cover its day-to-day operations, it's probably on shaky ground. Use the following formulas to find out whether a company has plenty of liquid (easily converted to cash) assets.

- *Current ratio* gives you a good idea whether a company will be able to pay any bills due over the next twelve months with assets it has on hand.

  Current ratio = Current assets ÷ Current liabilities

- *Quick ratio* or *acid test ratio* shows a company's ability to pay its bills using only cash on hand or cash already due from accounts receivable. It does not include money anticipated from the sale of inventory and the collection of the money from those sales.

  Quick ratio = Quick assets ÷ Current liabilities

- *Income gearing* lets you know whether a company is bringing in enough money to pay the interest on whatever outstanding debt it has.

  Income gearing = Interest paid ÷ operating profit

Cash Flow Formulas

Use the following formulas to make sure a company has plenty of cash to keep operating.

- *Free cash flow* shows you how much money a company earned from its operations that can actually be put in a savings account for future use.

  Free cash flow = Cash provided by operating activities − Net cash used in investing activities − Dividends paid − Interest paid − Tax paid

- *Cash return on sales* looks specifically at how much cash is being generated by sales.

  Cash return on sales = Cash provided by operating activities ÷ Sales

- *Current cash debt coverage ratio* lets you know whether a company has enough cash to meet its short-term needs.

  Current cash debt coverage ratio = Cash provided by operating activities ÷ Average current liabilities

- *Cash flow coverage ratio* finds out whether a company has enough money to cover its bills *and* finance growth.

  Cash flow coverage ratio = Cash flow from operating activities ÷ cash requirements

For Dummies: Bestselling Book Series for Beginners

Interpreting
Company Reports

FOR

DUMMIES®

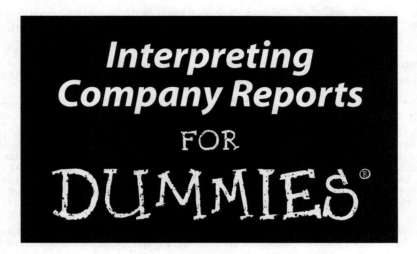

by Alan Bonham, Ken Langdon, and Lita Epstein

John Wiley & Sons, Ltd

Interpreting Company Reports For Dummies®

Published by
John Wiley & Sons, Ltd
The Atrium
Southern Gate
Chichester
West Sussex
PO19 8SQ
England

E-mail (for orders and customer service enquires): cs-books@wiley.co.uk

Visit our Home Page on www.wiley.com

For general information on our other products and services, please contact our Customer Care Department within the U.S. at 800-762-2974, outside the U.S. at 317-572-3993, or fax 317-572-4002.

For technical support, please visit www.wiley.com/techsupport.

Wiley also publishes its books in a variety of electronic formats. Some content that appears in print may not be available in electronic books.

British Library Cataloguing in Publication Data: A catalogue record for this book is available from the British Library

ISBN: 978-0-470-51906-6

Printed and bound in Great Britain by Bell & Bain Ltd., Glasgow

10 9 8 7 6 5 4 3 2 1

WILEY

About the Authors

Alan Bonham: Since qualifying as a Chartered Accountant, most of Alan's time has been spent training others. He was a Director at Anderson's Tutors Limited where he prepared students for ICAEW exams. From there, he joined Neville Russell where he became Training Manager. He then spent 16 years as a freelance lecturer and training consultant specialising in audit and accounting topics.

Most recently, Alan was Director of Training for SWAT Ltd. As part of his role, he was responsible for the development of SWAT's national programme of CPD training as well as presenting a number of courses himself. Alan had been Managing Director of Pentagon Training Ltd until the company was acquired by SWAT in October 2005.

Alan is now working again as a freelance lecturer – he is one of the few lecturers who can make auditing interesting. He also advises firms on their audit procedures and offers practical help in achieving compliance in a cost-effective manner. He has also worked with non-accountants, and is the co-author with Ken Langdon of *Smart Things to Know about Business Finance* which also demystifies the language of finance.

Ken Langdon: With a background in technology, Ken has been a trainer and consultant to many of the computer majors around the world. He has lectured in the USA, Australia, and all over the Far East and Europe.

In particular he has taught finance for non-financial managers and worked hard on explaining how the slightly esoteric world of finance reflects the real life world of businesses.

He is the author of a number of books on this and related topics.

Lita Epstein ran the financial accounting lab when she worked as a teaching assistant as she completed her MBA programme at Emory University's Goizueta Business School. After receiving her MBA, she managed finances for a small, non-profit organisation, and the facilities management section of a large medical clinic.

Now she enjoys helping people develop good financial, investing, and tax planning skills. She designs and teaches online courses on topics such as investing for retirement, getting ready for tax time, and finance and investing for women. She is the author of *Streetwise Crash Course MBA* and *Streetwise Retirement Planning* (Adams Media Corporation). Lita is the co-author of *Trading For Dummies* (Wiley), and *Teach Yourself Retirement Planning in 24 Hours* (Penguin Putnam).

Lita was the content director for a financial services Web site, MostChoice.com and managed the Web site Investing for Women. She also wrote TipWorld's Mutual Fund Tip of the Day in addition to columns about mutual fund trends for numerous Web sites. As a Congressional press secretary, Lita gained first-hand knowledge about how to work within and around the federal bureaucracy, which gives her great insight into how government programmes work. In the past, Lita has been a daily newspaper reporter, a magazine editor, and an associate director for development at The Carter Center.

For fun, Lita enjoys scuba diving and is certified as an underwater photographer. She hikes, canoes, and enjoys surfing the Web to find its hidden treasures.

Dedication

Alan and Ken: We would like to acknowledge the loyal support of our good friends Britney and Sol.

Lita: I would like to thank my father, Jerome Kirschbrown, an auditor and savings and loan examiner, who helped to hone my financial skills and taught me to be leery of what I see in financial reports.

Authors' Acknowledgements

Alan and Ken: We would like to thank our acquisitions editor, Samantha Spickernell, our development editor, Simon Bell, and the team at Wiley for the huge contribution they have made to this book. We would also like to thank our Technical Reviewer, Paul Gee of Smith & Williamson Solomon Hare LLP, for his help and suggestions.

Lita: I would like to thank all the people at Wiley who helped to make this book possible, especially my acquisitions editor, Stacy Kennedy, who first discussed this topic with me; my project editor, Traci Cumbay, who did a wonderful job of steering this book through the entire process and was always available to help me with any problems; and my copy editors, Michelle Dzurny and Trisha Strietelmeier, for their excellent work cleaning up the copy.

I also want to thank my agent, Jessica Faust, who finds all these great projects for me, and my outstanding technical editor, Shellie Moore, who helped keep all the technical accounting stuff accurate for this book. This is third time we've worked together on a book. And a special thank you to HG Wolpin who puts up with all my craziness as I rush to meet deadlines.

Publisher's Acknowledgements

We're proud of this book; please send us your comments through our Dummies online registration form located at www.dummies.com/register/.

Some of the people who helped bring this book to market include the following:

Acquisitions, Editorial, and Media Development

Acquisitions Editor: Samantha Spickernell

Development Editor: Simon Bell

Content Editor: Nicole Burnett

Developer: Kelly Ewing

Copy Editor: Martin Key

Proofreader: Christine Lea

Technical Reviewer: Paul Gee, Technical Director Smith & Williamson Solomon Hare LLP

Publisher: Jason Dunne

Assistant Production Manager: Daniel Mersey

Cover Photos: © PhotoAlto / Alamy

Cartoons: Ed McLachlan

Composition Services

Project Coordinator: Erin Smith

Layout and Graphics: Reuben W. Davis, Alissa D. Ellet, Melissa K. Jester, Christine Williams

Indexer: Claudia Bourbeau

Brand Reviewer: Janet Sims

Contents at a Glance

Introduction *1*

Part I: Getting Down to Financial Reporting Basics.........7
Chapter 1: Discovering What Reports Reveal...9
Chapter 2: Recognising Different Business Types...19
Chapter 3: Discovering How Company Structure Affects the Books.......................27
Chapter 4: Digging into Accounting Basics...43

Part II: Understanding Published
Information: Annual Reports...59
Chapter 5: Exploring the Anatomy of an Annual Report...61
Chapter 6: Balancing Assets Against Liabilities and Equity 77
Chapter 7: Using the Income Statement 95
Chapter 8: The Statement of Cash Flows...111
Chapter 9: Scouring the Notes to the Financial Statements 125
Chapter 10: Considering Consolidated Financial Statements...................................147

Part III: Analysing the Numbers 157
Chapter 11: Testing the Profits and Market Value...159
Chapter 12: Looking at Liquidity 179
Chapter 13: Making Sure the Company Has Cash to Carry On.................................189

Part IV: Understanding How Companies
Optimise Operations...203
Chapter 14: Using Basic Budgeting 205
Chapter 15: Turning Up Clues in Turnover and Assets 215
Chapter 16: Examining Cash Inflow and Outflow 227
Chapter 17: How Companies Keep the Cash Flowing...239

Part V: The Many Ways Companies
Answer to Stakeholders 247
Chapter 18: Finding Out How Companies Find Errors: The Auditing Process 249
Chapter 19: Checking Out the Analyst–Company Connection 259
Chapter 20: How Companies Soothe the Shareholders..271
Chapter 21: Keeping Score When Companies Play Games with Numbers.............283

Part VI: The Part of Tens 307

Chapter 22: Ten Financial Crises That Rocked the World..309
Chapter 23: Ten Signs That a Company's in Trouble...319
Chapter 24: Ten Top-Notch Online Resources..325

Part VII: Appendixes 331

Appendix A: Financial Statements..333
Appendix B: Glossary 349

Index 359

Table of Contents

Introduction *1*

   About This Book 2
   Conventions Used in This Book 2
   What You're Not to Read 3
   Foolish Assumptions 3
   How This Book Is Organised 4
      Part I: Getting Down to Financial Reporting Basics 4
      Part II: Understanding Published Information: Annual Reports 4
      Part III: Analysing the Numbers 4
      Part IV: Understanding How Companies Optimise Operations 5
      Part V: The Many Ways Companies Answer to Stakeholders 5
      Part VI: The Part of Tens 5
      Part VII: Appendixes 5
   Icons Used in This Book 6
   Where to Go from Here 6

Part 1: Getting Down to Financial Reporting Basics *7*

  Chapter 1: Discovering What Reports Reveal **9**
   Finding Out What Financial Reporting Is For 9
   Looking at Different Types of Reporting 11
      Keeping everyone informed 12
      Staying within the walls of the company: Internal reporting 13
      Preparing the reports 14
   Dissecting the Annual Report for Shareholders 15
   Understanding How the Number Crunchers Are Kept in Line 16

  Chapter 2: Recognising Different Business Types **19**
   Flying Solo: Sole Traders 19
      Keeping taxes personal 20
      Reviewing requirements for reporting 20
   Joining Forces: Partnerships 21
      Partnering up on taxes 21
      Meeting reporting requirements 21
   Shielding Your Assets: Public and Private Limited Companies 22
      Paying taxes the corporate way 23
      Getting familiar with reporting requirements 23

Seeking Protection with Limited Liability Partnerships 24
   Taking stock of taxes...24
   Reviewing reporting requirements 25

Chapter 3: Discovering How Company Structure Affects the Books .... .27
   Investigating Private Companies..27
      Checking out the benefits...28
      Defining disadvantages...29
      Figuring out reporting...30
   Understanding Public (Listed) Companies..33
      Meeting filing requirements 34
      Examining the perks...35
      Looking at the negative side 36
      Filing and more filing: Government and shareholder reports 37
   A Whole New World: How a Company Goes from Private to Public......39
      Teaming up with an investment banker 40
      Timetable for listing...41

Chapter 4: Digging into Accounting Basics 43
   Making Sense of the Accounting Method..43
      Cash-basis accounting 43
      Accrual accounting 44
      Why method matters 45
   Understanding Debits and Credits..46
      Double-entry bookkeeping...46
      Profit and loss statements...47
      The effect of debits and credits on sales 47
   Digging into Depreciation and Amortisation.....................................48
   Checking Out the Chart of Accounts..50
      Asset accounts..51
      Liability accounts 53
      Equity accounts 54
      Revenue accounts 55
      Expense accounts..56
   Differentiating Profit Types...57

Part II: Understanding Published Information: Annual Reports 59*

Chapter 5: Exploring the Anatomy of an Annual Report 61
   Meeting the Basic Parts of an Annual Report....................................61
   Everything but the Numbers 63
      Debunking the statements to shareholders................................63
      Making sense of the corporate message 64

Meeting the people in charge 64
Getting the real gen from management 64
Bringing the auditor's answers to light 69
Studying the standard auditor's report 69
Mulling over the modified auditor's report 70
Presenting the Financial Picture 73
Summarising the Financial Data..74
Finding the highlights 74
Reading the notes...75

Chapter 6: Balancing Assets against Liabilities and Equity 77
Understanding the Balance Equation..77
Introducing the Balance Sheet 78
Digging into dates...78
Nailing down the numbers 79
Comparing formats 80
Assessing Assets 82
Non-current assets 82
Current assets 85
Looking at Liabilities..88
Current liabilities 88
Net current assets 89
Non-current liabilities 90
Navigating the Equity Maze 91
Share capital..91
Other reserves 93
Retained earnings 93
Capital..93
Drawing..94

Chapter 7: Using the Income Statement 95
Introducing the Income Statement 96
Digging into dates...97
Comparing formats 97
Delving into the Tricky Business of Revenues 99
Defining revenue...100
Adjusting sales...101
Considering cost of sales 103
Gauging gross profit..104
Acknowledging Expenses 105
Sorting Out the Profit and Loss Types 107
EBITDA..107
Non-operating income or expense 108
Net profit or loss..109
Calculating Earnings Per Share 110

Chapter 8: The Statement of Cash Flows **111**

Digging into the Statement of Cash Flows......................................111
    The parts 112
    The sections of the cash flow statement using UK standards......113
    The formats 113
Checking Out Operating Activities 116
    Depreciation...116
    Inventory 117
    Accounts receivable...117
    Accounts payable 117
    The cash flow from activities section 118
Investigating Investing Activities 119
Understanding Financing Activities..120
    Issuing shares 120
    Buying back shares 121
    Paying dividends 121
    Incurring new debt 122
    Paying off debt 122
Recognising Special Line Items 122
    Discontinued operations..123
    Foreign currency exchange 123
Adding It All Up 123

Chapter 9: Scouring the Notes to the Financial Statements **125**

Deciphering the Small Print...126
Accounting Policies Note: Laying Out the Rules of the Road.................127
    Depreciation...128
    Revenue 128
    Expenses..129
Working Out Financial Borrowings and Other Liabilities 130
    Short-term borrowings 131
    Long-term borrowings 131
    Lease obligations...134
Accounting for Share-Based Payment: Something New in the
    Accountants' World..136
Mergers and Acquisitions: Noteworthy Information.............................137
Pondering Pension and Retirement Benefits 138
Breaking Down Business Breakdowns...140
Reviewing Significant Events 142
Finding the Red Flags...143
    Finding out about valuing assets and liabilities 144
    Considering changes in accounting policies 144
    Decoding obligations to pensioners and future pensioners.........145

Chapter 10: Considering Consolidated Financial Statements **147**

Getting a Grip on Consolidation...147
Looking at Methods of Buying Up Companies 150
Reading Consolidated Financial Statements 151
Looking to the Notes..153
    Mergers and acquisitions 154
    Goodwill...154
    Liquidations or discontinued operations..155

Part III: Analysing the Numbers 157

Chapter 11: Testing the Profits and Market Value **159**

The Price/Earnings Ratio 160
    Working out earnings per share 160
    Calculating the P/E ratio..161
    Practising the P/E ratio calculation 161
    Using the P/E ratio to judge company market value
       (share price)..163
    Understanding variation among ratios..164
Dividend Yield and Cover 166
    Determining dividend yield..166
    Digging into dividend cover 167
Return on Sales...169
    Figuring out ROS...170
    Reaching the truth about profits with ROS....................................171
Return on Assets 172
    Doing some dividing to get ROA...172
    Ranking companies with the help of ROA.......................................172
Return on Equity 173
    Calculating ROE 173
    Reacting to companies by understanding the ROE 174
The Big Three: Margins 175
    Dissecting gross margin...175
    Investigating operating margin...176
    Catching the leftover money: Calculating the net
       profit margin...177

Chapter 12: Looking at Liquidity **179**

Finding the Current Ratio..180
    Calculating the current ratio...180
    What do the numbers mean?..181

Determining the Quick Ratio 181
    Calculating the quick ratio 182
    What do the numbers mean? 182
Investigating Income Gearing 183
    Calculating historic income gearing 183
    What do the numbers mean? 184
Comparing Debt to Shareholders' Equity 184
    Calculating debt to shareholders' equity 185
    What do the numbers mean? 186
Determining Debt-to-Capital Ratio 186
    Calculating the ratio..186
    What do the numbers mean? 188

**Chapter 13: Making Sure the Company Has Cash to
Carry On 189**

Measuring Income Success...189
    Calculating free cash flow 190
    What do the numbers mean? 192
    Figuring out cash return on sales ratio 192
    What do the numbers mean? 193
Checking Out Debt 193
    Determining current cash-debt coverage ratio 194
    What do the numbers mean? 195
    Computing cash-debt coverage ratio...............................196
    What do the numbers mean? 198
Calculating Cash-Flow Coverage 198
    Finding out the cash-flow coverage ratio.......................198
    What do the numbers mean?...201

Part IV: Understanding How Companies Optimise Operations

....203

Chapter 14: Using Basic Budgeting 205

Peering Into the Budgeting Process..205
    Working out who does what 206
    Setting goals 207
Building Budgets 209
Providing Monthly Budget Reports 211
Using Internal Reports...213

Chapter 15: Turning Up Clues in Turnover and Assets 215

Exploring Inventory Valuation Methods 215
Applying Inventory Valuation Methods 219
    FIFO 219
    Average costing 220
    Comparing inventory methods and financial statements............220

Determining Inventory Turnover 221
    Calculating inventory turnover 221
    What do the numbers mean? 223
Investigating Tangible Fixed Assets Turnover 224
    Calculating fixed assets turnover...................................224
    What do the numbers mean? 225
Tracking Total Asset Turnover...225
    Calculating total asset turnover 225
    What do the numbers mean? 226

Chapter 16: Examining Cash Inflow and Outflow **227**

Assessing Trade-Receivable Turnover and Average
    Collection Period 227
    Calculating trade-receivable turnover 228
    What do the numbers mean? 230
Taking a Close Look at Customer Accounts 231
Finding the Accounts-Payable Turnover Ratio............................232
    Calculating the ratio...232
    What do the numbers mean? 233
Determining the Number of Days in Accounts-Payable Ratio 234
    Calculating the ratio...234
    What do the numbers mean? 235
Deciding Whether Discount Offers Make Good Financial Sense..........235
    For terms of 2/10 net 30..236
    For terms of 3/10 net 60..236
    What do the numbers mean? 237

Chapter 17: How Companies Keep the Cash Flowing **239**

Slowing Down Bill Payments..239
Collecting Accounts Receivables Faster 240
Borrowing on Receivables 242
Reducing Inventory...243
Getting Cash More Quickly 244

*Part V: The Many Ways Companies Answer
to Stakeholders* *247*

**Chapter 18: Finding Out How Companies Find Errors:
The Auditing Process** **249**

Meeting Mr or Ms Auditor...249
Delving Into the Auditing Process...251
    Gathering knowledge of the business.............................252
    Planning 253
    Performing fieldwork 254
    Creating an audit report 255

Filling the GAAP..256
Accounting standards: Four important qualities.......................257
Changing principles: More work for the IASB..........................258

Chapter 19: Checking Out the Analyst–Company Connection......259

Typecasting the Analysts..259
Buy-side analysts...260
Sell-side analysts...261
Independent analysts...264
Bond analysts...265
Regarding Bond Rating Agencies..265
Delving Into Share Rating...268
Looking at How Companies Talk to Analysts.............................269
Analyst briefings...269
Press releases...269
Road shows..270

Chapter 20: How Companies Soothe the Shareholders..........271

Knowing What to Expect from an Annual General Meeting..........272
Culling Information from the Annual General Meeting.................273
Listening between the lines..274
Looking towards the future..276
Checking Out How the Board Runs the Company.......................276
Speaking Out at Meetings: Proxy Votes.....................................278
Moving away from battling it out...279
Sorting through reports and proxy votes.............................280
Catching Up on Corporate Actions...280
Staying Up-to-Date Using Company Web Sites..........................282

Chapter 21: Keeping Score When Companies Play Games with Numbers......283

Getting to the Bottom of Creative Accounting...........................284
Defining the scope of the problem..285
Following recipes for cooked books.....................................285
Unearthing the Games Played with Earnings.............................287
Reading between the revenue lines.......................................288
Detecting creative revenue accounting................................292
Exploring Exploitations of Expenses...295
Advertising expenses..296
Research and development costs..296
Patents and licences...297
Asset impairment..297
Restructuring charges..299
Finding Funny Business in Assets and Liabilities.......................299
Recognising overstated assets...300
Looking for undervalued liabilities......................................302

Playing Detective with Cash Flow 304
Discontinued operations 304
Corporation tax paid...305

Part VI: The Part of Tens 307

Chapter 22: Ten Financial Crises That Rocked the World 309
Enron: Be Cautious of Explosive Growth 309
Adelphia and Hollinger: Be Wary of Lavish Lifestyles..............310
WorldCom/MCI: If It Looks too Good to Be True 311
Parmalat: Keep It Simple 312
Independent Insurance: Unreliable Info, Higher Risk.................313
Versailles: Don't Follow the Money-Go-Round 314
Barings Bank: Security, Accuracy, and Incompetence 314
Equitable Life: Spread Your Pension Bets....................................315
Robert Maxwell: Unfit to Lead...316
Northern Rock: Financial Problems Without Wrongdoing.........316

Chapter 23: Ten Signs That a Company's in Trouble 319
Lower Liquidity 319
Low Cash Flow..320
Disappearing Profit Margins 320
Revenue Game-Playing 321
Too Much Debt 321
Unrealistic Values for Assets and Liabilities................................322
A Change in Accounting Methods 322
Questionable Mergers and Acquisitions 323
Slow Inventory Turnover 324
Slow-Paying Customers 324

Chapter 24: Ten Top-Notch Online Resources 325
Companies House 325
IASB..326
Yahoo! Finance UK..326
Standard & Poor's 327
Biz/ed..327
Financial Times..327
Accounting Web: ICC 328
Find 328
Department of Business, Enterprise and Regulatory Reform 328
Reuters 329

Part VII: Appendixes..*331*

    Appendix A: Financial Statements *333*

    Appendix B: Glossary *349*

Index...*359*

Introduction

*W*hen you open an annual financial report today, one of the first things you ask yourself is, 'Can I believe the numbers that I'm seeing?' At one time no one doubted the numbers. Everyone believed that any corporate financial report, audited by a certified public accountant, was truly prepared with the public's interests in mind.

However, the financial scandals of the late 1990s and early 2000s destroyed public confidence in those numbers, including millions of investors who lost billions in the stock market crash that followed after many of those scandals came to light. Sure, a stock market bubble (a period of rising stock prices that stems from a buying frenzy) had burst, but financial reports that hid companies' financial problems fuelled the bubble and helped companies put on a bright, smiling face for the public. After these financial reporting scandals came to light, more than 400 public companies in the US alone had to restate their earnings.

Many people still wonder what government regulators and public accountants were thinking and doing during this entire fiasco. How did the system break down so dramatically and so quickly? Although a few voices raised the red flags, their pleas were drowned out by the euphoria of a building stock market bubble.

These financial scandals occurred partly because the City measures success based on a company's periodic results. Many in the City are more concerned about whether or not a company meets its short-term expectations than they are about a company's long-term prospects for future growth. Companies that fail to meet their expectations find their shares quickly beaten down on the market. To avoid the fall, companies 'massage' their numbers. And this short-sighted race to meet the numbers each period is a big reason why these scandals occurred in the first place.

Since the scandals broke, legislators and regulatory bodies have enacted new laws and regulations to attempt to correct the problems. In this book, we discuss these new regulations and show you how to read financial reports with an ounce of scepticism. We also give you a bunch of tools that can help you determine whether or not the numbers make sense. We help you see how companies can play games with their numbers and show you how to analyse the figures in a financial report so that you can determine the financial health of a company.

About This Book

In this book, you find detailed information about how to read the key financial statements – the balance sheet, the income statement, and the statement of cash flows – in a financial report as well as discover the other key parts of the report that you should scour. (Turn to Chapters 6, 7, and 8 to find out more about these important statements.)

Many people skim or skip over three crucial parts of annual reports – the auditor's report, the notes to the financial statements, and management's discussion and analysis. (See Chapters 5 and 9 for more info on these parts.) In fact, in these parts, you find most of the juiciest information. Unlike the fancy, glossy coloured pages that lead off the report and give only the information that a company *wants* you to know, these less graphically appealing black-and-white pages give the key data that you *need* to know.

Although we can't promise that you'll be able to detect every type of company problem or fraud, we can promise that your antennae will be up and you'll be more aware of how to spot possible problems. When you finish reading this book, you'll understand what makes up the parts of a financial statement and how to read between the lines, using the fine print to increase your understanding of a company's financial position. You'll find out about who regulates the companies and certifies the truth and fairness of financial reports and how the rules have changed since the corporate scandals broke.

Conventions Used in This Book

Our principle concern here is with public limited companies that you may choose to invest in. But we also include some information on different types of company, small as well as large. (To find out more about company types and structure, see Chapter 2.)

To help you practise the tools we show you in this book, we use the annual reports of two large retailers, Tesco and Marks and Spencer, and dissect their annual reports in various chapters throughout the book. We also include their financial statements in Appendix A so that you can practise with the actual reports. You can download a full copy of the reports by visiting the investor-relations section of the companies' Web sites: www.tesco.com and www.marksandspencer.com.

What You're Not to Read

Many of the topics discussed in this book are, by nature, technical. Dealing with finances can hardly be otherwise. But in some cases, we provide details that offer more than the basic stuff you need to know to understand the big picture. Because these explanations may not be up your alley, we mark them with a Technical Stuff icon (see the section 'Icons Used in This Book' later in this chapter) and invite you to skip them without even the slightest regret.

If you want, you can also skip over the sidebars (the grey shaded boxes) as these cover only example material or anecdotes. They're interesting to read through, but you won't miss the meat and veg by skipping them.

Even if you skip these items, you still get all the information you need. On the other hand, if you savour every financial detail or fancy yourself the bravest of all financial report readers, then dig in!

Foolish Assumptions

To write this book, we made some basic assumptions about who you are. We assume that you:

- ✔ Want to know more about the information in financial reports and how you can use it.
- ✔ Want to know the basics of financial reporting.
- ✔ Need to gather some analytical tools to more effectively use financial reports for your own investing or career goals.
- ✔ Need a better understanding of the financial reports that you receive from the company you work for to analyse the results of your department or division.
- ✔ Want to get a better handle on what goes into financial reports, how they're developed, and how to use the information to measure the financial success of your own company.

Both investors and company insiders who aren't familiar with the ins and outs of financial reports can benefit from the information and tools included in this book.

How This Book Is Organised

This book is organised into seven parts. After introducing the basics, we carefully dissect what goes into financial reports, giving you the tools you need to analyse those reports. We introduce you to the company outsiders who are involved in the financial reporting process and show you how to find red flags that might indicate deceptive or fraudulent reporting.

Part I: Getting Down to Financial Reporting Basics

Part I discusses the basics of accounting and financial reporting. If you need an introduction to these basics, or just a simple refresher course, you may want to begin here. In this part, you find information about the types of business structures, the differences between public and private companies, and the accounting basics necessary to understand financial reports.

Part II: Understanding Published Information: Annual Reports

This part introduces you to the key elements of an annual financial report. The first chapter in this part reviews the key sections of an annual report; the chapters that follow focus on each of these parts individually, explaining what you'll find in a financial report and how to use that information. Another chapter explains in more detail what you can expect to find in the notes to the financial statements and what all that small print means. In the last chapter of this part, we discuss consolidated statements and the information that goes into them.

Part III: Analysing the Numbers

In this part, we give you the tools you need to analyse the numbers in financial statements. We show you how to test profitability, liquidity, and cash flow. These tools help you determine whether or not the company is a good investment.

Part IV: Understanding How Companies Optimise Operations

This part focuses on using financial statements to measure how efficiently management is using its resources. We review the basics of budgeting and how to use financial reports in the budgeting process. You also find tools for testing how efficiently companies manage their assets and keep cash flowing.

Part V: The Many Ways Companies Answer to Stakeholders

In this part, we focus on the outsiders involved in the financial reporting process. We review the role of auditors and the accounting rules and look at the role analysts play in the world of financial reporting. We also talk about shareholders and what they should expect from the companies that they invest in. In addition, we discuss how some companies 'massage' the numbers when they compile their financial reports.

Part VI: The Part of Tens

In the *Part of Tens,* we give you quick-reference lists pointing out the top-ten online resources you can use to do your financial research about companies and the top-ten signs that indicate that a company is in financial trouble. We also outline some of the juicier financial reporting scandals of the past several years.

Part VII: Appendixes

Appendix A includes two actual financial reports from the retailers Tesco and Marks and Spencer. We refer to these reports throughout the text. Appendix A also contains the results of the analysis carried out in the chapters. And, because much of the language of financial reporting may be new to you, we include a glossary in Appendix B.

Icons Used in This Book

Throughout the book, we use icons to flag parts of the text that you'll want to notice. Here's a list of the icons and what they mean.

This icon points out ideas for improving your financial report reading skills. In these paragraphs, you find useful financial resources, too.

This icon highlights information you definitely want to remember.

This icon points out a critical piece of information that can help you identify the dangers and perils in financial reports. We also use this icon to emphasise information you definitely don't want to skip or skim when reading a financial report.

This icon highlights information that may explain the numbers in more detail than you care to know. Don't worry – you can skip these points without missing the big picture!

Throughout the book, we give examples from financial reports of real companies, particularly Tesco and Marks and Spencer, whose reports are featured in Appendix A of this book. We highlight these examples with the icon you see here.

From time-to-time we use this icon to show you differences in nomenclature or systems that apply to small companies after text in which we have discussed their equivalent big brother companies. In this context, when we use the term *small company,* we are referring to companies that are not listed on the stock market.

Where to Go from Here

You can start reading anywhere in this book, but if you're totally new to financial reports, start with Part I so you can get a good handle on the basics before delving into the financial information. If you already know the basics, turn to Part II to start dissecting the parts of a financial report. If you're ready to get started on the road to analysing the numbers, turn to Part III. If your priority is tools for optimising company operation, you might want to start in Part IV. Those of you who want to know more about company outsiders involved in the financial reporting process may want to start at Part V.

Part I

Getting Down to Financial Reporting Basics

'It's Company Financial Report time
again and we really need a hero – come in.'

Part I

Getting Down
to Financial
Reporting Basics

In this part . . .

If you're a complete novice to the world of financial reports, this part gives you the background you need to understand this complex world, which has a language and rules of its own. In this part, we discuss the key types of financial reports, both internal and external, as well as what you should expect to find in those reports. We also explore different types of business structures and talk about the differences between a public and a private company. Finally, we review the accounting basics you need to understand in order to read financial reports.

Chapter 1

Discovering What Reports Reveal

In This Chapter

▶ Reviewing the importance of financial reports

▶ Exploring the different types of financial reporting

▶ Discovering the key financial statements

*F*inancial reports give a snapshot of a company's worth at the end of a particular period, as well as a view of the company's operations and whether it made a profit. In the modern business world it's unthinkable that public, and some would say private, limited companies do not give the public some way to gauge their financial performance. Many stakeholders depend on this information.

Right now, nothing could possibly replace financial reports. Nothing could be substituted that'd give investors, financial institutions, and government agencies the information they need to make decisions about a company. And without financial reports, the people who work for a company wouldn't know how to make the company more efficient and profitable because they wouldn't have a summary of its financial activities during previous business periods. These financial summaries help companies look at their successes and failures, and help them make plans for future improvements.

This chapter introduces you to the many facets of financial reports and how internal and external stakeholders use them to evaluate a company's financial health.

Finding Out What Financial Reporting Is For

Financial reporting gives readers a summary of what happened in a company based purely on the numbers. The numbers that tell the tale include the following:

✔ **Assets:** The cash, amounts receivable from customers, stock awaiting sale, investments, buildings, land, tools, equipment, vehicles, copyrights, patents, and any other items needed to run a business that the company owns or has the use of.

✔ **Liabilities:** Money a company owes to outsiders, such as loans and unpaid bills.

✔ **Equity:** Shareholders' money invested in the company.

✔ **Sales:** Products or services sold to customers.

✔ **Costs and expenses:** Money spent to operate the business, such as money used for production, employee remuneration, and costs of operating the buildings and factories and supplies to run the offices.

✔ **Profit or loss:** The amount by which the revenue from sales exceeds (or is less than) the costs and expenses.

✔ **Cash flow:** The amount of money that flowed into and out of the business during the time period being reported.

Without financial reporting, nobody would have any idea where a company stands financially. Sure, the managers of the company would know how much money the company had in its bank accounts but even they wouldn't know how much is still due to come in from customers, how much inventory is being held in the warehouse and on the shelf, how much the company owes, or what the company owns. As an investor, if you don't know those details, you can't make an objective decision about whether the company is making money and whether it's worth investing in the future of the company.

Many people rely on the information companies present in financial reports. Here are some key groups of readers and why they need accurate information:

✔ **Executives and managers:** They need information to know how well the company is doing financially and to get information about problem areas so they can make changes to improve the company's performance.

✔ **Employees:** Employees need to know how well they're meeting or exceeding their goals and to know where they need to improve. For example, if a salesperson has to make £30,000 in sales every month, they need a financial report at the end of each month to gauge how well they did in meeting that goal. If they believe that they met their goal, but the financial report doesn't show that they did, they'd have to provide details to defend their level of productivity. Most salespeople are paid according to the level of their sales. Without financial reports, there would be nothing to base their bonuses on.

Employees also make career and pension decisions based on financial reports released by the company. If a company's financial reports are misleading or false, employees could lose most, if not all, of their pensions and their long-term financial futures could be at risk.

✔ **Creditors:** Suppliers need to understand a company's financial results to determine whether they should supply goods and services to the company. Banks and other lenders need to decide whether to risk lending more money to the company and to find out whether the company is meeting the minimum requirements of any existing loans. To find out how companies meet creditors' requirements, see Chapters 9 and 12.

If a company's financial reports are false or misleading, banks might lend money at an interest rate that doesn't truly reflect the risks being taken. They could miss out on a better opportunity because they trusted the information released in the financial reports.

✔ **Investors:** Investors need information to judge whether or not the company is a good investment. If investors think that a company is on a growth path because of the financial information it reports, but those reports turn out to be false, investors can make large losses. They may buy shares at inflated prices, risking the loss of capital as the truth comes out or missing out on better investment opportunities.

✔ **Government agencies:** These agencies need to be sure that the company is complying with regulations. They also need to be satisfied that the company is accurately informing the public about its financial position.

✔ **Analysts:** Analysts need information to develop analytical reviews for clients who are considering the company for investment or additional loans.

✔ **Financial reporters:** Financial reporters need to provide accurate coverage about a company's operations to the general public. Their commentaries help investors to be aware of the critical financial issues facing a company and any changes the company makes in its operations.

✔ **Competitors:** Every company's top people read the financial reports of their competitors. If these reports are based on false numbers, it distorts the financial playing field. A well-run company could make a bad decision to keep up with the false numbers of a competitor and end up reducing its own profitability.

Looking at Different Types of Reporting

Under UK company law, every company must prepare accounts for shareholders and file information on the public record at Companies House.

Small private companies will usually prepare one set of accounts for their shareholders but will file a simplified set of accounts known as abbreviated accounts at Companies House. In most cases, neither of these sets of accounts will need to be audited.

Medium-sized private companies require to have their accounts audited. Some minor concessions, to make things simpler, are available for the set of accounts which are filed.

Larger private companies receive no concessions.

Public limited companies, or PLCs, are not necessarily listed on the stock market. A PLC has the right to issue shares to the public but does not necessarily have to exercise that right. All PLCs are subject to more detailed reporting requirements than private companies but, except for listed entities, the extra requirements are minor.

There are three markets for trading shares in the UK. The full market is subject to very detailed listing rules which are considered briefly below and in more detail in Chapter 3. AIM (Alternative Investment Market) provides a lighter touch for companies seeking a listing for the first time. As AIM companies grow, they may progress to the full market. The third market is known as the Plus market (formerly OFEX) which exists to permit arranged (matched) deals between buyers and sellers as distinct from the open market dealings in shares for companies on the AIM or full markets.

All public companies and private companies (other than small private companies) require an audit by a firm of registered auditors which are firms of accountants regulated by the various professional bodies. More details about auditors and the audit are included in Chapter 18.

Keeping everyone informed

One big change to a company's operations after it decides to sell shares to the public is that the company must report publicly on a regular basis to its shareholders and the major financial institutions that help fund their operations through loans or bonds. As well as an annual report, listed companies in the UK currently need to produce the following:

- ✔ Interim reports (currently at the 6 month stage).
- ✔ Preliminary announcements (these are advance notices of the profit and other key information which will appear in the annual accounts).
- ✔ Notification of material events such as indications that the profit is going to fall significantly short of the previously announced expectations. These notifications would also include other matters such as proposed take overs, mergers, and so on.
- ✔ Notification of major changes in shareholdings.

Most major companies put a lot of money into producing glossy reports filled with information and pictures to make a good impression on the public. The marketing or public relations department, rather than the financial or accounting departments, writes much of the summary information. Too often, annual reports are puff pieces that carefully hide any negative information in the *notes to the financial statements,* which is the section that offers additional detail about the figures provided in those statements (see Chapter 9). Find out how to read between the lines – especially the tiny print at the back of the report – to get some critical information about the accounting methods used, any pending lawsuits, or other information that could negatively impact results in the future.

You can access reports filed with Companies House online at the Companies House Web site www.companieshouse.gov.uk.

Staying within the walls of the company: Internal reporting

Not all the finance department's reporting is done for public consumption. In fact, companies usually produce many more internal reports than external ones to keep management informed. Companies can design their internal reports in whatever way makes sense to their operations.

These internal reports help managers to:

- ✔ Find out which of the business's operations are producing a profit and which are operating at a loss.
- ✔ Determine which departments or divisions should receive additional resources to encourage growth.
- ✔ Identify unsuccessful departments or divisions and make needed changes to turn the troubled section around or, for example, kill a project.
- ✔ Determine the staff and inventory level they need to respond to customer demand.
- ✔ Review customer accounts to identify slow-paying or non-paying customers in order to devise the best collection methods and to develop guidelines for when a customer should be cut off from future orders.
- ✔ Prepare production schedules and review production levels.

Each department head usually receives a report from the top managers showing the department's expenses and revenues, sometimes called sales or turnover, and whether it's meeting its budget. If the department's numbers vary significantly from budget, the report indicates red flags. The department head usually needs to investigate the differences, or variations on budget, and report what the department is doing to correct any problems. Even if the difference is increased revenue (which can be good news), the manager still needs to know why the difference exists because an error in the data input may have occurred. We talk more about reports and budgeting in Chapter 14.

Reports on inventory are critical not only for managing the products in hand, but also for knowing when to order more inventory. We talk more about inventory controls and financial reporting in Chapter 15.

Tracking cash is vital to the day-to-day operations of any company. Some large companies actually provide cash reporting to their managers daily. The frequency of a company's reporting depends on the volatility of its cash status. The more volatile the cash, the more the company needs frequent reporting to make sure that it has cash in hand to pay its bills. We talk more about cash reporting in Chapters 16 and 17; Chapter 16 focuses on incoming cash, and Chapter 17 deals with outgoing cash.

These are just a few of the many uses companies have for their internal financial reports. The list is endless and is limited only by the imaginations of the executives and managers who want to find ways to use the numbers to make better business decisions. We talk more about using internal reports to optimise results in Chapters 14, 15, and 16.

Preparing the reports

The finance department is the key source of financial reports. This department is responsible for monitoring the numbers and putting together the reports. The numbers are the products of a process called *double-entry bookkeeping*, which requires a company to record resources and the assets it used to get those resources. For example, if you buy a chair you must spend another asset probably cash. An entry in the double-entry system would show both sides of that transaction. The cash account would be reduced by the cost of the chair and the furniture account value would be increased by the cost of that chair.

This crucial method of accounting gives companies the ability to record and track business activity in a standardised way. The principles of double-entry bookkeeping have stood the test of time, remaining unchanged for centuries but accounting standards are constantly updated to reflect the business environment as financial transactions become more complex. To find out more about double-entry bookkeeping, turn to Chapter 4.

Dissecting the Annual Report for Shareholders

The annual report gives more detail about the company's business and financial activities than any other report. This report is primarily for shareholders, although any member of the general public can request a copy or look at it online. Glossy pictures and graphics fill the front of the report, highlighting what the company wants you to know. After that, you find the full details about the company's business and financial operations.

The annual report is broken into the following parts (We summarise the key points of each of these parts in Chapter 5):

- ✔ **Mission statement:** Many companies put their statement of intent, or their mission statement, on the front cover, or in a key position on the first page. This succinct statement explains the company's key vision and strategy.

- ✔ **Financial highlights:** The inside cover and first page normally contain the company's view of their financial performance last year compared to the year before. This comparison is interesting, but carefully selected, information.

- ✔ **The chairman's statement:** This is always a key description of the intentions of the company. Whilst predicting what will be in any particular statement is impossible, in this section the chairman is expected to pick out the critical issues in the recent past and in the future.

- ✔ **Reports of the chief executive and directors:** These reports contain a number of matters required by law as well as describing the principal activities of the company.

  A recent development in the directors' report now requires the directors to state that they are not aware of any information of which the auditors are unaware (Yes! That is exactly what it says). A review of the business, including financial and non-financial key performance indicators, is also required to be included in the directors' report as a substitute for the information which would have been required in the OFR (see below).

- ✔ **Review of operations – also known as the operating and financial review (OFR):** This section has always been an important voluntary statement from which we can derive the company's strategy. The detection of the overall strategy should not be too difficult.

  Recently, the government got in a right pickle when it decided to make the OFR compulsory but then changed its mind soon after in order to cut red tape. In the meantime the Accounting Standards Board had written rules for the OFR and many companies had done so much work in gathering the necessary information that they went ahead and published their OFR's on a voluntary basis!

- ✔ **Directors' responsibilities:** This section covers a number of issues including the responsibilities of the directors in relation to the publishing of financial information.

- ✔ **Auditors report:** This statement is also nearly a standard with few particular variations. It's here to record the fact that the auditors have done their job, how they did the job, and what their considered opinion is of the prepared accounts.

- ✔ **The financial statement:** For those who want to know how well the company has done financially, the financial statement is the most critical part of the annual report as it includes the balance sheet, the income statement (also known as the profit and loss account), and the cash-flow statement.

  - The *balance sheet* gives a snapshot of a company's financial condition. On a balance sheet, you find assets, liabilities, and equity. The balance sheet got its name because the total assets must equal the total liabilities plus total equity (which in itself is a liability of the company). For more on the balance sheet, see Chapter 6.

  - The *income statement,* also known as the *profit and loss account* (P&L), gets the most attention from investors. This statement shows a summary of the financial activities of an entire year or any other period. Many companies prepare income statements on a monthly basis for internal use. Investors always focus on the exciting parts of the statement: sales revenue, net income, and earnings per share. To find out more about the information you can find in an income statement, go to Chapter 7.

  - The *cash-flow statement* is relatively new to the financial reporting game. The Accounting Standards Board didn't require companies to publish it with the other financial reports until 1991 – previous to that there was a requirement for a rather convoluted document known as the 'Source and Application of Funds'. Basically, the cash-flow statement is similar to the income statement in that it reports a company's performance over time. But instead of focusing on profit or loss, it focuses on how cash flowed through the business. This statement has three sections: cash from operations, cash from investing, and cash from financing. We talk more about the statement of cash flows in Chapter 8.

Understanding How the Number Crunchers Are Kept in Line

Every public company's internal accounting team, as well as its external auditors, must answer to government. The primary government entity responsible for overseeing corporate reporting and making sure that reporting is accurate is the Financial Reporting Council (FRC). Reports filed with Companies House may be reviewed by the Financial Reporting Review Panel which is a subsidiary body of the FRC. The Review Panel will also investigate complaints from members of the public concerning financial reports.

Another subsidiary body of the FRC is the Accounting Standards Board (ASB) which, as its name suggests, is responsible for setting accounting standards in the UK. The ASB's power has been reduced in recent years since UK listed companies are now required to prepare their consolidated accounts in accordance with International Accounting Standards as adopted by the European Community. There is much more about this regulatory hiatus in Chapter 18.

Finally, auditors of listed companies are visited by the Audit Inspection Unit – yet another public body answerable to the FRC. We now have the answer to the question 'Who audits the auditors?'

Financial statements filed at Companies House must adhere to Generally Accepted Accounting Principles (GAAP). To meet the demands of these rules, financial reporting must be understandable, relevant, reliable, and comparable with the financial reports of other similar entities. To find out more about GAAP, turn to Chapter 18.

You may wonder why so many accounting scandals have hit the front pages of newspapers around the country for the past few years with GAAP in place. Filing statements according to GAAP rules has become a game for many companies. Unfortunately, investors and regulators find that companies don't always engage in transactions for the economic benefit of the shareholders but to make their reports look better and to meet the expectations of the City. Many times, companies look financially stronger than they actually are. For example, as scandals have come to light, companies have been found to overstate income, equity, and cash flows while understating debt. We talk more about reporting problems in Chapter 21.

Chapter 2

Recognising Different Business Types

In This Chapter

▶ Exploring sole traders

▶ Taking a look at partnerships

▶ Figuring out the advantages of limited liability partnerships

▶ Discovering the differences between types of limited companies

All businesses need to prepare key financial statements, but some businesses can make less formal statements than others can. The way in which a business is legally organised greatly impacts on the way it must report to the public and the depth of that reporting. For a small business, financial reporting is needed only to monitor the success or failure of operations. But as the business grows, and more and more outsiders such as investors and creditors become involved, financial reporting becomes more formalised until the company reaches the point where audited financial statements are required.

Each business structure also follows a specific set of rules about what financial information the business must file with government agencies. In this chapter, we review the basics about how each type of business structure is organised, how taxation differs, what must be filed, and what types of financial reports are required.

Flying Solo: Sole Traders

The simplest business structure is the *sole trader* – a business owned and run by an individual. Most new businesses with only one owner start out as sole traders. Some never grow into anything larger. Others start adding partners and staff and may realise that incorporating is a wise decision for legal purposes. (Check out 'Seeking Protection with Limited Liability Partnerships' and 'Shielding Your Assets: Public and Private Limited Companies' later in this chapter to find out more about incorporating.)

Anyone who wants to start a business as a sole trader must inform Her Majesty's Revenue and Customs (HMRC) within three months. Weekly National Insurance Contributions (NICs) will need to be paid and, at the end of the tax year, the sole trader completes a self-assessment tax return. If turnover is expected to exceed the threshold for Value Added Tax (VAT) (currently £64,000 per annum), then VAT registration is also required.

The biggest risk for a sole trader is that the business isn't a separate legal entity. All debts or claims against the business are filed against the sole trader's personal property. If you are the owner of a sole tradership and are sued, then insurance is the only form of protection against losing everything you own.

Keeping taxes personal

Sole traders aren't taxable entities, and sole traders don't have to fill out separate tax forms for their businesses. Instead, sole traders simply add the self-employment forms about the business entity to their personal tax returns, and this is the only financial reporting they must do.

Sole traders will pay weekly National Insurance Contributions (NICs). NICs are fixed in amount (currently £2.20 per week) and are known as Class 2 National Insurance Contributions. If the trader's annual profits exceed a set amount (currently £5,225), then additional contributions known as Class 4 Contributions will be payable. These are calculated from the self-assessment tax return and collected along with income tax.

Reviewing requirements for reporting

Financial reporting requirements don't exist for sole traders. However, if they want to seek funding from outside sources, such as a bank, then the lender is likely to demand financial information. The lender is likely to need a statement of assets and liabilities and a basic profit and loss statement. Depending on the size of the loan, a sole trader may even have to submit a formal business plan stating goals, objectives, and implementation plans.

Even though financial reports aren't required for a sole trader who isn't seeking outside funding, completing periodic profit and loss statements lets you keep tabs on how well the business is doing and helps you find any problems before they become too huge to fix. These reports don't have to adhere to formal Generally Accepted Accounting Principles (GAAP; see Chapter 18), but honesty is the best policy. The only person being fooled is you if you decide to make your financial condition look better on paper.

Joining Forces: Partnerships

Any business started by more than one person is a *partnership*. The partners share the risks and rewards of being in business but, because more than one person is involved, the business set-up is more complicated than that of a sole trader. Partners have the same requirement to inform HMRC as the sole trader. A useful online interactive tool exists which you can access from the HMRC Web site to identify what you need to do when starting a business. See www.hmrc.gov.uk. Partners have to sort out the following legal issues:

- ✔ How they will divide profits.
- ✔ How they can sell the business.
- ✔ What happens if one of the partners becomes sick or dies.
- ✔ How the partnership will dissolve if one of the partners wants out.

Because of the number of options, a partnership is the most flexible business structure for a business that involves more than one person. But to avoid future problems that can destroy an otherwise successful business, partners should decide on all these issues before opening their business's doors.

The biggest risk for a partnership is that all the partners are jointly liable for the debts of the partnership and so are equally responsible for paying off the whole debt. If your partners disappear, you can end up picking up the entire tab.

Partnering up on taxes

Partnerships aren't taxable entities. Partners are self-employed in exactly the same way as sole traders. Therefore, they will each pay Class 2 and Class 4 NICs. Each individual partner must report their share of the partnership profit in their personal tax return.

Meeting reporting requirements

Similar to the sole trader, a partnership does not have to present its financial reports in any special way because it doesn't have to satisfy anyone but the partners. Partnerships do need reports to monitor the success or failure of business operations, but they don't have to be completed to meet GAAP standards (see Chapter 18). Usually, when more than one person is involved, the partners decide among themselves what type of financial reporting is required and who is responsible for preparing those reports.

Shielding Your Assets: Public and Private Limited Companies

Business owners seeking the greatest level of protection may choose to incorporate their businesses as limited companies. The courts have clearly determined that limited companies are separate legal entities, and their owners are protected from claims filed against the company's activities. An owner (shareholder) in a company can't get sued because of actions taken by the company.

Two types of limited company structure exist:

- ✔ **Private companies:** Whilst there is no limit to the number of shareholders in a private company, there will normally be just a handful. Typically, the private company is owned by a small number of people who are all involved in the day-to-day management of the business.

- ✔ **Public companies (PLCs):** A company that wishes to offer shares to the public must register as a PLC. All companies listed on the stock exchange are PLCs, but some owner-managed companies are also PLCs. That is, a company does not have to issue shares to the public just because it's a PLC.

Before incorporating, the first thing a business must do is form a board of directors, even if that board includes spouses and grown-up children on the board. (In a new rule brought in by the Companies Act 2006, directors must be at least 16 years of age.) Boards can be made up of both owners and non-owners. In private companies, the shareholders and directors are likely to be one and the same people but, as a company grows bigger, it often needs to raise money from outsiders.

Before incorporating, a company must also decide how many shares each of the shareholders will have. Private companies aren't allowed to sell their shares on an open exchange. Even selling shares privately to friends and investors may fall foul of the strict rules that exist in this area.

A limited company's veil of protection makes a powerful case in favour of incorporating. However, certain obligations come with incorporating, and the required legal and accounting services can be costly. Many businesses don't incorporate and choose instead to stay as sole traders or partnerships to avoid these additional costs.

When a company is first set up, its constitution is laid down in its Memorandum and Articles, which must be placed on public record at Companies House. Model Articles exist, and they can be adopted by any new company. The Articles set out the rules for the internal management of the company and cover matters such as rights of shareholders, rules for transfer of shares, rules for conducting meetings, and the appointment and removal of directors.

Paying taxes the corporate way

Limited companies are separate tax entities, so they must file tax returns and pay taxes or try to find ways to reduce them by using deductions.

You sometimes hear that company profits are taxed twice – once through the corporate entity and once as dividends paid to its owners. This is not true. If the shareholder is a basic rate tax payer then there is no further tax to pay when he receives his dividends. A higher rate tax payer will pay the extra tax – as is right and just!

Getting familiar with reporting requirements

Public reporting is achieved by placing records on file at Companies House. All companies must file an Annual Return giving:

- ✔ The address of the company's registered office
- ✔ The type of company it is and its principal business activities
- ✔ Details about the directors and company secretary
- ✔ A statement of capital
- ✔ Details about names and addresses of the members (shareholders) of the company

Companies must also keep Companies House informed about a range of matters such as a change in the directors or the Articles of the company or if a charge is given over the assets of the company.

Companies must also file a copy of their Financial Statements drawn up in accordance with the rules appropriate for their business. (For more details, see Chapter 3.)

The records at Companies House are available to be searched by the public. The easiest way to do this is to log on to the Companies House Web site www.companieshouse.gov.uk. Basic details of registered address and nature of business are available free of charge. Alternatively for a small fee, you can get copies of the Annual Return and/or the latest financial statements. While most of this information is available from the Investor Relations pages of the Web sites of large companies, Companies House is the only source of this information when dealing with smaller companies.

Seeking Protection with Limited Liability Partnerships

A partnership or sole proprietorship can limit its liability by using an entity called a *limited liability partnership,* or LLP. This business form actually falls somewhere between a limited company and a partnership or sole trader in terms of protection by the law. (For more on these business forms, see the sections earlier in this chapter.)

LLPs are quite a new business vehicle in the UK. Created by the Limited Liability Partnerships Act 2000, LLPs are growing rapidly in popularity. LLPs have a number of the benefits of the limited company – the partners (or, more properly, the members) are taxed in the same way as the partners in a partnership.

The benefits of the LLP stem from the fact that it is a separate legal entity; the LLP is treated like a single person. It can enter into contracts and hold property and continues in existence despite a change of membership, such as through the death of a member. A third party enters into a contract with the LLP rather than with an individual member. By contrast, in a partnership, the third party contracts with a partner as principal and on behalf of the other partners.

The upshot of this is that, in the traditional partnership, negligent advice by an individual partner will result in all the partners suffering their share of the loss arising from a court action – even to the extent that they can lose their homes and personal possessions. In the LLP, the members who were not party to the giving of the advice are protected. It is the LLP itself which will be sued – although the individual member who gave the negligent advice can still suffer an action under the law of tort.

Taking stock of taxes

LLPs have their cake and eat it, too: They get the same legal protection from liability as a limited company, but don't have to pay corporate taxes. In fact, HMRC treats LLPs as partnerships. (See the earlier section 'Shielding Your Assets: Public and Private Limited Companies' for more on these topics.)

Reviewing reporting requirements

Reporting requirements for LLPs are broadly similar to those of limited companies with some slight differences in the format of the main performance statements. LLPs classified as small enjoy the same exemptions as limited companies. We cover these matters in more detail in Chapter 3.

To shield themselves from liability, many large legal and accounting firms incorporate as LLPs rather than as limited companies.

Chapter 3

Discovering How Company Structure Affects the Books

In This Chapter

▶ Looking at the private side of business

▶ Investigating the public world of corporations

▶ Examining what happens when a company decides to go public

*N*ot every company wants to be under public scrutiny. Although some companies operate in the public arena by selling shares to the general public on the open market, others prefer to keep ownership within a closed circle of friends or investors. When company owners contemplate whether to keep their business private or to take it public, they're making a decision that can permanently change the company's direction.

In this chapter, we explain the differences between public and private companies, the advantages and disadvantages of each, and how the decision about whether to go public or stay private impacts on a company's financial reporting requirements. We also describe the process involved when company owners decide to make their company public.

A company that wishes to offer shares to the public must register as a PLC – a public limited company to give it its full title. All companies listed on the stock exchange are PLCs, but some owner-managed companies are also PLCs.

Many people use the term *public company* as a shorthand way of saying that the company is listed on the stock exchange. As a result, we also use that shorthand description in this chapter.

Investigating Private Companies

Private companies are not allowed to sell shares to the general public, so they don't have to worry about the reporting requirements that face the public company. A private company gives owners the freedom to make choices for the company without having to worry about outside investors' opinions. Of course, to maintain that freedom, the company must be able to raise the funds necessary for the business to grow – through profits, debt funding, or investments from family and friends.

However, private companies do have to place information on the public record at Companies House (refer to Chapter 2). When it comes to reporting financial performance, the extent of information required depends on the size of the company. See the section 'Figuring out reporting,' later in this chapter.

Checking out the benefits

Private companies maintain absolute control over company operations. With absolute control, owners don't have to worry about what the public thinks about its operations or the need to satisfy the City's profit watch. The company's owners are the only ones who worry about profit levels and whether the company is meeting its goals, which they can do in the privacy of a boardroom.

Keeping it in the family

You don't have to go public to go global. The Virgin Group of companies, one of the most recognised brands in Britain, is pretty much a global brand despite being a private company. The Virgin Group has been involved in planes, trains, finance, soft drinks, music, mobile phones, holidays, wines, publishing, space tourism, cosmetics, and probably a lot more by the time you read this. Virgin has more than 200 companies worldwide, employs over 35,000 people, and boasts total revenues measured in many billions of pounds.

Virgin's strategy, or rather that of its owner Richard Branson, is that the company stands for 'Value for money, quality, innovation, fun, and a sense of competitive challenge'. Like most entrepreneurial companies, Virgin is very customer-oriented. It does its homework before going into a new enterprise, looking at the industry from the customer's viewpoint and

asking the simple question 'How can we do this better?'

Virgin is an example of a company that has gone to the public market and found it not to its liking. Virgin Group – comprising its music, retail, property, and communications businesses – was floated on the stock exchange in 1986 (the airline and travel businesses, in contrast, remained privately owned). The stock witnessed limited capital growth after the launch date and, like the equity market as a whole, suffered in the stock market crash of 1987. Richard Branson also expressed disappointment with the short-term expectations of equity analysts and fund managers. This dissatisfaction culminated in the decision in 1988 to make the company private again through a management buy-out at precisely the same price at the launch in 1986.

Further advantages of private ownership include:

- ✔ **Confidentiality:** Private companies can limit the amount of information that they must file to the minimum laid down by law. Competitors can take advantage of the information disclosed by public companies. Private companies can leave their competitors guessing and even hide a short-term problem because they do not need to place information on record until several months after the end of the financial year affected.

- ✔ **Flexibility:** In private companies, family members can easily decide how much to pay one another, whether to allow private loans to one another, and whether to award lucrative fringe benefits or other financial incentives without having to worry about shareholder scrutiny. Public companies must answer to their shareholders for any bonuses or other incentives given to top executives. In a private company owners can take out whatever money they want without worrying about the best interests of outside stakeholders. Any disagreements the owners have about how they disperse their private company's assets remain behind closed doors.

- ✔ **Greater financial freedom:** Private companies can carefully select how to raise money for the company and whom to make financial arrangements with. After public companies offer their shares in the public markets, they have no control over who buys their shares and becomes a future owner.

Defining disadvantages

The biggest disadvantage a private company faces is its limited ability to raise large sums of cash. Because a private company doesn't sell shares or offer bonds to the general public, it spends a lot more time finding investors or creditors who are willing to risk their funds. And many investors don't want to invest in a company that's controlled by a small group of people without some sort of guarantee or control – such as a seat on the board. If a private company needs cash, it must perform one or more of the following tasks:

- ✔ Arrange for a loan with a financial institution.

- ✔ Sell additional shares to existing owners.

- ✔ Ask for help from an *angel,* a private investor willing to help a small business get started with some upfront cash.

- ✔ Get funds from a *venture capitalist,* which is someone who invests in start-up businesses, providing the necessary cash in exchange for some portion of ownership.

These options for raising money may present a problem for a private company because:

- ✔ **A company's borrowing capability is limited and based on how much capital the owners have invested in the company.** A financial institution may well require that a certain portion of the capital needed to operate the business – sometimes as high as 50 per cent – comes from the owners. Just like when you want to borrow money to buy a home, the bank requires you to put up some cash before it will lend you the rest. The same is true for companies that want a business loan. We talk more about this topic and how to calculate debt to equity ratios in Chapter 12.

- ✔ **Persuading outside investors to put up a significant amount of cash if the owners want to maintain control of the company is no mean feat.** Often, major outside investors seek a greater role in company operations by acquiring a significant share of the ownership and asking for seats on the board of directors.

- ✔ **Finding the right investment partner can be difficult.** When private-company owners seek outside investors, they must be careful that the potential investors have the same vision and goals for the company that the owners do.

Another major disadvantage that a private company faces is that the owners' net worth is likely to be tied almost completely to the value of the company. If a company fails, the owners may lose everything and may possibly even be left with a huge debt. If owners take their company public, however, they can sell some of their shares and diversify their portfolios, reducing the risk in their personal portfolios.

Figuring out reporting

Reporting requirements for a private company vary based on its size. The reporting requirements for a large private company are very similar to those which apply to an unlisted PLC.

Private companies will soon be required to file a copy of their financial statements at Companies House within nine months of the end of the financial year. (This was ten months until the change brought in by the Companies Act 2006 which will become effective during 2009.) The PLC will have to file the financial statements within six months of the year-end (previously seven months).

The financial statements consist of:

- ✔ Directors' Report – which includes a review of the business and a description of how the business uses financial instruments as well as a host of other interesting data such as donations to charities and political parties. In simple terms, the term financial instrument refers to any contract between the company and an outsider which is described in financial (that is, money) terms. Examples range from bank deposits, bank loans, trade receivables, and so on, through leases to more complicated contracts such as interest rate swaps or forward exchange contracts.

- ✔ Auditor's Report – which expresses an independent opinion on the truth and fairness of the accounts and is signed by an independent registered auditor.

- ✔ Profit and Loss Account – formatted in accordance with the Companies Act rather than the International Standards.

- ✔ Balance Sheet – also formatted in accordance with the Companies Act rather than the International Standards.

- ✔ Cash-Flow Statement – this is not a Companies Act requirement but was introduced into UK accounting by FRS 1 in the early 1990s.

- ✔ Notes to the accounts – to pick up the mass of other disclosure requirements laid down in the Companies Act and UK accounting standards.

Note that small companies (as defined by the Companies Act) are exempt from the requirement to prepare a cash-flow statement and can produce a simplified Directors' Report.

Medium-sized companies

Medium-sized companies are given very few concessions compared with larger private companies. In the past, they would not need to disclose turnover in their filed accounts nor would they need to prepare group accounts. Both of these concessions are in the process of being removed by the Companies Act 2006.

With respect to any financial year, a company satisfies the size criteria to be medium-sized if two out of the three following conditions are met:

- ✔ Turnover is not more than £22.8 million.
- ✔ Gross assets (fixed assets plus current assets) are not more than £11.4 million.
- ✔ Number of employees is not more than 250.

To qualify as a medium-sized company, the company must usually satisfy the conditions in two consecutive years. Further, a company is ineligible to be medium-sized if it is a PLC or if it is involved in financial services or if it is a member of a group containing an ineligible company.

The financial limits increase at regular intervals and another increase is expected to take effect in 2008.

Small companies

This is one of the few times in this book when the small company icon carries its literal meaning. The definition is similar to that for the medium-sized company. With respect to any financial year, a company satisfies the size criteria to be small if two out of the three following conditions are met:

- Turnover is not more than £5.6 million.
- Gross assets (that is, fixed assets plus current assets) are not more than £2.8 million.
- Number of employees is not more than 50.

The limits for turnover and balance sheet increase at regular intervals and another increase is expected to take effect in 2008.

Again, the company must usually satisfy the conditions in two consecutive years and the company is ineligible to be small if it is a PLC or a member of a group containing an ineligible company. The restrictions concerning ineligibility of financial services entities are less restrictive for the small company definition.

Being a small company is good news on the filing front. The small company doesn't need to have an audit and can file abbreviated accounts which don't contain a directors' report or profit and loss account. The balance sheet in the filed accounts is much the same as any other private company but the notes are restricted to details about accounting policies, share capital and debentures, fixed assets, transactions with directors, and details of loans.

Although small companies may file abbreviated accounts, they must still issue full accounts to their shareholders – although these accounts are simplified when compared with medium-sized or larger companies. Small companies are entitled to follow the Financial Reporting Standard for Small Entities (FRSSE) which is a cut-down version of full UK GAAP. All Companies Act requirements are included in the FRSSE as are almost all of the rules regarding the way that items are measured in accounts. Where the small company benefits is that the FRSSE omits a lot of the detail which larger companies have to include in the notes to the accounts.

A multitude of partners

One company is neither a public nor private limited company despite having a turnover of over £6 billion. The founder of the John Lewis Partnership, John Spedan Lewis, wanted to create a company that combined a staff-friendly environment with a commercial edge that would allow it to move quickly and stay ahead in a competitive industry. All 68,000 permanent staff are Partners owning 26 John Lewis department stores, 183 Waitrose supermarkets, an online and catalogue business, and more. Its constitution is a democratic one giving every Partner a voice in the business they co-own – an unusual combination of commercial acumen and corporate conscience. Partners share in the benefits and profits of a business that is dedicated to putting them first.

Understanding Public (Listed) Companies

A company that offers shares on the open market is a *public* or *listed company*. Public-company owners don't make decisions based solely on their preferences. They must always consider the opinion of the company's outside investors.

In the UK, there are three markets where shares can be traded:

- **London Stock Exchange – Main Market:** This is the market for the established company. It has the most onerous requirements as concerns standards of corporate governance and reporting. For the rest of this chapter, whenever we refer to public companies, we mean companies listed on the Main Market.

- **London Stock Exchange – Alternative Investment Market (AIM):** AIM offers all the benefits of being traded but within a regulatory environment designed specifically for smaller companies. There are no minimum criteria covering size, track record, or number of shares which need to be available to the public. A company wishing to join AIM must appoint a nominated advisor (Nomad) from a list of such advisors approved by the market. The Nomad will ensure that the company is suitable for AIM and ready to be admitted to a public market. AIM is seen as the best market for the smaller but growing company.

> ✔ **PLUS:** Plus Markets Group (PMG) is an independent provider of primary and secondary market services and currently trades over 850 small and mid-capitalised company shares. To be traded on PLUS, the company may already be listed on AIM or the Main Market – in which case, the PLUS market offers an alternative trading platform offering greater market exposure, Alternatively, the company may float on PLUS and therefore be traded on PLUS. The key difference from trading on the London Stock Exchange is that buying and selling shares on PLUS is supported by a quote-driven equity trading system. Market makers will quote the price at which they are prepared to deal and this is then transmitted to the market. Deals can then be executed immediately. Competing market makers should improve the prices that can be obtained and offer improved liquidity in shares that might otherwise be difficult to trade on the other markets.

Meeting filing requirements

Before a company goes public, it must meet certain criteria. Generally, investment bankers (who are actually responsible for selling the stock) require that a private company generates at least £10–20 million in annual sales, with profits of about £1 million. (Exceptions to this rule exist, however, and some smaller companies do go public.)

Before going public, company owners must ask themselves the following questions:

> ✔ Can my company maintain a high growth rate to attract investors?
>
> ✔ Does enough public awareness of my company and its products or services exist to make a successful public offering?
>
> ✔ Is my company operating in a hot industry that will help attract investors?
>
> ✔ Can my company perform as well as, and preferably better than, its competition?
>
> ✔ Can my company afford the ongoing cost of financial reporting and auditing requirements?

If company owners are confident in their answers to these questions, they may want to take their company public. But they need to keep in mind the advantages and disadvantages of going public. Going public is a long, expensive process that takes months, or even years.

Companies don't take themselves public alone. They hire investment bankers to steer the process to completion. Investment bankers usually get multimillion-pound fees or commissions for taking a company public. We talk more about the process in the upcoming section 'A Whole New World: How a Company Goes from Private to Public'.

REAL WORLD EXAMPLE

Going public, losing jobs

Public company founders who don't keep their investors happy can find themselves out on the street and no longer involved in the company that they started. Steve Jobs and Steve Wozniak, who started Apple Computer, found out the hard way that selling shares on the public market can ultimately take the company away from the founders.

Jobs and Wozniak became multimillionaires after Apple Computer went public, but shareholders ousted them from their leadership roles in a management shake-up in 1984 following an industry-wide sales slump towards the end of 1984 and Wozniak decided to leave Apple soon after the shake-up. Apple's new CEO announced that he couldn't find a role for Steve Jobs in the company's operations in 1985.

Interestingly, Steve Jobs ended up as the head of Apple again in 1998, when the shareholders turned to him to try to rescue the company from failure. He has since engineered a comeback for Apple.

Examining the perks

If a company goes public, the primary benefit is that it gains access to additional capital (more cash), which can be critical if it's a high-growth company that needs money to take advantage of its growth potential. A secondary benefit is that company owners can become millionaires, or even billionaires, overnight if the initial public offering (IPO) is successful. When Google announced its decision to go public, initial news reports indicated that the IPO was expected to net $2.7 billion for the company and its small circle of investors.

Being a public company has a number of other benefits:

- ✔ **New corporate cash:** At some point, a growing company usually maxes out its ability to borrow funds, and it must find people willing to invest in the company. Selling shares to the general public can be a great way for a company to raise cash without being obligated to pay interest on the money.

- ✔ **Owner diversification:** People who start a new business typically put a good chunk of their assets into starting the business and reinvest most of the profits earned in the business in order to grow the company. Frequently, founders have a large share of their assets tied up in the company. Selling shares publicly allows owners to take out some of their investment and diversify their holdings in other investments, which reduces the risks to their personal portfolios.

✔ **Increased liquidity:** *Liquidity* is a company's ability to quickly turn an asset to cash if it isn't already cash. People who own shares in a closely held private company may have a lot of assets but little chance to actually turn those assets into cash. Selling privately owned shares is very difficult. Going public gives the shares a set market value and creates more potential buyers for the shares.

✔ **Company value:** Company owners benefit by knowing their company's worth for a number of reasons. If one of the key owners dies, a value must be placed on the company for inheritance tax purposes. If these values are set too high for private companies, this can cause all kinds of problems for other owners and family members. Going public sets an absolute value for the shares held by all company shareholders and prevents problems with valuation. Also, companies that want to offer shares to their employees as incentives find that recruiting with this incentive is much easier when the shares are traded on the open market.

Looking at the negative side

Regardless of the many advantages of being a public company, a great many disadvantages also exist:

✔ **Costs:** Paying the costs of providing financial statements that meet the appropriate requirements can be very expensive. Investor relations can also add significant costs in employee time, printing, and mailing expenses.

✔ **Control:** After the shares are traded on the open market, it would be unusual for the original owners and investors to retain enough shares to keep absolute control of the company. As shares sell on the open market, more and more shareholders enter the picture, giving each one the right to vote on key company decisions.

✔ **Disclosure:** Competitors can access detailed information about a public company's operations by getting copies of the required public financial reports. Although a private company can hide difficulties it may be having, a public company must report its problems, exposing any weaknesses to competitors. In addition, the net worth of a public company's owners is widely known because their holdings of stock must be disclosed as part of these reports.

✔ **Cash control:** In a private company, the owner's salary and benefits – as well as the salary and benefits of any family member or friend involved in running the company – can be decided on by the owner independently. In a public company, the remuneration committee – usually made up of non-executive directors – has to approve and report salary and other benefits of the directors. Public companies are not permitted to give loans to directors or their families.

✔ **Lack of liquidity:** When a company goes public, a constant flow of buyers for the shares isn't guaranteed. In order for a share to be liquid, a shareholder must be able to convert shares into cash. Small companies that don't have wide distribution of their shares can find that selling them on the open market is difficult. The market price may even be lower than the actual value of the company's assets because of a lack of competition for shares. When not enough competition exists, shareholders have a hard time selling their shares and converting them to cash, making the investment non-liquid.

A failed IPO or failure to live up to shareholders' expectations can change what may have been a good business for the founders into a bankrupt entity. Although founders may be willing to ride the losses for a while, shareholders rarely are. Many IPOs that raised millions before the Internet stock crash in 2000 are now defunct companies.

Filing and more filing: Government and shareholder reports

Just as private companies must file their financial statements at Companies House (see the section 'Investigating Private Companies', earlier in this chapter), public companies must fulfil the same requirements.

For public companies that are not listed there are only a few additional requirements when compared with private companies. However, listed public companies have to provide a lot more information to their shareholders and the market. The requirements vary somewhat between the three markets but the key continuing obligations of companies listed on the Main Market can be summarised as follows:

✔ The company must comply with the Combined Code on Corporate Governance – or explain why they do not. The Combined Code is so called because it is based on the recommendations over the years of a number of committees starting with the Cadbury Committee in 1992. It is now produced and monitored by the Financial Reporting Council (FRC) and includes requirements such as:

  • The chairman should not also be the chief executive.

  • Non-executive directors should be appointed so that a balanced board is achieved.

  • Directors' remunerations should be set by a remuneration committee consisting of non-executive directors.

  • The board should maintain a sound system of control to safeguard shareholders' investments and the company's assets.

✔ An audit committee should be established consisting of non-executive directors.

✔ The company must publish:

  • Interim statements – currently at the half-year stage. Interim statements should contain the main financial statements – balance sheet, summarised income statement, cash-flow statement, statement of

TECHNICAL STUFF

The Sarbanes-Oxley Act

The Sarbanes-Oxley Act is a bill passed by Congress in the US in 2002 in the wake of various corporate scandals such as Enron and Tyco. This bill affects any UK company with a listing in the US. It has added significant costs to the entire process of completing financial reports, affecting the following components:

✔ **Documentation:** Companies must document and develop policies and procedures relating to their internal controls over financial reporting. Although an outside accounting firm can assist with the documentation process, management must be actively involved in the process of assessing internal controls. They can't delegate this responsibility to an external firm.

✔ **Audit fees:** Independent audit firms now look a lot more closely at the financial statements and the internal controls in place over financial reporting, and the Securities and Exchange Commission (SEC) and the Public Company Accounting Oversight Board (PCAOB) now regulate the accounting profession in the US. The PCAOB inspect accounting firms annually to be sure that they're in compliance with the Sarbanes-Oxley Act and SEC rules. These inspections have increased audit fees substantially.

✔ **Legal fees:** Because companies need lawyers to help them comply with the new provisions of the Sarbanes-Oxley Act, their legal expenses are increasing.

✔ **Information technology:** Complying with the Sarbanes-Oxley Act requires both hardware and software upgrades to meet the internal control requirements and the speedier reporting requirements.

✔ **Board of directors:** Most companies must restructure their board of directors and audit committees to meet the requirements of the Sarbanes-Oxley Act, ensuring that independent board members control key audit decisions. The structure and operation of nominating and compensation committees must eliminate even the appearance of conflicts of interest. Companies must make provisions to give shareholders direct input in corporate governance decisions. Companies also must provide additional education to board members to be sure that they understand their responsibilities to shareholders.

The rules imposed by Sarbanes-Oxley may be such a significant burden on small companies in the US that a number of them may decide to buy out shareholders and make the companies private again, merge with larger companies, or even liquidate. If a private company is considering the possibility of going public, it may decide that the process isn't worth the costs.

As regards UK companies, they may decide to de-list from the US stock exchange to avoid the need to comply with Sarbanes-Oxley.

changes in equity – and a commentary on the results. Interim statements do not need to be audited. The Transparency Directive, which has recently been introduced into UK law adds new requirements for quarterly statements.

- Annual report and accounts – which are covered in great detail in chapters 5 to 10 of this book. Prior shareholder approval must be obtained for Class 1 transactions – these occur if the company acquires or disposes of a major asset (such as a subsidiary company) where the amounts involved exceed 25 per cent of a range of financial indicators. Prior approval is also required for certain employee share schemes.

✔ Shareholders must be informed of Class 2 and Class 3 transactions which are similar to Class 1 but where the amounts involved are less.

✔ The company must comply with the Model Code which is part of the FSA's listing rules. The Model Code lays down the rules concerning when directors and others can deal in the company's shares. These rules are designed to stop *insider dealing*. Insider dealing is the name given to the situation where an individual, being aware of inside information which if it were known to the public at large would affect the share price of the company, uses that information to gain an unfair advantage over other investors.

✔ Directors must notify the company of dealings in the company's shares and these must be reported to the market as soon as possible.

✔ Shareholders owning more than 3 per cent of the shares of the company must notify the company of that fact and this must be reported to the market.

In addition to regular reports, public companies must inform the market of any major events that could have a significant impact on the financial position of the company. A major event may be the acquisition of another company, the sale of a company or division, bankruptcy, the resignation of directors, or a change in the financial year.

A Whole New World: How a Company Goes from Private to Public

So a company has finally decided to sell its stock publicly. Now what? In this section we describe the role of an investment banker in helping a company sell its stock. We also explain the timetable for listing.

A company must be a PLC before it can become a listed company. To convert a private limited company into a public limited company is fairly straightforward:

1. Shareholder approval needs to be obtained.

2. The issued share capital of the company must be at least £50,000 – although only a quarter of this needs to be paid up.

3. The most recent accounts of the company must show that the capital has not been eroded by losses.

4. When all the documents have been delivered to the registrar then the company's name is changed to end with those three special letters – PLC.

Teaming up with an investment banker

A major step for a company deciding to go public is to choose who will handle the sales and which market to sell the stock on. Few firms have the capacity to approach the public stock markets on their own. Instead, they hire an investment banker or other advisor to help them through the complicated process of going public. A well-known investment banker can help lend credibility to a little-known small company, which makes selling the stock easier.

Investment bankers help a company in the following ways:

- ✔ **They prepare the required documents and the prospectus for the sale of shares.** There are very detailed requirements as to the contents of the prospectus. It will include, for example, information about the company (its products, services, and markets) and its officers and directors. Additionally, information must be given about the risks the company faces; how the company plans to use the money raised; any outstanding legal problems; holdings of company insiders; and, of course, audited financial statements.

- ✔ **They price the shares to be attractive to potential investors.** If the shares are priced too high, the offering could fall flat on its face, with few shares sold. If priced too low, the company could miss out on potential cash that investors, who buy IPO shares, can get as a windfall from quickly turning around and selling the shares at a profit.

- ✔ **They negotiate the price at which the shares will be offered to the general public and the guarantees the investment banker will give to the company owners for selling the stock.** An investment banker can give an *underwriting guarantee,* which guarantees the amount of money that will be raised. In this scenario, the banker buys the shares from the company and then resells them to the public. Usually, an investment banker puts together a syndicate of investment bankers that helps find buyers for the stock.

Another method that's sometimes used is called a *best efforts agreement*. In this scenario, the investment banker tries to sell the stock but doesn't guarantee the number of shares that will sell.

- ✔ **They decide which stock exchange to list the stock on.** The Main Market has the highest level of requirements. If a company wants to list on this exchange, it must normally have a minimum market capitalisation of £700,000, at least 25 per cent of the shares must be in public hands and it would normally have at least a three-year trading record. AIM and PLUS have lower requirements.

Responsibility for the approval of prospectuses and admission of companies to the official list lies with the UK Listing Authority (UKLA) which is a division of the Financial Services Authority (FSA). The London Stock Exchange is responsible for the admission to trading of companies to the Main Market. As a result, joining the Main Market involves two parallel processes. A company applies for its securities to be admitted to the Official List through the UKLA and the listing is dependent on those securities gaining admission to trading on the Main Market through satisfying the Exchange's admission and disclosure standards.

Timetable for listing

In their guide to joining the Main Market, the London Stock Exchange sets out a timetable for listing. They describe the main activities in each phase as follows:

Pre-float preparation:

- ✔ **36–24 months:** Develop a robust business plan and a detailed review of ownership and tax issues, customer/supplier contracts, management information systems, and operational and compliance controls.

- ✔ **24–12 months:** Acquire information about what a Main Market flotation involves, review corporate governance, and complete any strategic initiatives or acquisitions.

- ✔ **12–6 months:** Develop an investor relations strategy and ensure that the necessary financial statements and non-executive directors are in place. Decide on the method of flotation and interview potential advisors.

The listing process:

- ✔ **6–3 months:** Appoint and instruct advisors and agree on the timetable.

- ✔ **12–6 weeks:** The company and its advisors review pricing issues, host analyst presentations and produce drafts of key documents – including the prospectus.

✔ **6 weeks–1 week:** UKLA sees and approves all documents. The company and advisors complete their checking of the documentation, hold PR meetings and analyst roadshows.

✔ **1 week–admission:** The company makes its formal application for listing and admission. Once this is granted trading begins.

Chapter 4

Digging into Accounting Basics

In This Chapter
▶ Understanding accounting methods
▶ Following debits and credits
▶ Differentiating between assets and liabilities

A h, the language of financial accounting – debits, credits, double-entry accounting! Just reading the words makes your heart beat faster, doesn't it? The language and practices of accountants can get the best of anyone, but there's a method to the madness, and working out that method is a crucial first step to understanding financial reports. In this chapter, we help you understand the logic behind the baffling and unique world of financial accounting. And you won't even need a pocket calculator!

Making Sense of the Accounting Method

Officially, there are two types of *accounting methods,* which dictate how the company's transactions are recorded in the company's financial books: cash-basis accounting and accrual accounting. The key difference between the two types is how the company records cash coming into and going out of the business. Within that simple difference lies a lot of room for error – or manipulation. In fact, many of the major corporations involved in financial scandals have got into trouble because they played games with the nuts and bolts of their accounting method. We talk more about those games in Chapter 22.

Cash-basis accounting

In *cash-basis accounting,* companies record expenses in financial accounts when the cash is actually laid out, and they book revenue when they actually hold the cash in their hot little hands or, more likely, in a bank account. For example, if a painter completed a project on 30 December 2007, but doesn't get paid for it until the owner inspects it on 10 January 2008, the painter reports those cash earnings in the accounts for the year ended 31 December 2008 – not 2007, even though that's the year the painter did the work. In cash-basis accounting, cash earnings include cash, cheques, credit-card receipts, or any other form of revenue from customers.

In the past, smaller businesses, such as sole traders, might have used cash-basis accounting because the system is easier for them to use on their own, meaning they don't have to hire accounting staff. However, HMRC make it clear that they expect all accounts – be they for sole traders, partnerships, or companies – to be prepared in accordance with Generally Accepted Accounting Principles (GAAP), and that means accrual accounting.

If you're a sole trader, partnership, or company, don't even think about using cash-basis accounting. You must use accrual accounting (see the next section).

Accrual accounting

A company using *accrual accounting* records revenue when goods are delivered or work is performed, not when it receives the cash. That is, the company records revenue when it earns it, even if the customer hasn't paid yet. For example, a carpentry contractor who uses accrual accounting records the revenue earned during the job, even if the customer hasn't paid the final bill yet.

A recent and very controversial change to UK GAAP dictates that the carpenter would need to accrue revenue if the job was part completed at the financial year-end. For example, suppose a carpenter has a financial year-end of 31 December 2007 but was only part way through a contract to build an expensive bookcase. Assuming that the quotation for the job was £2,000 (excluding materials which were to be supplied by the customer), and that only 75 per cent of the work is completed at the end of December, then the accounts must show a revenue of £1,500 for the year ended 31 December 2007, even if no payment is actually received in the 2007 calendar year. This change in UK GAAP brought UK standards into line with the International Accounting Standard IAS 18 which is the standard relevant to listed companies.

Expenses are handled the same way as revenue. The company records any expenses when they're incurred, even if it hasn't paid for the supplies yet. For example, when a carpenter buys timber for a job it is probably paid for on account and no cash is laid until a month or so later when the bill arrives.

All companies must use accrual accounting according to Generally Accepted Accounting Principles (GAAP). If you're reading a company's financial reports, what you see is based on accrual accounting.

Why method matters

The accounting method a business uses can have a major impact on the total revenue the business reports as well as on the expenses that it subtracts from the revenue to get the bottom line. Here's how:

- **Cash-basis accounting:** Expenses and revenues aren't carefully matched on a month-to-month basis. Expenses aren't recognised until the money is actually paid out, even if the expenses are incurred in previous months, and revenues earned in previous months aren't recognised until the cash is actually received. However, cash-basis accounting excels in tracking the actual cash available.

- **Accrual accounting:** Expenses and revenue are matched, providing a company with a better idea of how much it's spending to operate each month and how much profit it's making. Expenses are recorded (or accrued) in the month incurred, even if the cash isn't paid out until the next month. Revenues are recorded in the month the project is performed or the product is shipped, even if the company hasn't yet received the cash from the customer.

The way a company records payment of payroll taxes, for example, differs with these two methods. In accrual accounting, each month a company sets aside the amount it expects to pay toward its monthly tax bills for employee taxes using an *accrual* (paper transaction in which no money changes hands, which is called an accrual). The entry goes into a *tax liability account* (an account for tracking tax payments that have been made or must still be made). If the company incurs £1,000 of tax liabilities in March, that amount is entered in the tax liability account even if it hasn't yet paid out the cash. That way, the expense is matched to the month it's incurred.

In cash accounting, the company doesn't record the liability until it actually pays the government the cash. Although the company incurs tax expenses each month, the company will always be a month behind.

To see how these two methods can result in totally different financial statements, imagine that a carpenter contracts a job with a total cost to the customer of £2,000. The carpenter's expected expenses for the supplies, labour, and other necessities are £1,200, so the expected profit is £800. The work starts on 23 December 2007 and is completed on 31 December 2007. No payment is received until 3 January 2008. The contractor takes no cash upfront and instead agrees to be paid in full at completion.

Using the cash-basis accounting method, because no cash changes hands, the carpenter doesn't have to report any revenues from this transaction in 2007. But if cash is paid out for expenses in 2007 the bottom line is £1,200 less with no revenue to offset it. The result is that the net profit (the amount of money the company earned, minus its expenses) for the business in 2007 is lower.

This scenario is not necessarily a bad thing if the carpenter is trying to reduce the tax hit for 2007 – which is, of course, why Her Majesty's Revenue and Customs (HMRC) outlawed it!

If the same carpenter uses accrual accounting, the bottom line is different. In this case, the carpenter books the expenses when they're actually incurred. The income for the complete job is recorded on 31 December 2007, even though no cash payment is received until 2008. As a result the net income is increased by this job. Chapter 7 covers the ins and outs of reporting income on the income statement.

Understanding Debits and Credits

You probably think of the word 'debit' as a reduction in your cash. Most non-accountants see debits only when they're taken out of their bank account. Credits probably have a more positive connotation in your mind. You see them most frequently when you've returned an item and your account is credited.

Forget everything you *think* you know about debits and credits! You're going to have to erase these assumptions from your mind in order to understand *double-entry bookkeeping*, which is the basis of most accounting done in the business world.

The reason that people so often get confused about debits and credits is that their only experience of debits and credits is on their bank statement. The point about the bank statement is that it has been prepared from the bank's point of view – and they are looking at the transaction from the opposite side to you.

Double-entry bookkeeping

When you buy something, you do two things: You get something new (say, a chair), and you have to give up something to get it (most likely, cash or you take a loan). Companies that use double-entry bookkeeping show both sides of every transaction in their books, and those sides must be equal.

For example, if a company buys office supplies with cash, the value of the Office Supplies account increases, while the value of the Cash account decreases. If a company purchases £100 in office supplies, here's how it records the transaction on its books:

Account	*Debit*	*Credit*
Office supplies	£100	
Cash		£100

In this case, the transaction increases the value of the Office Supplies account and decreases the value of the Cash account. Both accounts are *asset accounts,* which means both accounts represent things the company owns that are shown on the balance sheet. (The *balance sheet* is the financial statement that gives you a snapshot of the assets, liabilities, and shareholders' equity as at a particular date. We cover balance sheets in greater detail in Chapter 6.)

Most businesses use double-entry bookkeeping. In the past, double-entry involved the business in writing the same figure twice into the accounting records – hence double-entry was a way of checking that the entries had been made accurately. These days the balance is enforced by a computer package – that is, the value is only entered once and the computer expects the operator to input the two accounts which are to be debited and credited. This may seem to be a good thing because the books will always balance but, in fact, the accuracy check of the entry is lost in computerised systems.

The assets are balanced or offset by the *liabilities* (claims made against the company's assets by creditors, such as loans) and the *equity* (claims made against the company's assets, such as shares held by shareholders). Double-entry bookkeeping seeks to balance the assets and claims against the assets. In fact, the balance sheet of a company is developed using this formula:

Assets = Liabilities + Owner's Equity

Profit and loss statements

In addition to establishing accounts to develop the balance sheet and make entries in the double-entry system, companies must also set up accounts that they use to develop the *income statement* (also known as the *profit and loss statement,* or P&L), which shows a company's revenue and expenses over a set period of time. (See Chapter 7 for more on revenue and expenses.) The double-entry bookkeeping method impacts not only the way assets and liabilities are entered, but also the way revenue and expenses are entered.

The effect of debits and credits on sales

If you're a sales manager tracking how your department is doing for the year, you want to be able to decipher debits and credits. If you think an error may exist, your ability to read reports and understand the impact of debits and credits is critical. For example, any time you think the income statement isn't accurately reflecting your department's success, you have to dig into the debits and credits to be sure your sales are being booked correctly. You also need to be aware of the other accounts, especially revenue and expense accounts, that are used to book transactions that impact your department.

A common entry that impacts both the balance sheet and the income statement keeps track of the amount of cash customers pay to buy the company's products. If the customers pay £100, here's how the entry looks:

Account	*Debit*	*Credit*
Cash	£100	
Sales revenue		£100

In this case, both the Cash account and the Sales Revenue account increase. One increases using a debit, and the other increases using a credit. Yikes – this can be so confusing! Whether an account increases or decreases from a debit or a credit depends on the type of account. See Table 4-1 to find out when debits and credits increase or decrease an account.

Table 4-1	Effect of Debits and Credits	
Account	*Debits*	*Credits*
Assets	Increases	Decreases
Liabilities	Decreases	Increases
Income	Decreases	Increases
Expenses	Increases	Decreases

Make a copy of Table 4-1 and tack it up where you review your department's accounts until you become familiar with the differences.

Digging into Depreciation and Amortisation

Depreciation and amortisation are accounting methods which track the use of assets that are used in the business and, as they age, their cost in the balance sheet is reduced. Tangible assets (physical assets such as machines or motor vehicles) are *depreciated* (reduced in value by a certain percentage each year to show that the tangible asset is being used up). Intangible assets (things like intellectual property or patents) are *amortised* (reduced in value by a certain percentage each year to show that the intangible asset is being used up).

For example, each vehicle owned by a company loses value throughout the normal course of business each year. Cars or lorries might be estimated to have five years of useful life. Suppose a company paid £30,000 for a car.

To calculate its depreciation on a five-year schedule, divide £30,000 by 5 to get £6,000 per year in depreciation. Each of the five years this car is in service, the company records a depreciation expense of £6,000.

When the company makes the initial purchase of the vehicle using a loan, the company records the purchase this way:

Account	*Debit*	*Credit*
Motor vehicles	£30,000	
Loans payable		£30,000

In this transaction, both the debit and credit increase the accounts affected. The debit recording the car purchase increases the total of the assets in the motor vehicles account, and the credit recording the new loan also increases the total of the loans payable account.

The company records its depreciation expenses for the car at the end of each year this way:

Account	*Debit*	*Credit*
Depreciation expense	£6,000	
Accumulated depreciation – Vehicles		£6,000

The debit in this case increases the expense for depreciation. The credit increases the amount accumulated for depreciation. When you see *Motor vehicles* listed in the notes to the balance sheet, the line item *Accumulated depreciation – Motor vehicles* will be listed directly below the asset *Motor vehicles* and will be shown as a negative number to be subtracted from the value of the *Motor vehicles* assets. This way of presenting the information in the notes helps the financial report reader see quickly how old the assets are and how much value and useful life remain for the asset.

On the balance sheet itself, the net book value of all the tangible assets used in the business is shown. The net book value is the total cost of all of these assets less the total of all of the accumulated depreciation.

A similar process, *amortisation,* is used for intangible assets, such as patents. Just like with depreciation, a company must write down the value of a patent during the patent's lifetime. Amortisation expenses appear on the income statement, and the value of the asset is shown on the balance sheet. The line item *Patent* is shown in the notes to the balance sheet with another line item called *Accumulated amortisation* below it. The *Accumulated amortisation* line shows how much has been written down against the asset in the current year plus in any past years. This gives the financial report reader a way to quickly calculate how much value is left in a company's patents.

On the balance sheet itself, just like tangible assets, the net book value of all of the intangible assets used in the business is shown. The net book value is the total cost of all of these assets less the total of all of the accumulated amortisation.

Checking Out the Chart of Accounts

A company groups the accounts it uses to develop the financial statements in the *Chart of Accounts,* which is a listing of all open accounts that the accounting department can use to record transactions, according to the role of the accounts in the statements. All businesses have a Chart of Accounts, even if it's so small that they don't even realise they have one and have never formally gone about designing their Chart of Accounts.

The Chart of Accounts for a business will sort of build itself as the company buys and sells assets for its use and records revenue earned and expenses incurred in its day-to-day operations.

If you're working inside a company and have responsibility for company transactions, you will have a copy of the Chart of Accounts, so you know which account you need to use for each transaction. If you're a financial report reader with no internal company responsibilities, you won't get to see this Chart of Accounts, but you do need to understand what goes into these different accounts to understand what you're seeing in the financial statements.

Each account in a Chart of Accounts is given a number. This clearly defined structure helps accountants move from job to job and still quickly get a handle on the Chart of Accounts. Also, because most companies use computerised accounting, the software is developed with these numerical definitions. Some companies make up an alphabetical listing of their Chart of Accounts with numbers in parentheses to make finding accounts easier for managers who are unfamiliar with the structure.

The accounts in the Chart of Accounts will often appear in the following order:

- ✔ Balance sheet asset accounts (usually in the number range of 1000–1999).
- ✔ Liability accounts (with numbers ranging from 2000–2999).
- ✔ Equity accounts (3000–3999).
- ✔ Income statement accounts/revenue accounts (4000–4999).
- ✔ Expense accounts (5000–6999).

The granddaddy of bookkeeping

Every transaction a company makes during the year eventually finds its way into the general ledger. Although companies often use the *general ledger* just for a summary of what happens in each of their accounts, some companies include details about specific transactions in their sub-ledgers. For example, accounts receivable is likely to be summarised in the general ledger by just putting the end-of-month totals for outstanding customer accounts. The actual detail of the transactions that took place during the month involving accounts receivables will be in an accounts receivable sub-ledger – often known as the Sales Ledger. In addition, accounting records will show details for each customer including what they bought and how much they still owe.

In the old days, these accounts were recorded on paper, and finding a specific transaction on the dozens, or even hundreds, of pages used to record activity was a nightmare. Today, because most companies use computerised accounting, you can easily design a report to find most types of transactions electronically, by grouping them by account type, customer, salesperson, product, or almost any other configuration that helps you decipher the entries.

To help you become familiar with the types of accounts in the Chart of Accounts and the types of transactions in those accounts, we review the most common accounts in this section in the order in which you'll most likely read them in a financial report. We assign the accounts numbers that are most commonly generated by computer programs, but you may find that your company uses a different numbering system.

Asset accounts

Asset accounts come first in the Chart of Accounts, with the long-term accounts (those that the company will use in more than 12 months) listed before the most current accounts (those that the company will use in less than 12 months).

Tangible assets

Physical assets that you can touch are termed *tangible assets* and include long-term assets and current assets.

Long-term assets (also known as fixed assets) are assets that will be held for more than 12 months. The following are common long-term asset accounts:

- **Land:** This account is used to record any purchases of land as a company asset. Companies should list land separately because it doesn't depreciate in value like the building or buildings sitting on it do.

- **Buildings:** This account lists the value of any buildings the company owns. This value is always a positive number.

- **Accumulated depreciation:** This account tracks the depreciation of company-owned buildings. Each year the company deducts a portion of the value of the building based on the building's costs and the number of years the building will have a productive life.

- **Leasehold improvements:** This account tracks improvements to buildings that the company leases rather than buys. In most cases, when a company leases retail or warehouse space, it must pay the costs of improving the property for its unique business use. These improvements are also depreciated, so the company uses a companion depreciation account called **Accumulated depreciation – Leasehold improvements**.

- **Motor vehicles:** This account tracks the cars, lorries, and other vehicles owned by the business. The initial value added to this account is the value of the vehicles when put into service. Vehicles are also depreciated, and the depreciation account is **Accumulated depreciation – Motor vehicles**.

- **Furniture and fixtures:** This account tracks all the desks, chairs, and other fixtures a company buys for its offices, warehouses, and retail shops. Yes, these items, too, are depreciated, and the depreciation account is named **Accumulated depreciation – Furniture and fixtures**.

- **Plant and machinery:** A company uses this account to track any equipment purchased for the business that it expects will have a useful life of more than one year. This equipment includes computers, copiers, cash registers, and any other equipment needs. The depreciation account is **Accumulated depreciation – Plant and machinery**.

Current assets are assets that will be used up in the next 12 months. The following are examples of current-asset accounts:

- **Inventory (or Stock):** This account tracks the costs of products a company has available for sale, whether it purchases the products from other companies or produces them in-house. Although some companies use a computerised inventory system that adjusts the account almost instantaneously, others adjust the account only at the end of an accounting period.

- **Accounts receivable (or Trade debtors):** In this account, businesses record transactions in which customers bought products on credit.

✔ **Cash in bank:** Businesses use this account most often, depositing their cash received as revenue and their cash paid out to cover bills and debt.

✔ **Cash on deposit:** This account is where businesses keep cash that isn't needed for daily operations. This account usually earns interest until the company decides how it wants to use this surplus cash.

✔ **Cash on hand (or Petty cash):** This account tracks the actual cash the company keeps at its business locations. Cash on hand includes money in the cash registers, as well as petty cash. Most companies have several different Cash-on-hand accounts. For example, a shop may have its own account for tracking cash in the registers, and each department may have its own petty-cash account. How these accounts are structured depends on the company and the security controls it has in place to manage the cash on hand. Companies always leave plenty of room for additions in this account category.

Intangible assets

Companies also hold intangible assets, which have value to the company but are often difficult to measure. The following are the most common intangible assets in the Chart of Accounts:

✔ **Goodwill:** A company needs this account only when it has bought another company or unincorporated business. Frequently, the company that purchases another company pays more than the actual value of its assets minus its liabilities. The premium paid, which may account for things such as customer loyalty, exceptional workforce, and great location, is listed on the books as goodwill.

✔ **Intellectual property:** Intellectual property is copyrights and patents, and written work or products for which the company has been granted exclusive rights. For example, the government grants patents to a company or individual that invents a new product or process.

Having exclusive rights to a product allows a company to hold off competition, which can mean a lot of extra profits. Patented products often can command a much higher price.

Liability accounts

Money a company owes to creditors, vendors, suppliers, contractors, employees, government entities, and anyone else who provides products or services to the company are *liabilities*.

Current liabilities

Current liabilities include money owed in the next 12 months. The following accounts are used to record current-liability transactions:

- ✔ **Accounts payable (or Trade creditors):** This account includes all the payments to suppliers, contractors, and consultants that are due in less than one year. Most of the payments made on these accounts are for invoices due in less than two months.

- ✔ **VAT account:** This account tracks Value Added Tax (VAT) collected for the government on sales by the company – known as output tax. It also records VAT that can be reclaimed on purchases – known as input tax. Companies record daily transactions in this account as they make sales and purchases. The balance on the account will then be payable to the government – usually at quarterly intervals.

- ✔ **Accrued payroll taxes:** This account includes any Pay As You Earn (PAYE) income tax and national insurance (NI) that has been deducted from employees' wages and salaries. It will also include the company's national insurance contributions. The balance is paid over to the collector of taxes on a monthly basis.

- ✔ **Credit card payable:** This account tracks the payments to corporate credit cards. Some companies use these accounts as management tools for tracking employee activities and set them up by employee name, department name, or whatever method the company finds useful for monitoring credit card use.

Long-term liabilities

Long-term liabilities include money due beyond the next 12 months. The following are accounts companies use to record long-term liability transactions:

- ✔ **Loans payable:** This account tracks debts, such as mortgages or loans on vehicles, that are incurred for longer than one year.

- ✔ **Bonds payable (previously known as Debentures):** This account tracks corporate bonds that have been issued for a term longer than one year. Bonds are a type of debt sold on the market that must be repaid in full with interest.

Equity accounts

Equity accounts reflect the portion of the assets that isn't subject to liabilities and is, therefore, owned by the company shareholders. If the business isn't incorporated, the ownership of the partners or sole proprietors is represented in this part of the balance sheet in an account called *Owner's equity* or *Capital.* The following is a list of the most common equity accounts:

✔ **Share capital:** This account reflects the nominal value of the ordinary shares in issue. Each share represents a portion of ownership. Even companies that haven't sold shares in the public marketplace list the nominal value of their shares on the balance sheet. Each ordinary shareholder has a vote in the operation of the company.

✔ **Preference share capital:** This account reflects the nominal value of preference shares in issue. These shares fall somewhere between bonds and ordinary shares. Although the company has no obligation to repay the preference shareholder or to pay dividends, the preference shareholders always receive payment before the ordinary shareholder – even on a winding up of the company. If the dividends can't be paid in a particular year for some reason on some preference shares, they're accrued for payment in later years. Such preference shares are called cumulative preference shares. Any unpaid preference dividends must be paid before a company pays ordinary shareholders' dividends. Preference shareholders don't normally get a vote in the operation of the company but this depends on the company's Articles. We deal with preference shares in more detail in Chapter 6.

✔ **Share premium:** All shares have a nominal value. If, when purchasing shares, the shareholder pays the company more than the nominal value, then the excess (or premium) is recorded in this account.

✔ **Retained Earnings:** This account tracks the profits or losses for the company each year. These numbers reflect earnings retained rather than paid out as dividends to shareholders and show a company's long-term success or failure.

Revenue accounts

At the top of every income statement is the revenue brought in by the company. This revenue is offset by any costs directly related to it. The top section of the income statement includes sales, cost of goods sold, and gross margin. Below this section, before the profit and loss section, expenses are shown. In the following section we review the key accounts in the Chart of Accounts that make up the income statement (see Chapter 7).

Revenue

All sales of products or services are recorded in revenue accounts. The following are the accounts used to record revenue transactions:

✔ **Sales of goods or services:** This account tracks the company's revenues for the sale of its products or services.

✔ **Sales discounts:** This account tracks any discounts the company has offered to increase its sales. If a company is heavily discounting its products, it may be competing intensely or interest in the product may be falling. A company outsider won't see these numbers, but if you're reading the reports prepared for internal management purposes, this account gives you a view of how discounting is used.

✔ **Sales returns and allowances:** This account tracks problem sales from unhappy customers. A large number here may reflect customer dissatisfaction which could be the result of a quality-control problem. These reports are not available to those outside the company but internal management financial reports show this information. A dramatic increase in this number is usually a red flag for company management.

Cost of goods sold (or Cost of Sales)

The costs directly related to the sale of goods or services are tracked in cost of goods sold accounts. Cost of goods sold is usually shown as a one-line item but includes the transactions from all these accounts.

✔ **Purchases:** This account tracks the cost of merchandise bought by the company for sale. A manufacturing company has a much more extensive tracking system for its cost of goods that includes accounts for items, such as raw materials, components, and labour, that are used to produce the final product.

✔ **Purchase discounts:** This account tracks any cost savings the company is able to negotiate because of accelerated payment plans or volume buying. For example, if a supplier offers a 2 per cent discount when a customer pays an invoice within 10 days rather than the normal 30 days, the supplier tracks this cost saving in purchase discounts.

✔ **Purchase returns and allowances:** This account tracks any transactions involving the return of any products to the manufacturer or vendor because they were damaged during shipping or were defective.

✔ **Freight charges:** This account tracks the costs of shipping the goods sold.

Expense accounts

Any costs not directly related to generating revenue are considered *expenses*. Expenses fall into four categories: operating, interest, depreciation or amortisation, and taxes. A large company can have hundreds of expense accounts, so we don't name each one but give you a broad overview of the types of expense accounts that fall into each of these categories:

✔ **Operating expenses:** The largest share of expense accounts falls under the umbrella of operating expenses, which include advertising, subscriptions, equipment rental, property rental, insurance, legal and accounting fees, meals, entertainment, salaries, office expenses, postage, repairs and maintenance, supplies, travel, telephone, utilities, vehicle repairs, and just about anything else that goes into the cost of operating a business and isn't directly involved in the cost of a company's products.

Expenses that fall into this area, rather than into the cost of goods sold, relate to spending that isn't specific to the sale of a particular product but to the overall operation of the company.

✔ **Interest expenses:** Interest paid on the company's debt is reflected in the accounts for interest expenses – from credit cards, loans, bonds, or any other type of debt the company may carry.

✔ **Depreciation and amortisation expenses:** We discuss how depreciation is calculated in 'Digging Into Depreciation and Amortisation' earlier in this chapter. The process for amortisation is similar. The amount written off each year for any type of asset is tracked in the depreciation and amortisation accounts, and the expenses related to depreciation and amortisation in each individual year are shown on the income statement.

✔ **Taxes:** A company pays numerous types of taxes. VAT is not listed as an expense because it is paid by the customers and accrued as a liability until paid. Taxes withheld from employees are also accrued as a liability and aren't listed as an expense.

The types of taxes that become expenses for a company include the employer's national insurance contributions and corporation tax. We talk more about taxes and company structure in Chapter 3.

Differentiating Profit Types

A company doesn't actually make different kinds of profits, but it has different ways to track a profit and compare its results with those of similar companies. The three key profit types are gross profit, operating profit, and net profit. In Chapter 11, we discuss how these different profit types are used to test the viability of a company.

✔ **Gross profit:** Reflects the revenue earned minus any direct costs of generating that revenue, such as costs related to the purchases or production of goods before any expenses, including operating, taxes, interest, depreciation, and amortisation. The gross profit isn't actually part of the Chart of Accounts. You calculate the number for the income statement to show the profit made by your company before expenses.

✔ **Operating profit:** The next profit figure you see on the income statement. This number measures a company's earning power from its ongoing operations. The operating profit is calculated by subtracting operating expenses from gross profit. Some companies include depreciation and amortisation expenses in this calculation, calling this line item *EBIT,* or *earnings before interest and taxes.*

Others add an additional line called *EBITDA,* or *earnings before interest, taxes, depreciation, and amortisation.* Accountants started using EBITDA in the 1980s because it provided analysts with a number that they could use to test profitability among companies and eliminated the effects of financing and accounting.

Companies don't actually pay out cash for depreciation and amortisation expenses. Instead, depreciation and amortisation are an accounting requirement that comes into play when determining the value of assets.

Interest is a financial decision. A company has the choice to finance new product development or other major projects by selling bonds, taking loans, or issuing shares. If a company chooses to raise money using bonds or loans, it has to pay interest. Money raised by issuing shares doesn't have interest costs. We talk more about this difference and the impact on a company's profits in Chapter 12.

Taxes, believe it or not, are also an accounting game. Most corporations report different tax numbers on their financial statements than they actually pay to the government because of differences between tax law and GAAP. We explain this further in Chapter 6.

✔ **Net profit:** The bottom line after all costs, expenses, interest, taxes, depreciation, and amortisation. Net profit reflects how much money the company makes. The company can pay out the profit to shareholders or it can reinvest the money in growing itself. Companies add money reinvested to the retained earnings account on the balance sheet.

Part II
Understanding Published Information: Annual Reports

'The rose-tinted spectacles if you
please, Miss Houndsfoot.'

In this part . . .

You can't analyse a financial report until you understand all its pieces. In this part, we help you put together the puzzle of financial reporting. We delve into the key financial statements – the balance sheet, income statement, and cash flow statement. We also explore the other parts of an annual report, particularly how to read the small print in the notes to the financial statements. In addition, we discuss what makes up consolidated financial statements.

Chapter 5

Exploring the Anatomy of an Annual Report

In This Chapter
▶ Decoding company messages
▶ Getting management's view
▶ Hearing the auditor's opinions
▶ Summing up the financial report

*T*he financial statements are the meat of any annual report, but they contain lots of trimmings that you need to be able to read and understand. Although companies must follow set rules for how they format the key financial statements, how they present the rest of the report is left to their creativity.

In this chapter, we explain the six standard parts of an annual report and why they're so critical. We also define the other parts of an annual report and their purposes.

Meeting the Basic Parts of an Annual Report

Some companies spend a lot of money putting on a glossy show with colour pictures throughout the report. Others just put out a pretty ordinary black and white version without pictures. Most are trying to present a useful report on the state of their business. The major components of an annual report are standard, although the order in which companies present them may vary.

When you see a fat, glossy annual report from a company, you can be certain that you'll find a lot of froth and spin about all the good things that it has accomplished. No matter how fancy or plain the annual report is you, as a careful reader, need to focus on these key parts:

- ✔ **Chairman's statement**: A report from the chairman about progress during the preceding year and prospects for the future. (See the section 'Everything but the Numbers', later in this chapter, for more on what to look for in this statement.)

- ✔ **Operating review**: Sometimes called the Operating and Financial Review or OFR, this is a report by the key directors of the main divisions of the company giving management's view on progress. The Finance Director or Chief Financial Officer will, for example, write the finance part of the report. (See 'Getting the real gen from management' in this chapter.)

- ✔ **Directors' report and Directors' remuneration report**: These reports give information required by the Companies Act or the stock exchange. (See 'Share-based payments' in this chapter.)

- ✔ **Auditor's report:** A statement by the auditor regarding the findings of their audit of the company's books. (See 'Bringing the auditor's answers to light' in this chapter.)

- ✔ **Financial statements:** These include the balance sheet, income statement, and the statement of cash flows. (See 'Presenting the Financial Picture' in this section.)

Translating the language of reports to shareholders

Maintaining a long and proud tradition, reports to shareholders present companies in the best possible light, minimising whatever trouble may lie under the surface. A careless reader may feel reassured by the 'everything's-hunky-dory' tone, but a few often-used niceties may indicate that things aren't what they seem and can tip off careful readers.

- ✔ 'Challenging' is frequently used when a company is facing significant difficulties selling its product or service.

- ✔ 'Restructuring' means something isn't working. Be sure to find out what that something is and how much the company is spending to fix the problem.

- ✔ Sometimes, reports to shareholders gloss over mistakes by using a phrase like 'corrective actions are being taken'. Look for details about the cause of the problem and the plan for corrective actions in the notes to the financial statements or further management discussion and analysis.

- ✔ If you come across the term 'difficulties', look for details about the difficulties highlighted in the management reviews or notes to the financial statements.

For more on the reports and statements parts of the annual report, go to the sections 'Getting the real gen from management' and 'Reading the notes' later in this chapter.

✔ **Notes to the financial statements:** The notes give additional information about the contents of the financial statements. (See 'Reading the notes' in this chapter.)

✔ **Corporate Governance Report:** This report is about how the company applies the principles of good corporate behaviour as outlined in the Companies Act and the UK Combined Code on Corporate Finance.

Everything but the Numbers

Most people think of numbers when they hear the words *annual report,* but an investor with savvy can find a lot more useful information in the text. Some parts of the report are fluff pieces written for public consumption, but others can give you great insight into the company's prospects, as well as highlighting areas of management concern. You just need to be like a detective: Read between the lines, and read the small print.

Debunking the statements to shareholders

What would an annual report be if not an opportunity for the head honchos to tout their company's fabulousness? Near the front of most annual reports you find statements to the shareholders from the chairman of the board, and possibly, other key executives.

In these statements, you usually find information about the key business activities for the year, or at least, the most successful ones, a general statement about the company's financial condition, performance summaries of key divisions or subsidiaries that are the shining stars, and what the company's key prospects are.

Don't put too much stock by these statements, no matter how appealing they look and how exciting their message. While the chairman and other executives are heavily involved in writing the reports to shareholders, the company's public relations department usually carefully designs them to highlight the positive aspects of the company's year. Negative results, when mentioned at all, are usually hidden in the middle of a paragraph somewhere in the middle of the report. These statements *will* focus on the positive news and try to minimise the bad news. Do read the company's optimistic view, but don't depend on these statements to make a decision about whether or not you should invest in the company. You can find more definitive information in other parts of the report that can help you make investment decisions.

Making sense of the corporate message

After the reports to shareholders but before the juicy information, you often find more 'rah-rah' text in the form of a summary about the company's key achievements throughout the year. Like the Chairman's statement, these pages present the messages the company wants to portray, which may or may not give you the true picture. Few companies include much information about negative results in this section. Often chock-full of glossy, colourful images, this section is public relations fluff focusing on the best performance highlights of the year. Having said all that, the managers of the business don't want to be caught out with a straight lie: that's why it's generally possible to detect what's really going on as long as you can read between the lines like the examples in 'Translating the language of reports to shareholders'.

Although this section is basically advertising, it may give you a good overview of what the company does and the key parts of its operations. The company will present its key divisions or units, what the top products are within these divisions, and a brief summary of the financial results of the main divisions. In addition, you usually find some discussion of market share and position in the market of the company's key products or services.

Meeting the people in charge

Want to find out who's running the show? After the corporate statements and financial review section, one or two pages list the members of the board of directors and, sometimes, a brief bio of each member. You also find a listing of top executives or managers and their responsibilities. If you want to complain to someone at the top, this is the place where you can find out where to send your letters!

But seriously, reviewing the backgrounds of the company's leaders can help you get an idea of the experience these leaders bring to the company. If they don't impress you, that may be a good sign that you should walk away from the investment.

Getting the real gen from management

The Operating and Financial Review (OFR) section is one of the most important sections of an annual report. It may not be the most fun section to look at but in this section you find the key discussions about what went smoothly over the year as well as what went wrong.

The OFR has been a part of UK reporting for many years based on a code of best practice. However, a couple of years ago, the government set out to make the OFR compulsory and, to this end, the Accounting Standards Board (ASB) produced a standard setting out the required contents of such a report. At the last minute the legislation was repealed on the grounds of cutting red tape. The ASB converted their standard into a best practice statement and things went on much as before.

But the government reintroduced the compulsory OFR by a back-door route by including most of the previous requirements in a new extended business review which is now part of the Directors' Report. Welcome back red tape!

Read the OFR section carefully. It has a lot of the meat-and-potatoes information that gives you details about how the company's doing. Remember that the information may be split between the OFR and the Directors' Report.

Investors monitor the OFR section closely to make sure that companies present all critical information about current operations, capital, and liquidity. Management should also include forward-looking statements about known market and economic trends that could impact the company's liquidity and material events. These statements also include uncertainties that can mean that the reported information doesn't necessarily reflect future operating results or future financial conditions. For example, if a company manufactures its products in a country that's facing political upheaval or labour strife, those conditions may impact the company's ability to continue manufacturing its products at the same low cost. The company must report this information, indicating how this situation may impact the company's future earning potential.

Investors pay special attention to a number of key factors that the OFR and Directors' Report generally cover, including:

- **Revenue recognition:** In a retail store, recognising revenue can be a relatively straightforward process: A customer buys a product off the shelves, and the revenue is *recognised,* that is, recorded in the company's books. But things aren't that cut and dried in many complex corporate deals. For example, in the computer and hardware industry, revenue recognition can be complex because purchase contracts frequently include multiple parts, such as software, hardware, services, and training. The point at which the revenue is actually recognised for each of these parts can vary, depending on the terms of a contract. If a contract goes over the boundaries of two company years, the rules state that the point at which the revenue is recognised depends on the stage of completion of the contract.

The timing of revenue recognition is currently a very live issue in the UK and has been perceived as an area of potential abuse. Two recent standards on the subject have been issued by the Accounting Standards Board. We deal with this topic in more detail in Chapter 22.

When reading financial reports for a particular industry, reviewing how management describes its revenue recognition process compared to other similar companies in the same industry may be important.

✔ **Restructuring charges:** When a company restructures a portion of its firm – which can include shutting down factories, disbanding a major division, or enacting other major changes related to how the company operates – management discusses the impact the changes have had or may have in the future on the company. Costs for employee redundancy, facility shutdowns, and other costs related to restructuring are explained in this portion of the report.

✔ **Impairments of assets:** Investors expect companies to report any losses to assets in a timely manner. If an asset is damaged, destroyed, or for any reason loses value, companies must report that loss to shareholders. Look for information about the loss of value of assets in the OFR. Also look for information about the depreciation of these assets (refer to Chapter 4 for more details on depreciation, amortisation, and impairment).

✔ **Pension valuations:** Accounting for pension plans includes many assumptions, such as the amount of interest or other gains that the company expects to make on the assets held in its pension plans and the expenses a company anticipates paying out when employees retire. If a company has a pension plan for its employees, you should find discussion about how the company finances this plan and whether or not the company expects to have difficulty meeting its plan's requirements. This discussion may be here or in the notes to the accounts where a detailed description of pension obligations is given. This problem of valuing pension schemes is limited to defined benefit final salary schemes where the pension fund guarantees the pensioner a certain percentage of final salary. This is why many firms are changing to 'money purchase' schemes where the pension paid is defined solely by the value of the pensioner's own pension fund.

✔ **Environmental and product liabilities:** All companies face some liability for products that fail to operate as expected or possibly could cause damage to an individual or property. In some industries – such as oil, gas, and chemical companies – an error can cause considerable environmental damage. You've probably heard stories about a chemical spill destroying a local stream or drinking water supply, or an oil spill wiping out an area's entire ecological system. In the OFR section, a company must acknowledge the liabilities it faces and the way it prepares financially for the possibility of taking a loss after the liability is paid. The company must estimate its potential losses and disclose the amount of money it has set aside or the insurance it has to protect against such losses.

✔ **Share-based payments:** In order to attract and keep top executives, many companies offer *share incentives* (such as awarding shares as bonuses) as part of an employee remuneration package. This part of the annual report normally mentions a summary of any share-based payments as part of the discussion about equity. Where the executives are directors of the company then the full details of their pay and benefits will be included in the Directors' Remuneration Report.

Many recent scandals have included disclosures of unusually high share-based remuneration packages for top executives. Keep a watchful eye (or ear) out for discussion of bonuses or other employee compensation that involves giving employees shares or share options which result in them being able to buy shares below the market value.

✔ **Allowance for doubtful debts:** Any company that offers credit to customers will encounter some non-payers. If it is a significant sum, for example in the accounts of a bank, management will discuss what level of loss it is allowing for on accounts that aren't paid and whether or not this allowance is an increase or decrease from the previous year. If the allowance for doubtful debts increases, it may indicate a problem with collections or may be a sign of significant problems in the industry as a whole.

The discussion in this section of the annual report can get very technical. If you find things you don't understand, you can always ring the investor relations department to ask for clarification. Investor relations departments are more forthcoming than they used to be, but some will still only give you statutorily mandatory information. Whenever you're considering an investment in a company's shares, be certain that you understand the key points being discussed in the OFR. Any time you find the information beyond your comprehension, don't hesitate to research further and ask a lot of questions before investing in the stock.

In the OFR, managers usually focus on three key areas: company operations, capital resources, and liquidity.

Company operations

Management commentary on this topic focuses on the income generated and expenses related to the company's operations. To get some idea of how well the company may perform in the future, look for:

✔ Discussion about whether sales increased or decreased

✔ How well its various product lines performed

✔ Discussions about economic or market conditions that may have impacted the company's performance

The OFR section also discusses:

- ✔ **Distribution systems:** How products are distributed.

- ✔ **Product improvements:** Changes to products that improve their performance or appearance.

- ✔ **Manufacturing capacity:** The number of manufacturing plants and their production capability. The OFR may also mention the percentage of the company's manufacturing capacity that it is using.

  If a company uses only 50 per cent of its manufacturing capacity, that may be an indication that the company has lots of extra resources that are idle. If a company is using 100 per cent of its manufacturing capacity, that may indicate that the company has maxed out its resources and may need to expand. Sometimes manufacturing capacity is referred to in a comment rather than a stated percentage.

- ✔ **Research and development projects:** The research or development the company is doing to develop new products or improve current products.

The manager also comments on key profit results and how they may have differed from the previous year's projections. You should also look for cost information related to product manufacturing, purchasing or the costs of providing services. Cost-control problems can mean that future results may not be as good as the current year's, especially if management mentions that the cost of raw materials and commodities, such as oil, isn't stable. Look for statements about interest expenses, major competition, inflation, or other factors that may impact the success of future operations.

Capital resources

You will expect to see an indication of whether the company can fund its operations for the long term. In addition to a statement whether the company is in a strong financial position or not, you find discussions about:

- ✔ Acquisitions or major expansion plans.

- ✔ Any major capital expenditure carried out over the past year or planned in future years.

- ✔ Company debt (amounts that the company owes to outsiders).

- ✔ Plans the company may have for taking on new debt.

- ✔ Other key points about the company's cash flow. This information varies depending on the industry; the discussion may focus on items that are unique to the operation of the particular company.

Liquidity

A company's liquidity is its cash position and its ability to pay its bills on a short-term or day-to-day basis. We cover how to analyse liquidity in Chapters 12, 15, and 16.

Bringing the auditor's answers to light

Any company other than a small company must provide financial reports that have been audited by an outside auditor. (We talk more about the audit process in Chapter 18.) You usually find the *auditor's report* before the financial information or immediately following it.

Before you read the financial statements or the notes to the financial statements, be sure that you've read the auditor's report. Read the auditor's report first to find out whether the auditor raised any red flags about the company's financial results. Then you know whether the auditor expressed concerns about any aspect of the company's financial results and what those questions are. You won't find answers to the questions raised in the auditor's report. To find the details, you need to read the OFR, financial statements, and the notes to the financial statements. But if you haven't read the auditor's report, you may overlook some critical details. In the majority of cases the auditor's report is standard and contains no reservations on the auditor's part.

To lend credibility to management's assurances, and to conform with their statutory duty, the company calls in independent auditors from an outside accounting firm to audit a company's internal controls and financial statements. Auditors don't check every transaction, so their reports don't provide you with 100 per cent assurance that the financial statements don't include misstatements about the company's assets and liabilities. Auditors don't endorse a company's financial position or give indications about whether or not a company is a good investment.

Studying the standard auditor's report

The auditor's report is usually standard with few, if any, particular variations. The purpose of the report is to record the fact that the auditors have done their job, how they did the job, and what is their considered opinion of the prepared accounts.

Most standard auditor's reports include these paragraphs:

- **Introductory paragraph:** In the introductory paragraph, you find information about the time period that the audit covers, and the sections of the report that the auditor is reporting on. The auditors often take this opportunity to disclaim any liability to any user of the accounts other than the shareholders of the company.

- **Respective responsibilities of the directors and auditor:** This paragraph states that management is responsible for the financial statements and that the auditors only express an opinion about the financial statements based on their audit. Essentially, this is a 'protect-your-ass' paragraph where the auditors attempt to limit their responsibility for possible inaccuracies.

- **Basis of audit opinion (or scope paragraph):** In this paragraph, the auditors describe how they carried out the audit, including a statement that they used the generally accepted audit standards which currently are the International Standards on Auditing (ISAs) – as adapted by the Auditing Practices Board for use in the UK and Ireland. These standards require that auditors plan and prepare their audit to be reasonably sure that the financial statements are free of material misstatements. A *material misstatement* is an error that significantly impacts the company's financial position. For example, if the company reported a significant amount of revenue before it was actually earned, that'd be a material misstatement.

- **Opinion paragraph:** In the opinion paragraph, the auditors state their opinion of the financial statements. If the auditors don't find any problems with the statements, they simply say that these statements are prepared 'in accordance with IFRS as adopted by the EU'. For more on IFRS (International Financial Reporting Standards), see Chapter 18.

When an auditor's report follows the outline described here, it's called a *standard auditor's report*. And because the auditors have not found any alarming situations, it's also an *unmodified audit report*. The company must print the report as the auditors presented it and there are strict rules limiting their ability to fire an auditor whose report they do not like.

Mulling over the modified auditor's report

If the auditors modify their report then they will explain the reasons why. The modified report may be a qualified report in which the auditors report a disagreement over the figures or the information provided in the notes to the accounts. An alternative form of modification (not a qualification) is where the auditors wish to draw attention to an important matter in the accounts – not because they disagree with what the company has said but because they want to make sure the reader gets the message. (We discuss possible problems auditors may encounter later in this section.) A non-standard auditor's report and a standard auditor's report have the same structure; the only difference is that the non-standard report includes information about the problems the auditors found.

When you see a modified auditor's report, be sure that you find a discussion of the problems in the OFR and in the notes to the financial statements. Also, when reading the OFR, be certain that you understand how management is handling the problems noted by the auditors and how these problems could impact the long-term financial prospects of the company before you invest your hard-earned money. (Call the investor relations department to ask for clarification, if you need to.) If you've already invested, look carefully at the issues to be sure you want to continue holding shares in the company.

A modified auditor's report may include paragraphs that discuss problems that the auditors found such as the following:

- ✔ **Accounting policy changes:** If a company decides to change its accounting policies or how it applies an accounting method, they report this fact in the list of accounting policies in the notes to the accounts. These changes may not indicate a problem. For example, if a company changes how it reported an asset because that change is required by a new accounting standard then that's a good reason for making the change. If the auditors agree that the company had a good reason for making the change, then there will be no reference to the change in the auditor's report.

  If there is a change in accounting policy, be sure to look in the notes portion of the annual report for the full explanation of the change and how it could impact the financial statements. When companies change an accounting policy or method, they need to adjust the results of previous years by means of a prior period adjustment so that you can still compare the previous year's results to the current year's. You should look for a note to the accounts which indicates the effect of the adjustment. In the case of a major change, such as the introduction of International Financial Reporting Standards (IFRS), there may be a reconciliation showing what the figures would have been under previous practices.

  If the auditors disagree with the company's decision to change accounting methods, they question the change and provide a *qualified opinion* (which we discuss later in this section).

✔ **Significant uncertainties:** The best example of a significant uncertainty is the damages the company must pay if it loses a pending lawsuit. Life is full of uncertainties and this is true of the financial world also. The directors must make their best estimate of the financial effect of uncertainties and include their estimates in the accounts. Taking the example of the pending lawsuit, the directors may include a provision in the balance sheet for their best estimate of the potential liability which they then explain by way of a note. Alternatively, if the directors are confident that the lawsuit will be won then they don't include a provision but will simply refer to the lawsuit in the notes to the accounts. If the auditors disagree with the directors' treatment of the uncertainty then they qualify their opinion. If, on the other hand, they consider that the directors have done the best they can but believe that the uncertainties could have a significant impact on the company, the auditors include a paragraph drawing the situation to the attention of the readers. This statement is known as an emphasis of matter and is not a qualified opinion.

✔ **Going-concern problems:** Another example of a significant uncertainty is going concern. If the auditors have substantial doubt that a company has the ability to stay in business, they'll draw attention to this by an emphasis of matter paragraph. Problems that can lead to this type of paragraph in the auditor's report include ongoing losses, capital deficiencies, or a significant contract dispute. If the auditors mention going-concern then it's a major red flag. You should examine the OFR and the notes to see what the company is doing about the problem. Unless they tell a very good story, you should be very hesitant about investing in this company.

✔ **Qualified opinion – limitation of scope:** A qualified opinion doesn't always mean that you should be alarmed, but it does mean that you should do additional research to make sure that you understand the qualification. Sometimes, there's no problem at all; a qualified opinion may simply indicate that there wasn't sufficient information available at the time of the audit to determine whether or not the issue raised will have a significant financial impact on the company. The auditor's report indicates whether the problem is limited to a particular issue or whether the effect is so great that they can't express an opinion on the accounts. You should look in the notes to the financial statements or the OFR for any explanation of the matter that caused the auditors to issue a qualified opinion on the grounds of limitation of scope.

✔ **Qualified opinion – disagreement:** A disagreement is obviously a serious matter. The auditor may disagree with the figures or the disclosures in the notes. You can be sure that there was a lot of discussion between the company and the auditor before the auditor made the decision to qualify since the repercussions for the company may be serious. In the event that there is a disagreement, the auditor will indicate the extent of that disagreement. They might say that 'except for' the particular problem identified the accounts still show a true and fair view. Alternatively, if the problem is too great then they will express an 'adverse' opinion which is that the accounts do not show a true and fair view. It should be noted that qualified opinions on the grounds of disagreement aren't common.

✔ **Work performed by a different auditor:** In many cases, work being done by a different auditor isn't a problem and won't be mentioned in the report. In the UK, if a different auditor handles the audit of a subsidiary then the auditor of the parent company has the responsibility of forming the overall view. Reference to reliance on the other auditors shouldn't be necessary. Similarly, if a company changes auditors, the incoming auditor has the responsibility to form the overall view of the accounts – including the balances audited at the end of the previous year by the outgoing auditor. If there are no problems then there might not be any reference in the auditor's report to the change of auditor.

As an investor, you need to know why the company changed auditors, and you should research the issue. You probably won't find the reason for the change in the annual report, so you may have to research the change in news reports or analysts' reports about the company. Because changing auditors can negatively impact a company's share price, companies are very careful about changing auditors. The City usually gets concerned whenever a change of auditors occurs because it can be a sign of a major accounting problem that hasn't surfaced yet.

Presenting the Financial Picture

The main course of any annual report is the financial statements. In this part, you find out what the company owns, what the company owes, how much revenue the company took in, what expenses it paid out, and how much profit it made or how much it lost. We cover each of the following statements in great detail throughout the book, so we mention them briefly here and indicate in which chapters you can find additional information.

When looking at a company's financial results, make sure that you're comparing periods of similar length or a similar collection of months. For example, a retail store usually has much better results in the last quarter of the year (from October to December) because of the Christmas season than it does in the first quarter (from January to March). Comparing these two quarters doesn't make sense when you're trying to determine how well a company is doing. To judge a retail company's growth prospects, compare the fourth quarter of one year with the fourth quarter of another year. We talk more about income statements in Chapter 7 and tell you how to analyse these statements in Part III.

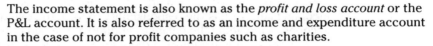

✔ **Balance sheet:** The balance sheet gives a snapshot of a company's assets and liabilities at a specific point in time. We discuss all the parts of a balance sheet in Chapter 6, and talk about analysing the financial reports in Part III.

✔ **Income statement:** The income statement reviews a company's operations over a specific period of time. In an annual report this statement covers activities in the 12 months of the previous company year. We discuss the income statement in Chapter 7 and how to analyse that statement in Part III.

The income statement is also known as the *profit and loss account* or the P&L account. It is also referred to as an income and expenditure account in the case of not for profit companies such as charities.

✔ **Statement of cash flows:** The statement of cash flows discusses the actual flow of cash into and out of the company. The statement has three sections focusing on changes to cash status from operations, investing, and financing. Like the income statement, the statement of cash flows reflects what has happened over a specific period of time. We discuss this statement in greater detail in Chapter 8, and we talk about cash-flow analysis in Chapter 13.

Summarising the Financial Data

Knowing that most people won't spend the time reading all the way through the annual report, many companies summarise their numbers in various ways. The two most common ways to summarise are to highlight the financial data presented in the financial statements and to summarise some key information in the notes to the financial statements. But beware: Some summaries highlight the good news and skip over the bad.

Finding the highlights

The highlights to the financial data summarise the financial results for the year being reported. Typically, this summary is called the *financial highlights,* but companies can be creative because they aren't a required part of the report. And because the highlights aren't a required part of the financial statement, they're not always presented according to generally accepted rules, so don't count on their accuracy. You usually find the financial highlights at the front of the annual report after the report from the chairman of the board. Some companies include them inside the back cover of the annual report.

You frequently find financial highlights at the front of the annual report, designed in a graphically pleasing way. Most companies show a 5-year or 10-year summary that doesn't include much detail but allows you to see the growth trends of the company. Although this type of summary can be a good historical overview, don't count on it. Instead, do your own research of a company's financial history to be sure that you're aware of both the good and bad news. Remember that even outstanding companies have some bad years that they want to gloss over.

The directors' report includes *key performance indicators* (KPIs) but since the directors are free to choose which KPIs to publish, they are hardly likely to choose KPIs which show the company in a bad light.

Reading the notes

The notes to the financial statements is the section where you find any warts on a company's financial record. The notes to the financial statement are a required part of the annual report that give you the details behind the numbers presented in the financial statements. Companies like to hide their problems in this part of the financial report. In fact, some companies even print this part of the annual report in smaller type.

The notes to the financial statements section cover a wide range of issues some of which are:

- ✔ Accounting methods used
- ✔ Changes to accounting methods
- ✔ Key financial commitments that can impact current and future operations
- ✔ Lease obligations
- ✔ Pension and retirement benefits

If any red flags pop up in a company's annual report, this part is where you can find the financial details and explanations. You may also find problems mentioned in the OFR section, but the full explanations for these problems are probably covered in greater detail in the notes section.

Don't get turned off by the visually unpleasing presentation. The notes to the financial statement is one of the most critical parts of the annual report. We cover the importance of the notes to the financial statements in more detail in Chapter 9.

Chapter 6

Balancing Assets against Liabilities and Equity

In This Chapter

▶ Defining assets, liabilities, and equity

▶ Exploring the basics of balance sheets

▶ Reviewing assets

▶ Understanding liabilities

▶ Examining equity

*P*icture a tightrope walker tentatively stepping along a tightrope. As if that isn't challenging enough, imagine that the tightrope walker is carrying plates of equal weight on both sides of a wobbling rod. What would happen if one of those plates were heavier than the other? You don't have to understand anything about physics to know it isn't going to be a pretty sight.

Just as the tightrope walker must be in balance, so must a company's financial position. If the assets aren't equal to the claims against those assets, then that company's financial position isn't in balance, and everything topples over. In this chapter, I introduce you to the balance sheet, which gives the financial-report reader a snapshot of the company's position at a certain point in time.

Understanding the Balance Equation

A company keeps track of its financial balance on a *balance sheet,* a summary of a company's financial standing at a particular point in time. A company's balance sheet contains the following items:

✔ **Assets:** Anything the company owns, from cash to stock of products for sale, to the paper it prints the reports on.

✔ **Liabilities:** Debts the company owes.

✔ **Equity:** Money owed to the owners of the company, such as the cash they have put in as share capital plus the profits the company has retained.

The assets that a company owns are equal to the claims against that company, by creditors (liabilities) or owners (equity). The claims side must equal the assets side in order for the balance sheet to stay in balance. The parts always balance according to this formula:

Assets = Liabilities + Equity

As a company and its assets grow, its liabilities or equities grow in similar proportion. For example, whenever a company buys a major asset, such as a building, the company has to use another asset to pay for it, like cash in the bank, or use a combination of assets and liabilities (such as overdrafts or mortgages) or equity (owner's money, perhaps obtained by selling more shares).

Introducing the Balance Sheet

Trying to read a balance sheet without having a grasp of its parts is a little like trying to translate a language you've never spoken – you may recognise the letters, but the words don't mean much. Unlike a foreign language, however, a balance sheet is pretty easy to get a fix on as soon as you work out a few basics.

Digging into dates

The first things you should notice when looking at the financial statements are the dates at the top. You need to know on what date or during what period of time the financial statements are relevant. This information is particularly critical when you start comparing results among companies. You don't want to compare the 2007 results of one company with the 2006 results of another company. Economic conditions are certainly different, and the comparison doesn't give you an accurate view of how well the companies competed in similar economic conditions.

On a balance sheet, the date at the top is written after 'as at', meaning that the balance sheet reports a company's financial status on that particular day. A balance sheet differs from other kinds of financial statements, such as the income statement or statement of cash flows, which show information for a period of time such as a year, a quarter, or a month. We discuss income statements in Chapter 7 and statements of cash flows in Chapter 8.

If a company's balance sheet states 'As at 31 December 2007', the company is most likely operating on a calendar year. Not all companies end their business year at the end of the calendar year, however. Many companies operate on a fiscal year instead, which means the company picks a 12-month period that more accurately reflects its business cycles. For example, a number of retail companies end their fiscal year on 31 January. The best time of year for major retail sales is during the holiday season and post-holiday season, so stores close the books after those periods end. Many companies end their year at the same time as the end of the tax year – end of March or 5 April in the case of the UK.

To show you how economic conditions might make it very difficult to compare the balance sheets of two companies with two different fiscal years, we'll use the terrorist attacks on 11 September 2001. If one company reports its fiscal year from 1 September to 31 August, and another company reports its fiscal year from 1 January to 31 December, the results could be very different. The company that reported from 1 September 2000 to 31 August 2001, would not have felt the impact of that devastating event. Its Christmas-season sales from October 2000 to December 2000 are likely to have been much different from those of the company that reported from 1 January 2001 to 31 December 2001, because those results would include sales after 11 September, when the world economy slowed considerably. The company's balance sheet for 1 September 2001 to 31 August 2002, would show the full impact of the attacks on the company's financial position.

Nailing down the numbers

As you start reading financial reports for large corporations, you see that they don't use big numbers to show billion-pound results (1,000,000,000) or state the amount to the penny, such as 1,123,456,789.99. Imagine how difficult it would be to read such detailed financial statements!

At the top of a balance sheet or any other financial statement, you see a statement indicating that the numbers are in millions, thousands, or however the company decides to round the numbers. For example, if a billion-dollar company indicates that numbers are in millions, you see 1 billion represented as 1,000 and 35 million as 35. The 1,123,456,789.99 figure would be shown as 1,123.

Rounding off numbers makes a report easier on the eye, but be sure you know how the company is rounding its numbers before you start comparing financial statements among companies. This is particularly crucial when you compare a large company with a smaller one. The large company may round to millions, whereas the smaller company rounds to thousands.

Comparing formats

You are likely to come across two main formats for balance sheets, the UK format and the US format. We've compiled samples of each format using very simple numbers to give you an idea of what you can expect to see. Of course, real balance sheets have much larger and more complex numbers.

You can see the balance sheets for two companies, Tesco and Marks and Spencer, in Appendix A. Both companies use the UK format.

The *UK format,* the type of format you see most often, is a vertical presentation of the numbers, as Table 6–1 shows.

Table 6–1	The UK Format
Non-current assets	200
Current assets	300
Total assets	500
Current liabilities	200
Non-current liabilities	100
Total liabilities	300
Net assets	200
Equity	200

In the UK, a balanced sheet shows net assets equal to equity.

The *US format* is normally a horizontal presentation of the numbers although they also use the vertical format. You can see it in Table 6–2.

Table 6–2	The US Format
Current assets	$300
Long-term assets	$150
Other assets	$50
Total assets	$500
Current liabilities	$200

Long term liabilities	$100
Shareholders' equity	$200
Total liabilities/equity	$500

In the US format, a balanced sheet shows total assets equal to total liabilities plus equity.

The UK format is different from the US in that it may have two significant lines that don't appear in the US format:

- ✔ **Net current assets:** This line is the current assets the company has available to pay bills. You calculate net current assets by subtracting the current liabilities from the current assets.

- ✔ **Net assets:** This line shows what is left for the company's owners, or shareholders, after all liabilities have been subtracted from total assets.

(Keep in mind that Non-current assets in the UK are known as long-term assets plus Other assets in US balance sheets.)

As investing becomes more globalised, you may start comparing UK companies with foreign companies. Or perhaps you may consider buying shares directly in US, European or other foreign companies. You will find that the UK format is closer to other European countries because all listed companies within the European Economic Area prepare their accounts based on International Accounting Standards.

Companies that are not listed still follow UK standards and the Companies Act. The format of their accounts is shown in Table 6–3:

Table 6–3	The UK Format
Fixed assets	200
Current assets	300
Current liabilities	200
Net current assets	100
Liabilities due beyond one year	100
Net assets	200
Equity	200

Assessing Assets

Anything that the company owns is considered an asset. An asset can be something as basic as cash or as massive as a factory. A company must have assets in order to operate the business. The asset side of a balance sheet gives you a summary of what the company owns.

Non-current assets

Assets that the company plans to hold for use in the business rather than for sale are placed in the *non-current assets* section of the balance sheet. Non-current assets, described in the following sections, include intangible assets; land and buildings; capitalised leases; plant and equipment; furniture and fixtures; and investments. This section of the balance sheet shows you the assets that a company has to build its products and sell its goods.

Intangible assets

Any assets that aren't physical, such as patents, copyrights, trademarks, and goodwill, are considered *intangible assets.* Patents, copyrights, and trademarks are actually registered with the appropriate government department, and the company holds exclusive rights to these items. If another company wants to use something that is patented, copyrighted, or trademarked, it must pay a fee to use those assets.

Patents give the companies the right to dominate the market for a particular product. For example, pharmaceutical companies can be the sole source for a drug that is still under patent. Copyrights also give companies exclusive rights for sale. Books that are copyrighted can be printed only by the publisher or individual who owns that copyright or by someone who has bought the rights from the copyright owner.

Goodwill is a different type of asset, reflecting things like the value of a company's locations, customer base, or consumer loyalty. Companies essentially purchase goodwill when they buy another company for a price that's higher than the value of a company's tangible assets – its market value. The premium that's paid for the company's assets is kept in an account called goodwill shown on the balance sheet. Goodwill is dealt with in more detail in Chapter 10.

Property, plant, and equipment

These assets are known as tangible fixed assets in the accounts of small companies. They're shown as a single figure on the face of the balance sheet although further analysis of the different classes of assets is provided in the notes to the accounts. Property, plant, and equipment includes:

✔ **Property:** Any land and buildings the company own are included under this heading. Companies must *depreciate* (show that the asset is gradually being used up by deducting a portion of the value) the value of their buildings each year. The land portion of ownership isn't depreciated because its value is not used up by the passage of time. Adopting a policy of revaluation is possible if the company wishes to do so. Revaluation might seem to be a good idea when the value goes up significantly from the purchase price. However, once the decision has been taken to revalue property then that valuation must be kept up-to-date – even if it falls.

If property is leased, then the value of the property is not usually included in the balance sheet. However, any amounts spent on improving a leasehold property are included and depreciated in the same way as other assets.

Property that is not used in the business but is kept for its potential to earn rental income or for capital gain is known as investment property. Under International Accounting Standards (IAS) 40, investment property can be included in the balance sheet at cost less depreciation or fair value.

Strangely, small companies have less choice on this matter than listed companies. The only permitted treatment under UK GAAP is to include investment properties at open market value.

Sometimes you see an indication that a company holds *hidden assets* – they're hidden from your view when you read the financial reports because you have no idea what the true market value of the buildings and land might be. For example, an office building that was purchased for £390,000 and held for 20 years without being revalued may have a market value of £1 million if it were sold today but has been depreciated to £190,000 or left at its original purchase price over the past 20 years.

✔ **Plant and equipment:** Companies track and summarise all machinery and equipment used in their facilities or by their employees under the sub-heading *plant and equipment*. These assets depreciate just like buildings but for shorter periods of time, depending on the company's estimate of their useful life. IT equipment may be included in this category or may be shown as a separate class of assets in the notes to the accounts.

✔ **Furniture and fittings:** Some companies have a separate class for *furniture and fittings* or *fixtures and fittings*, whereas others group these items in plant and equipment. You're more likely to find furniture and fixture line items in major retail chains that hold significant furniture and fixture assets in their retail outlets than you are to find the line item on balance sheets for manufacturing companies that don't have retail outlets.

Capitalised leases

If a company acquires an asset, such as a machine, under a lease agreement where that agreement covers most of the asset's life, then the asset will be included in plant and equipment. The same method of accounting is used for a hire purchase agreement that contains an option to purchase the asset at some point in the future. You can find more details about the leases in the notes to the financial statements.

Accumulated depreciation

In an important note to the accounts you can find out the cost of the non-current assets, their depreciation charge this year and the accumulated depreciation since the asset was obtained. We explain depreciation in greater detail in Chapter 4.

The note shows each non-current category, such as property, plant, and equipment separately so that you can get some idea which of the asset types are oldest by recognising how much depreciation has been charged against it.

The age of machinery and factories can be significant factors in trying to determine a company's future cost and growth prospects. A company with mostly aging plants needs to spend more money on repair or replacement than a company that has mostly new facilities. Look for discussion of this in the manager's commentary or the notes to the financial statements. If you don't find this information there, you have to dig deeper by reading analyst reports or reports in the financial press.

If you look at Tesco's and Marks and Spencer's balance sheets in Appendix A, you will see that Tesco has an item goodwill and intangible assets whereas Marks and Spencer only mentions goodwill in Note 13 to the accounts. In both cases you have to go to the notes to the accounts to find the detail about the land and property they currently own.

Investments in associates and joint ventures

A *subsidiary* is an entity that is controlled by another entity. A company will prepare consolidated accounts to include all of its subsidiaries. (We talk more about consolidation in Chapter 10.)

Investments in associates are included in the balance sheet under the heading of non-current assets. An associate is an entity over which the company has significant influence but which does not fall into the definition of a subsidiary or a joint venture. It is presumed (unless the presumption can clearly be demonstrated to be false) that significant influence exists if the company holds, directly or indirectly, 20 per cent or more of the voting rights in the associate.

If a company controls less than 20 per cent of another entity's voting rights then it is presumed that there is no significant influence – unless, again, this presumption can be clearly demonstrated to be false. Such an investment is included within non-current assets or current assets depending on the intentions of the investing company, (see the section 'Current asset investments' later in this chapter). Long before a company reaches even the 20 per cent mark, you usually find discussion of the company's buying habits in the financial press or in analyst reports. Talk of a possible merger or acquisition often begins when a company reaches the 20 per cent mark.

You usually don't find more than a line item in the balance sheet that shows the total of all associates. More detail is mentioned in the notes to the financial statements.

A *joint venture* is an entity which is under the joint control of two or more other parties. Joint ventures are accounted for by proportional consolidation (see Chapter 10) or by the same method as associates.

Current assets

Anything that a company owns that it can convert to cash in less than a year is a current asset. Without these funds, the company would not be able to pay its bills and would have to close its doors. Cash, of course, is an important component of this part of the balance sheet, but there are other assets that will be used during the year to pay the bills.

Inventory (also known as stock)

Any products held by the company ready for sale are considered *stock*. The term stock has always been used in the UK but the correct name is now *inventory* in accordance with IAS 1. We will use the terms interchangeably as is very common in UK business. The stock on the balance sheet is normally valued at the cost to the company, not at the price the company hopes to sell the product at. However, if an item of stock has lost value so that the company will suffer a loss on sale, then that item is valued at net realisable value which is selling price less any expenditure necessary to bring the item to a saleable condition.

Companies can pick any of four different methods to calculate the cost of their stock (depending on their business and location), and the method they choose can significantly impact the bottom line. The four methods of costing coincide with the way that the company keeps track of stock. The following are the different stock-costing systems:

- **First in, first out (FIFO):** This system assumes that the oldest goods are sold first. This system is used when the company is concerned about spoilage or obsolescence. Food stores use FIFO because items that sit on the shelves too long spoil. Computer firms use it because products become quickly outdated, and they need to sell the older products first. Assuming that older goods cost less than newer goods, FIFO makes the bottom line look better, because the lowest cost is assigned to the goods sold, increasing the net profit from sales. FIFO is the system most commonly used in the UK.

✔ **Last in, first out (LIFO):** This system assumes that the newest stock is sold first. Companies with products that don't spoil or become obsolete can use this system. The bottom line can be significantly affected if the cost of goods to be sold is continually rising. The most expensive goods that come in last are assumed to be the first sold. LIFO increases the cost of goods sold, which in turn lowers the net profit from sales and decreases a company's tax liability because its profits are lower after the higher costs are subtracted. Hardware stores that sell hammers, nails, screws, and other items that have been the same for years and won't spoil are good candidates for LIFO. We have included LIFO because it is a term you will still hear, but companies cannot use LIFO under International Accounting Standards. LIFO continues to be used in the United States.

✔ **Average costing:** This system reflects the cost of stock most accurately and gives the company a good view of the cost trends for its stock. As a company receives each new shipment of stock, it calculates an average cost for each product by adding in the new stock. If a company is frequently faced with stock prices that go up and down, average costing can help level out the peaks and valleys of stock costs through the year. Because the price of petrol rises and falls almost every day, petrol stations usually use this type of system.

✔ **Specific identification:** This system is a system that tracks the actual cost of each individual piece of stock. Companies that sell big-ticket items or those with differing accessories or upgrades (such as cars) commonly use this system. Each car that comes into the showroom has a different set of features, so the price of each car differs.

After a company chooses a type of stock system, it must use that system for the rest of its corporate life or it must explain the reasons for changing systems in its accounting policies. Because the way companies track stock costs can have a significant impact on the profit before tax and therefore the amount of taxes due, Her Majesty's Revenue and Customs monitors any changes in stock-tracking methods closely.

Trade and other receivables also known as Accounts receivable or Debtors

Any company that allows its customers to buy on credit has an accounts receivable line on its balance sheet. *Accounts receivable* is a collection of individual customer accounts listing money that customers owe the company for products or services they've already received.

A company must carefully monitor not only whether the customer pays, but also how quickly they pay. If a customer makes payments later and later, the company must determine whether to allow the late-paying customer gets additional credit or whether it should block further purchases. Although the sales may look good, a non-paying customer hurts the company because they're taking out – and failing to pay for – stock that another customer could've bought. Too many non-paying or late-paying customers can severely hurt a company's cash-flow position, which means the company may not have the cash it needs to pay the bills.

Comparing a company's accounts receivable line over a number of years gives you a very good idea of how well the company is doing in collecting late-paying customers' accounts. Although you may see a company report very positive sales numbers and a major increase in sales, if the accounts-receivable number is rising more rapidly in proportion, the company may be having trouble collecting the money on these accounts. We show you how to analyse accounts receivable in Chapter 16.

Current asset investments

Securities that are bought by a company primarily as a place to hold assets until the company decides how to use the money for its operations or growth are included in current assets. A company must report these assets at their fair value based on the market value of the share or bond on the day the company prepares its financial report. This means that the company must report any *unrealised losses or gains* – changes in the value of a holding that has not yet been sold – on current asset investments on the company's balance sheet to show the impact of those gains or losses on the company's earnings.

This method of accounting is optional for small companies who can instead include current asset investments at cost.

Cash

For companies, cash is basically the same thing you carry around in your pocket or keep in your current and savings accounts. Keeping track of money is a lot more complex for companies, however, because they usually keep it in many different locations. Every multimillion corporation has numerous locations, and every location needs cash in the appropriate currency.

Even in a *centralised accounting system*, in which all bills are paid in the same place and all money is collected and put in the bank at the same time, a company keeps cash in more than one location. Keeping most of the money in the bank and having a little cash on hand for incidental expenses doesn't work for most companies.

For example, retail outlets or banks need to keep cash in every cash register or under the control of every cashier to be able to transact business with their customers. Yet the company must have a way of tracking its cash and knowing exactly how much it has at the end of every day (and sometimes several times during the day for high-volume businesses). Anyone handling cash for a company must count out his cash drawer before leaving for the day and show that the amount of cash matches up with the figure that the day's transactions indicate should be there.

If a company has a number of locations, each location is likely to need a bank in which it can deposit receipts and get cash as needed. So a large corporation is going to have a maze of bank accounts, cash registers, petty cash, and other places where cash is kept daily. At the end of every day, each company location calculates the cash total and reports it to the centralised accounting area.

The amount of cash that you see on the balance sheet is the amount of cash found at all company locations on the particular day for which the balance sheet was created.

Managing cash is one of the hardest jobs because cash can so easily disappear if proper internal controls aren't in place. Internal controls for monitoring cash are usually among the strictest in any company. If this subject interests you, you can find out more about it in any basic accounting book, such as *Understanding Business Accounting For Dummies* by John A Tracy and Colin Barrow (Wiley).

Other types of current asset

The rule is that an asset is current if it is the intention of the company to convert it into cash within 12 months and that there is a good likelihood that they will be able to do so. You may, for example, see *Taxation receivable* in current assets if the company is likely to recover tax in cash during the next year, or in non-current assets if not.

The balance sheet is a presentation for general consumption, but the notes to the financial statements are where you find the small print that most people don't read. You find lots of juicy details in the notes that you shouldn't miss. We talk more about the notes and their importance in Chapter 9.

Looking at Liabilities

Companies must spend money in order to conduct their day-to-day operations. Whenever a company makes a commitment to spend that money on credit, whether it be short-term using a credit card or long-term using a mortgage, those commitments become debts or liabilities.

Current liabilities

Current liabilities are any obligations that a company must pay during the next 12 months. These include short-term borrowings, the current portion of long-term debt, accounts payable, and accrued liabilities. If the company can't pay these bills, it could go out of business or go into bankruptcy.

✔ **Trade and other payables:** Companies list money they owe to others for products, services, supplies, and other short-term needs (invoices due in less than 12 months) in *accounts payable*. They record payments due to suppliers, contractors, and other companies they do business with.

✔ **Accrued liabilities:** Liabilities that are accrued but aren't yet paid at the time a company prepares the balance sheet are called *accrued liabilities* and are included in trade and other payables. For example, companies include royalties, advertising, payroll, management incentives, or employee taxes that aren't yet paid in this line item. Sometimes a company breaks down items like income taxes payable individually without using a catch-all line item called accrued liabilities. When you look in the notes, you see more detail about the types of company financial obligations included and the total of each type of liability.

✔ **Short-term borrowings:** *Short-term borrowings* are usually credit facilities the company takes to manage cash flow and will include bank overdrafts. When a company borrows this way, it isn't much different from when you use a credit card or personal loan to pay bills until your next pay day. As you know, these types of loans usually carry the highest interest-rate charges, so if a company can't repay them quickly, it converts the debt to something longer term with lower interest rates.

This type of liability should be a relatively low number on the balance sheet compared with other liabilities. If the number isn't low, it could be a sign of trouble, indicating that the company is having difficulty securing long-term debt or meeting its cash obligations.

✔ **Current portion of long-term borrowings:** Payments due on long-term debt during the coming financial year are shown in this line of the balance sheet. Any portion of the debt that's owed beyond the current 12 months is reflected in the long-term liabilities section. There are many ways for a company to borrow money and these are detailed in the notes to the accounts.

✔ **Current tax payable:** This tax, probably corporation tax, relates to the profits of the year being reported and will be paid during the next 12 months.

✔ **Provisions:** Most balance sheets have an element of these liabilities that will probably have to be paid. Provisions may be short-term or long-term depending on their timing.

Net current assets

This line shows the difference between current assets and current liabilities. If this figure is positive and the difference is large it shows that the company will have no short-term trouble in meeting its financial commitments. However, what figure represents a comfortable net current assets figure depends on the industry.

Non-current liabilities

Any money the company must pay out more than 12 months in the future is considered a long-term liability. Long-term liabilities won't throw a company into bankruptcy, but if they become too large, the company could have trouble paying its bills in the future.

- **Long-term borrowings:** The items under this heading include bank loans and other long term borrowings such as debentures or mortgages. In a recent change to accounting principles, preference shares may also be included in liabilities. The detail of the nature and timing of long-term borrowings is in the notes to the accounts.

- **Post employee benefit obligations:** There are two types of pension scheme – defined contribution and defined benefit. Companies with a defined contribution scheme pay the correct amount into each employee's scheme each year. As such, the company has no future obligation and there will be no reference to pension schemes in the balance sheet.

  In a defined benefit scheme, the employer commits to paying a future pension based on length of service and salary during service. Amounts will be paid into the pension scheme throughout the employees' working lives but, in the event that the amounts put aside are insufficient, the company remains liable to make up the difference. It is the actuary's best estimate of the shortfall that shows in the balance sheet. Clearly, this estimate is highly subjective and, in the event of a downturn in the stock market, can be a very large figure. In the event that the actuary assesses a surplus in the scheme then that will be included in the balance sheet as an asset.

- **Deferred tax liabilities:** Deferred tax is a device used by accountants to reflect the fact that tax is calculated not on the profits in the income statement but on profits adjusted for tax purposes. This calculation is explained further in Chapter 7.

In Appendix A, you can see that both Tesco and Marks and Spencer give the financial report reader little detail of these liabilities on the balance sheet. Instead, you must dig through the notes and managers' commentary to find the detail of the liabilities.

You can find more detail about what the company actually groups in the other liability category in the notes to the financial statement. (Guess you're getting used to that phrase!)

Navigating the Equity Maze

The final piece of the balancing equation is equity. All companies are owned by somebody, and the claims that these owners have against the assets owned by the company are called *equity*. In a non-corporate entity, the equity owners are individuals or partners. In a corporation, the equity owners are shareholders.

Share capital

A *share* represents a portion of ownership in a company. Each share has a nominal value of say 25 pence or £1 but normally shares in public companies are sold to investors at a higher price than the nominal value. The difference between the nominal value and the selling price is known as a *premium*. The amount recorded in the balance sheet as share capital is the number of shares issued multiplied by the nominal value of the share. This price isn't affected by the current market value of the share. Any increase or decrease in a share's value after its initial offering to the public isn't reflected in the accounts. The market gains or losses are actually taken by the shareholders and not the company when shares are bought and sold on the market.

Some companies issue two types of shares: ordinary and preference.

Ordinary (or equity) shareholders

These shareholders own a portion of the company and have a vote on issues taken to the shareholders. If the board decides to pay *dividends* (a certain portion per share paid to ordinary shareholders from profits), ordinary share-holders get their portion of those dividends after the preference shareholders have been paid in full.

Small companies may have different classes of equity shares to enable different groups of shareholders to have different rights concerning voting or dividends. This is unusual in a listed company where shareholders would expect to be treated equally.

When the utilities formerly owned by the government were privatised, the government retained a *golden share* that permits it to step in and take control again if the situation warrants it. The golden share has no dividend rights but immense voting rights.

Preference shareholders

These shareholders own stock that's actually somewhere in-between ordi-nary shares and a *bond* (a long-term liability to be paid back over a number of years).

Preference shares come in all shapes and sizes. Thirty years ago, most preference shares were a permanent part of the company's capital. A fixed dividend was payable each year (subject to the approval of the directors) and the term 'preference' referred to the fact that the dividend on the preference shares would be paid before any dividend on ordinary shares. Similarly, if the company was wound up, preference shareholders would receive their capital before the ordinary shareholders.

Note that preference shareholders are not guaranteed a dividend each year since the directors may consider that it is not in the best interests of the company to pay one. Some preference shares are cumulative which means that if, for some reason, the company doesn't pay a preference dividend in one year then these dividends are accrued for in the current year's accounts and paid when the company has enough money. Accrued dividends for preference shareholders must be paid before ordinary shareholders get any money. Usually, preference shareholders do not have voting rights in the company.

These days, preference shares may well be convertible and/or redeemable. If they are redeemable, the company has the right or obligation to buy the shares back. The date of redemption may be fixed or it may be at the option of the shareholder or the company. The redemption amount may be par or at a premium.

If the shares are convertible, they can be converted into equity shares. Again, the date of conversion may or may not be fixed and the right to enforce conversion may belong to the shareholder or the company.

Legally, preference shares are a type of share (and subject to the requirements of the Companies Act) but sometimes they have characteristics that make them more like bonds. In a recent change to accounting principles, the directors of the company must decide whether the preference shares issued by the company should be classified with equity or liabilities. This will depend on whether the rights of the preference shareholders give the company an obligation to make payments which it can't avoid.

The old-fashioned preference shares still exist in some small companies. If the share is non-redeemable and the dividends are at the discretion of the directors then the preference shares will be classed as equity.

Preference shares have become the financial instrument of choice for venture capitalists since they permit great flexibility in the arrangements between the company and the provider of funds. By juggling the percentage dividend and the premium on redemption, the venture capitalist can obtain the required return over a period of time but the repayments can be spread to suit the needs of the company. The right to convert will then kick in if the company fails to meet its obligations at any stage and this then gives the venture capitalist a stake in the equity – or even control of the company.

Most modern preference shares are classified as part of liabilities but in an unwelcome complication, the relevant accounting standard (IAS 39) requires that, in appropriate circumstances, the preference shares should be treated as compound instruments and split between liabilities and equity.

Share premium account

If a growing company decides to raise capital by selling more shares it will issue them at a price somewhere near the current market value not at its nominal value. This line in the balance sheet shows the difference between the two. So if a share with nominal value of 25p is trading at £1.50 pence on the market and the company issues new shares at say, £1.20, then 25 pence is added to Issued capital and 95 pence into the share premium account.

Other reserves

The most common balance that you will see under this heading is the Revaluation Reserve. If a property is revalued, then the assets in the balance sheet will go up. To keep the balance, equity must also be increased. If the property had been sold, then a profit would be realised and this would be shown in the income statement and would affect retained earnings. Since the property has only been revalued, the profit is unrealised and therefore the increase in equity is shown in the revaluation reserve.

Retained earnings

Each year, a company makes a choice to pay out its net profit to its share-holders or to retain all or some of it for reinvesting in the company. Any profit not paid to shareholders over the years is accumulated in an account called *retained earnings*.

Capital

You won't find the Capital line item on a company's financial statement, but if you work for an unincorporated entity such as a sole trader or partnership, you are likely to find this line item on the balance sheet. *Capital* is the money that was initially invested by the founders of the company.

If you don't see this line item on the balance sheet of a partnership, it is likely that the owners didn't invest their own capital to get started, or they already took out their initial capital when the company began to earn money.

Drawing

Drawing is another line item you don't see on a company's financial statement. Only unincorporated businesses have a drawing account. This line item tracks money that the owners take out from the yearly profits of a business. After a business is incorporated, owners can take money as salary or dividends, but not on a drawing account.

Chapter 7

Using the Income Statement

· ·

In This Chapter

▶ Getting acquainted with the income statement

▶ Considering different types of revenue

▶ Determining a company's expenses

▶ Analysing a company's finances using profits and losses

▶ Working out earnings per share

· ·

*B*usinesspeople need to know how well their businesses have done over the past month, quarter, or year. Without that information, they have no idea where their businesses have come from and where they might go next. Even a small business that has no obligation to report to the public is likely to do income statements on at least a quarterly basis to find out whether the business is making a profit or a loss.

The income statement you see in published annual reports is likely to be very different from the one you see if you work for the company. The primary difference is the detail in certain line items. In this chapter we review the detail that goes into an income statement – but don't be surprised if some of the detail never shows up in the financial reports you get as a company outsider. Much of the detail is considered confidential and isn't given out to people outside the company. We include this detailed information in this chapter so that you know what's behind the numbers that you do see. If you're a company insider, this additional information helps you understand the internal reports you receive.

Introducing the Income Statement

The *income statement* is where you find out whether the company made a profit or a loss. You also find information about the company's revenues, sales levels, the costs it incurred to make those sales, and the expenses it paid to operate the business. The key parts of the income statement are:

- ✔ **Sales or revenues:** How much money the business took in from its sales to customers.

- ✔ **Cost of sales:** What it cost the company to produce or purchase the goods it sold.

- ✔ **Expenses:** How much the company spent on advertising, administration, rent, salaries, and everything else that's involved in operating a business to support the sales process.

- ✔ **Profit or loss for the year:** This is the bottom line that tells you whether the company made a profit or operated at a loss.

The income statement is one of the three main reports required by the International Accounting Standards Board (IASB); we describe their role in the preparation of financial statements in Chapters 18 and 19. The IASB publishes and updates the standards for reporting in documents called International Financial Reporting Standards (IFRS) and International Accounting Standards (IAS). These standards do not currently apply to small companies or large unlisted companies. For this reason we point out some differences in what you might find in small business reports where they are different from IFRS.

The IASB specifies that all items of income or expense recognised in a period should be included in the income statement except where an IAS or IFRS requires otherwise. Examples of items that affect equity but do not appear in the income statement of the current period are items relating to previous periods which have been adjusted in the current period – such as correction of errors or the effect of changes in accounting policies. Another example mentioned in Chapter 6 is a revaluation of a property which changes equity but is not shown in the income statement. In order that the financial statements reflect all changes during a period of time to the equity of a business IAS 1 requires a statement of changes in equity which include the profit or loss from the income statement but also gather together all other changes affecting equity.

When looking at an income statement, you can expect to find a report of either

✔ **Excess of revenues over expenses:** This report means the company earned a profit, or

✔ **Excess of expenses over revenues:** This report means the company faced a loss.

Income statement is the standard term under IFRS. Small business reports frequently refer to it as the Profit and Loss account.

Digging into dates

Income statements reflect an *operating period,* which means that they show results for a specific length of time. At the top of an income statement, you see the phrase 'Year Ended' and the month the period ended for an annual financial statement. You may also see 'Quarters Ended' or 'Months Ended' for reports prepared based on shorter periods of time. Companies are required to show at least two periods of data on their income statements. So if you're looking at a statement for Last Year, you'll also find columns for the Previous Year.

Many people believe you should analyse at least four years' worth of data if you're thinking about investing in a company. You can easily get hold of this data by ordering a two-year-old annual report along with the current one. You can also find most annual and quarterly reports online at a company's Web site or by visiting the UK Companies House Web site. One slight complication to this is that IFRS were introduced in 2005. Previous to that reports were governed by UK GAAP so you are not comparing like with like when you compare the Annual Report for 2005, for example, with the Annual Report for 2003. However, many companies include a five-year record in their annual report and, if they do so, the results from previous periods will have been adjusted so that all results are stated on the same IFRS basis.

Comparing formats

The UK format divides the income statement into several sections and gives the reader some critical subtotals to make analysing the data quicker and easier. Even though the UK and US income statements include the same revenue and expense information, they may group the information differently. Table 7–1 shows the format for a simple UK income statement.

Table 7–1	The UK Format for the Income Statement
Revenue	1,000
Cost of sales	500
Gross profit	500
Marketing and distribution expenses	200
Administrative expenses	150
Other operating expenses	50
Operating profit	100
Financial income	200
Financial expenses	50
Profit before taxation	250
Taxation	50
Profit for the year	200

The critical subtotals in the UK format are:

✔ **Gross profit:** This reflects the profit generated from sales minus the cost of the goods sold.

✔ **Operating profit or loss:** This reflects the income earned by the company after all its operating expenses have been subtracted.

✔ **Profit/Loss before taxation:** This reflects all income earned – which can include gains on equipment sales, interest revenue, and other revenue not generated by sales – before taxes are subtracted.

✔ **Profit/Loss for the period:** This reflects the bottom line – whether or not the company made a profit.

Many companies add even more profit lines, like earnings before interest, taxes, depreciation, and amortisation, known as EBITDA for short (see the section 'EBITDA' later in this chapter).

Some companies that have discontinued operations include those in the line item for continuing operations. But it's better for the financial report reader if that information is on a separate line; otherwise, the reader won't know what the actual profit or loss is from continuing operations. (You can find Tesco and Marks and Spencer financial reports in Appendix A.) We delve a bit deeper into these various profit lines in 'Sorting Out the Profit and Loss Types' later in this chapter.

There is more than one format for the Income Statement in the US. Table 7–2 shows an example of a simple US format:

Table 7–2	A Simple US Format for the Income Statement
Revenues	
Sales	$1,000
Interest income	200
Total Revenue	**$1,200**
Expenses	
Cost of goods sold	$500
Depreciation	50
Advertising	50
Salaries and wages	100
Insurance	50
Research and development	100
Supplies	50
Interest expense	50
Income taxes	50
Total expenses	**$1,000**
Net income	**$200**

Delving into the Tricky Business of Revenues

You may think that deciding when to count something as revenue is a relatively simple procedure. Well, forget that. Revenue acknowledgement is one of the most complex issues on the income statement. In fact, you may have noticed that with the recent corporate scandals, a significant reason for companies getting into trouble has to do with the issue of misstated revenues.

In this section, we define revenue and explain the three line items that make up the revenue portion of the income statement: sales, cost of sales, and gross profit.

Defining revenue

When a company recognises something as *revenue* that doesn't always mean that cash changed hands or that the product was delivered or even completed. Accrual accounting leaves room for deciding when revenue is actually recorded. A company recognises revenue when it earns it and recognises expenses when it incurs them, without regard to whether or not cash changes hands. You can find out more about accounting basics in Chapter 4.

Because accrual accounting allows a company to count something as revenue even if it doesn't actually have the cash in hand, senior managers can play games to make the bottom line look the way they want it to look by counting or not counting income. Sometimes they acknowledge more income than they should to improve the financial reports; other times, they reduce income to reduce the tax bite. We talk more about these shenanigans in Chapter 22.

When a company wants to count something as revenue, several factors can make that decision rather muddy, leaving questions about whether or not a particular sale should be counted:

- ✓ **If the seller and buyer haven't agreed on the final price for the merchandise and service, the seller can't count the revenue collected.** For example, when a company is in the middle of negotiating a contract for the sale of a major item, such as a car or appliance, it cannot include that sale as revenue until the final price has been set and a contract obligating the buyer is in place.

- ✓ **If the buyer doesn't pay for the merchandise until the company resells it to a retail outlet (which may be the case for a company that works with a distributor) or to the customer, the company can't count the revenue until the sale to the customer is final.** For example, publishers frequently allow bookshops to return unsold books within a certain amount of time. If there's a good chance that some portion of the product may be returned unsold, companies must take this into account when reporting revenues. For instance, a publisher uses historical data to estimate what percentage of books will be returned and adjusts sales downward to reflect those likely returns.

- ✓ **If the buyer and seller are related, then the company cannot ever count it as revenue.** No, we're not talking about blood relatives here. We're talking about when the buyer is the parent company or subsidiary of the seller; in that case, revenue isn't acknowledged in the same way. Instead, companies must handle it as an internal transfer of assets.

✔ **If the buyer isn't obligated to pay for the merchandise because it's stolen or physically destroyed before it's delivered or sold, the company can't acknowledge the revenue until the merchandise is actually sold.** For example, a toy company works with a distributor or other middleman to get its toys into retail stores. If the distributor or middleman doesn't have to pay for those toys until they're delivered or sold to retailers, the manufacturer can't count the toys it shipped to the middleman or distributor as revenue until the distributor or middleman completes the sale.

✔ **If the seller is obligated to provide significant services to the buyer or aid in reselling the product, the seller can't count the sale of that product as revenue until the sale is actually completed with the final customer.** For example, many manufacturers of technical products offer installation or follow-up services for a new product as part of the sales promotion. If those services are a significant part of the final sale, the manufacturer can't count that sale as revenue until the installation or service has been completed with the customer. Items shipped for sale to local retailers under these conditions wouldn't be considered sold, so they can't be counted as revenue.

✔ **If the seller is providing a combination of products and services to the buyer which are bundled together into a single contract.** For example, many sellers of IT equipment provide hardware, software and after-sales support and updates. In this case, the seller should try to separate the contracts into its constituent parts so that revenue can be recognised on the parts of the contract which have been delivered. For example, a contract for the sale of a computer may include a year's 'free' support. The total revenue should be split between the two separate contracts. The revenue from the sale of the hardware and software should be recognised immediately and the revenue from the service contract should be recognised as the contract progresses.

Adjusting sales

Not all products sell for their list price. Companies frequently use discounts, returns, or allowances to reduce the prices of products or services. Sometimes, in order to make a sale, a company must sell the product at a discounted price. Whenever a company sells a product at a discount it should keep track of those discounts as well as its returns. That's the only way a company can truly analyse how much money it's making on the sale of its products and how accurately it's pricing the products to sell in the marketplace.

If a company is offering too many discounts, that's usually a sign of a weak or very competitive market. If a company has a lot of returns, that may be a sign of a quality-control problem or a sign that the product isn't living up to customers' expectations. The sales adjustments we talk about here help a company track and analyse its sales and recognise any negative trends.

As a financial-report reader, you won't see the specifics about discounts offered in the income statement, but you may find some mention of significant discounting in the notes to the financial statements. The most common types of adjustments companies make to their sales are:

- **Volume discounts:** To get more items in the marketplace manufacturers offer major retailers *volume discounts,* which means that these retailers agree to buy a large number of the manufacturer's product in order to save a certain percentage of money off the price. One of the reasons you get such good prices at discount sellers like Asda and TKMaxx is because they buy products from the manufacturer at greatly discounted prices. Because they purchase for thousands of stores, they can buy a very large number of goods at one time. Volume discounts reduce the revenue of the company that gives them.

   Notice that some volume discounts do not kick in until a certain level of sales is reached. This can cause a problem in establishing the correct revenue to recognise if a customer reaches a trigger point after the end of the accounting period.

- **Returns:** *Returns* are arrangements between the buyer and seller that allow the buyer to return goods for a number of reasons. I'm sure you've returned goods that you didn't like, that didn't fit, or that possibly didn't even work. Returns are subtracted from a company's revenue. At the period end, the company needs to make its best estimate of future returns of goods sold before the end of the period.

- **Allowances:** Gift vouchers and similar types of accounts that a customer pays for upfront without taking merchandise are types of *allowances.* Allowances are actually liabilities for a store because the customer hasn't yet selected the merchandise and the sale isn't complete. Revenues are collected upfront, but at some point in the future, merchandise will be taken off the shelves and additional cash won't be received.

Most companies don't show you the details of their discounts, returns, and allowances, but they do track them and adjust their revenue accordingly. The *sale, net sales,* or *revenue* figure (the sales made by the company net of any adjustments) at the top of an income statement is shown after the company has adjusted the figure for these items.

Internally, managers see the detail about these adjustments in the sales area of the income statement, so they can track trends for discounts, returns, and allowances. Tracking such trends is a very important aspect of the managerial process. If a manager notices that any of these line items show a dramatic increase, he or she should investigate the reason for the increase. For example, an increase in discounts could mean that the company consistently has to offer its products for less money, which could mean the market is softening and fewer customers are buying fewer products. Or, if a manager notices a dramatic increase in returns, the products he or she is selling may have a defect that needs to be corrected.

Considering cost of sales

Like the sales line item, *cost of sales* (what it costs to manufacture or purchase the goods being sold) also has many different pieces that make up its calculation. You don't see the detail for this line item unless you're a manager of the company concerned. Few companies report their cost of sales in detail to the general public.

Items that make up the cost of sales vary depending on whether the company manufactures the goods in-house or purchases them. If the company manufactures them in-house, you track the costs all the way from the point of raw materials and include the cost of labour involved in building the product. A fair proportion of the manufacturing overheads of the company is added to the cost of each item manufactured. If a company purchases its goods, it tracks the purchases of the goods as they're made.

In fact, a manufacturing firm tracks several levels of stock, including:

✔ **Raw materials:** The materials used for manufacturing.

✔ **Work-in-progress:** Products in the process of being constructed.

✔ **Finished goods:** Products ready for sale.

Tracking begins from the time the raw materials are purchased, with adjustments based on discounts, returns, or allowances given. Companies also add freight charges, and any other costs involved directly in acquiring goods to be sold, to the cost-of-sales section of the income statement.

When a company finally sells the product, the product becomes a cost of sales line item. Managing costs during the production phase is critical for all manufacturing companies. Managers in this type of company receive regular reports that include this type of detail. Trends that show dramatically increasing costs must be investigated as quickly as possible, because the company must consider a price change to maintain its profit margin.

Even if a company is only a service company, it is likely to have costs for the services provided. In this case, the line item may be called 'cost of services sold' rather than 'cost of goods sold'. You may even see a line item called 'cost of goods or services sold' if a company gets revenue from the sale of goods as well as from the sale of services. In this book, to keep it simple, we use the term 'product' to describe what the company sells. In every case 'product' implies the term 'products and/or services'.

Gauging gross profit

The gross profit line item in the revenue section of the income statement is simply a calculation of net revenue or net sales minus the cost of sales. Basically, this number shows the difference between what a company pays for its products and services and the price at which the company sells them. This summary number tells you how much profit a company makes selling its products before deducting the expenses of the operation. If there's no profit or not enough profit here, it's not worth being in business.

Managers, investors, and other interested parties closely watch the trend of a company's gross profit because it indicates the effectiveness of a company's purchasing and pricing policies. Analysts frequently use this number not only to gauge how well a company manages its product costs internally, but also to gauge how well a company manages its product costs compared with other companies in the same business.

If gross profit is too low, a company can do one of two things – find a way to increase sales revenue or find a way to reduce the cost of the goods it's selling.

To increase sales revenue, a company can raise or lower prices in order to increase the amount of money it's bringing in. Raising the prices of its product brings in more revenue if the same number of items are sold, but it could bring in less revenue if the price hike turns away customers and fewer items are sold.

Lowering prices to bring in more revenue may sound strange to you, but if a company determines that a price is too high and is discouraging buyers, doing so may increase its volume of sales and, therefore, its gross profit. This scenario is especially true if the company has a lot of *fixed costs* (such as manufacturing facilities, equipment, and labour) that aren't being used to full capacity. A company could use its manufacturing facilities more effectively and efficiently if it has the capability to produce more product without a significant increase in the *variable costs* (such as raw materials or other factors, like overtime).

A company can also consider using cost-control possibilities for manufacturing or purchasing if its gross profit is too low. The company may find a more efficient way to make the product or may negotiate a better contract for raw materials to reduce those costs. If the company purchases finished products for sale, it may be able to negotiate better contract terms to reduce its purchasing costs.

Acknowledging Expenses

Expenses include the items a company must pay for to operate the business that aren't directly related to the sale and production of specific products. These differ from cost of sales, which can be directly traced to the actual sale of a product. Even when a company is making a sizable gross profit, if management doesn't carefully watch the expenses, the gross profit can quickly turn into a net loss.

Expenses make up the second of the two main parts of the income statement; revenues make up the first part.

Advertising and promotion, administration, and research and development are all examples of expenses. Although many of these expenses impact the ability of a company to sell its products, they aren't direct costs of the sales process for individual items. The following are details about the key items that fit into the expenses part of the income statement:

- **Distribution expenses:** This category is a catch-all for any selling and distribution expenses, including salespeople's and sales managers' salaries, commissions, bonuses, and other compensation expenses. The costs of sales offices and any expenses related to those offices also fall into this category. It is sometimes referred to as Marketing Expenses.

  For many companies, one of the largest expenses is advertising and promotion. Advertising includes TV and radio ads, print ads, and poster ads. Promotions include product giveaways, such as hats, T-shirts, pens with the company logo on it, or name identification on a sports stadium. If a company helps promote a charitable event and has its name on T-shirts or posters as part of the event, these expenses must be included in the advertising and promotion expense line item.

- **Administrative expenses:** This category includes expenses such as administrative salaries, expenses for administrative offices and supplies, insurance, and anything else needed to run the general operations of a company. Expenses for human resources, management, accounting, and security also fall into this category.

✔ **Other operating expenses:** If a company includes line-item detail in its financial reports, you usually find that detail in the notes to the financial statement. All operating expenses that aren't directly connected to the sale of products or administrative expenses fall into the other-operating-expenses category, including:

  • **Royalties:** Any *royalties* (payments made for the use of other peoples' property) paid to individuals or other companies fall under this umbrella. Companies most commonly pay royalties for the use of patents or copyrights owned by another company or individual. Companies also pay royalties when they buy the rights to extract natural resources from another person's property.

  • **Research and product development:** Any costs for developing new products are listed in this line item. Most likely you'll find details about research and product development in the notes to the financial statements or in the managers' commentary. Any company that makes new products has research and development costs because, if it isn't always looking for ways to improve its product or introduce new products, it's at risk of losing out to a competitor. Note, however, that some development expenditure must be carried forward as an asset so that the costs of development are matched with the future expected revenues from the new products. The IASB have set out detailed rules in IAS 38 for when R&D expenditure should be listed and when it should be carried forward as an asset.

✔ **Finance income:** This category includes interest from deposit accounts or bonds held by the company, or dividends received from another company.

✔ **Finance expenses:** Expenses paid for interest on long- or short-term debt are shown in this line item. You usually find some explanation for the interest expenses in the notes to the financial statements.

✔ **Depreciation and amortisation expenses:** Depreciation on buildings, machinery, or other items as well as amortisation on intangible items may be shown as a separate line item. However, in most income statements, depreciation and amortisation fall into the separate headings – cost of sales, distribution, and administrative – depending on the nature of the assets. If you look in the notes to the financial statements, you always find more details about depreciation and amortisation. To find out how these expenses are calculated, go to Chapter 4.

✔ **Taxes:** All corporations have to pay tax on their income. In the taxes category, you find the amount of tax that the company needs to pay on its profits for the year. The standard rate of tax may be set at, say, 30 per cent but this does not mean that the tax charge is 30 per cent of the profit before tax. The reason for this is that the tax rules treat some items differently from accounting rules.

For example, some expenses like entertaining are not allowable for tax purposes so the tax is calculated on a higher profit figure. These differences are known as *permanent differences*. Depreciation is also not allowable for tax purposes but is replaced by capital allowances in the tax computation. This means that, in any particular period, the tax relief for the purchase of a fixed asset does not match the depreciation of the asset. Over the whole life of the asset, the total depreciation equals the total capital allowances received but the timing is different. Quite reasonably, these differences are known as timing differences.

Deferred tax is the device used by accountants to adjust the accounts for the effect of timing differences. Many companies and their investors complain that corporate income is taxed twice – once directly as a corporation and a second time on the dividends that the shareholders receive. In fact, the shareholder only pays tax on dividends if they are a higher rate tax payer since dividends are treated as though basic rate income tax has been deducted at source.

Sorting Out the Profit and Loss Types

When you hear earnings or profits reports on the news, most of the time the financial news reporters are discussing the net profit, net income, or net loss. For readers of financial statements, that bottom-line number doesn't tell the entire story of how a company is doing. Relying solely on the bottom-line number is like reading the last few pages of a novel and thinking that you understand the entire story. All you really know is the end, not how the characters got to that ending.

Because companies have so many different charges or expenses unique to their operations, different profit lines are used for different types of analysis. We cover the types of analysis in Part III, but in this section, we review what each of these profit types includes or doesn't include. For example, gross profit is the best number to use to analyse how well a company is managing its sales and the costs of producing those sales; however, you have no idea how well the company is managing the rest of its expenses. Using operating profit, which shows you how much money was made after considering all costs and expenses for operating the company, allows you to analyse how efficiently the company is managing its operating activities, but you don't get enough detail to analyse product costs.

EBITDA

A commonly-used measure to compare companies is *earnings before interest, taxes, depreciation, or amortisation,* also known as EBITDA. With this number, analysts and investors can compare profitability among companies or industries because it eliminates the effects of the companies' activities to raise cash outside their operating activities, such as by selling stock or bonds. EBITDA also eliminates any accounting decisions that could impact the bottom line, such as the companies' policies relating to depreciation methods. Investors reading the financial report can use this figure to focus on the profitability of each company's operations. If a company does include this term it is in the notes or, for example, the five-year record.

How a company chooses to raise money can greatly impact its bottom line. Selling equity has no annual costs if dividends aren't paid. Borrowing money means interest costs must be paid every year, so a company will have ongoing required expenses.

EBITDA gives financial report readers a quick view of how well a company is doing without considering its financial and accounting decisions. This number became very popular in the late 1990s to support companies that were pursuing an acquisition policy. It is also used to support decisions to make leveraged buyouts. A *leveraged buyout* takes place when an individual or company buys a controlling interest (which means more than 50 per cent) in a company using primarily debt. Many times, the individual or company pays 70 per cent or more of the purchase price using debt. This leaves many companies in a situation where investors have to carefully watch that the company earns enough from operations to pay its huge debt load.

Today, EBITDA is frequently touted by technology companies or other high-growth companies with large expenses for machinery and other equipment. In these situations, the companies like to discuss their earnings before the huge write-offs for depreciation, which can make the bottom line look pretty small. EBITDA can actually be used as an accounting gimmick to make a company's earnings sound better to the general public or to investors who don't take the time to read the fine print in the annual report.

Some commentators jokingly refer to this number as '*earnings before all the bad stuff*'.

Companies can get pretty creative when it comes to their income-statement groupings. If you don't understand a line item, be sure to look for explanations in the notes to the financial statements. If you can't find an explanation there, call investor relations and ask questions.

Non-operating income or expense

If a company earns income from a source that isn't part of its normal revenue-generating activities, it usually lists this income on the income statement as *non-operating income*. Amounts in this area are presented straight after the Operating Profit line. Finding a gain on the sale of a building, manufacturing facility, or division in this section of the income statement is common. Companies also group one-time expenses in the non-operating section of the income statement. For example, the severance and other costs of closing a division or factory are shown in this area of an income statement or, in some cases, a separate section on discontinuing operations is shown on the statement. Other types of expenses may include losses from theft, vandalism, or fire; loss from the sale or abandonment of property, plant, or equipment; and loss from employee or supplier strikes.

Whilst non-operating income or expense items are commonly shown in statements, IAS 1 does not actually include any reference to operating profit and therefore, by extension, does not consider it necessary to distinguish operating and non-operating items. What IAS 1 does indicate is that if an entity chooses to distinguish operating items from non-operating items then this should be done in such a way as would normally be considered to be appropriate.

You usually find explanations for income or expenses from non-operating activities in the notes to the financial statements. In our view, separating non-operating activities is helpful, otherwise, investors, analysts, and other interested parties can't gauge how well a company is doing with its core operating activities. The core-operating-activities line item is where you find a company's continuing income. If those core activities aren't raising enough income, the company may be on the road to significant financial difficulties.

A major gain may make the bottom line look great, but it can send the wrong signal to outsiders, who may then expect similar earnings results the next year. When the company can't repeat the results, the City may hammer its shares. A major one-time loss also needs special explanation so that the City doesn't downgrade the share price unnecessarily if the one-time non-operating loss won't be repeated in future years.

Whether a gain or a loss, separating non-operating income from operating income and expenses helps to prevent sending the wrong signal to analysts and investors about a company's future earnings and growth potential.

Net profit or loss

The bottom line of any income statement is net profit or loss. This number means very little if you don't understand the other line items that make up the income statement. Few investors and analysts look solely at net profit or loss to make a major decision about whether or not a company is a good investment.

Calculating Earnings Per Share

In addition to profit for the year, the other number you hear almost as often about a company's earnings results is earnings per share. *Earnings per share* is the amount of profit for the year the company made per share available on the market. For example, if you own 100 shares of stock in ABC company, and the company earned £1 per share, £100 of those earnings would be yours unless the company decided to reinvest them in the company for future growth. In reality, a company rarely pays out 100 per cent of its earnings; it usually pays out a very small fraction of those earnings.

You find the earnings-per-share after profit for the year on the income statement. The calculation for earnings per share is relatively simple: You take the number of outstanding shares (which you can find on the balance sheet or in the notes to the accounts) and divide it into the net earnings (which you find on the income statement).

Basically, earnings per share shows you how much money each shareholder made for each of their shares. In reality, this money doesn't get paid back to the shareholder. Instead, most is reinvested in future operations of the company. The profit or loss for the year is added to the retained earnings number on the balance sheet.

At the bottom of an income statement, you see two numbers:

✔ The *basic earnings per share* is a calculation based on the number of shares outstanding at the time the income statement was developed.

✔ The *diluted earnings per share* includes other potential shares that could eventually be outstanding. This category includes shares designated for things like share options or warrants (financial instruments which give the holder a right to buy shares at a set price, usually below the share's market value), and *convertibles* (shares promised to a holder of bonds or preference shares that are convertible to ordinary shares).

These numbers give you an idea of how much the company earned per share. You can use them to analyse the profitability of a company, which we show you how to do in Chapter 11.

Dividends declared per share are sometimes shown at the foot of the income statement under the earnings-per-share information. Otherwise these details are in the notes to the accounts. The company's board of directors may declare dividends quarterly, biannually, or annually.

Chapter 8

The Statement of Cash Flows

In This Chapter

▶ Exploring the statement of cash flows

▶ Understanding operating activities

▶ Getting a grip on investments

▶ Figuring out the financing section

▶ Looking at other line items

▶ Finding net cash from all company activities

Cash is a company's lifeblood. If a company expects to manage its assets and liabilities and to pay its obligations, it has to know the amount of cash flowing into and out of the business, which isn't always easy to figure out when using accrual accounting. (You can find out more about accrual accounting in Chapter 4.)

Accrual accounting makes it hard to pinpoint exactly how much cash a company actually holds, because cash doesn't have to change hands for a company to record a transaction. The *statement of cash flows* is the financial statement that helps the financial report reader understand a company's cash position by adjusting for differences between cash and accruals. (Refer to Chapter 4 for more information on cash and accruals.) This statement tracks the cash that flows in and out of a business during a specified period of time and lays out the sources of that cash. In this chapter, we explore the basic parts of the statement of cash flows.

Digging into the Statement of Cash Flows

Basically, a *statement of cash flows* gives the financial report reader a map of the cash receipts, cash payments, and changes in cash that a company holds minus the expenses that arise from operating the company. In addition, the statement looks at money that flows into or out of the company through investing and financing activities. As with the income statement (go to Chapter 7), a company provides two years' worth of information on the statement of cash flows.

When reading the statement of cash flows, look for answers to these three questions:

- ✔ **Where did the company get the cash needed for operation during the period shown on the statement – from revenue generated, funds borrowed, issue of new shares, or the proceeds of sales of fixed assets?**

- ✔ **What cash did the company actually spend during the periods shown on the statement?**

- ✔ **What was the change in the cash balance during each of the years shown on the statement?**

Knowing the answers to these questions helps you determine whether the company is thriving and has the cash needed to continue and grow its operations, or whether the company appears to have a cash-flow problem and could be nearing a point of fiscal disaster. In this section, we show you how you can use the statement of cash flows to find the answers to these questions.

The parts

Transactions shown on the statement of cash flows prepared under International Financial Reporting Standards are grouped in three parts:

- ✔ **Operating activities:** This part includes cash transactions that involve revenue that was taken into the company through sales of its products or services and expenses that were paid out by the company to carry out its operations. (For more on operating activities, see the upcoming section 'Checking Out Operating Activities'.)

- ✔ **Investing activities:** This part includes the purchase or sale of the company's investments and can include the purchase or sale of long-term assets, such as a building or a company division. Spending on *capital improvements* (upgrades to assets held by the company, such as the renovation of a building) also fits in this category, as does any buying or selling of short-term invested funds. (For more on this topic, see the upcoming section 'Investigating Investment Activities'.)

- ✔ **Financing activities:** This part involves raising cash through long-term debt or by issuing new shares. It also includes using cash to pay off debt or buy back shares. Companies also include any dividends paid in this section. (For more on operating activities, see the upcoming section 'Understanding Financing Activities'.)

The sections of the cash flow statement using UK standards

Companies following UK standards have an amazing nine sections in the cash-flow statement:

- ✔ Operating activities
- ✔ Dividends from joint ventures and associates
- ✔ Returns on investments and servicing of finance
- ✔ Taxation
- ✔ Capital expenditure and financial investment
- ✔ Acquisitions and disposals
- ✔ Equity dividends paid
- ✔ Management of liquid resources
- ✔ Financing

On the other hand, companies satisfying the *legal* definition of a small company (refer to Chapter 3) do not need to prepare a cash-flow statement at all!

Operating activities is the most important section of the statement of cash flows. In reading this section of the statement, you can determine whether the operations of a company are generating enough cash to keep the business viable. We discuss how to analyse this statement and make these determinations in Chapter 12.

The formats

A company can choose between two different formats when preparing its statement of cash flows, both of which arrive at the same total but use different information to get there:

- ✔ **Direct method:** The International Accounting Standards Board (IASB; see Chapter 18) prefers the direct method, which groups major classes of gross cash receipts and gross cash payments. The IASB says that the direct method provides information that may be useful in estimating future cash flows and that is not available under the indirect method. The direct method is easier for the user to understand. Figure 8-1 shows you the direct method.

> ✔ **Indirect method:** The indirect method starts with the figure for profit or loss in the income statement and adjusts it for the effect of transactions of a non-cash nature, deferrals, or accruals of past or future operating cash receipts or payments, and items of income or expense associated with investing or financing cash flows. The indirect method is easier for the company to prepare. Figure 8-2 shows you the indirect method.

The direct and indirect methods differ only in the operating activities section of the report. The investing-activities and financing-activities sections are the same, as shown in Figures 8-1 and 8-2. Despite the fact that the direct method is easier for the user to understand and is preferred by the IASB, it is rarely used in practice because the figures which are needed to prepare the statement are not usually readily available from the accounting system. Ease of preparation wins out over quality of information.

Figure 8-1:
The direct method.

Cash receipts from customers	£ XXX
Cash paid to suppliers and employees	£ XXX
Cash generated from operations	£ XXX
Interest paid	£ XXX
Corporation tax paid	£ XXX
Net cash from operating activities	£ XXX

Figure 8-2:
The indirect method.

Profit before taxation	£ XXX
Adjustments for:	
Depreciation	£ XXX
Foreign exchange loss	£ XXX
Investment income	£ XXX
Interest expense	£ XXX
	£ XXX
Increase/decrease in trade and other receivables	£ XXX
Increase/decrease in inventories	£ XXX
Increase/decrease in trade payables	£ XXX
Cash generated from operations	£ XXX
Interest paid	£ XXX
Corporation tax paid	£ XXX
Net cash from operating activities	£ XXX

You can easily calculate the information in the indirect method by using two years of financial statements. Anyone who reads the balance sheet and compares the data between the current and previous year can calculate most of the numbers shown by using the indirect method. The rest of the numbers can be obtained from the notes to the accounts.

For example, you can calculate changes in accounts receivable, inventories, and accounts payable by comparing the totals shown on the balance sheet for each of the two years. If a company shows £1,500,000 in inventory in 2006 and £1,000,000 in 2007, the change in inventory is shown using the indirect method 'Decrease in Inventory – £500,000'. The statement of cash flows for the indirect method summarises information already given in a different way, but it doesn't reveal any new information.

With the direct method, a company has to reveal the actual cash it receives from customers and the cash it pays to suppliers and employees. Someone reading the balance sheet and income statement can't find these numbers in other parts of the financial report.

According to the IASB, cash flows from interest and dividends received and paid can be classified in any of the three parts of the cash-flow statement – as long as the approach adopted is followed consistently from year-to-year. Tesco follows the example included in International Accounting Standards (IAS) 7 by putting interest paid in the operating section, interest received and dividends received in the investing activities section, and dividends paid in the financing section. By contrast, Marks and Spencer put interest paid in the financing section.

The investing-activities and financing-activities sections for both the direct and indirect methods look something like Figures 8-3 and 8-4, both of which show some of the basic line items. (If you're interested in finding out about line items that make their way onto the statement only in special circumstances, see 'Recognising Special Line Items' later in the chapter.)

Figure 8-3: The investing-activities section.

> **Cash flows from investing activities**
> Acquisition of subsidiary
> Purchase of property, plant and equipment
> Proceeds from sale of equipment
> Interest received
> Dividends received

Figure 8-4: The financing-activities section.

> **Cash flows from financing activities**
> Proceeds from issue of share capital
> Proceeds from long-term borrowings
> Payment of finance lease liabilities
> Dividends paid

You can find samples of Tesco's and Marks and Spencer's statements of cash flows in Appendix A.

Checking Out Operating Activities

The operating-activities section is where you find a summary of how much cash flowed into and out of the company during the day-to-day operations of the business.

Operating activities is the most important section of the statement of cash flows. If a company isn't generating enough cash from its operations, it isn't going to be in business for long. Although new companies often don't generate a lot of cash in their early years, they can't survive that way for long before going bust.

The primary purpose of the operating-activities section is to adjust the net income by adding or subtracting entries that were made in order to abide by the rules of accrual accounting that don't actually require the use of cash. In this section, we describe several of the accounts in the operating-activities section of the statement and explain how they're impacted by the changes required to revert accrual accounting entries to actual cash flow.

Depreciation

A company that buys a lot of new equipment or builds new facilities has high depreciation expenses that lower its net income. This is particularly true for many high-tech companies that must always upgrade their equipment and facilities to keep up with their competitors.

The bottom line may not look good, but all those depreciation expenses aren't necessarily using cash. In reality, no cash changes hands to pay depreciation expenses. These expenses are actually added back into the equation when you look at whether a company is generating enough cash from its operations, because the company didn't actually lay out cash to pay for these expenses.

For example, if a company's net income is £200,000 for the year and its depreciation expenses are £50,000, it adds the £50,000 back in to find the net cash from operations, which is £250,000. Essentially, this company is in better shape than it looked to be before the depreciation expenses because of this non-cash transaction – in other words, the cash generated by operations is higher than it might at first appear. Remember, when the company buys the equipment it must lay out the cash price in full, but this cost is reflected in the investing-activities section of the cash-flow statement.

Inventory

Another adjustment shown on the statement of cash flows that would add cash to the mix is a decrease in inventory. If a company's inventory on hand is less in the current year than in the previous year, then some of the inventory sold was actually bought with cash in the previous year.

On the other hand, if a company's inventory increases from the previous year, then the company spent more money on inventory in the current year and it subtracts the difference from the net income to find its current cash holdings. For example, if inventory decreases by £10,000, the company adds that amount to net income.

Accounts receivable

Accounts receivable is the summary of accounts of customers who bought their goods or services on credit provided directly by the company.

Customers who bought their goods by using credit cards from banks or other financial institutions aren't included in accounts receivable. Payments by outside credit sources are counted as cash instead, because the company receives cash from the bank or financial institution. The bank or financial institution collects from those customers, so the company that sold the goods or services doesn't have to worry about collecting the cash.

When accounts receivable increase during the year, a company sells more products or services on credit than it collects in actual cash from customers. In this case, an increase in accounts receivable means a decrease in cash available.

The opposite is true if accounts receivable are a lower number during the current year than the previous year. In this case, a company collects more cash than it adds credit to customers' credit accounts. In this situation, a decrease in accounts receivable results in more cash received, which adds to the net income.

Accounts payable

Accounts payable is an account that summarises the bills due that haven't yet been paid, which means cash must still be laid out in a future accounting period to pay those bills.

When accounts payable increases, a company uses less cash to pay bills in the current year than it did in the previous one, so more cash is on hand. An increase in accounts payable has a positive effect on the cash situation.

Expenses are shown on the income statement because they have been incurred, which means net income is lower. But in reality, the cash hasn't yet been laid out to pay those expenses, so an increase is added to net income to find out how much cash is actually on hand.

Conversely, if accounts payable decreases, a company pays out more cash for this liability. A decrease in accounts payable means the company has less cash on hand, and it subtracts this number from net income.

The cash flow from activities section

To give you a taste of what all of these line items look like in the statement of cash flows in Table 8-1, we roll together the information from the previous sections to show you how it all comes together.

Table 8-1	Cash Flows from Operating Activities
Line Item	*Cash Received or Spent*
Net income	£200,000
Depreciation	£50,000
Increase in accounts receivable	(£20,000)
Decrease in inventories	£10,000
Decrease in accounts payable	(£10,000)
Net cash provided by (used in) operating activities	£230,000

In Table 8-1, the company has £30,000 more in cash from operations than it reported on the income statement, so the company actually generated more cash than you may have thought if you just looked at net income.

If you compare the statements for Tesco and Marks and Spencer (check out Appendix A) you can see that Tesco's net cash from operating activities totalled £2,611 million after adjustments on £1,899 million profit for the year ended February 2007. This is a rate of £1.37 of cash for every £1 of profit, Marks and Spencer's net cash was £1,293 million on £660 million of profit for the year – in other words, £1.96 of cash for every £1 of profit. Adjusting for the scale of the companies in this way, it looks as though Marks and Spencer did a better job of generating cash from its operations. But Marks and Spencer includes interest paid in the financing section rather than the operating section, which can make comparison tricky. However, in this case, working out an adjusted ratio for Marks and Spencer of £1.77 is relatively easy to do by reducing the operating cash flow by the amount of interest paid.

When performing ratio analysis, you must make sure to compare like with like. In Chapter 13, when we look at cash ratios, we use the figure from the top of the cash flow-statement – before deductions for interest and tax – so that we are comparing like with like.

Investigating Investing Activities

The investment activities section of the statement of cash flows, which looks at the purchase or sale of major new assets, is usually a drainer of cash. Consider what's typically listed in this section:

- ✔ Purchases of new buildings, land, and major equipment
- ✔ Mergers or acquisitions
- ✔ Major improvements to existing buildings
- ✔ Major upgrades to existing factories and equipment
- ✔ Purchases of new marketable securities, such as bonds or shares

The sale of buildings, land, major equipment, and marketable securities is also shown in the investment-activities section. When any of these major assets are sold, they're shown as cash generators rather than as cash drainers.

The primary reason to check out the investments section is to see how the company is managing its *capital expenditure* (money spent to buy or upgrade assets) and how much cash it's using for this expenditure. If a company shows large investments in this area, be sure to look for explanations in the Operating and Financial Review (or in some companies, a report with a different title, for example 'Business Review')and the notes to the financial statements (see Chapter 9) to get more details about the reasons for the expenditure.

If you believe that a company is making the right choices to grow the business and improve profits, investing in its shares may be worthwhile. If the company is making most of its capital expenditure to keep old factories operating as long as possible, it may be a sign that the company isn't keeping up with new technology.

Compare companies in the same industry to see what type of expenditure each lists in investment activities and the explanations for this expenditure in the notes to the financial statement. Comparing the company with one of its peers helps you determine whether the company is budgeting its capital expenditures wisely.

In comparing the statements of Tesco and Marks and Spencer (see Appendix A), you can see that Tesco spent considerably more on purchases of property, plant, and equipment. Tesco's spending totalled more than £2.8 billion, whereas Marks and Spencer spent about £700 million. However, Tesco's sales are five times those of Marks and Spencer so on a pro rata basis Marks and Spencer spent more. In this case, both companies are investing adequately in the future and you would not consider one to be performing better than the other.

Understanding Financing Activities

Companies can't always raise all the cash they need from their day-to-day operations. Financing activities are another means of generating cash. Any cash raised through activities that don't include day-to-day operations can be found in the financing section of the statement of cash flows.

Issuing shares

When a company sells shares, it shows the money raised in the financing section of the statement of cash flows. The first time a company sells shares to the general public this sale is called an *initial public offering* (IPO; refer to Chapter 3 for more information about an IPO). If a company wants to raise cash later by selling more shares it normally does this by offering shares to its existing shareholders by means of a *rights issue* which is cheaper than offering shares to the general public. The term rights issue is used to describe the situation where existing shareholders are given the right to buy more shares in the company but this offer is not given to non-shareholders. The price set for a rights issue will be below the current market value of the shares to encourage existing shareholders to take up the rights. If they don't wish to then they could sell the rights to somebody else.

Usually, when companies decide to raise extra capital by a rights issue, they do so to raise cash for a specific project or group of projects that they can't fund by ongoing operations. The finance department must determine whether it wants to raise funds for these new projects by borrowing money (new debt) or by issuing shares (new equity). If the company already has a great deal of debt and finds that borrowing more is difficult, it may try to sell additional shares to cover the shortfall. We talk more about debt versus equity in Chapter 12.

Buying back shares

Sometimes you see a line item in the financing section indicating that a company has bought back its shares. Companies that announce a share buyback are usually trying to accomplish one of two things:

- ✔ Increase the market price of their shares. (If companies buy back their shares, fewer shares remain on the market, thus raising the value of shares still available for purchase.)

- ✔ Meet internal obligations regarding employee share options which guarantee employees the opportunity to buy shares at a price that's usually below the price outsiders must pay for the shares.

Sometimes, companies buy back stock with the intention of going private (look at Chapter 3). In this case, company executives and the board of directors decide that they no longer want to operate under the watchful eyes of investors and the stock market. Instead, they prefer not to have to worry about satisfying so many company outsiders. We discuss the advantages and disadvantages of staying private in Chapter 3.

For many companies, an announcement that they're buying back shares is an indication that they're doing well financially and that the executives believe in their company's growth prospects for the future. Because buybacks reduce the number of outstanding shares, a company can make its per-share numbers look better even though a fundamental change hasn't occurred in the business's operations.

If you see a big jump in earnings per share, look for an indication of share buyback in the financing-activities section of the statement of cash flows.

Paying dividends

Whenever a company pays dividends, it shows the amount paid to shareholders in the financing-activities section of the statement of cash flows. Companies aren't required to pay dividends each year, but a company rarely stops paying dividends after the shareholders have become used to their dividend cheques.

If a company reneges on its decision to pay dividends, the market price of the share is sure to tumble. A company's decision not to pay dividends after paying them in the previous quarter or previous year usually indicates that it's having problems, and it raises a huge red flag.

Incurring new debt

When a company borrows money for the long term, this new debt is shown in the financing-activities section of the statement of cash flows. This type of new debt includes the issuance of bonds; notes; or other forms of long-term financing, such as a mortgage on a building.

When you read the statement of cash flows and see that the company has taken on new debt, be sure to look for explanations about how the company is using this debt in the Operating and Financial Review (OFR) and in the notes to the financial statements (see Chapter 9 for more information about the notes to the financial statements).

Paying off debt

Debt pay-off is usually a good sign, often indicating that a company is doing well. However, it may also be an indication that a company is simply rolling over existing debt into another type of debt instrument.

If you see that a company paid off one debt and took on another debt that costs about the same amount of money, this sign likely indicates that the company simply refinanced the original debt. Ideally, that refinancing involved lowering the company's interest expenses. Look for a full explanation of the debt pay-off in the notes to the financial statement.

If you compare the financing activities of Tesco and Marks and Spencer (see Appendix A), you see that Tesco increased their long-term borrowing by £184 million but, on the other hand, bought back shares for £490 million and paid dividends of £467 million. Marks and Spencer paid down their long-term borrowings by £479 million as well as paying dividends of £261 million. Adding in the other smaller amounts in the financing section Tesco used £533 million of its cash for its financing activities, and Marks and Spencer used £876 million of its cash on hand for its financing activities.

When you look at the financing activities on a statement of cash flows for younger companies, you usually see financing activities that raise capital. Their statements include borrowing funds or issuing shares to raise cash. Older, more established companies begin paying off their debt when they've generated enough cash from operations.

Recognising Special Line Items

Sometimes you see line items on the statement of cash flows that appear unique to a specific company. Companies use these line items in special circumstances, such as the discontinuation of operations. Companies that have international operations use a line item that relates to exchanging cash among different countries, which is called *foreign exchange*.

Discontinued operations

If a company *discontinues operations* (stops the activities of a part of its business), you usually see a special line item on the statement of cash flows that shows whether the discontinued operations have increased or decreased the amount of cash a company takes in or distributes. Sometimes discontinued operations increase cash because the company no longer has to pay the salaries and other costs related to that operation.

Other times, discontinued operations can be a one-time hit to profits because the company has to make significant severance payments to laid-off employees and has to continue paying the costs of the manufacturing and other fixed costs related to those operations. For example, if a company leased space for the discontinued operations, the company is contractually obligated to continue paying for that space until the contract is up or the company finds someone to sublease the space.

Foreign currency exchange

Whenever a company has global operations, it's certain to have some costs related to the cost of moving currency from one country to another. The pound, as well as currencies from other countries, can experience changes in currency exchange rates – sometimes 100 times a day or more.

Each time the exchange rate between two countries changes, moving currency between those two countries can result in a loss or a gain. Any losses or gains related to foreign currency exchanges are shown on a special line item on the statement of cash flows called 'Effect of exchange rate changes'. Both Tesco and Marks and Spencer show the effects of currency exchange at the foot of their statements (see Appendix A). Tesco's net cash reduced by £18 million, and Marks and Spencer's reduced by £1.5 million.

Adding It All Up

This number is the big one, the highlight, the bottom line: 'Cash and cash equivalents at end of year'. This number actually shows you how much cash or cash equivalents a company has on hand for continuing operations the next year.

Cash equivalents are any holdings that a company can easily change to cash, such as cash in current and deposit accounts, and money-market funds. Investments that can be converted to a known amount of cash within three months of acquisition are also included as cash equivalents. Investments in shares are excluded from cash equivalents since their realisable value may change.

The top line of the statement starts with cash flows from operating activities which is a figure derived from profit for the year. Adjustments are made to show the impact on cash from operations, investing activities, and financing. These adjustments result in the calculation of actual cash available for continuing operations. Remember that this is the cash on hand that the company can use to continue its activities the next year.

If you look at the statement of cash flows for Tesco and Marks and Spencer in Appendix A, you can see that Tesco had about £1 billion on hand at the end of February 2007 on profit for the year of about £1.9 billion. Marks and Spencer had only about £47 million in cash and cash equivalents at the end of March 2007 on profit for the year of £660 million. Both companies cash on hand actually decreased during the year.

In Part III, we delve more deeply into how the cash results of these two companies differed. We also show you how you can use the figures on the statement of cash flows and other statements in the financial reports to analyse the results and make judgements about a company's financial position.

Chapter 9

Scouring the Notes to the Financial Statements

- -

In This Chapter

▶ Describing the notes and their importance

▶ Understanding the fine print of accounting methods

▶ Finding out about financial commitments

▶ Getting acquainted with mergers and acquisitions

▶ Reading notes about pensions and retirement

▶ Detailing segmented businesses

▶ Keeping an eye out for red flags

- -

*W*ould you ever sign an important contract without reading the fine print first? Probably not. Remember this philosophy when you read financial statements because the corporate world certainly doesn't escape the cliché about sweeping dust under the carpet. Hiding problems in the notes to the financial statements is a common practice for companies in trouble.

In this chapter we explain the role of notes as part of the financial statements, discuss the most common issues addressed in the notes, and point out some key warning signs that should raise a red flag if you see them mentioned in the notes. And to help you become a note-reading expert, we refer to the financial reports of Tesco and Marks and Spencer (both retailers) throughout the chapter. (See Appendix A for these companies' financial statements. To view their complete annual reports, you can find Tesco's at www.tesco.com by looking at the section called 'Investor Relations' and then 'Annual Reports'. For Marks and Spencer go to www.marksandspencer.com and then to the section about the company and then to 'Investors'.)

When searching for a company's financial reports on its Web site, you usually need to find the corporation information section, and within that section, you find investor relations. Links to the annual and quarterly reports for a company are in the investor-relations section of the company's Web site.

Deciphering the Small Print

Learning how to read and understand the small print of the notes to the financial statements can be a daunting task. Companies usually present these notes in the least visually appealing way and fill them with accounting jargon so that they're hard for the general public to understand. By publishing these notes, the company fulfils its obligations to give the required financial report to the reader, but it's hard for the reader to actually understand the information presented.

But don't give up. There's lots of important information in these notes that you need to know, including accounting methods used, red flags about the company's finances, and any legal entanglements that may threaten the company's future. We point out the key sections of the notes to the financial statements and what types of information to pluck out of these sections.

The notes to Tesco's accounts run close to 50 pages. A typical unlisted entity may have 15 pages of notes – not because the requirements are fundamentally different but because the business has less complicated circumstances than the listed entity. A typical FRSSE set of accounts might contain 6 to 8 pages of notes.

The first indication that you'll see that there are notes to the financial statement is at the bottom of the financial statements. You see a comment that the accompanying notes form part of the financial statements. Also, the various line items in the income statement, balance sheet and cash-flow statement will have a number next to them which refers to the number of the relevant note. You find the actual notes on numerous pages after the financial statements.

The information on the financial statement is just a listing of numbers. To really analyse how well a company is doing financially you need to understand what the numbers mean and what decisions the company made to get the numbers. Sometimes a line item refers you to a specific note but normally you see only a general reference to the notes at the bottom of the statement.

The notes have no specific format, but you're likely to find at least one note regarding several key issues in every company's financial report.

Small doesn't matter

You won't see this icon very often in this chapter since the disclosure requirements for listed companies are very similar to those for unlisted companies. In fact, as UK accounting standards converge with the international standards, the differences will reduce even further. Where there are differences at the moment, they tend to be in the detail, not the broad principles. Almost everything we say in this chapter applies to both listed and unlisted entities.

The only significant difference in disclosure requirements is for those companies that satisfy the legal definition to be small (basically turnover less than £5.6 million, total assets less than £2.8 million and less than 50 employees – but look at the technical stuff in Chapter 3 for the details). These companies follow their own standard – the Financial Reporting Standard for Small Entities (FRSSE) which lays out much reduced disclosure requirements.

Accounting Policies Note: Laying Out the Rules of the Road

The first note in almost every company's financial report gives you the ammunition to understand the accounting policies used to develop the financial statements. This note explains the accounting rules the company used to develop its numbers. The note is usually called 'Accounting policies'.

Issues discussed in this note include:

- ✔ **Basis of consolidation:** The way in which the company deals with other companies in which it has an investment. (See Chapter 10 for more information about consolidation.)

- ✔ **Asset types:** The types of things owned by the company. (Refer to Chapters 4 and 6 for more information on assets.)

- ✔ **Method of valuation:** How the company values its assets. (Refer to Chapters 4 and 6 for more information on valuation.)

- ✔ **Methods of depreciation and amortisation:** The methods the company uses to charge for the use of its assets. (Refer to Chapters 4 and 6 for more information on depreciation and amortisation.)

- ✔ **How revenue and expenses are recognised:** The method that the company uses to record the money it takes in from sales and the money it pays out to cover its expenses. (Refer to Chapters 4 and 7 for more information on revenue and expenses.)

- ✔ **Pensions:** The obligations the company has to its current and future pensioners.

✔ **Financial instruments:** The company's use of financial instruments such as loans as well as more esoteric instruments such as derivatives or hedges.

✔ **Share-based payment:** Employee incentive plans involving share ownership.

✔ **Taxes:** The company's methods for dealing with current tax and deferred tax. (Refer to Chapter 7 for more details about deferred tax.)

Read the summary of significant accounting policies carefully. If you don't understand a policy, research it further so you can make a judgement about how this policy may impact the company's financial position. You can research the issue yourself on the Internet or call the company's investor-relations office to ask questions. Also, compare policies among the companies you're analysing. You want to see whether the differences in the ways companies handle the valuation of assets or the recognition of revenues and expenses makes it more difficult for you to analyse and compare the results.

For example, if companies use different methods to value their inventory, this could have a major impact on net income. (We explain the impact of inventory valuation on net income in Chapter 15.) Many times, you won't actually have enough detail to make apples to apples comparisons of two companies that use different accounting policies, but you need to be aware that the policies differ as you analyse the company's financial results and be alert to the fact that you may be comparing apples to oranges.

Depreciation

One significant difference in accounting policies that can affect the bottom line is the amount of time a company allows for the depreciation of assets. Whilst one company may use a 15–25 year timeframe, another may use a 10–40 year span. The timeframe used for depreciation directly impacts the value of the assets on the balance sheet. A faster depreciation method reduces the value of these assets more quickly on the balance sheet.

Depreciation expenses are also charged as an expense against revenue. A company that writes off its buildings more quickly, say in 25 years rather than up to 40 years, has higher depreciation expenses and lower net income than if it takes longer to write off its buildings. We discuss how depreciation works in greater detail in Chapter 4.

Revenue

You can find some noteworthy differences between companies by reading the revenue-recognition section of the summary of significant accounting policies. Differences between the timing of revenue recognition can impact the total revenues reported. For example, one company might indicate that it recognises revenue when the product is shipped to the customer. Another company might recognise revenue upon the customer's receipt of the product. If products are shipped at the end of the month, a company that includes shipped products includes the revenues in that month, but a company that only recognises revenue when the product is received might not include the revenue until the following month.

Revenue recognition is an area where a company's results can be massaged (see Chapter 22). As a taster, here are a couple of examples of policy differences you should pay attention to:

- ✔ **Rights of return:** Some companies expect a significant level of returns from their customers – think mail order, for example. When does the company recognise revenue on such sales? On despatch? Or after the return period has passed? Or do they make a provision for expected returns?

- ✔ **Collectibility:** The amount of income reported depends on whether or not all the revenue is likely to be collected. Successful collection can depend on the business environment, a customer's financial condition, historical collection experience, accounts receivable aging, and customer disputes. If collectibility is uncertain, the revenue isn't reported.

There is clearly great scope for the company to form a range of different judgements as to what revenue should be recognised. We talk more about accounts-receivable collections and how to analyse them in Chapter 16.

Expenses

Expenses differ widely among companies. As you read this part of the accounting policies note, be sure to notice the types of expenses a company chooses to highlight. Sometimes the differences between companies can actually give you an insight into how the company operates. Here are two key areas where you may see differences in how a company reports expenses:

- ✔ **Product development:** Some companies develop all their products in-house, whereas others pay royalties to inventors, designers, and others to develop and market new products. In-house product development is reported as research and development expenses. The cost of research activities are written off as incurred but when the research reaches the development phase, then the costs may be included in the balance sheet as an asset. International Accounting Standards (IAS) 38 has detailed rules and conditions to cover this point. If the company primarily develops new products by using outside sources, the costs appear as royalty expenses once production starts.

✔ **Advertising:** Some companies indicate that all advertising is expensed at the time the advertising is printed or aired. Others may write off advertising over a longer period of time. IAS 38 indicates that advertising costs should normally be written off as incurred, but companies may want to claim that an asset has been created by advertising expenditure. For example, one company that depends on catalogue sales might like to spread out the expense of this type of advertising over several months, or even a year, if it can prove that sales continued to come in during that longer period of time. Other companies in the same industry might consider that all of the costs should be expensed immediately.

As you compare two companies' financial reports, look for both the similarities and differences in their accounting policies. You may need to make some assumptions regarding the financial statements in order to compare apples to apples when trying to decide which company is the better investment. For example, if the companies depreciate assets differently, you must remember that their asset valuations aren't the same, nor are their depreciation expenses (based on the same assumptions).

Working Out Financial Borrowings and Other Liabilities

How a company manages its borrowings is critical to its short- and long-term profitability. You can find out a lot about a company's financial management by reading the notes related to financial liabilities. You always find at least one note about the financial borrowings and other liabilities that impact the short- and long-term financial health of the company.

IAS 32 requires companies to disclose information about their exposure to interest rate risk which includes maturity dates and effective interest rates. However, the method of displaying the information may well vary.

In Table 9–1, Tesco presents all loans with their maturity dates and interest rates. The Marks and Spencer situation is a lot more straightforward and the company provides maturity dates and interest rates as a footnote to the analysis of their borrowings as shown in Table 9–2.

No matter how a company structures its notes related to financial borrowings and other liabilities, as you read the notes, break the information down into two piles: long-term borrowings and short-term borrowings. The *long-term borrowings* involve financial obligations of more than one year, and the *short-term,* or *current borrowings* involve obligations due within the 12-month period following the year of the accounts which are presented in the financial report.

Short-term borrowings

Short-term borrowings can have a greater impact on a company's earnings each year, as well as on the amount of cash available for operations, than long-term borrowings. The reason is that a company must pay back short-term borrowings over the next 12 months, whereas for a long-term loan, a company must pay only interest and, possibly, some of the principal in the next 12 months.

The type of short-term borrowings you see on a company's balance sheet varies greatly, depending on the type of company but the most common form of short-term borrowing in the UK is the *bank overdraft*. Companies whose sales are seasonal may carry a lot more short-term borrowings to get themselves through the slow times than companies that have a consistent cash flow from sales throughout the year.

Seasonal companies carry large lines of credit (or large overdraft limits) to help them buy or produce their products during the off-season times so that they can have enough product to sell during the high season. For example, a company that sells toys sells most of its product during the Christmas or other peak toy-selling seasons; during the other times of the year it has fewer sales.

Another way that companies raise cash if they don't have enough on hand is to sell their accounts receivable. To get immediate cash, the company can sell the receivables to a bank or other financial institution and get immediate cash rather than wait for the customer to pay. (Accounts receivable involve credit extended to customers, which sometimes results in short-term cash-flow problems. By selling these receivables, companies can raise cash for immediate needs rather than wait until they collect the money.) We talk more about accounts-receivable management in Chapter 16.

Be sure to look for a statement in the financial-obligations notes that indicates how a company is meeting its cash needs and whether it's having any difficulty meeting those needs. Some companies use 'financial obligations' in the title for the note; others may have one note on short-term obligations and another on long-term (or non-current) obligations.

Long-term borrowings

Both medium- and long-term notes or bonds fall into the long-term-borrowings category. *Medium-term notes or bonds* are amounts that a company borrows for 2–10 years. *Long-term notes or bonds* include all amounts borrowed for over 10 years.

In the discussion of long-term financial borrowings, you find two key pieces of information. One shows the terms of the borrowings, and the other permits you to work out the amount of cash that a company must pay toward its debt for each of the next five years and beyond. Table 9–1 shows Tesco's long-term borrowings. Note that MTN stands for Medium Term Note.

Table 9–1	Tesco's Non-Current Borrowings					
	Par value	Effective interest rate %	Effective interest ate after hedging trans- actions %	Maturity year	2007 £m	2006 £m
Finance leases	-	9.2	9.2	-	147	84
7.5%MTN	£325m	-	-	-	-	344
6%MTN	£125m	6.0	5.9	2008	130	268
5.25%MTN	EU500m	5.3	6.0	2008	352	366
5.125%MTN	£192m	5.1	5.8	2009	190	355
6.625%MTN	£150m	6.7	6.7	2010	153	153
4.75%MTN	EU750m	4.8	6.2	2010	525	548
3.875%MTN	EU500m	3.9	5.9	2011	340	-
4% RPI MTN	£238m	6.6	6.6	2016	244	236
5.5%MTN	£350m	5.6	5.6	2019	349	349
5%MTN	£350m	5.1	5.1	2023	361	-
3.322%LPI MTN	£241m	5.9	5.9	2025	243	236
6%MTN	£200m	6.0	6.0	2029	198	214
5.5%MTN	£200m	5.6	5.6	2033	197	213
2%RPI MTN	£204m	4.6	4.6	2036	206	-
5%MTN	£300m	5.1	5.1	2042	306	-
Other MTNs		2.2	2.2	-	176	278
Other loans		4.9	4.9	2008	29	98
					4,146	3,742

In the notes below Table 9–1, Tesco indicate that there has been a partial redemption of two of the Notes, namely the 6 per cent MTN maturing in 2008 and the 5.125 per cent MTN maturing in 2009.

The company also explains the details relating to two of the MTNs which seem to be somewhat different from the others. The 4 per cent RPI MTN is redeemable at par indexed for increases in the Retail Price Index (RPI) over the life of the MTN. The 3.322 per cent LPI MTN is similarly redeemable at par indexed for increases in RPI but has the added condition that the maximum indexation in any one year is 5 per cent. They have omitted to explain the terms attaching to the 2 per cent RPI MTN – perhaps they are the same as the 4 per cent RPI MTN?

The *par value* of a loan is the amount originally borrowed and is normally the amount to be repaid (redemption value) unless there is an agreement to the contrary. The amount included in the balance sheet for any loan is based on the amount borrowed and the redemption value but also takes into account any transaction costs – this is why the balance sheet value is usually slightly different from the par value.

Notice that Tesco refer to the effect on interest rates of hedging transactions. To understand what is happening here you need to read the Operating and Financial Review where the company explains its objectives when managing interest rate risk – to limit their exposure to interest rate increases while retaining the opportunity to benefit from interest rate reductions.

Marks and Spencer is a bit more straightforward with its long-term-borrowings information, as Table 9–2 shows.

Table 9–2	Marks and Spencer's Non-Current Borrowings	
	2007 £m	*2006 £m*
Medium term notes	1,177.3	779.0
Securitised loan notes	-	307.3
Finance lease liabilities	57.2	47.5
Total non-current borrowings and other financial liabilities	1,234.5	1,133.8

Marks and Spencer explain that the balance for medium term notes relates to fixed rate bonds of £375 million at a rate of 6.375 per cent repayable on 7 November 2011, £400 million at a rate of 5.625 per cent repayable on 24 March 2014 and £400 million at a rate of 5.875 per cent repayable on 29 May 2012.

Further, the securitised loan notes related to three separate bonds securitised against 45 of the group's properties which were redeemed on 12 March 2007 in order to release the properties for use in the limited partnership with the group's pension scheme. This is explained further in a separate note to the accounts.

The notes to the accounts contain more information on the borrowings of the two companies. One issue is the extent to which the interest rates on borrowings are fixed.

A fixed interest rate is a good thing when interest rates are going up because your outgoings are set. The quid pro quo is that when interest rates go down, the company loses the opportunity to borrow more cheaply.

Tesco's financial statements show that, for banks and other loans, £1,791 million are at fixed rates and £3,726 million are at floating rates. Overdrafts are always at floating rates and the Tesco overdraft explains £1,052 million of the balance. This means that, if we remove the overdraft from the figures, then about 60 per cent of the borrowings are at floating rates down from 67 per cent in the previous year. This brings them in line with the objective stated in their OFR that a minimum of 40 per cent of borrowings should be on fixed or capped interest rates.

For Marks and Spencer, the equivalent figures are fixed rate loans £1,375 million, floating rate loans £321 million. They have an overdraft of £160 million, so the percentage of borrowings which are at floating rates is only 10 per cent. This is down from 46 per cent in the previous year as a result of the maturation during the year of about £900 million of medium term notes whose interest rates were linked to bank rate.

We take a closer look at this issue and how it impacts the companies' liquidity in Chapter 12. We also show you how potential lenders analyse a company's borrowing habits.

Lease obligations

Rather than purchase plants, equipment, and facilities, many companies choose to lease them. You usually find at least one note to the financial statements that spells out a company's lease obligations. Whether the lease is shown on the balance sheet or in the notes depends on the type of lease:

✔ **Finance leases:** These leases give the *lessee* (the company leasing the asset for use in its business) substantially all the risks and rewards of ownership. At the end of the lease, legal ownership may pass to the lessee or may remain with the original owner (the lessor). *Hire purchase contracts* are finance leases where ownership does pass to the lessee at the end of the HP contract. This type of lease is shown as a long-term obligation on the balance sheet, whilst the cash price of the asset is included within the property, plant, and equipment heading in the balance sheet.

✔ **Operating leases:** Any lease that does not satisfy the definition of a finance lease is classified as an operating lease. This type of lease is mentioned in the notes to the financial statements but isn't shown on the balance sheet.

Companies that must constantly update certain types of equipment to avoid obsolescence use operating leases rather than capital leases. At the end of the lease period, companies return the equipment and replace it by leasing new, updated equipment.

When reading the notes, be sure to look for an explanation about the types of leases a company has and what percentage of its fixed assets is under operating leases. Some high-tech companies have higher obligations in operating-lease payments than they do in long-term liabilities (but remember they don't show as liabilities on the balance sheet). When calculating *debt ratios* (ratios that show the proportion of debt versus the type of asset or equity being considered), many analysts use at least two-thirds, and sometimes the entire amount, of these hidden operating-lease costs in their debt-measurement calculations to judge the liquidity of a company. We show you how to calculate debt ratios in Chapter 12.

In the Tesco accounts, the company discloses total commitments under operating leases of £6,661 million. Although this figure seems very large (in fact, larger than the amount of long-term borrowings), remember that it is spread over a long period of time because a lot of the leases relate to properties. In fact over 70 per cent of the obligation is due more than five years after the balance sheet date.

When you see operating lease commitments that total close to 50 per cent of a company's net fixed assets, or that exceed the total of its long-term liabilities, be sure to use at least two-thirds of the obligations, if not all the payments, in your debt-measurement calculations. The fact that these obligations are only mentioned in the notes to the financial statements doesn't negate their potential role in creating future cash problems for a company.

Accounting for Share-Based Payment: Something New in the Accountants' World

Share-based payment is not new but the way we account for it is. By share-based payment, we mean that payment is made by the issue of shares or share options rather than cash. Such payment is sometimes used for suppliers when a start-up business is short of cash but the most common use of share-based payment is for employees through the use of incentives.

Here's a simple example: X PLC has agreed that its managing director can buy shares in the company. This is achieved by granting the MD an option. The option says that the MD can buy 10,000 shares at a price of £20 per share as long as the MD is still employed by the company in three year's time. These conditions are known as the *vesting conditions*. The £20 price is actually the current price of the shares and the idea is that the MD benefits from any growth in the share price over the three-year period. Why not, the MD helped to create that growth? If the value of the share goes down, the option isn't exercised and lapses. If the share price goes up, the MD pays the company £200,000 for the shares and, of course, can immediately sell them for the higher market price.

For many years, companies have been required to disclose such agreements with directors. Indeed, in the directors' remuneration report, there is a mass of information concerning options granted, exercised or lapsed with respect to each individual director.

What is new is that the share option's fair value at the date it is granted has to be figured out and reflected in the income statement and balance sheet. This is how it works.

The starting point is to place a value on the option. It is unlikely that an identical option is available on the open market and so the first problem is to try to estimate what a reasonable market price for such an option would be. This may involve employing an external expert to use one of the complicated mathematical models which apply in this situation.

Suppose the expert says that the options are worth £6 each. The total value of the MD's options at the date of grant is therefore £60,000. This cost is charged as part of payroll costs but spread over the three years of the options life – so £20,000 is charged each year as a cost in the income statement with a corresponding credit to a new reserve account within equity.

This calculation is straightforward (if a bit bizarre) but consider the complications that arise where the company grants share options to 5,000 employees who must meet various targets before the shares can vest at the end of the three-year period. Now, the valuation of the option is the easiest bit of the calculation. Each year during the three-year period, the company must estimate how many share options will eventually be exercised taking into account the expected number of leavers and the progress towards achievement of the targets. An appropriate charge is made in the income statement each year so as to ensure that the amount included in equity always reflects the best estimate of the number of shares options that will ultimately vest.

Mergers and Acquisitions: Noteworthy Information

Sometimes one company decides to buy another. Other times, two companies decide to merge into one. In the past, different method of accounting were used depending on whether an acquisition or a merger took place. Recently, the IASB decided that it would be better to treat all business combinations in the same way. Merger accounting was banned and all business combinations are now accounted for using the purchase method (also known as acquisition accounting). For the moment, companies following UK GAAP are still permitted to use both merger accounting and acquisition accounting depending on the detailed situation.

If a company acquired another company or merged during the year covered by the annual report, a note to the financial statements is dedicated to the financial implications of that transaction. In this note, you see information about:

- ✔ The market value of the company purchased
- ✔ The amount paid for the company
- ✔ Any exchange of shares involved in the transaction
- ✔ Information about the transaction's impact on the bottom line

When a company acquires another company, it frequently pays more for that acquisition than for the total value of its assets. The additional money spent to buy the company falls into the line item called 'goodwill'. Goodwill includes added value for customer base, locations, customer loyalty, and intangible factors that increase a company's value. If a company has goodwill built over the years from previous mergers or acquisitions, you see that indicated on the balance sheet as an asset. We discuss goodwill in greater detail in Chapter 4.

In an acquisition, the acquired company's net income from the date of acquisition is added to the new parent company's bottom line. A note to the accounts will then disclose what the effect on group profit would have been if the subsidiary had been owned throughout the year. This note should help you estimate the potential impact of mergers and acquisitions on future net income.

A merger or acquisition may positively impact the bottom line for a year or two, and then the company's performance drops dramatically as the merged company sorts out various issues regarding overlapping operations and staff. Many times, the announcement of a merger or acquisition generates excitement, causing share prices to skyrocket temporarily before dropping back to a more realistic value. Don't get caught up in the short-term euphoria of a merger or acquisition when you're considering the purchase of shares. Read the details in the notes to the financial statements to find out more about the true impacts of the merger or acquisition transaction.

Pondering Pension and Retirement Benefits

You may not think of pension and other retirement benefits as types of debt, but they might be. In fact, for most companies that offer pension benefits, the amount of money they owe their employees is higher than the amount they owe to bondholders and banks. Some companies offer both *pensions* (which are an obligation to pay pensioners a certain amount for the rest of their lives after they leave the company) and other retirement benefits such as private health care.

When looking at the note about pension and other retirement benefits, find out which type of plan the company offers:

- **Defined benefit plan:** The company promises a retirement benefit to each of its employees who are members of the plan and is obligated to pay that benefit. This type of plan includes traditional retirement plans in which employees get a set monthly or annual benefit from the company after retirement. Usually, the pension is based on the number of year's service with the company and the final salary earned (or the average of a number of years of service towards the end of employment). These schemes are often known as *final salary schemes* for obvious reasons.

  Defined benefit plans carry obligations for the company for as long as an employee lives and, sometimes, for as long as both the employee and his spouse live. Determining how much that benefit will cost in the future is based on assumptions regarding how much return is expected from the retirement portfolios and how long the employees and their spouses live after retirement. As people live longer, pension obligations become much greater for those companies that offer defined benefit plans.

  In the UK, most companies who offer a defined benefit pension scheme pay contributions into a separate legal entity – a trust – which invests the funds and pays pensions. The company has a responsibility to make contributions sufficient to meet its eventual obligations. It is the responsibility of an actuary (a statistician who looks at lifespan and other risk factors to make assumptions about a company's long-term pension obligations) to determine how big those contributions should be.

✔ **Defined contribution plan:** The employer and, usually, the employee both make contributions to a company scheme or to the employee's personal pension plan. In the UK, all companies, other than the very smallest, are obliged to set up a pension scheme – but they are not, at present, compelled by law to make payments in to it.

Usually, the employer commits to pay an amount into the scheme each year based on a percentage of the employee's wages until the employee leaves or retires. In the defined contribution scheme, the company isn't required to pay any additional money to the scheme after the employee retires and there is no guarantee on the level of pension that is finally paid.

In the notes to the financial statement, you find a description of any pension schemes offered by the company. If the only scheme is defined contribution then you simply see a statement of the amount paid into the fund.

If, on the other hand, the company is offering a defined benefit scheme then the notes go on for page after page. You find a description of the assumptions made by the *actuary* in establishing the contribution rates and the current funding position of the scheme.

Prior to the publication of Financial Reporting Standard (FRS) 17: Retirement benefits, the surplus or deficit of a pension scheme did not appear in the company's accounts because the thinking was that these assets were owned by a separate legal entity. The UK Accounting Standards Board took the view that the pension fund may be a separate legal entity but the company had the obligation to fund a shortfall and therefore it should appear in the company's accounts. A surplus is also recognised but only to the extent that the company can recover it through a reduction in future contributions.

You need to compare a number of figures that companies use in calculating their estimates for pension obligations. You should see similar assumptions used by companies in similar industries. Numbers to watch include

✔ **Discount rate:** The interest rate used to determine the present value of the projected benefit obligations.

✔ **Rate of return on assets:** The expected long-term return the company expects to earn on the assets in the retirement investment portfolio.

✔ **Rate of increases in salaries:** The estimate the company makes related to salary increases and the impact those increases have on future pension obligations.

How safe is your pension really?

In the 1990s, most pension funds were *overfunded* – meaning that they had more than enough money to meet future needs. This led to companies taking contribution holidays – on the advice of the actuary. The government was particularly concerned that pension schemes should not be over-funded because they were giving tax relief on contributions and therefore tax-relief is not available when a fund becomes significantly over-funded.

Then, with the stock market crash of the early 21st Century, funds lost billions of pounds. Also, life expectancy was increasing and, all of a sudden, most pension schemes became underfunded – some to a massive extent. It was at about the same time that the UK Accounting Standards Board brought in a new rule that required companies to recognise in their balance sheets the surplus or deficit on a defined benefit scheme. Some companies reacted by increasing contributions to try to remove deficits; others closed schemes to new employees – or even to existing employees – to reduce the problem.

At the time of writing, the stock market is improving and a lot of schemes are moving back into the black. Indeed the majority of company schemes are now properly funded. But, as we all know, investments can go down as well as up, and we have now seen how the volatility in the stock market is translated into very large surpluses or deficits in company accounts. The trend to close defined benefit pension schemes is likely to continue in order to reduce the risk for the company.

For example, Tesco's retirement scheme shows a deficit of £950 million at February 2007 – down from £1,211 million at the start of the year. Marks and Spencer's deficit stands at £283 million down from £795 million.

Each of these rates requires that assumptions be made about unknown future events involving the state of the economy, interest rates, investment returns, and employee life spans. A company can do no more than make an educated guess – guided by the actuary. To be sure that a company's guesses are reasonable, all you can do is check that the company makes similar guesses to those of other companies in the same industry. You also should look for information in the notes about whether the company's retirement savings portfolio is sufficient to meet its expected current and future pension obligations. If the company's retirement savings portfolio falls short, it may be a red flag that future cash-flow problems are possible.

Breaking Down Business Breakdowns

Can you imagine what it takes to manage a multibillion-pound company? Just reading the numbers can be a daunting task. Think about how many products are sent out to make that many sales and how many people are needed to keep the business afloat.

Most major companies deal with their massive size by splitting up the company into manageable segments. This division makes managing all aspects of the business, from product development, to product distribution, to customer satisfaction easier so that the company can better track the performance of each of its product lines.

In the *Operating and Financial Review,* you may find some detail about:

- **Target markets:** These are the key market segments that a company targets, such as age group (teens, tots, adults), locations (UK, Europe, US, for instance), or interest groups (such as sportsmen, hobbyists, and so on). Target markets are limited only by the creativity of the marketing team, which develops the groups of customers that they want to win over.

- **The largest customers:** The company usually names its top customers that buy their product. For example, a manufacturer that sells a large portion of its products to major retailers such as Tesco or Marks and Spencer usually gives some details about these relationships.

- **Manufacturing and other operational details:** A company gives you information about how it groups its product manufacturing and where its products are manufactured. If the company manufactures its products internationally, look for indications about problems that may have occurred during the year related to those operations. Sometimes labour or political strife can have a great impact on a company's manufacturing operations. Also, weather conditions can greatly impact manufacturing conditions. For example, if the company's manufacturing for a certain product line is in Singapore, and Singapore experienced numerous damaging storms, the company may indicate that the problem occurred and that it had difficulty producing enough product for market.

- **Trade sanctions:** All companies that operate internationally must deal with trade laws, which differ in every country. Some countries impose high tariffs on products coming from outside their borders to discourage importing. Sometimes countries impose sanctions on other countries for actions taken by politicians they disagree with. For example, the US doesn't allow trade with Cuba for political reasons, so a company that buys products from Cuba can't import into the US.

In the notes to the financial statements, you find at least one note related to the segment breakdowns. This note gives you details about how each of a company's segments is doing. IAS 14 requires disclosure of segmental information covering both business and geographical segments although how a company defines its defines its segments is a matter for the judgement of management within the limitations laid down by the standard.

The existing standard IAS 14 is being replaced by a new standard, IFRS 8 which will be compulsory for financial statements for years ending on or after 31 December 2009. This new standard is one of the first standards that has been amended by the IASB so as to converge with the standard used in the USA. IFRS 8 has already caused considerable controversy mainly because it permits companies to give less geographical information than was previously required.

If a company faces a specific marketing or manufacturing problem, you also find details about these problems in the note about segment breakdowns. Don't skip over this note!

Reviewing Significant Events

Each year, companies face significant challenges. One year a company may find out that its customers are suing it for a defective product. Another year a company may get notice from the government that one of its manufacturing facilities is polluting the environment. You may also find mention in the notes about significant events that are not related to external forces – for example, the decision to close a factory or combine two divisions into one.

You can look in a number of places in the notes for information on significant events. Sometimes an event has its own note, such as a note about the discontinuation of operations. Other times, it is just part of a note called 'Commitments and Contingencies'. Scan the notes to find significant events that impact a company's financial position.

You're most likely to find significant events mentioned in the notes regarding topics such as:

- **Lawsuits:** Lawsuits (which you usually find in 'Commitments and Contingencies') that are pending against the company are explained. These suits can sometimes have a huge impact on a company's future. For example, GlaxoSmithKline has a general statement in its annual report declaring that it has a number of product liabilities lawsuits impending. You would need to read the notes to the accounts to make a judgement on the potential damage that these might do.

- **Environmental concerns:** These concerns can become a significant event if the company is involved in a major environmental cleanup because of discharges from one of its plants. Clean-up can cost millions of dollars. For example, Exxon has paid more than $900 million in compensation related to damages from the *Valdez* oil spill in Alaska's Prince William Sound in 1989 and will still have to pay more in reparations.

✔ **Restructuring:** Any time a company decides to regroup its products, close down a plant, or make some other major change to the way it does business, this is restructuring. You usually find an individual note explaining the restructuring and how that impacts the company's income during the current year and all other years in which there is an impact from the decision to restructure.

✔ **Discontinued operations:** Sometimes a company decides not to restructure but to close down an operation entirely. When this happens, you're likely to find a separate note on the financial impact of the discontinued operations, which likely includes the costs of closing down facilities and laying off or relocating employees.

Many times the information included in these notes discusses not only the financial impact of an event in the current year, but also any impact expected on financial performance in future years.

When a company discusses lawsuits and potential environmental liability cases in the notes, it commonly indicates that in the opinion of management, the matter in question won't result in a material loss to the company. Use your own judgement after reading the details management provides. If you think the company may be facing bigger problems than the company mentioned, do your own research on the matter before investing in a company.

If a company faces a lawsuit, this matter isn't necessarily something of great concern. Given the litigious nature of society, most major corporations face lawsuits annually. But these suits do raise red flags sometimes, as described in the next section.

Finding the Red Flags

As you probably know by now, some companies love hiding their dirty washing in the small print of the notes to the financial statements. As you read through the notes, keep an eye out for possible red flags.

Whenever you see notes titled 'restructuring', 'discontinued operations', and 'accounting changes' look for red flags that could mean continuing expenses for a number of years. The companies detail the costs of any of these changes. Be sure to consider long-term financial impacts that could be a drain on future earnings for the company – which may mean share prices suffer.

Also be on the lookout for potential lawsuits that could result in huge settlements. If you see a lawsuit has been filed against a company, search for stories in the financial press that discuss the lawsuit in greater detail than the company might include in the notes. The financial press usually covers major lawsuits filed against a company.

Significant events aren't the only things that can raise red flags. You may also see signs of trouble in the way that a company values assets or in decisions made to change accounting policies. The notes involving the long-term obligations a company has to its pensioners may also be a good spot to find some potential red flags.

 The financial press often mentions the red flags that analysts spot in companies' financial reports. Read the financial press to pick up the potential problem spots and then look for the details in the financial statements and the notes to those financial statements. These problems can be related to how a company values its assets and liabilities or to a decision to change accounting policies.

Finding out about valuing assets and liabilities

Valuing assets and liabilities leaves room for accounting creativity. If assets are overvalued, you may be led to believe that the company owns more than it actually does. If liabilities are undervalued, you may think the company owes less than it actually does. Either way, you get a false impression about the company's financial position.

 When you don't understand something, ask questions of the company's investor relations staff (who are responsible for answering investors' questions) until they present the information in a manner that you understand. If you're confused about the presentation about asset or liability valuation, we guarantee that other financial readers are as well. We often find that the more convoluted a company's explanation is, the more likely you are to find out that the company is hiding something.

Considering changes in accounting policies

How a company puts together its numbers is just as critical as the numbers themselves. The accounting policies adopted by the company drive these numbers. Whenever a company indicates in the notes to the financial statements that it's changing accounting policies, your red flag should go up. We discuss the key accounting policies and how they can impact income in the section 'Accounting Policies Note: Laying Out the Rules of the Road' earlier in this chapter. You can find more detail about accounting policies in Chapter 4.

Changes in accounting policies aren't always a sign of a problem. In fact, many times the change is related to requirements specified by the International Accounting Standards Board (IASB). No matter what the reason for the change, be sure you understand how that change impacts your ability to compare year-to-year or quarter-to-quarter results.

If you see a change in accounting methods and there's no indication that the IASB required it, dig deeper into the reasons for the change and find out how the change impacts the valuation of assets and liabilities or the net income of the company. You can find some explanation in the accounting policies note, but if you don't understand the explanation there, call the investor relations department and ask questions.

Decoding obligations to pensioners and future pensioners

As noted in 'Pondering Pension and Retirement Benefits' earlier in this chapter, obligations to pensioners and future pensioners can be a bigger drain on a company's resources than debt obligations. The note to the financial statements related to pension benefits is probably one of the most difficult to understand. Look specifically at the notes that show a company's long-term payment obligations to pensioners and the cash available to pay those obligations. If you find any indication that the company may have difficulty meeting these obligations mentioned in the note, this could be the sign of a major cash-flow problem in the future. Don't hesitate to call and ask questions if you don't understand the presentation.

Chapter 10

Considering Consolidated Financial Statements

. . . .

In This Chapter

▶ Understanding consolidation

▶ Figuring out how companies buy companies

▶ Exploring consolidated financial statements

▶ Turning to the notes for details

. . . .

*L*ike couples who marry and work to combine two incomes – two sets of financial obligations and two ways of managing money – things get complicated when companies decide to join forces or buy other companies and their financial statements become one. This new arrangement makes finding out how each of the pieces of this new entity perform financially much harder for you. In this chapter, we discuss how to read the more complex financial reports that arise when companies consolidate.

Getting a Grip on Consolidation

One of the ways companies grow is by buying or merging with other companies. When a company is bought by another, it gets gobbled up in the new company and loses all its independence. But when companies decide to merge, they usually decide jointly on how the new company operates.

In the past, when companies combined their operations in a merger, they were permitted to use the method known as *merger accounting*. This method simply added together the accounts of the two separate entities and was, for a time, very popular. The problem was that the standard setters saw it as an area where abuse could occur because companies might use merger accounting when the reality of the business combination was that an acquisition had taken place rather than a merger. The UK Accounting Standards Board brought in stringent conditions to try to stem the abuse way back in 1994 but the International Accounting Standards Board thought that the easier approach was to simply ban the merger accounting method which they did in 2005.

Now, under international standards, if two entities combine in what would previously have been referred to as a merger, then one of them quite simply must be designated to be the acquirer.

Small companies in the UK are still permitted to use merger accounting subject to a set of stringent conditions designed to ensure that the merger accounting technique is only used in appropriate circumstances.

Major corporations produce consolidated accounts that include all or part of the results of any other entity in which they own a share. These entities include subsidiaries, associates, and joint ventures. Here are some details:

- *Subsidiaries* are entities controlled by another entity, usually a company. The company controlling the subsidiary is called the *parent company*. We discuss the various ways a company can become a subsidiary in the next section 'Looking at Methods of Buying Up Companies'.

- *Joint ventures* are entities in which *venturers* (usually two or more companies) share joint control over the economic activity of the entity.

- *Associates* are entities over which the parent company has significant influence but which are not subsidiaries or joint ventures.

The parent company's financial report gives considerable detail about subsidiaries, associates, and joint ventures in the notes to the financial statements (refer to Chapter 9 for more on notes). However, you know immediately that a company has subsidiaries, associates, or participates in joint ventures if you look at the balance sheet (refer to Chapter 6) or income statement (refer to Chapter 7) and see 'Consolidated' noted at the top of the page.

The European Union (EU) requires all listed companies in the European Economic Area to prepare their consolidated accounts using International Accounting Standards (IAS) as approved by the EU. In reality, this means that almost all listed companies use IAS because almost all listed companies have subsidiaries. Where a listed company has no subsidiaries it can still prepare its accounts using local Generally Accepted Accounting Principles (GAAP) – in other words, a UK company can still follow UK standards.

One other thing, UK corporation tax is based on the accounts of the individual company, not the group. Therefore, the parent company, and every other company within the group, can choose to prepare their own individual accounts using UK GAAP if they think that this will be advantageous from a tax point of view. All of these accounts would then have to be converted to IAS as part of the consolidation into group accounts.

If you look at Tesco's or Marks and Spencer's statements in Appendix A, you see that each statement indicates that it represents the financial results of the parent company and its subsidiaries. Tesco refer to the income statement as 'group income statement' whereas Marks and Spencer refer to it as 'consolidated income statement'. These two phrases mean exactly the same thing.

You don't see any listing of what those subsidiaries are on the balance sheet or income statement. In fact, unless a company discusses an acquisition or sale of a subsidiary in the notes to the financial statements, you probably won't see them mentioned individually in the current year's financial report. If no financial transactions occur in the year being reported, the company probably highlights only some of its subsidiaries' successes in the narrative pages in the front of the financial report.

However, UK company law requires that the parent company prepares its own individual accounts as well as consolidated accounts. These accounts are simpler than the group accounts and are subject to some exemptions – most notably that the company does not have to prepare a separate income statement or cash-flow statement because its own income and cash flow have been included in the group figures. The separate accounts of the parent company will include a listing of significant investments in subsidiaries, joint ventures, and associates.

Both Tesco and Marks and Spencer include the financial statements of the parent company at the back of the annual report for the group. Marks and Spencer include a list of significant subsidiaries in the notes to the accounts of the parent company. By contrast, Tesco include such a list in the group accounts and simply cross-refer to it in the accounts of the parent. Both companies make the point that the list of subsidiaries contains only the principal subsidiaries but a full list can be obtained by examining the annual return filed at Companies House.

In some parts of the world (including the UK until 2005), groups can exclude subsidiaries from consolidation on the grounds that the business activities of the subsidiary are so different from the parent that to consolidate the results would be potentially misleading. However, IAS 27 addresses this issue explicitly and says that consolidation must occur and where activities of a subsidiary are significantly different then this should be dealt with by disclosing additional information.

Looking at Methods of Buying Up Companies

One of the most common ways companies grow is by buying up smaller businesses. These smaller businesses either get completely gobbled up with no outward sign that they ever existed, or they become subsidiaries, operating under the umbrella of the company that bought them.

Companies can take control over another business by two methods: They can acquire the assets and liabilities of the other business or they can acquire a majority of its shares. Only when a company buys another by acquiring a majority of its shares does that other company become a subsidiary. Here's a brief overview of the ways one company can buy another:

- **Acquisition of the business:** This occurs when one company acquires all the assets of another and accepts the responsibilities of all the liabilities of that company. As part of this deal, the acquiring company will take over the business activities of the other entity and this will usually involve the payment of an agreed amount for goodwill. This is known as purchased goodwill and appears in the balance sheet as an intangible non-current asset. If the entity being taken over is a sole trader or partnership then this is the only way to acquire the business.

- **Share acquisition:** In this case, two companies combine, but both companies remain separate legal entities after the transaction. The company that buys the shares of the other merges as the parent company, and the other company becomes the subsidiary. The financial statements of the two are consolidated into the parent company's financial statements.

  Two types of share acquisition exist:

  - **Majority interest:** When a company buys more than 50 per cent of another company's equity shares, the company has what is termed a *majority interest*. When a company buys 100 per cent of another company's equity shares, the subsidiary is called a *wholly-owned subsidiary*.

  - **Minority interest:** When a company owns less than 50 per cent of another company's equity shares, the company has a *minority interest*. When a consolidated balance sheet indicates minority interest, a consolidated balance sheet shows the interests of minority shareholders as a part of total equity but distinguished from the equity interests of the shareholders in the parent company.

Subsidiaries are the entities that are left in place after a company is acquired by another company using the share acquisition method. If you were a shareholder in the subsidiary before it was bought out, you are still able to track the results of the company that you originally owned because the company is still required to prepare its own separate financial statements.

When an individual or a company wants to acquire a listed company they may first buy shares on the open market. Once they own 3 per cent of that target company they need to notify the company of their holding. They must also notify the company every time their holding increases by another percentage point. Obviously, the financial press show interest in the intentions of the entity which is building up such a substantial holding. As the holding of shares increases, the City code on takeovers and mergers takes effect when the percentage of shares owned passes the 30 per cent mark. At that point the acquirer of the shares is required to make an offer for the rest of the share capital of the company on terms no less favourable than the recent acquisitions.

Reading Consolidated Financial Statements

Most major corporations are made up of numerous companies bought along the way to create their empires. The consolidated financial statements reflect the financial results for all these entities that it bought as well as the original assets of the company.

After a share acquisition by the parent company, the subsidiary continues to maintain separate accounting records. But in reality, the parent company controls the subsidiary, so it no longer operates completely independently.

Because the parent company now fully controls the subsidiary, by accounting rules, the parent company must present its subsidiary's, and its own, financial operations in a consolidated manner (even though the two companies are separate legal entities). The parent company does so by publishing a *consolidated financial statement,* which combines the assets, liabilities, revenue, and expenses of the parent company as well as those of its subsidiaries, associates, and joint ventures.

If you hold a minority interest (see the previous section for more information on minority interest) in the subsidiary of a parent company, the consolidated financial statement won't give you the information you need to make decisions about your holdings. A subsidiary with minority shareholders must report its financial results separately from its parent company's in addition to having its report included in the consolidated financial statements.

When a company owns all the equity shares of its subsidiaries, the company doesn't really need to publish reports about its subsidiaries' individual results for the general public to peruse. Shareholders don't even need to know the results of these subsidiaries. However, the requirement to file accounts at Companies House still applies to wholly-owned subsidiaries just as it does to individual companies which are not part of a group.

In preparing consolidated financial statements, the parent company must eliminate those transactions that have taken place between the parent and its subsidiaries (or between one subsidiary and another) before presenting the consolidated financial statements to the public. Key transactions that a parent company must eliminate when preparing consolidated financial statements are:

- **Investments in the subsidiary:** The parent company's books show its investments in a subsidiary as an asset account. The subsidiary's books show the shares that the parent company holds as shareholders' equity. The parent company must eliminate these amounts in the consolidated accounts by matching the investment off against the share capital and reserves in the subsidiary at the date of acquisition. The cost of the investment in the parent's books probably doesn't exactly balance with the total of the share capital and reserves in the subsidiary's books at the time of acquisition. The difference between them is goodwill.

- **Advances to subsidiary:** If a parent company advances money to a subsidiary or a subsidiary advances money to its parent company, both entities carry the opposite side of this transaction on their books (that is, one entity gains money while the other one loses it, or vice versa). Again, on consolidation, these two balances are matched against each other and are thus cancelled out.

- **Interest revenue and expenses:** Sometimes a parent company lends money to a subsidiary or a subsidiary lends money to a parent company; in these business transactions, one company may charge the other one interest on the loan. On the consolidated statements, any interest revenue or expenses that these loans generate must be eliminated.

- **Dividend revenue or expenses:** If a subsidiary declares a dividend, the parent company receives some of these dividends as revenue from the subsidiary. Any time a parent company records revenue from its subsidiaries on its books, the parent company must eliminate any dividend expenses that the subsidiary recorded in its books.

- **Management fees:** Sometimes a subsidiary pays its parent company a *management fee* for the administrative services it provides. These fees are recorded as revenue on the parent company's books and as expenses on the subsidiary's books. Again, both must be cancelled out.

- **Sales and purchases:** Parent companies frequently buy products or materials from their subsidiaries, or their subsidiaries buy products or materials from them. In fact, most companies that buy other companies do so within the same industry as a means of getting control of a product line, a customer base, or some other aspect of that company's operations.

However, the consolidated income statements shouldn't show these sales as revenue and shouldn't show the purchases as expenses. Otherwise, the company would be earning a profit just by moving goods about within the group. Accounting rules require that parent companies eliminate these types of transactions.

Whilst preparing consolidated accounts may appear complicated, all that we are doing is preparing accounts for the group as if it were a single entity and so any transactions between members of the group must be cancelled out.

Looking to the Notes

The eliminations to adjust for reporting subsidiary results mentioned in the previous section don't show up in the group's financial reports unless some portion of the share acquisition took place in the year that's being reported. When the acquisition or some financial impact of that acquisition did take place in the year that's being reported, you need to look to the notes to the financial statements to get details about any financial impacts (refer to Chapter 9 for more about notes).

In the accounting policies note in the consolidated financial statements, the company indicates that the financial statements represent the results of the parent company and the companies within the group. The notes also include some statement about the transactions that were eliminated. Just to give you an example of how this is worded, here's the information from Tesco's notes:

> *The Group financial statements consist of the financial statements of the ultimate parent company (Tesco plc), all entities controlled by the company (its subsidiaries) and the group's share of its interests in joint ventures and associates.*

Note that you don't find out what subsidiaries fall under Tesco in this explanation – the principal subsidiaries are listed in note 13 to the accounts.

A further extract from the Tesco accounting policies:

> *Intragroup balances and any unrealised gains and losses or income and expenses arising from intragroup transactions are eliminated in preparing the consolidated financial statements.*

You can see that the note mentions eliminations, but it doesn't provide much detail, and just by looking at the notes, you don't really know what was eliminated. In fact, even if you had the financial statements of the parent and all the subsidiaries, you'd have a very difficult time unwinding the information to figure out the eliminations. And doing so probably isn't worth your time: It could take hours and probably won't help you make any decisions about whether the company is a good investment. We don't explain how to calculate eliminations, but some analysts do attempt to do so in their reports about the company and its subsidiaries.

Mergers and acquisitions

If a company completed a merger or acquisition in the year that's reported in the consolidated financial statements, you'll find a special note in the notes to the financial statements. Otherwise, if you want to find out any details about how the mergers and acquisitions may still be impacting the company financially, you have to start digging.

For example, if a company issued additional shares to buy a subsidiary, the value of the shares held by shareholders before the acquisition is *diluted*, which means that the same earnings or assets must be divided among a greater number of shareholders. To see how this works, imagine an example involving 100 shares and a company profit of £100. In this scenario, each share claims £1 of earnings. If, after the acquisition, 150 shares are outstanding, each share of stock can claim only 67p of the £100 of earnings. This diluted ownership impacts the amount of dividends or the portion of ownership you have in the company for the rest of the time you own those shares. However, with any luck, as a result of the acquisition, the profits of the group will have increased to compensate for the dilution in your shareholding!

You can see how you need to play a game of cat-and-mouse to find all the little pieces of cheese laid out in the financial statements. Companies don't necessarily make information easily accessible, and might even hide the financial impact of an acquisition or merger on the value of your shares by writing the notes to the financial statements in such a convoluted way that you have to be a detective to sort out the relevant details.

Goodwill

Another important note you can check out to find the impact of mergers and acquisitions on the consolidated financial statements is the note that explains 'goodwill'. *Goodwill* is the amount of money a company pays in excess of the value of the assets when it buys another company (go to Chapters 4 and 6 for more details).

For example, suppose that a company has £100 million in net assets, but another company offers to buy it for £150 million. That extra £50 million does not represent tangible assets like inventory or property, but instead represents extra value because of customer loyalty, store locations, or other factors that add value.

Liquidations or discontinued operations

Whenever a company sells a subsidiary or significant joint venture or associate, or discontinues its operations, a note to the financial statement regarding this transaction appears in the year in which the sale or discontinuance first occurred. After the first year, any impact that a sale or a discontinuance of operations has on a company's operating results is usually buried in other notes. Just like with mergers and acquisitions, you have to play detective to find out any ongoing impact that these changes have had on the company.

The company includes information about any profits or losses related to the liquidation of an asset or discontinued operations in the notes to the financial statement. Because these transactions can impact financial statements over a number of years, the detail includes financial impacts for the years prior to the year being reported, as well as future financial impacts anticipated.

When reading the consolidated financial statements and their related notes, be sure you look for any mention of the impact of previous acquisitions or disposals and how those transactions may still be impacting the financial statements.

You may find notes related to impacts on the balance sheet, income statement, shareholders' equity, or cash flows. Transactions involving acquisitions and disposals can impact any of these statements.

Part III
Analysing the Numbers

'The managing director - he's very busy,
involving himself with the liquidity of
the company'

In this part . . .

We show you how to crack the numbers so you can find out whether the company whose report you're reading is truly in a healthy financial position. We explain how to analyse the financial statements to test whether the company is profitable and liquid enough to continue operating. We also give you tips on how to test the company's cash-flow situation.

Chapter 11

Testing the Profits and Market Value

In This Chapter

▶ Getting a handle on the price/earnings ratio

▶ Diving into dividend yield and cover

▶ Examining return on sales

▶ Realising return on assets

▶ Taking a look at return on equity

▶ Working with margins

*W*ell, did the company make any money? That's the question everyone, and we mean *everyone* with a financial stake in the company – executives, investors, creditors, employees – wants the answer to. Investors especially want to know whether or not the company's shares are worth the price they would have to pay for them.

You may think the answer should be a simple 'yes' or 'no', but actually the answer always depends on many factors. How well did the company make use of its resources in order to make a profit? Was that profit high enough based on the resources the company had at hand and compared with that of similar companies? Did the company pay out a fair share of its earnings to its investors? Did it reinvest the right amount of the money in its coffers for future growth?

In this chapter, we show you how to answer these key questions with calculations that help you to test a company's profitability and market value: price/earnings ratio (P/E), dividend yield, and return on sales (ROS), return on assets (ROA), and return on equity (ROE). We also review how to calculate the profit margins – both the operating margin and the net margin.

To help you understand the validity of these profitability tests, we compare the results of two leading retailing companies, Tesco and Marks and Spencer, and compare their results with those of the retail industry in general. (See Appendix A for these companies' financial statements.)

The Price/Earnings Ratio

The profit term you hear discussed most often in the financial news is the *price/earnings ratio,* or the *P/E ratio.* Basically, the P/E ratio looks at the price of the shares in a company against its earnings. For example, P/E ratios of 10 means that for every £1 in company earnings per share, people are willing to pay £10 to buy a share. If the P/E is 20, that means people are willing to pay £20 per share for each £1 of company earnings.

Why are people willing to pay more per pound of earnings on some shares? Because the people who buy the more expensive shares believe that the share has greater potential for growth. This ratio is used when valuing shares and is one of the oldest measurements in the world of stock exchanges.

On its own, the P/E ratio means very little, but as part of an overall evalua-tion of a company, the P/E ratio helps you interpret earnings results. Never make a decision about whether to buy or sell shares based solely on the P/E ratio. Nonetheless, a negative P/E or a P/E of zero is a major trouble sign, indicating that a company isn't profitable.

To help put the P/E ratio into perspective, check out the section 'Using the P/E ratio to judge company market value (share price)', later in this chapter.

Working out earnings per share

Earnings per share represent the amount of income a company earned per share on the stock market. The company calculates the *earnings per share* (EPS) by dividing the Profit for the Year on the Income Statement by the number of shares outstanding.

Companies often use a *weighted average* of the number of shares outstanding during the reporting period because the number of shares outstanding can change as a company sells new shares to outside investors or company employees. In addition, companies sometimes buy back shares from existing shareholders, reducing the number of shares available to the general public. A weighted average is calculated by totalling the number of shares available during a certain period of time and dividing that number by the number of periods included. For example, if the weighted average is based on a monthly average, the number of shares outstanding on the stock market at the end of each month is totalled and divided by 12 to find the weighted average. If the company has not published this calculation in the annual report you have to use a cruder method to find the weighted average. Simply add the number of shares at the end of 2007 to the number at the end of 2006 and divide by two.

Calculating the P/E ratio

To get the P/E ratio, divide the share price by earnings per share:

Share price/earnings per share of stock = P/E ratio

You can find share prices on many Web sites. Yahoo! Finance (`finance.yahoo.co.uk`) is good for easily finding historical stock data.

The P/E formula comes in two flavours, which vary according to how earnings per share are calculated: on historic or projected earnings.

- ✔ **Historic P/E:** You calculate a historic P/E by using earnings per share from the last four quarters or 12 months of earnings. This number gives you a view of a company's earnings ratios based on accurate historical data.

- ✔ **Projected P/Es:** The other two types of P/E ratios are calculated using analysts' expectations, so they're sometimes called 'leading' or 'projected P/Es'.

  - The *current P/E ratio* is calculated using earnings expected by analysts during the current year.

  - A *forward P/E ratio* is based on analysts' projections for the next year or years further ahead.

Any P/E ratio that uses future projected results is only as good as the analyst making those projections. So be careful when you see the terms *leading*, *projected*, *current*, or *forward P/E*.

Any type of P/E ratio is just one of many profitability ratios you should consider. This ratio gives you a good idea of what the public is willing to pay for a share based on the company's historical earnings or what the analysts project you can consider paying for a share based on future earnings (current P/E or forward P/E). However, the figure gives you no guarantees about what the company will earn or what the share price will be in the future.

Practising the P/E ratio calculation

Here's how you can calculate the P/E ratio using real-world numbers from Tesco and Marks and Spencer. To calculate the P/E ratio you first need to obtain the earnings per share (EPS) figure, which represents the Profit for the year divided by the number of shares outstanding (see the previous section 'Working out earnings per share'). Remember that the number of shares outstanding can change as the company sells new shares to investors or buys them back from existing shareholders.

When a company reports its earnings per share, it usually shows two numbers: basic and diluted. The company calculates the *basic EPS* using a weighted average of all shares currently on the market. The *diluted EPS* takes into consideration all future obligations to sell shares. For example, this number takes into account employees who have options to buy shares in the future or bondholders who hold bonds that are convertible into shares.

To practise using the formula to calculate P/E ratios, we use numbers from Tesco's and Marks and Spencer's income statements. Table 11–1 shows Tesco's basic and diluted EPS for 2007 and 2006. Table 11–2 shows the same information for Marks and Spencer.

Table 11–1	Tesco's Earnings Per Share (EPS)	
	Net Income (Loss)	*Earnings Per Share*
	2007	*2006*
Basic	23.84p	20.07p
Diluted	23.54p	19.79p

Table 11–2	Marks and Spencer's Earnings Per Share (EPS)	
	Net Income (Loss)	*Earnings Per Share*
	2007	*2006*
Basic	39.1p	31.4
Diluted	38.5p	31.1

Notice that the diluted EPS of Marks and Spencer has made more progress from 2006 to 2007 as a percentage than Tesco.

In the following examples, to calculate how the public valued the results for Tesco and Marks and Spencer at the time of writing (June 2007) using the 2007 annual report (see Appendix A), we looked up the share price online while writing this section of the book. We also use the diluted earnings per share, which more accurately represents the company's outstanding shareholder obligations. The Tesco share price was 457.75p, and Marks and Spencer was 674.00p.

Here's Tesco's P/E ratio:

457.75p (share price) ÷ 23.54p (2007's diluted EPS) = 19.4 (P/E ratio)

So Tesco investors are willing to pay 19.4p for every 1p of earnings by Tesco in 2007.

The following is Marks and Spencer's P/E ratio:

674p (share price) ÷ 38.5p (2007's diluted EPS) = 17.5 (P/E ratio)

Marks and Spencer investors are willing to pay 17.5p for every 1p of earnings by Marks and Spencer in 2007.

Using the P/E ratio to judge company market value (share price)

In comparing Tesco's and Marks and Spencer's P/E ratios, you can conclude that in June 2007, investors believed that Tesco had slightly better chances of improving its earnings performance than Marks and Spencer and, therefore, were willing to pay a higher price for a Tesco share. You must dig deeper into the numbers, the quarterly reports for the first half of 2008, and general financial press coverage to determine why investors are more bullish on Tesco than Marks and Spencer. But this one quick calculation lets you know which company investors favour. Tesco has the more consistent growth of profit performance and is, of course, a much bigger company.

How do you know what a reasonable P/E ratio is for a company? Historically, the average P/E ratio for shares falls between 12 and 20 for large companies. This ratio depends on economic conditions and the industry the company's in. Some industries, such as technology, regularly maintain higher P/E ratios in the range of 30 to 40.

In addition to comparing two companies, you should compare the P/E calculation you did to the industry in which the companies fall. Doing so allows you to compare share price or market value, not only for the companies whose annual reports you're analysing, but also to compare the companies you're focusing on with others in the same business.

Probably the easiest way to find average P/E's is to look in the _Financial Times_. Supermarket companies come under the retail food and drug industry sector. The average P/E for the food and drug retail industry was 22.15 in June 2007, so Tesco was a bit below that average. The average P/E for general retailers was 19.84 and Marks and Spencer was slightly below that average as well. Bear in mind, though, that no large company is in exactly the same business as the ones that make up the average. The conclusion is that neither company has a major discrepancy within its industry average.

The P/E is a good quick ratio for picking potential investment candidates, but you shouldn't use this ratio alone to make a buying or selling decision. After you pick your targets, read and analyse the annual reports and other information about the company before making a decision to invest.

If you want to start your research on potential investment opportunities based on leaders or laggards in an industry, you can find a summary for all industry statistics at uk.biz.yahoo.com/sectors. You may wonder why someone would even consider laggards as investment opportunities. Well, that's where you can sometimes find a company that many investors think is a dog, but in reality is terribly undervalued and doing the right things to recover from its current slump. This style of investing is called *value investing*.

When investors are bullish, they tend to bid up the price of shares and end up paying higher prices for shares than they may actually be worth. This price-bidding war also drives up the P/E ratio.

Share prices are set by the market based solely on the price at which someone is willing to sell a share and the price at which someone is willing to buy a share.

During the Internet and technology share bubble of the late 1990s and early 2000s, P/E ratios hit highs in the 100s and tumbled dramatically after the bubble burst. Even big names, such as Microsoft, had P/E ratios over 100 that dropped back to realistic levels when the bubble burst. In June 2007, Microsoft's P/E was 26.9, so you can see that even a top company can from time to time be seriously overpriced by investors.

Be careful when you see P/Es creeping above their historical averages. Usually you're seeing a sign that a correction is looming, which will bring share prices back down to realistic levels.

Understanding variation among ratios

You probably find varying P/E ratios for the same company because the number used for EPS can differ depending on which method for calculating EPS is chosen. The diluted EPS is the one you should generally use. This figure is based on the current number of shares on the market as well as those promised to employees for purchase in the future and those promised to creditors who may decide to convert a debt into a shareholding (if that's part of the debt agreement). So diluted earnings gives you the most accurate picture of the actual earnings per share available on the market or committed for sale in the future.

When reporting EPS in the accounts, companies are constrained by the rules in IAS 33 and will produce figures consistent with the explanations given in this chapter. However, companies are permitted to report additional EPS figures in the notes to the accounts as long as they explain how the earnings figures have been arrived at.

When companies put out a press release, they might be tempted to use whatever EPS looks most favourable for them. Companies can choose among four basic ways to calculate EPS:

- **Reported EPS:** Companies calculate this EPS number by using general accounting principles and report it on the financial statements. They show it in two formats: basic and diluted. Usually, the diluted EPS number is the best one to use, but sometimes it can be distorted by one-time events, such as the sale of a division or a one-time charge for discontinued operations. So you need to read the notes to the financial statements to determine whether the EPS figure needs to be adjusted for unusual events. Chapter 9 discusses the notes to the financial statements in great detail.

- **Pro forma EPS:** You often find this EPS in a company's press release because it makes the company look its best. In most cases, this figure excludes some of the expenses or income the company used in the official financial reports. The company adjusts these official numbers to take out income that won't recur, such as a one-time gain on the sale of marketable securities, or expenses that won't recur, such as the closing of a large division.

When a company mentions Pro forma EPS or statements in its press release, be sure that you compare these numbers with what the company calculates using Generally Accepted Accounting Principles (GAAP) in financial statements filed at Companies House.

- **Headline EPS:** This EPS is the one you hear about on television and read about in the newspapers. The earnings per share numbers used could be basic EPS, diluted EPS, Pro forma EPS, or some other EPS calculated based on analysts' projections, so you have absolutely no idea what's behind the numbers or the P/E ratio calculated using it. It's likely to be the most unreliable EPS, and you shouldn't use it for your evaluation.

- **Cash EPS:** Companies calculate this EPS by using *operating cash flow* (cash generated by company operations to produce and sell its products and services). Operating cash can't be manipulated by accounting rules as easily as net income, so some analysts believe this EPS is the purest. When you see this number, be sure it's based on operating cash and isn't just a fancy way of saying EBITDA (earnings before interest, taxes, depreciation, and amortisation). You can judge by calculating the cash EPS using the EBITDA reported in the financial statements and the net cash from operations reported in the statement of cash flows. Only the net cash figure gives you a true picture of cash flow.

The P/E ratio is an ever-changing number based on the day's market price and is also a number that's hard to depend on unless you know the calculations behind it. Companies can calculate the earnings per share in many different ways – using basic EPS, diluted EPS, pro forma EPS, cash EPS, headline EPS, and projected EPS. Reading the financial reports and checking the calculation for yourself is the only way that you can truly determine a company's P/E and what's included in its calculation.

Dividend Yield and Cover

Dividend yield looks at the amount a company pays out to investors as dividend as a percentage of the price they would have to pay for a share. Using this ratio, you can predict the actual cash return you'll get by buying and holding a share.

Some companies pay a portion of their earnings directly to their shareholders as dividends. Growth companies, which reinvest all their profits, rarely pay out dividends, but older, mature companies usually do. Older companies that no longer need to reinvest large sums in growing their businesses pay out the highest dividends.

To determine how well investors did with their stock holding, you can calculate the dividend yield yourself.

Determining dividend yield

To find the dividend yield, divide annual dividend per share (the total amount per share paid out to investors during the year in dividends) by share price:

annual dividend per share ÷ share price = dividend yield

You can use numbers from Tesco's 2007 annual report (see Appendix A) to practise calculating the dividend yield. The dividend payout is in the notes to the financial statements. The share price is on the company's Web site or in the financial pages of a newspaper:

8.91p (dividends per share) ÷ 457.75p (share price) = 1.9 per cent (dividend yield).

The following are numbers from Marks and Spencer's 2007 income statement (see Appendix A) and the Web site for the share price. You can use them to calculate dividend yield.

15.5p (dividends per share) ÷ 674p (share price) = 2.3 per cent (dividend yield).

Marks and Spencer offers investors a higher return on an investment in their shares at the current price than Tesco. Notice that it is only in the notes to the Marks and Spencer accounts that you see the actual dividend paid according to IFRS rules. In the financial review they have claimed dividend paid of 18.3p. This figure represents, probably fairly, what the company will pay in dividend out of the profits for 2007. Part of the dividend was paid during 2007 (an interim dividend) and the rest (the final dividend) will be paid in 2008 after approval by the shareholders at the AGM. In the past, the dividend shown in the accounts would include amounts not yet paid at the year end but, in 1985, the Companies Act was altered and now UK GAAP, in line with IFRS rules, insist that the amount shown in the accounts is the amount actually paid in 2007 – which of course now includes the final dividend for 2006.

Depending on the particular requirement of an investor, dividend yield could help determine which of the two shares to purchase. If, for example, an old-age pensioner needs income, then the share with the higher yield may be attractive. On the other hand, young high earners may not want dividend returns at this time because of the tax they will have to pay: they may accept a lower-yielding share in expectation of a capital gain from an increase in the value of their shareholding: In this case, the higher P/E ratio of Tesco may suggest that the market is expecting Tesco to be the faster grower.

Digging into dividend cover

Dividend cover, the number of times profits 'cover' the dividend. So, if profits were 100 and the dividend payment were 25 then dividend cover would be 4 times. Dividend cover helps an investor to answer two questions:

- ✔ What proportion of its earnings is a company paying out as opposed to retaining in the business to fund growth?
- ✔ How likely is the company to be able to maintain its dividend strategy in the future?

To find the dividend cover, divide earnings per share by dividend per share (the total amount per share paid out to investors during the year in dividends):

earnings per share ÷ annual dividend per share = dividend cover

You can use the EPS figure from Tesco's 2007 income statement (see Appendix A) to practise calculating the dividend payout ratio:

23.54 (diluted EPS) ÷ 8.91p (dividends per share) = 2.64 (dividend cover).

The following are numbers from Marks and Spencer's 2007 income statement (see Appendix A). You can use them to calculate dividend yield.

38.5p (diluted EPS) ÷ 15.5p (dividend per share) = 2.48 (dividend cover).

Both Tesco and Marks and Spencer have a very reasonable level of dividend cover. There would have to be a dramatic fall in profits in the future for the companies to have to reduce or pass their dividend payments.

Lower dividend cover means that a company is paying out a larger proportion of its earnings to its shareholders. Should the amount a company pays out in dividends, compared to how much of its earnings it keeps back to fund growth, make a difference to you? In the past, investors expected dividend payouts. In fact, dividends made up as much as 40 per cent of most investors' portfolio returns about 20 years ago. But investors' priorities have changed in the past 20 years. Today, investors look toward *capital gains* – the profits investors make when selling shares for more than they paid for them – for portfolio growth.

The big question is what better serves the investor and the company – immediate cash payouts of dividends or long-term growth resulting from reinvesting profits each year? The answer to this question isn't an easy one. Younger companies rarely pay dividends because they need the money for growth, but as companies mature, the correct answer is more difficult to determine. For example, high technology companies who need many millions to spend on research and development and good reserves to employ if their complicated products prove expensive to introduce and install at the beginning of their life, tend to pay out a very small proportion of their earnings to shareholders. Investors accept this dividend strategy and high dividend cover knowing that if the high-tech company enjoys spectacular growth they will get a good return from the rising price of the shares.

You should definitely check how a company's dividend strategy compares with that of similar companies. If dividend cover is considerably higher than that of other similar companies, be sure you understand what the company does with the money and whether the company is making good use of the funds it's reinvesting. If the company pays out a significantly larger portion of earnings to investors than most other companies in the industry, the company may not have any good ideas for growth and is therefore just milking the cash cow, which may eventually run dry. If dividend cover moves towards 1 it may well become increasingly difficult for the company to maintain its high level of dividend distribution.

Low dividend cover could be a sign that a decrease in dividends may soon be on the way. If a company continually increases its dividend pay out even as profits fall, the figure for dividend cover is a warning sign that future trouble is brewing.

Who pays the highest dividends?

Investors who purchase shares primarily for current income look to industries that traditionally have high dividend yields. Utility companies traditionally have some of the highest dividend yields, but you find good dividend payers in many mature, older industries. If you want to look for a good share to buy based on dividend pay out, here are two key factors to consider:

✔ **Cash stash:** When you read the annual report, pay close attention to how much cash the company reports in its books. Remember that the dividend comes from extra cash flow. Most companies need to hold on to some of their cash so that they have money for acquisitions, research and development, and other capital needs to keep the company competitive, even if it's not in a high-growth industry. Use your calculation of dividend cover to determine how much cash the company is using to cover its dividends and how much cash it's saving for future needs. If the company is paying out most

of its cash and saving very little, that may be a sign that the cash could run out at some point because the company is no longer reinvesting anything in maintaining its market or updating its products. Eventually, the company will lose out to competition and earn less, bringing in less cash.

✔ **Dividend consistency:** As you read the annual report, also look for information about dividends paid out over the past few years. You can find that information for the past two years in the annual report and possibly longer if the company has a Five Year Record table in the notes to the accounts. You can get information for more than two years by looking up the company at Yahoo! Finance and other financial Web sites. You want to find companies that pay dividends at a consistent level or, even better, that are able to increase their dividend pay outs regularly.

If dividend cover looks extremely high or extremely low, look at the financial statements before you get too concerned. Did some extraordinary event dramatically impact net income, such as a significant loss from a plant closing or the sale or purchase of a subsidiary? A one-time event that impacts net income can explain an unusually high or low dividend pay-out ratio and needn't raise a red flag for investors.

Return on Sales

You can test how efficiently a company runs its operations (that is, the making and selling of its products) by calculating its *return on sales* (ROS). This ratio measures how much profit the company is producing per pound of sales. By analysing the numbers you're seeing in the income statement using ROS, you can get a picture of its profit per pound of sales and gauge how much extra cash the company is bringing in per sale.

Remember, the company needs that cash to cover its expenses, develop new products, and keep itself competitive. Investors also hope that at some point in the future they may even be paid some dividends. At the very least, investors want to be sure that the company is generating enough cash from sales to keep itself competitive in the market through advertising, new product development, and new market development.

Figuring out ROS

To calculate ROS, divide the profit before taxation by sales. You can find both numbers on the income statement. Sales (sometimes called revenue) is the top number on the income statement. This figure for sales is sometimes referred to as net sales since it is shown in the accounts net of VAT. Profit before taxation is in the expense section of the income statement just before tax expenses are reported.

> profit before taxation ÷ sales = return on sales

You can calculate Tesco's ROS based on information in its income statement for 2007 (see Appendix A):

> £2.653 million (profit before taxation) ÷ £42,641 million (sales) = 6.22 per cent (ROS)

Tesco made 6.22 per cent on each pound of sales. Compare that number with Marks and Spencer's ROS (using numbers on its income statement in Appendix A):

> £936.7 million (profit before taxation) ÷ £8,588.1 million (sales) = 10.91 per cent (ROS)

Marks and Spencer made 10.91 per cent on each pound of sales.

Investors can use the ROS ratio to determine how much profit is being made on a pound of sales. In comparing Tesco and Marks and Spencer, you can see that Marks and Spencer made almost double the amount per pound of sales than Tesco did.

As well as comparing Marks and Spencer with Tesco, comparing each company with its performance in the previous year is also useful. Note that in Appendix A we have given previous year ratios (known as *comparatives*) for all ratios where it's possible to perform the calculation.

When comparing with previous years, you must consider any changes which have occurred to the accounting policies, or any unusual events that may have occurred in one year and not the other. Marks and Spencer provide a good example of this. In the financial year to 2007, they disclose that some of the interest charge is exceptional in nature. Therefore, if we want to make a fair comparison between 2007 and 2006, we need to adjust the ratio to remove the exceptional cost from the profit before tax figure. This results in a revised ROS of 11.26 per cent as against the original calculation of 10.91 per cent. The figure of 11.26 per cent is the correct figure to use when making a comparison with the 2006 ratio which was 9.56 per cent.

This exceptional item will affect all calculations of ratios which use a profit figure. For simplicity, in the following ratios, we use the figures as stated and will not adjust for the exceptional costs.

If you want to know more about exceptional items you need to look at the notes to the accounts. In this case, note 5 to the Marks and Spencer accounts reveals that the exceptional interest cost arose as a result of the early redemption of long-term borrowings.

Reaching the truth about profits with ROS

In reading analysts' reports on Tesco and Marks and Spencer, we found that Marks and Spencer's historical ROS has been climbing so the results for Marks and Spencer in the preceding section are expected. Tesco is experiencing a continued improvement in its operating income. Its ROS in 2007 was 6.22 per cent, a good advance on the previous year. There's no question that Marks and Spencer is making more per pound on sales than Tesco, so why do investors see Tesco as the better buy measured by P/E ratios? You need to consider the fact that Tesco sells primarily food while Marks and Spencer is very big in the garment business. The garment business is known to be more risky because of the risk associated with what is fashionable and what is not. When you see a disconnect between the ratios and the market's view of a share's worth, you need to research further using the information you find in the notes to the financial statements as well as in reports from analysts and the financial press. Because Marks and Spencer shares are selling at a lower P/E, even though it's earning more per pound on sales than Tesco's, we knew we needed to dig deeper to find out why. Perhaps the answer is in the segmentation of the businesses between food and garments that you can find in the notes to the accounts.

Once you're armed with the information about why investors have a positive or negative view about a particular share, you can determine for yourself whether or not the share is a good investment. Even Marks and Spencer's stronger ROS is just one part of the puzzle. You need to analyse fully the information you see in the annual reports to find all the pieces and make a determination about whether to invest in a company. This chapter focuses on profitability. You also need to analyse a company's liquidity, discussed in Chapter 12, and its cash flow, covered in Chapter 13.

Return on Assets

You can judge how well a company uses its assets by calculating the *return on assets* (ROA). The ROA ratio shows you how much a company earned from its assets or capital invested. If the ROA is a high percentage, the company is likely to be managing its assets well. As an investor, that's important because your shares represent a claim on those assets. You want to be sure that your claim is being used wisely. If you haven't invested yet, be sure your investment goes toward shares in a company that invests its assets well. As with all ratios, you need to compare results with those of similar companies in an industry for the numbers to mean anything.

To calculate ROA, divide profit for the year by total assets. You can find profit for the year at the bottom on the income statement, and you can find total assets by adding together the figures for non-current assets and current assets from the assets section of the balance sheet.

> profit for the year ÷ total assets = return on assets

Doing some dividing to get ROA

Using the numbers from Tesco's income statement and balance sheet (see Appendix A), you can determine its ROA:

> £1,899 (profit for the year) ÷ £24,807 (total assets) = 7.66 per cent (ROA)

So Tesco made 7.66 per cent on each pound of assets. Compare this number with Marks and Spencer's ROA (using numbers from its income sheet in Appendix A):

> £659.9 (profit for the year) ÷ £5,381.0 (total assets) = 12.26 per cent (ROA)

Marks and Spencer made 12.26 per cent on each pound of assets. Marks and Spencer earned about 60 per cent more on each pound of assets compared with Tesco.

Ranking companies with the help of ROA

The ROA ratio gives investors and creditors a clear view of how well a company's management uses its assets to generate a profit. Both *shareholders' equity* (claims on assets by shareholders) and *debt funding* (claims on assets by creditors) are factored into this calculation, meaning that the ratio looks at the income generated using money raised by borrowing funds from creditors and selling shares to shareholders. From looking at the examples in the preceding section, you can see that Marks and Spencer generated more income on its invested capital than Tesco.

ROA can vary significantly depending on the type of industry. Companies that must maintain manufacturing operations with expensive machinery have a much lower ROA than companies that don't require to put much of the capital they raise from selling shares, borrowing funds, or generating income into expensive assets, such as factories and production equipment. Service companies don't require spending on these expensive types of assets. Companies with low asset requirements have an ROA of up to 20 per cent or higher, whereas companies that require a large investment in assets can have ROAs below 5 per cent.

Return on Equity

Return on equity (ROE) measures how well the company did earning money for its investors. ROE looks at the profit left for the shareholders after meeting all other liabilities.

In fact, you'll probably find it easier to determine an ROE for a company than an ROA. Although the ROE is an excellent measure of how profitable the company was in comparison with other companies in the industry, you should look at the ROA as well, because that ratio looks at returns for both investors and creditors.

Calculating ROE

You calculate ROE by dividing net income earned by the company (which you find at the bottom of the income statement) by the total shareholders' equity (which you find at the bottom of the equity section of the balance sheet):

profit for the year ÷ shareholders' equity = return on equity

Note that shareholders' equity includes minority interests because the profit for the year is stated before any payments (dividends) are made to the minority shareholders.

You can figure out Tesco's ROE based on its 2007 income statements and balance sheets (see Appendix A):

£1,899 (profit for the year) ÷ £10,571 (shareholders' equity) = 17.96 per cent (ROE)

Tesco made17.96 per cent on each pound of shareholders' equity. The following is Marks and Spencer's ROE, also based on its 2007 income statements and balance sheets (see Appendix A):

£659.9 (profit for the year) ÷ £1,648.2 (shareholders' equity) = 40.04 per cent (ROE)

Marks and Spencer made 40.04 per cent on each pound of equity. Comparing Tesco and Marks and Spencer, you can see that Marks and Spencer generated more than twice as much profit on its shareholders' equity.

Reacting to companies by understanding the ROE

Investors most often cite the ROE ratio when they want to see how well a company is doing for them. But is ROE really the best measure? Comparing ROE to ROA for Tesco and Marks and Spencer, you can see that both companies' ROEs look better than their ROAs.

	ROA	*ROE*
Tesco	7.66 per cent	17.96 per cent
Marks and Spencer	12.26 per cent	40.04 per cent

The reason that ROE is a higher figure than ROA is that the same figure for profit is being used in both ratios. This profit figure is then divided by a higher figure in ROA than in ROE. This figure is bound to be higher because the total assets figure used in ROA is equal to the shareholders' equity (used in ROE) plus total liabilities. You should not seek to compare ROA with ROE. They are measuring different things.

ROA considers all of the assets that the company own. What if the company took the whole lot, turned them into cash and put the money in the bank? The ROA would then probably be of the order of 5–6 per cent. If the company can't earn a better return on its assets than that then it might as well throw in the towel.

When you see comparisons of company statistics, you frequently find an ROE but no mention of an ROA, because many companies believe ROA is primarily a statistic to be used by management and the company's creditors. Take the extra time to determine the company's ROA, and compare it with that of other companies in the industry. You'll have a much better idea of how well a company generates its profit when you take both debt and equity into consideration.

The Big Three: Margins

You need to investigate three types of margins when you evaluate a company based on its financial reports. *Margins* show you how much financial safety the company has after its costs and expenses. Each of the three margins we discuss – gross margin, operating margin, and net profit margin – shows what the company has left to work with at various stages of the profit calculation.

Dissecting gross margin

Gross margin is the profit margin based solely on sales and the cost of producing those sales. It gives you a picture of how much revenue is left after all the direct costs of producing the product have been subtracted. These costs can include discounts offered, returns, allowances, production costs, and purchases. We talk about these costs in greater detail in Chapter 7.

To calculate gross margin, divide gross profit by sales or revenues:

gross profit ÷ sales or revenues = gross margin

You can find gross profit at the bottom of the sales or revenue section of the income statement. Sales are at the top of the same section.

Using numbers from Tesco's income statements (see Appendix A), you can calculate its gross margin:

£3,463 (gross profit) ÷ £42,641 (net sales) = 8.12 per cent (gross margin)

Tesco made a gross profit of 8.12 per cent on each pound of sales. Compare this number with Marks and Spencer's gross margin (using numbers from its income statement in Appendix A):

£3,341.2 (gross profit) ÷ £8,588.1 (net sales) = 38.9 per cent (gross margin)

Marks and Spencer has about 30 pence in every pound of sales more revenue left after it subtracts its direct costs than Tesco has. You may think therefore that Marks and Spencer has better cost controls on the purchase or production of the products it's selling but you need to remember that Tesco operate in a much more competitive market. The gross margin is a crucial number in a comparison of these two companies. Tesco has to run the gamut of price wars with its competitors and runs with a much lower gross margin as a result.

Investigating operating margin

The *operating margin* takes the financial report reader one step further in the process of finding what is left over for future use and looks at how well a company controls costs, factoring in any expenses not directly related to the production of a particular product. These costs include advertising, selling (sales staff, sales offices, sales materials, and other items directly related to the selling process), distribution, administration, research and development, royalties, and any other expenses not directly related to the cost of producing a particular product.

Just to be absolutely clear, selling and advertising expenses aren't factored into the cost of goods sold. Only at the stage of calculating operating profit are selling costs deducted. Divide operating profit by sales or revenues to calculate the operating margin:

> operating profit ÷ sales or revenues = operating margin

You can find sales or revenues at the top of the income statement and the operating profit at the bottom of the expenses-from-operations section on the income statement.

Using numbers from Tesco's income statements (see Appendix A), you can calculate the operating margin:

> £2,648 (operating profit) ÷ £42,641 (net sales) = 6.21 per cent (operating margin)

Tesco made an operating margin of 6.21 per cent on each pound of sales. Compare this number with Marks and Spencer's operating margin (using numbers from its income statements in Appendix A):

> £1,045.9 (operating profit) ÷ £8,588.1 (net sales) = 12.18 per cent (operating margin)

Marks and Spencer made an operating profit of 12.18 per cent on each pound of sales.

You can see the profitability gap is closing. Now that all indirect expenses are factored into the equation, Tesco appears to have a better handle on expenses than Marks and Spencer. Marks and Spencer's operating margin is only twice as much as Tesco although their gross margins were apart by about four times. Again, remember that while the two companies are in the same sector (retail), they are facing different challenges because of the products they sell and the market that they sell them to.

Companies with an operating margin that's higher than the industry average are usually better at holding down their cost of goods sold and operating expenses. Maintaining a higher operating margin means the company has more price flexibility during hard times. If a company with a higher operating margin must lower prices to stay competitive, more room is available to continue earning profits even when products must be sold for less.

Catching the leftover money: Calculating the net profit margin

The *profit for the year* looks at a company's bottom line. This calculation shows you how much money the company has left after it has deducted all expenses – whether from operations related to the production and selling of a company's products or from non-operating expenses or revenue not related to the company's sales of products or services.

For example, a non-operating revenue would be interest or dividends earned on a company's investments. That money wasn't generated by operations but is still considered earnings for the company. After the operating income line on the income statement, you usually see a line for finance costs. This line represents the interest the company paid out on corporate borrowings and overdrafts. You also see taxation, which indicates the amount that the company will be paying in corporation tax on the profits for the year. These are two of the biggest charges left to subtract from operating income. The only exception to this rule is if a large exceptional charge from a special event, such as discontinued operations or the purchase or sale of a division, appears on the income statement. These items also appear after the operating profit line.

To find net profit margin, divide profit for the year by sales or revenues:

profit for the year ÷ sales or revenues = net profit margin

You can find the profit for the year at the bottom line of the income statement; it may also be called 'net profit' or 'net loss'. Sales or revenue is on the top line of the income statement.

You can calculate the net profit margin using numbers from Tesco's income statements (see Appendix A):

£1,899 (profit for the year) ÷ £42,641 (sales) = 4.45 per cent (net profit margin)

Tesco made a net profit of 4.45 per cent on each pound of sales. Now calculate Marks and Spencer's net profit margin using numbers from its income statements (see Appendix A):

£659.9 (profit for the year) ÷ £8,588.1 (sales) = 7.68 per cent (net profit margin)

Marks and Spencer made a net profit of 7.68 per cent on each pound of sales. Comparing Tesco's and Marks and Spencer's net profit margins, Marks and Spencer appears to be more successful at generating a net profit per pound of sales than Tesco. The key question investors must then ask themselves is whether or not Marks and Spencer will perform as well in the future. They need more than just figures to do this. They need to think about the products and markets the companies are dealing with and whether, in their opinion, they will still thrive into the future. They take into account the quality and reputation of directors and managers.

Chapter 12

Looking at Liquidity

In This Chapter

▶ Calculating debt ratios

▶ Checking out interest payments

▶ Comparing debt to equity

▶ Looking at the debt-to-capital ratio

Making money is great, but if a company ties up too much of its money in non-liquid assets (such as factories it can't easily sell) or carries too much debt, it won't be around long to make more money. A company absolutely must have the cash it needs to carry out day-to-day operations and pay its debt obligations if its owners want to stay in business.

Lenders who have money wrapped up in the company follow debt levels closely. They want to be absolutely sure that they're going to get their money back, plus interest. As an investor, you need to take a close look at a company's debt, too, because your investment can get wiped out if the company goes bankrupt. So if you're investing in a company, you want to be certain that the company is liquid and isn't on the road to debt troubles.

So how do you make sure that the company you're investing in, or are about to invest in, isn't on the verge of spiralling down the drain, taking all your money with it? Well, you need to check out the company's ability to pay its bills and pay back its creditors. But looking at one company doesn't give you much information. You need to compare the company with similar companies, as well as the industry average, to get a better idea of where the company stands.

In this chapter, we show you how to calculate a company's ability to pay its bills by looking at debt ratios, comparing its debt to its equity and its debt to its total capital. (If you're starting to sweat and/or your brain is shutting down because of the impending mathlete workout, don't worry – things aren't as difficult as they sound!)

Finding the Current Ratio

One of the most commonly used debt measurement tools is the *current ratio*, which measures the assets a company plans to use over the next 12 months with the debts that it must pay during that same period. This ratio lets you know whether a company will be able to pay any bills due over the next 12 months with assets it has on hand. You find the current ratio by using two key numbers:

- **Current assets:** Cash or other assets (such as accounts receivable, inventory, and marketable securities) that the company is likely to convert to cash during the next 12-month period.

- **Current liabilities:** Debts that a company must pay in the next 12-month period. These liabilities include accounts payable, short-term loans, accrued taxes, and any other payments that the company must pay in the next 12-month period.

We talk more about current assets and current liabilities in Chapter 6.

Calculating the current ratio

The formula for calculating the current ratio is:

current assets ÷ current liabilities = current ratio

Using information from the balance sheets for Tesco and Marks and Spencer (see Appendix A), here are their current ratios for the year ending in 2007:

Tesco:

£4,576 (current assets) ÷ £8,152 (current liabilities) = 0.56

So Tesco has 56p of current assets for every £1 of current liabilities.

Marks and Spencer:

£846.40 (current assets) ÷ £1,606.20 (current liabilities) = 0.53

So Marks and Spencer has 53p of current assets for every £1 of current liabilities.

What do the numbers mean?

For most industries, the key question is 'Does a company's current ratio show that the company will be able to cover its short-term obligations?' Generally, the rule is that any current ratio between 1.2 and 2.0 is sufficient for a company to operate. However, keep in mind that the ratio varies among industries, which is particularly true of the retail industry that we are studying.

Think about it: Customers pay both these companies in cash. Debit cards are the same as cash, and credit cards are only a little slower for the payment to hit the retailers' bank accounts. (Both these companies have their own credit cards so they may not get the cash immediately, but they get a high rate of interest on it a month after the transaction if the customer does not pay off the debt immediately – clever, huh?). They also don't pay their suppliers in cash (see Chapters 16 and 17). On the contrary, both companies pay as late as they can, thanks to their muscle as major retailers, and they push their suppliers to their limits, and sometimes beyond. As they are in the retail business these companies are operating with very effective current ratios.

If the current ratio is below 1, anywhere apart from a few industries such as retailing, this is a strong danger sign that the company is heading for trouble. A ratio below 1 means that the company is operating with *negative working capital;* in other words, its current debt obligations exceed the current amount of money it has available to pay those debts.

A company can also have a current ratio that's too high. Any ratio over 2 means that the company isn't investing its assets well. The company can probably put some of those short-term assets to better use by investing them in growth opportunities for the company.

However, many lenders and analysts believe that the current ratio isn't a good enough test of a company's debt-paying ability because it includes some assets that aren't easy to turn into cash, such as inventory. A company must sell the inventory and collect the money before it has cash it can work with, and doing so can take a lot more time than using cash that's already on hand in the company's bank accounts or just collecting money due for accounts receivable, which represents customer accounts for items already purchased. Such lenders and analysts prefer the quick ratio.

Determining the Quick Ratio

Stricter than the current ratio is a test called the *quick ratio* or *acid test ratio,* which measures a company's ability to pay its bills without taking inventory into consideration. The calculation includes only cash on hand or cash already due from accounts receivable. Unlike the current ratio, it does not include money anticipated from the sale of inventory and the collection of the money from those sales. To calculate this ratio, you use a two-step process.

Calculating the quick ratio

Here's the two-step process you use to find the quick ratio:

1. **Determine the quick assets**

   quick assets = current assets – inventory

2. **Calculate the quick ratio**

   quick assets ÷ current liabilities = quick ratio or acid test ratio

Using information from Tesco's and Marks and Spencer's balance sheets, we take you through the two-step process.

Tesco:

quick assets = £4,576 – £1,931 = £2,645

£2,645(quick assets) ÷ £8,152 (current liabilities) = 0.32 (quick ratio)

So Tesco has 32p of quick assets for every £1 of current liabilities.

Marks and Spencer:

quick assets = £846.40 – £416.30 = £430.10

£430.10 (quick assets) ÷ £1,606.2 (current liabilities) = 0.27 (quick ratio)

So Marks and Spencer has 27p of quick assets for every £1 of current liabilities.

Marks and Spencer is, strangely enough, in a slightly better position than Tesco based on the quick ratio. They are making even better use of 'the receive cash pay with credit' retail strategy. Most companies operate with a quick ratio greater than 1 so that they have no problem paying their bills.

What do the numbers mean?

A company is usually considered to be in a good position as long as its quick ratio is over 1. When the quick ratio falls below 1, it's a sign that the company will probably have to sell some short-term investments to pay bills or take on additional debt until it sells more stock.

If you're looking at statements from companies in the retail sector, you're more likely to see a quick ratio under 1. Retail stores often have a lot more money tied up in inventory than other types of businesses do. As long as the company you're evaluating is operating at or near the quick ratio of similar companies in the industry, you're probably not looking at a problem situation, even if the quick ratio is well under 1.

Remember that a quick ratio of less than 1 can be a sign of trouble ahead if the company is not able to sell its inventory quickly. Also, if customers are slow payers, and accounts receivable aren't collected when billed, these issues can cause problems, too. In Chapters 15 and 16, we take a closer look at how you can assess inventory and accounts-receivable turnover.

Investigating Income Gearing

You also need to check out whether or not a company generates enough income to pay its interest obligations. Although the current and quick ratios look at a company's ability to pay back creditors by comparing items on the balance sheet, the interest coverage ratio looks at income to determine whether the company is generating enough profits to pay its interest obligations. If the company doesn't make its interest payments on time to creditors, its ability to get additional credit will be hurt, and eventually, if non-payment goes on for a long time, the company could end up in bankruptcy.

Historic interest gearing uses two figures, one that you can find on the company's income statement (operating profit; check out Chapter 7 for more information) and one on the cash-flow statement (interest paid – refer to Chapter 8).

Calculating historic income gearing

Here's the formula for finding income gearing:

interest paid ÷ operating profit = income gearing ratio

Tesco and Marks and Spencer both show the interest paid line separately; so we can calculate interest gearing.

Tesco:

£376 (interest paid) ÷ £2,648 (operating profit) = 0.14 (income gearing)

Tesco uses 14 per cent of its operating profit to pay its interest obligations.

Marks and Spencer:

$145.00 (interest paid) ÷ $1,045.9 (operating profit) = 0.14 (income gearing)

Marks and Spencer also uses 14 per cent of its operating profit to pay its interest obligations.

If you're trying to use income gearing to consider the company's ability to meet future interest payments, then you need to be careful to ensure that the interest commitments will continue into the future. In the case of Marks and Spencer, this is not the case. We have included in the interest paid figure an amount of $21.6 million which is recorded in the cash-flow statement (see Appendix A) as 'exceptional interest paid'. Presumably, this will not continue in the following year and therefore we could recompute the (future) income gearing ratio to be 12 per cent.

The sharp-eyed, thorough reader will notice that the exceptional interest figure referred to here ($21.6 million) is not the same as the figure quoted in Chapter 11 ($30.4 million). This is a good example of the accruals principle. The figure in Chapter 11 was taken from the profit and loss account and includes interest owed but not yet paid; the figure in this chapter was taken from the cash-flow statement which only includes interest paid.

What do the numbers mean?

Both companies clearly generate more than enough income to make their interest payments. Obviously, the nearer this figure gets to 1, the more difficulty the company has in paying the interest it owes. A figure of 0.25 and below is low income gearing, 0.50 medium and 0.75 is high gearing.

Lenders believe the lower the interest gearing, the better. You should be concerned about a company's fiscal health any time you see interest gearing above 0.66. This figure means that the company generates only about $1.50 for each pound it pays out in interest. That's operating on a tight budget. Any type of emergency or drop in sales could make it difficult for the company to meet its interest payments.

Comparing Debt to Shareholders' Equity

How a company finances its operations involves many crucial decisions. When a company uses debt to pay for new activities, it has to pay interest on that debt, plus pay back the principal amount at some point in the future. If a company uses shareholders' equity (shares sold to investors) to finance new activities, it doesn't need to make interest payments or pay back investors.

Finding the right mix of debt and equity financing can have a major impact on a company's cost of capital. Too much debt can be both risky and costly. However, if a company has too high a level of equity, investors may believe that a company isn't properly leveraging its money. *Leverage* is the degree to which a business uses borrowed money. For example, a company typically buys a new building by using a combination of a mortgage (debt) and cash (from a new share issue or retained earnings, which is the equity side of the equation).When a company uses leverage, its cash can go a lot further.

For example, imagine that you have £50,000 to pay for a home. This amount isn't enough to buy the home you want, so you use that money as a deposit on the home and get a mortgage for the rest of the money due. If the house price is £250,000, and you put down £50,000, you can use the mortgage to leverage that cash so you can afford the home. In this scenario, the mortgage covers 80 per cent of the purchase price. You can use any cash you earn beyond your monthly mortgage payment to pay your other bills and buy food, as well as other things you want to own.

The real benefit of leverage is seen when the house price goes up with inflation. Suppose that the house value increases by 20 per cent to £300,000 at which point you sell it and pay back the mortgage of £200,000. Your capital has doubled from £50,000 to £100,000.

As an investor, you want to know how a company allocates its debt versus equity. To determine this, use the *debt to shareholders' equity ratio*. You also want to check the company's *debt-to-capital ratio* (see the upcoming section 'Determining Debt-to-Capital Ratio') which lenders use to determine how much they'll lend. They also use this ratio to monitor a company's debt level.

Calculating debt to shareholders' equity

To calculate debt to shareholders' equity, divide the total liabilities by the shareholders' equity. This ratio shows you what proportion of the company's capital assets is paid by debt and what proportion is financed by equity.

Here's the formula you use to calculate debt to shareholders' equity:

total liabilities ÷ shareholders' equity = debt to shareholders' equity

We use the numbers from Marks and Spencer and Tesco's last year balance sheets to show you how to calculate the debt to shareholders' equity ratio.

In the case of Tesco, you first need to add current liabilities £8,152 to non-current liabilities £6.084 to give total liabilities of £14,236.

£14,236 (total liabilities) ÷ £10,571 (shareholders' equity) = 1.35 (debt to shareholders' equity)

Tesco used £1.35 from creditors for every £1 it had from investors. Therefore, Tesco depends a bit more on money raised by borrowing than on money raised by selling shares to investors.

Marks and Spencer:

> £3,732.80 (total liabilities which is given on the face of the balance sheet)
> ÷ £1,648.20 (shareholders' equity) = 2.26 (debt to shareholders' equity)

Marks and Spencer used £2.26 from creditors for every £1 it had from investors. Therefore, the company used a greater proportion of borrowed money from creditors to operate its company than Tesco did.

What do the numbers mean?

When you see a debt to shareholders' ratio that's greater than 1, it means that the company finances a majority of its activities with debt. If you see a ratio under 1, it means that the company depends more on using equity than debt to finance its activities.

In most industries, a 1:1 ratio is best, but it varies by industry. You can best judge how a company is doing by comparing it with similar companies and the industry averages.

 As the ratio creeps higher and higher above 1, a company's finances get more risky, especially if interest rates are expected to rise. Alarm bells should sound when you see a company near or above 2. Lenders consider a company that carries a debt load this large a credit risk – which means the company has to pay much higher interest rates to finance its capital activities.

Determining Debt-to-Capital Ratio

Lenders take another look at debt using the *debt-to-capital ratio,* which measures a company's leverage by looking at what portion of its capital comes from debt financing. This ratio is concerned only with borrowings and does not include other long-term liabilities such as liabilities to meet future pensions.

Calculating the ratio

You use a three-step process to calculate the debt-to-capital ratio:

   1. **Find the total debt.**

total debt = short-term borrowing + long-term debt + current portion of long-term debt + notes payable

2. **Find the capital.**

capital = total debt + equity

3. **Calculate the debt-to-capital ratio.**

total debt ÷ capital = debt-to-capital ratio

To show you how to calculate the debt-to-capital ratio, we use the information from Tesco and Marks and Spencer's 2007 balance sheets.

To find out Tesco's total debt, add up Tesco's short-term and long-term debt obligations:

short-term borrowings		£1,554
current portion of long-term debt	£0	
long-term debt		£4,146
Total debt		£5,700

Next, add the total debt to total equity to figure the number for capital:

£10,571 (equity) + £5,700 (debt) = £16,271 (capital)

Finally, calculate the debt-to-capital ratio:

£5,700 (total debt) ÷ £16,271 (capital) = 0.35 (debt-to-capital ratio)

So Tesco's debt-to-capital ratio was 0.35 to 1 in 2007. This ratio is often expressed as a percentage – for example, 35 per cent of total capital is debt.

To find out Marks and Spencer's total debt, add up Marks and Spencer's short-term and long-term debt obligations:

short-term borrowings		£461.00
current portion of long-term debt	£0	
long-term debt		£1,234.50
Total debt		£1,695.50

Then add the total debt to total equity to find out the number for capital:

£1,648.20 (equity) + £1,695.50 (debt) = £3,343.70 (capital)

Finally, calculate the debt-to-capital ratio:

£1,695.5 (total debt) ÷ £3,343.7 (capital) = 0.51 (debt-to-capital ratio)

So Marks and Spencer's debt-to-capital ratio of 51 per cent is higher than Tesco's at 35 per cent. Notice, however, that in the previous year, Marks and Spencer had a debt-to-capital ratio of 64 per cent; so it's improving rapidly.

Remember that both these companies have a strong and long history so their credit ratings are probably as good as you can get and their debt-to-capital ratios are reasonably low. Look at smaller and newer companies with a bit more scepticism.

What do the numbers mean?

Lenders often place debt-to-capital ratio requirements in the terms of a credit agreement for a company to maintain its credit status. (Some companies indicate that requirement in their notes to the financial statements.) If a company's debt creeps above what its lenders allow for the debt-to-capital ratio, the lender can *call* the loan, which means the company has to raise cash to pay off the loan. Usually companies take care of a call by finding another lender. The new lender is likely to charge higher interest rates because the company's higher debt-to-capital ratio makes the company appear as though it's a greater credit risk.

Generally, companies are considered to be in good financial shape with a debt-to-capital ratio of 35 per cent or less. Once a company's debt-to-capital ratio creeps above 50 per cent, lenders usually consider the company a much higher credit risk, which means the company has to pay higher interest rates to get loans.

Take note of the ratio and how it compares with the ratios of similar companies in its industry. If the company has a higher debt-to-capital ratio than most of its competitors, lenders probably see it as a much higher credit risk.

A company with a higher than normal debt-to-capital ratio faces an increasing cost of operating as it tries to meet the obligations of paying higher interest rates. These higher interest payments can spiral into more significant problems as the cash crunch intensifies.

Chapter 13

Making Sure the Company Has Cash to Carry On

In This Chapter

▶ Determining a company's solvency

▶ Gauging financial strength by looking at debt

▶ Checking cash sufficiency

No business can operate without cash. Unfortunately, the balance sheet (refer to Chapter 6) and income statement (refer to Chapter 7) don't tell you how well a company is managing its cash flow, which is critical for finding out about a company's ability to stay in business. To find this important information, you need to turn to the *statement of cash flows*, which looks at how cash flowed into and out of the business through its operations, investments, and financing activities.

In this chapter, we show you some basic calculations that help you determine the cash flow from sales and help you find out whether the cash flow is sufficient to meet the company's cash needs. Throughout the chapter, we use Tesco and Marks and Spencer (two leading retail companies) as examples to help you learn how to use these tools to evaluate a company's financial health. (See Appendix A for these companies' financial statements. You can find Tesco's complete annual report at www.tesco.com/investor and Marks and Spencer's at www.marksandspencer.com and click on 'The company'.

Measuring Income Success

Looking at whether a company is generating enough cash income can help you determine the company's *solvency* – its capability to meet its financial obligations (in other words, its ability to pay all its outstanding bills). If a company can't pay its bills, its creditors won't be happy, and it could be forced into bankruptcy or to discontinue operations. In this section, we show you two ratios that can help you determine a company's solvency based on its sales success.

Calculating free cash flow

The first step in determining a company's solvency is to find out how much money the company earned from its operations that can actually be put into a savings account for future use – in other words, a company's *discretionary cash,* which is also called the *free cash flow.*

A company with significant cash flow has a lot of flexibility to decide whether it wants to use its discretionary cash to purchase additional investments, pay down more debt, or add to its liquidity – which means to deposit additional funds in cash and *cash equivalent accounts* (including current accounts, savings accounts, and other holdings that can easily be converted to cash). The formula for calculating the free cash flow is a simple one:

> cash provided by operating activities – net cash used in investing activities – dividends paid – interest paid – tax paid = free cash flow

You can find cash flows from operating activities at the top of the operating activities section of the statement of cash flows. Net cash flow from investing activities is a line item on the statement of cash flows. Dividends, interest, and tax paid are also line items on the statement, but, unfortunately, are not always in the same place.

Tesco

Using Tesco's 2007 and 2006 cash-flow statements, Table 13-1 shows how to calculate the free cash flow:

Table 13-1	Calculating Tesco's Free Cash Flow	
	2007	*2006*
Cash flow provided by operating activities	3,532	3,412
Net cash used in investing activities	2,343	(1,962)
Dividends paid	467	(441)
Interest paid	376	(364)
Tax paid	545	(216)
Free cash flow	−199	216

As you can see, Tesco's free cash flow dropped significantly from 2006 to 2007. The increase in dividends accounts for £26 million and explains a small portion of that drop, but the total drop in free cash flow between the 2006 and 2007 is about £415 million.

Clearly, Tesco is not maintaining its 2006 cash levels. That could mean that the company decided to maintain lower cash levels and invest in new opportunities, or it could mean that it's having difficulty generating new cash. But you can't determine that with this calculation. What you do find out from this formula is that you must seek additional information by continuing the financial analysis of other line items (such as accounts receivable and inventory) and by reading the notes to the financial statements (refer to Chapter 9) or management's discussion and analysis in the Operating and Financial Review (go to Chapter 5). This formula is used as a red flag that there's a problem, but it doesn't give you a specific answer as to what the problem might be. Remember too the business Tesco is in: The company generates a lot of cash every day because customers pay cash but payment to suppliers is made after a period of time.

Marks and Spencer

Using Marks and Spencer's 2007 and 2006 cash-flow statements, Table 13-2 shows how to calculate the free cash flow:

Table 13-2: Calculating Marks and Spencer's Free Cash Flow		
	2007	*2006*
Cash flow provided by operating activities	1,442.6	1,183.6
Net cash used in investing activities	650.8	253.4
Dividends paid	260.6	204.1
Interest paid	145.0	142.8
Tax paid	150.8	101.5
Free cash flow	235.4	481.8

Marks and Spencer's free cash flow is much stronger than Tesco's for 2007. Also, Marks and Spencer's free cash flow wasn't hit as hard as Tesco's from 2006 to 2007. Although Marks and Spencer's free cash flow dropped about £246 million, that loss was a good bit less than the loss to cash flow that Tesco suffered. What this means is that Marks and Spencer is having less trouble maintaining its cash-flow levels.

What do the numbers mean?

No question, the more free cash flow a company has, the better the company is doing financially. A company with significant free cash flow is in a much stronger position to weather a financial storm, whether it be a recession, a slow down in sales, or another type of financial emergency.

If the free-cash-flow number is negative, the company must seek external financing to fund its growth. Negative or very low free-cash-flow numbers for young growth companies that need to make significant investments in new property, plant, or equipment are most likely not an indication of a big problem. But you should still look deeper into the financial reports and especially the notes to the financial statements (refer to Chapter 9) to find out why. If you see a negative free cash flow for an older company, you certainly should consider that it might be a red flag and look more deeply into the notes to the financial statements to find out why the free cash flow is so low.

Figuring out cash return on sales ratio

You can test how well a company's sales are generating cash using the *cash return on sales ratio*. This ratio looks at profitability from cash rather than from the accrual-based income prospective. Remember, in the accrual-based income perspective (which means income and expenses are recognised when the transaction is complete), there's no guarantee that cash has been received. (We talk more about cash-based and accrual accounting methods in Chapter 4.)

Making sure a business is properly managing its cash flow is critical when assessing a company's ability to stay in business and pay its bills. Sales are the primary way a company generates its cash. The following formula looks specifically at the cash that's being generated by its sales.

Here's the formula for calculating the cash on sales ratio:

cash provided by operating activities ÷ sales = cash return on sales

To calculate cash return on sales, you need to use the line item called 'cash provided by operating activities' on the cash-flow statement in the operating activities section and 'sales' or ' revenue' at the top of the income statement.

Tesco

Using Tesco's cash-flow and income statements here's how to calculate the cash return on sales ratio:

£3,532 (cash provided by operating activities) ÷ £42,641 (net sales) = 8.3 per cent (cash return on sales)

From looking at this equation, you can see that 8.3 per cent of the pounds that Tesco generates from its sales results are in cash for the company. Tesco's *net profit margin* (the bottom line, or how much the company made after all costs and expenses are calculated), which we show you how to calculate in Chapter 11, was 4.45 per cent. Tesco's cash return on sales is higher than its net profit margin, which is a good sign. The only time you need to worry is if you find that the sales ratio from cash is less than the net profit margin.

Marks and Spencer

Using Marks and Spencer's cash-flow and income statements, here's how to calculate the cash return on sales ratio:

£1,442.60 (cash provided by operating activities) ÷ £8,588.10 (net sales) = 16.8 per cent (cash return on sales)

You can see that 16.8 per cent of the pounds that Marks and Spencer generates from its sales provides cash for the company. Marks and Spencer's net profit margin was 7.68 per cent (look at Chapter 11), less than half of its cash return on sales, which is a strong sign that Marks and Spencer is efficiently converting its sales to cash.

What do the numbers mean?

The cash return on sales looks at the efficiency with which the company turns its sales into cash. Marks and Spencer's results show that it's more efficient at turning its sales into cash for the company than Tesco is. Add the fact that Tesco's cash flow was negatively impacted by decreases in cash from 2006 to 2007 (see 'Calculating free cash flow' earlier in the chapter), and you get a clearer picture that Tesco may have a problem converting its sales to cash. Given, however, the nature and success of their business, Tesco almost certainly is in control of this line item.

Tesco's cash return on sales is higher than its profit margin, so the company is unlikely to have a serious problem. A cash return on sales ratio that's lower than the profit margin ratio can be a major red flag. The company may be using aggressive accrual accounting practices that enable it to report higher net profit. We discuss these types of practices in Chapter 22.

Checking Out Debt

In addition to how much cash the company is generating from sales, you need to look at the cash flow going out of the company to pay its debts. Whenever a company cannot pay its bills, or the interest on its debt, it runs the risk of supply cut-offs and possible insolvency. Few suppliers continue delivering products to a company that doesn't pay its bills, and most creditors seek ways to collect a debt if they don't receive the interest and principal due on that debt.

You can check out a company's ability to pay this debt by looking at the company's debt levels and the cash available to pay that debt. You do this by collecting numbers related to debt levels from the balance sheet and comparing them with cash-outflow numbers from the statement of cash flows.

Determining current cash-debt coverage ratio

You can determine whether a company has enough cash to meet its short-term needs by calculating the *current cash-debt coverage ratio*. You calculate this number by dividing the cash provided by operating activities by the average current liabilities.

Here's the two-step formula for calculating the current cash-debt coverage ratio:

1. **Find the average current liabilities.**

   current liabilities for 2007 + current liabilities for 2006 ÷ 2 = average current liabilities

2. **Find the current cash-debt coverage ratio.**

   cash provided by operating activities ÷ average current liabilities = current cash-debt coverage ratio

You can find current liabilities for 2007 and 2006 on the balance sheet. You can find cash provided by operating activities on the statement of cash flows.

Tesco

Using the cash provided by operating activities from Tesco's 2007 cash-flow statement and the average of its current liabilities from its 2007 and 2006 balance sheets, we show you how to calculate the current cash-debt coverage ratio. Using the two-step process, first calculate the average current liabilities. Then use that number to calculate the ratio:

1. **Calculate average current liabilities**.

   £8,152 (2007 current liabilities) + £7,518 (2006 current liabilities) ÷ 2 = £7,835 (average current liabilities)

2. Calculate the ratio for the current reporting year.

£3,532 (cash provided by operating activities, 2007) ÷ £7,835 (average current liabilities) = 0.45 (current cash-debt coverage ratio)

 To determine whether a company's cash provided by activities is improving, you should also calculate the ratio for the 2006 reporting year. You need to go on to the company's Web site to find the numbers for 2005 in order to calculate average current liabilities. In this case:

£3,412 (cash provided by operating activities, 2006) ÷ £6,599 (average current liabilities) = 0.52 (current cash-debt coverage ratio)

This comparison shows you that Tesco's cash position worsened from the end of 2006 to the end of 2007. A ratio of 0.45 in 2007 shows that less than a half of its current liabilities were paid for by cash taken in from sales, while in 2006, the ratio of 0.52 shows that slightly more than half of its current liabilities were paid for by cash taken in from sales.

Marks and Spencer

Now we use the cash provided by operating activities from Marks and Spencer's 2007 cash-flow statement and the average of its current liabilities from its 2007 and 2006 balance sheets to show you how to calculate the current cash-debt coverage ratio:

1. Calculate average current liabilities.

£1,606.20 (2007 current liabilities) + £2,017.00 (2006 current liabilities) ÷ 2 = £1,811.60 (average current liabilities)

2. Calculate the ratio for the current reporting year.

£1,442.60 (cash provided by operating activities, 2007) ÷ £1,811.60 (average current liabilities) = 0.80 (current cash-debt coverage ratio)

For comparison's sake, calculate the ratio for the 2006 reporting year as well:

£1,183.60 (cash provided by operating activities, 2006) ÷ £1,627.20 (average current liabilities) = 0.73 (current cash-debt coverage ratio)

Marks and Spencer ended 2007 in a stronger cash position than Tesco. Its current cash-debt coverage improved over the two years.

What do the numbers mean?

The current cash-debt coverage ratio looks at the company's ability to pay its short-term needs. The higher the ratio, the better.

A negative 'cash provided by operating activities' number is a possible danger sign that a company isn't generating enough cash from operations. You need to investigate why its cash from operations is insufficient. You should look for explanations in the notes to the financial statements or in management's discussion and analysis. If you don't find the answers there, call the company's investor relations department. Also look at analysis written by the financial press or independent analysts.

It's not unusual for growth companies to report negative cash from operations because they're spending money to grow the company. However, a negative cash flow can't be sustained for long, so be sure you understand the company's long-term plans to improve its cash position.

Computing cash-debt coverage ratio

You also want to look at the company's ability to pay its debt that will be due over the long term. Current liabilities include only debt that a company must pay in the next 12 months. Long-term liabilities are debt that a company must pay beyond that 12-month period. If there are signs that the company may have difficulties meeting long-term debt: That, too, is a major cause for concern. Although you may find that a company is generating enough cash to meet its current liabilities, if long-term debt levels are too high, the company eventually will run into trouble paying off its debt and meeting its interest obligations. You can test a company's cash position to meet long-term debt needs by using the *cash-debt coverage ratio*.

The formula for the cash-debt coverage ratio is a two-step process:

1. **Find the average total liabilities.**

   (2007 total liabilities + 2006 total liabilities) ÷ 2 = average total liabilities

2. **Find the cash-debt coverage ratio.**

   cash provided by operating activities ÷ average total liabilities = cash-debt coverage ratio

You can find the last- and previous-year total liabilities on the balance sheet. You can find cash provided by operating activities on the statement of cash flows.

Tesco

Using the cash provided by operating activities from Tesco's 2007 cash-flow statement and the average of its total liabilities from its 2007 and 2006 balance sheet, we show you how to calculate the cash-debt coverage ratio. Using the two-step process, first calculate the average total liabilities. Then use that number to calculate the ratio:

1. **Calculate average total liabilities.**

   £14,236 (2007 total liabilities) + £13,119 (2006 total liabilities) ÷ 2 = £13,678 (average total liabilities)

2. **Find the cash-debt coverage ratio.**

   £3,532 (2007 cash provided by operating activities) ÷ £13,678 (average total liabilities) = 0.26 (cash-debt coverage ratio)

To judge whether a company's cash provided by activities is improving or not, you calculate the ratio for both the last reporting year and the 2006 reporting year:

   £3,412 (2006 cash provided by operating activities) ÷ £12,310 (average total liabilities) = 0.28 (cash-debt coverage ratio)

This ratio serves as further evidence that Tesco's cash position worsened from the end of 2006 to the end of 2007. Tesco's long-term debt increased between 2006 and 2007 by £483 million according to its balance sheet (see Appendix A).

Marks and Spencer

To show you how to calculate the cash-debt coverage ratio, we use the cash provided by operating activities from Marks and Spencer's 2007 cash-flow statement and the average of its total liabilities from its 2007 and 2006 balance sheet:

1. **Calculate average total liabilities.**

   £3,732.80 (2007 total liabilities) + £4,055.20 (2006 total liabilities) ÷ 2 = £3,894.00 (average total liabilities)

2. **Calculate the cash-debt coverage ratio for the current reporting year.**

   £1,442.60 (2007 cash provided by operating activities) ÷ £3,894.00 (average total liabilities) = 0.37 (cash-debt coverage ratio)

Calculate the ratio for 2006 as well:

   £1,183.60 (2006 cash provided by operating activities) ÷ £4,006.70 (average total liabilities) = 0.30 (cash-debt coverage ratio)

Taking total liabilities into consideration, Marks and Spencer ended 2007 in a stronger cash position than Tesco. Notice also the improvement in this ratio from 0.30 to 0.37 over the two years.

What do the numbers mean?

The cash-debt coverage ratio looks at a company's ability to pay its long-term debt obligations. As you can see, when long-term debt was taken into consideration, Marks and Spencer's position remains stronger than Tesco's. So calculating only one ratio or the other – current cash-debt coverage ratio or cash-debt coverage ratio – won't give you the full picture of a company's financial health. You need to look at both ratios to be certain that the company is generating enough cash to cover both its short-term and long-term debt. In Chapter 9 we talk more about this debt-structure difference when looking at the explanations given in the notes to the financial statements.

Like the current cash-debt coverage ratio, if you find a negative cash from operations number being reported, be sure to look for explanations in the notes to the financial statements or management's discussion to find out why the cash flow from operations is negative. If you don't find it there, call the investor relations office of the company to get the answers to your questions.

Calculating Cash-Flow Coverage

Debt and the interest paid on that debt are not a company's only cash requirements. A company also needs cash for capital expansion to grow the company (including new plants, tools, and equipment) and pay dividends to shareholders.

As a shareholder, the only way you make money is when the company's shares go up in price. The stock market rewards a company with good growth potential by bidding up the price of its shares. Companies that show low growth prospects usually have few buyers and end up with lower share prices. So you want to invest in companies that not only are generating enough cash to pay their bills, interest, and the principals on their long-term debts, but also have money left over to pay dividends to their shareholders and grow their company. Remember that many growth companies do not pay dividends at all but instead reinvest all profits toward future growth.

You want to test whether the company is generating enough cash to cover its capital expenditures, pay its dividends, and pay its debt obligations by calculating the cash-flow coverage ratio.

Finding out the cash-flow coverage ratio

You use a two-step process to calculate the cash-flow coverage ratio:

1. **Calculate the company's cash requirements.**

   Add the following:

   Net cash used in investing activities (listed in the investing activities section of the cash-flow statement)

   Cash dividends paid (listed in the financing activities section of the cash-flow statement

   Interest paid (which may be listed in any of the sections of the cash-flow statement)

   Tax paid (listed in the operating activities section of the cash-flow statement)

2. **Calculate the cash-flow coverage ratio.**

   Cash provided by operating activities ÷ cash requirements = cash-flow coverage ratio

You can find cash provided by operating activities on the statement of cash flows.

Tesco

We use the financial statements for Tesco to show you how to calculate the cash-flow coverage ratio:

1. **Find Tesco's cash requirements.**

Net cash used in investing activities	2,343
Cash dividends paid	467
Interest paid	376
Tax paid	545
Cash requirement	3,731

2. **Calculate the cash-flow coverage ratio.**

   £3,532 (cash flows from operating activities) ÷ £3,731 (cash requirements) = 0.95 (cash-flow coverage ratio)

Tesco didn't generate enough cash from its operations to pay all its cash requirements for 2007. This means that Tesco generated only enough to cover 95 per cent of the cash it needed to meet all its cash requirements. To cover the rest of its cash needs, it had to draw down cash on hand from activities in 2006 or borrow money. Any company that must draw down savings to maintain its operating activities may be showing signs of trouble. Because

Tesco has a large cash stash, it has enough to cover, but how long can it do that before the cash runs out and it gets in trouble? Tesco probably has the situation under good control.

With the exception, perhaps, of large well run retailers, any time a company cannot meet its cash requirements, you should seriously reconsider investing in that company.

Tesco had to find sources other than operations to meet the shortfall in their cash requirements. Tesco used cash on hand at the beginning of the year to make up the cash shortfall, which you can see when you look at the cash and short-term investments on hand (in the balance sheet in Appendix A) at the beginning of the year versus what was on hand at the end of the year.

Marks and Spencer

Now we use the financial statements for Marks and Spencer to show you how to calculate the cash-flow coverage ratio:

1. **Find Marks and Spencer's cash requirements.**

Net cash used in investing activities	650.80
Cash dividends paid	260.60
Interest paid	145.00
Tax paid	150.80
Cash requirement	1,207.20

2. **Calculate the cash-flow coverage ratio.**

£1,442.6 (cash flows from operating activities) ÷ £1,207.2 (cash requirements) = 1.19 (cash-flow coverage ratio)

Marks and Spencer improved its cash-flow ratios from 2006 to 2007 and had no need of further borrowings in 2007. Unlike Tesco (see preceding section), Marks and Spencer generated enough cash from its operations to pay all its cash requirements for 2007. This ratio shows that Marks and Spencer generated enough cash to cover 119 per cent of its cash requirements, which means Marks and Spencer could add to its cash reserves in 2007 or (as it actually did) choose to pay off part of its loans.

What do the numbers mean?

If you're trying to use the cash-flow coverage ratio to assess future cash needs then you must consider adjusting the cash requirements figure to remove any one-off costs. For example, in the case of Marks and Spencer (see preceding section), there is an amount of £21.6 million shown in the cash-flow statement (see Appendix A) as 'Exceptional interest paid'. Presumably, this will not need to be paid next year and so future cash requirements should be £21.6 million lower than in the current year.

However, life is not that simple. In Chapter 12, we refer to the fact that the amount included in the cash-flow statement was the actual amount paid but the profit and loss account showed the higher figure for exceptional interest of £30.4 million because of amounts accrued. Presumably therefore the accrued amount of £8.8 million (that is the difference between £30.4 million and £21.6 million) will need to be paid in the next year – leading to yet another adjustment in the cash requirements figure.

However, there may be different exceptional items in the future that we cannot predict so, perhaps, on balance, it's not worth making the adjustment to the ratio at all!

Long term you should expect Tesco to improve these ratios and return to a positive free cash flow. It's worth keeping an eye on though: In the end, no company can run with negative ratios for ever.

Companies that generate more than enough cash have a cash-flow coverage ratio of more than 100 per cent. The higher the ratio, the better. If you see a company that wasn't able to cover its cash requirements and has little left in cash and short-term investments, you should raise the red flag.

Part IV
Understanding How Companies Optimise Operations

'Here come the auditors'

In this part . . .

We show you how to analyse the company's operations to find out whether the management team is effectively using its resources. After discussing the role that financial reporting plays in the basic budgeting process, we show you how to assess management's effectiveness. We also give you the tools for measuring asset- and cash-management efficiency.

Chapter 14

Using Basic Budgeting

In This Chapter

▶ Examining the budgeting process

▶ Working out how budgets are created

▶ Understanding the importance of monthly budget reports

▶ Putting internal budget reports to work

*N*o matter how good the numbers look, you don't know how well a company is doing until you compare the actual numbers with the company's expectations. *Expectations* (the budget targets a company hopes to meet) are spelled out during the *budgeting process,* in which the company projects its financial needs for the next year. At different times throughout the year these budgets are used, along with periodic financial reports, by managers looking to determine how close the company is to meeting its budget targets.

As an outsider, you don't have access to the company's budgets or the reports related to them. But for those of you seeking to find out more about internal financial reports and how to use them effectively, understanding the budgeting process is critical.

A well-planned budgeting process not only helps a company plan for the next year, but it also provides managers with key information throughout the year to be sure that the company is meeting its goals and raising red flags when it doesn't reach its goals. The sooner managers recognise a problem, the greater their ability is to fix it before the end of the year. This chapter discusses the budgeting process and how it complements financial reporting.

Peering Into the Budgeting Process

The budget that a company sets for itself relies on a lot of careful calculations – and some guesswork – in order to predict the revenue that can be expected from the sales of products and services during the forthcoming year, and the expenses that will be incurred, including manufacturing and purchase of materials as well as other operating costs. Creating a budget is a lot more complicated than just making a list of expected revenues and expenses. We talk more about the basics of revenue and expenses in Chapters 4 and 7.

Two approaches to budgeting are used:

- ✔ **Top-down approach:** Budgets are set by key executives and given to department heads to meet. Most employees are not involved in the budgeting process; instead, the numbers are imposed on the employees by those at the top, and the employees are expected to meet them. The big problem with this type of budget process is that the employees don't feel any ownership of the budget presented by the executives and frequently complain that the budget handed down to them was unrealistic, which is why they couldn't meet expectations.

  Few large corporations use the top-down approach today. You are more likely to find this approach in small businesses run by one person or a small group of partners.

- ✔ **Bottom-up approach:** Budgets are created at the department level based on overall companywide goals and guidelines set by the board of directors and top executives. This approach encourages employee participation in the budgeting process, so the employees have more of a sense of ownership in the budget. Because they helped develop the budget, they can't later claim that the budget was unrealistic if it turns out that they couldn't meet expectations.

Most management studies have shown that the bottom-up approach works better because managers and staff members are more likely to take a budget seriously and follow that budget if they have some involvement in developing it. We focus on the process for bottom-up budget development, which is the most commonly used budgeting process in large corporations today.

Working out who does what

Everyone has a role to play in bottom-up budgeting. Top executives who are part of a budget committee set companywide goals and objectives. In some companies, the budget committee may consist of the entire board of directors with other staff seconded. Then, starting at the lowest staff levels, each department determines its budget needs. These budgets work their way through the management tree to the top, where numbers from each department are pulled together to develop a companywide budget.

The budget committee manages the entire process and is responsible for determining budget policies and co-ordinating budget preparation among departments. Usually this committee includes the chairman, chief financial officer (CFO), financial controller, and directors of various functions, such as marketing, sales, production, and purchasing.

Even before the departments start to develop their budgets, the budget committee develops rules that all departments must follow. These rules are likely to include a request to hold all budgets to a certain percentage increase in costs and possibly even a reduction in costs. These guidelines help departments develop budgets that meet company needs while proposing something they can live with throughout the year.

The budget committee doesn't mandate what the actual departments' budgets should be or how the departments should find a way to keep their costs down; that decision is left to each individual department. One department might decide it can cut costs by reducing staff; another may determine to cut costs by getting better control of the use of supplies; another might decide that cutting back on the use of rental equipment or temporary help can meet its cost-cutting goals. By leaving these choices to the departments rather than mandating the numbers from the top, companies give employees a stake in meeting their budget goals. After the budgets are developed at the section and department levels, the budget committee gives final approval for all budgets.

The budget committee also resolves any disputes that may arise in the budget process. Budget disputes can occur when different departments have conflicting goals to meet. For example, say the manufacturing department is mandated to cut costs, while the sales department must increase sales to meet its goals. The manufacturing manager may make a decision to cut costs in a way that lowers product-quality standards. However, the sales manager may believe that this cost-cutting method will create problems in maintaining customer satisfaction and damage sales. The budget committee acts as the mediator for this decision-making process.

Setting goals

To develop companywide budget guidelines, the budget committee must first determine the goals for the company. Before they can set those goals, they gather information about where the company stands financially, how the company fits into the bigger economic picture, and how it stacks up against its competitors. This information forms the basis for what the committee determines it needs to accomplish during the next year, such as increasing market share, increasing profit, or entering a new market area completely. Sections and departments can then estimate the resources they need to meet those goals.

The first critical step for goal setting is to develop a *sales forecast* (a projection of the number of sales the company will make during the year), usually involving the staff of several departments, including marketing, sales, and finance. Much of the data collected by these people is from industry research reports as well as from actual company numbers from the accounting, finance, and marketing departments.

Factors that must be considered to develop an accurate sales forecast include

✓ **Past sales success:** By looking at a breakdown by product of sales for the past three to five years, a company can look for trends and make a best guess about future sales growth potential.

✓ **Potential pricing policy:** By looking at past sales, companies can determine whether the current pricing policy is viable or whether changes are needed. Products that are moving quickly off the shelves may be able to sustain a price increase, while those that are not moving may need a price cut to stimulate sales. Pricing isn't set solely by sales success or failure, of course. Costs for producing the product are a key factor as well.

✓ **Data about unfilled orders and backlogs:** This information helps companies determine which product lines may need to be modified to meet demand.

✓ **Market research:** This research includes potential sales and competitive data for the entire industry, as well as the forecasts for the individual company. This information lets the committee know where the company fits in the industry and what potential the industry may have in the next year.

✓ **Information about general economic conditions:** This research gives the budget committee an overview of expected economic conditions for the next year so they know whether there is potential for growth or a possible reduction in sales. For example, if the economy has seen a slowdown during the past three years, but economists are now predicting a market recovery, the company may need to increase manufacturing goals to meet anticipated increasing demand.

✓ **Industry economic conditions:** A company monitors these conditions to determine whether the industry or industries in which it operates are set for a growth spurt or a downturn or are expected to perform at the same level in the next year.

✓ **Industry competition data:** Reviews of competitors' marketing strategies, advertising, and other competitive factors must also be considered when developing future goals in order to stay competitive within the industry. This information must be reviewed to determine where the company sits in relation to its competitors and whether new competitors are on the horizon that could challenge the company's products.

✓ **Market share data:** A company collects this data, which is the percentage of the market held by the company's products and services, to help set goals – whether to increase market share or maintain current levels. Growth potential is dependent on increasing market share, but if a company already holds nearly 100 per cent of the market, like Microsoft more or less does in the operating systems market for personal computers, room for growth may not exist. In that case, marketing strategists focus on tactics for maintaining that market share.

In addition to the hard numbers, information from staff members at all levels of the organisation is collected to get a first-hand view of what is actually happening in the field. This information includes reports about discussions with customers, suppliers, and contractors. Real world data collected from sales staff, customer-service staff, purchasers, and other employees gives a company additional information and allows it to test the numbers collected.

Building Budgets

After the budget committee finishes data collection (see the preceding section), the committee can determine sales goals for the company. After the committee determines goals, it uses them to develop *strategies* – the actual methods used to reach the goals – and build budgets that reflect the resources needed to carry out the strategies. Although the budget committee sets companywide goals and global strategies, each section and department translates these broad goals and strategies into specific goals and strategies for their own people.

Armed with its goals and strategies, each department develops its specific budget. Not all departments develop their budgets at exactly the same time because some departments are dependent on others to make budget decisions. For example, sales revenue must be projected before the company can make decisions about production levels and just about every other aspect of its operations.

Common budget categories include the following, organised according to the order in which they're produced:

- ✔ **Sales budget:** Sales managers start their budget planning by forecasting sales levels and the gross revenue they anticipate to be generated by these levels. Most other budgets depend on the goals set by sales, so this budget is usually the first to be developed. Without a sales budget, production managers don't know how many products to produce, and purchasing managers don't know how many items to buy.

- ✔ **Production budget:** If the company manufactures its own product, the next budget to be developed is the production budget. The production department looks at the beginning inventory left over from the previous planning period and then plans what additional inventory is needed, based on the forecasts in the sales budget. Production planning can be a difficult development task. Making sure that they have just the right level of inventory means that production managers must plan for the right amount of raw materials, the efficient use of production facilities, and the appropriate number of staff members to produce the products to meet customer needs on time.

- ✓ **Product purchasing budget:** For companies that don't manufacture their own products, the budgeting process focuses on purchasing needed products and being sure that they're delivered on time to meet customer needs. Similar issues to those the production team faces drive purchasing concerns because a company wants to be sure it has enough product on hand to meet customer demand. But at the same time, it doesn't want too many products left over because that means resources were wasted on inventory and could have been better used to meet other company needs.

- ✓ **Direct materials budget:** This budget controls the raw materials needed to meet the production schedule. The last problem any company wants to face is not having enough materials on hand to keep the product line moving, thus risking a shutdown of the factory. But the company also wants to avoid keeping too many materials on hand, because doing so increases warehousing expenses. Also, holding raw materials too long can result in material spoilage.

- ✓ **Direct labour budget:** The direct labour budget is unique to manufacturing companies and is dependent on the production budget. Companies work hard to determine how much staff they need to meet production needs. If they hire too few people, they have to deal with overtime charges or, in the worst cases, they face production shortfalls. Hire too many people and companies end up spending more than necessary on salaries or have to lay off employees – which is a huge blow to morale.

- ✓ **Selling and administrative expense budgets:** Many smaller departments are involved in getting a product or service to market and supporting those sales. These departments include accounting, finance, marketing, human resources, administration, and materials management. After sales revenue is known and the costs of selling those goods have been determined, the remaining resources are divided up among the selling and administrative needs of the company.

- ✓ **Master budget:** After everyone signs off on each of the department and section budgets, the accounting department prepares a master budget for the company. The company uses this budget as a road map to test how well each department is doing in meeting its budget expectations.

- ✓ **Cash budget:** After all the budgets are completed and combined into a master budget, the accounting department develops a cash budget that estimates the monthly cash needs for each department. Based on this budget, the finance department determines whether enough cash will be generated by operations to meet the cash needs or whether other financing is needed to maintain the company's cash flow.

When all the budget planning is complete, a budgeted income statement (refer to Chapter 7 for more information on income statements) is developed by the accounting department to test whether the budgeting process has created a budget that truly meets profit-planning goals. If the answer is no, the budget committee then has to decide where budget changes are needed to meet company goals. A lot of negotiating between the budget committee and its top managers is often necessary to determine budget changes.

If the budget committee imposes unrealistic changes on the budget for a department, little budget compliance from that department is likely to happen, and financial difficulties could develop throughout the year. Developing budgets that department and section managers can live with have a better chance of producing expected results and meeting goals.

Providing Monthly Budget Reports

No matter how thoroughly prepared, a budget is useless if it's not matched to actual revenue and expenses. So throughout the budget period, the accounting department prepares monthly *internal financial reports* (reports that summarise financial results) for each of the managers who use these reports to identify where the budget is going right or wrong. Many of these internal financial reports have a system of red flags that identify areas where the actual results aren't meeting budget expectations.

Each company has its own style for internal reports, but most reports include similar types of information. The report is usually broken into five columns:

- ✔ **Red flag:** A symbol, such as an asterisk, is usually used in the first or last column to identify problem items in a budget.

- ✔ **Line item:** This column lists the budget categories as they appear on the section or department budget.

- ✔ **Budget amount:** This column states the amount allocated for the period of the internal financial report.

- ✔ **Actual amount:** This column states how much the company actually spent during the period of the internal financial report.

- ✔ **Variance:** This column shows how close (or far apart) the actual and budgeted numbers are.

Many companies also include a year-to-date section on internal financial reports that shows the same information on a year-to-date basis in addition to the information specific to the month or quarter.

Figure 14–1 shows an internal report for March 2008 for a fictitious company called the ABC Company. In this example, a flag appears automatically on the report if the variance is greater than £100,000, but in real life, each company determines its own designated levels for red flags. A small company may flag items for a variation of just £5,000, and a large corporation may flag items for variations at much higher levels. An alternative approach to variances is to set a percentage variance above which the red flag applies.

| | | Income Statement – ABC Company – March 2008 | | |
| | | Confidential | | For Internal Use |

Flag	Line Item	Budget	Actual	Variance
•	**Sales**	£1,400,000	£1,200,000	(200,000)
	Cost of Goods Sold	(700,000)	(650,000)	50,000
•	**Gross Margin**	700,000	550,000	(£150,000)
	Expenses			
	Advertising	(150,000)	(150,000)	—
	Administrative	(300,000)	(275,000)	25,000
	Interest	(25,000)	(35,000)	(10,000)
•	**Net Income**	£225,000	£90,000	(£135,000)

Figure 14–1:
A sample income statement.

Although Figure 14–1 uses an income statement format, internal reports have no required format, and each company develops its own report format depending on what works best for the company.

In Figure 14–1, you can see that flags have been marked next to Sales, Gross Margin, and Net Income. Flags were thrown because those line items show differences of more than £100,000, and therefore, need to be investigated by management.

A glance at Figure 14–1 shows that the key problem is lower-than-expected sales revenue. Sales were budgeted for £1.4 million, and the actual sales were £200,000 less at £1.2 million. That difference is shown on the first line of the internal report. Management first needs to determine why sales are lower than forecast and then develop strategies for correcting the problem. Given the fact that cost of goods sold and administrative expenses are lower than budgeted, this could be a sign that management recognised the problem after a previous month's report and had already initiated cost-cutting programmes.

After looking at the report in Figure 14–1, managers have to determine what the problem is and what other changes may be needed to get the budget back in line. If external factors, such as economic conditions, are to blame, the best the company can do is revise the budget to meet current economic conditions so that further slippage in net income can be avoided.

Internal financial reports aren't important only to find out about the bad news. Good news can also require critical actions. For example, if sales had been much higher than expected, plans may need to be put in place to be sure the company can meet the unexpected demand without losing sales. Few customers want to wait weeks or months to get their products and instead may seek out a competitor to fulfil their needs if products aren't available when they're ready to buy.

If conditions change from expectations, companies can more easily make a mid-year correction if budgets have been accurately prepared. The company knows what was expected, and it can tweak its revenues or expenses to correct a problem long before the shortfall becomes disastrous for the company.

In Chapter 17, we talk about strategies companies use to keep cash flowing when internal financial reports don't meet expectations.

Using Internal Reports

Inside your company, you probably see much more detailed reports than the sample in Figure 14–1. A department head sees only the budget line items related to his or her department, and only the board, budget committee, and departments responsible for developing budget reports have access to companywide internal reports.

The internal financial report you receive as a manager is usually based on the budget you developed. The line items listed are those directly related to your department functions. Any line item whose difference exceeds those allowed by the company is flagged, and you need to find out why. Sometimes, the answer is clear. For example, if you know sales were higher or lower than expected, you simply need to report why and what you are doing to correct any problems. At other times, the answer will require some digging on your part.

After a report arrives at your office, you don't have much time to figure out what the variances are and what they mean for your department. If the differences are big, you can probably expect a call from your manager as soon as she or he sees a copy. When one of the authors of this book was managing the finances for five departments, she knew that she could expect a call from her manager even before her manager had received her copy of the report. An entire day's activities could be changed if a major variance showed up on an internal financial report, and she had to find out why.

Your best bet is to keep a good working relationship with someone in the accounting department who can help you sort through the details. Hopefully, you'll find that the variance was solely based on a coding error, and the revenue or expense was just put in the wrong place. When that's not the case, you'll have to come up with some solution to correct the problem rather quickly.

Chapter 15

Turning Up Clues in Turnover and Assets

In This Chapter

▶ Tracking inventory

▶ Counting inventory turnover

▶ Measuring fixed assets turnover

▶ Assessing total assets turnover

*T*esting how well a company manages its assets is a critical step in measuring how effectively a company uses its resources. Inventory is the most important asset used for generating cash for any company that sells a product.

Many factors directly impact the cost of selling a product. These factors include producing the product, purchasing the products or materials not produced in-house, storing the product until it's sold, and shipping the product to the customer or store where it's sold. And if the company doesn't sell its product fast enough, the product may become obsolete or damaged before it's sold.

In this chapter, we review the measures you can use to gauge how well a company manages its assets, especially its inventory and how quickly a company sells it.

Exploring Inventory Valuation Methods

A company must know the value of its inventory in order to complete its balance sheet. In addition, a company must set a value for the items it sold in order to include a *cost of sales number* (the amount of money spent to produce or manufacture products to be sold) on its income statement. Calculating that value depends on the method the company uses. Five different accounting methods are available for determining the value of inventory, and each one can result in a different *net income* (the amount of profit earned by the company).

These methods include

- ✓ **Last In, First Out (LIFO) inventory system:** We have included LIFO because it is a term in common use; but under international standards, it's not a permitted system. This system assumes that the last item put onto the shelf is the first item sold. Each time a product is purchased or manufactured to be put on the shelves, it costs a different amount. Usually, the cost goes up, so the last item put on the shelf is likely to cost more than the first item put on the shelf. Therefore, the goods sold first in the LIFO system are the highest-priced goods, which raises the cost of sales and lowers the net income. Stocking a shelf by leaving the older items in place and just adding the newly received products in front of it is a lot quicker. For example, hardware stores often use this method when restocking products that rarely change, such as hammers and wrenches.

- ✓ **First In, First Out (FIFO) inventory system:** This system assumes that the first items put on the shelf are the first items sold. The cost of goods purchased or manufactured differs each time they're bought or made. Usually, prices increase, so in the case of FIFO, the first item put on the shelf is likely to have a lower cost than the last item put on the shelf. Because the first item is the one sold first, the cost of goods sold is most likely to be lower than in a company that uses the LIFO method. Therefore, the cost of sales is lower, and the net income is higher. For example, grocery stores have to consider spoilage, so they put the newly received products behind the older ones to be sure that the older products sell first before they spoil. It would be logical therefore for the grocery store to use the FIFO system.

- ✓ **Average-costing inventory system:** This system doesn't try to specify which items sell first or last but instead calculates the average cost of each unit sold. This method gives a company the best picture of its inventory cost trends. Using this valuation method, the ups and downs of prices don't impact a company's inventory. Instead, the inventory value levels out through the year. The net income actually falls somewhere between the net income figures calculated based on LIFO and FIFO. It would be logical for a company to use this system if the items in a particular stock line were indistinguishable. For example, a company holding stock of a plastic moulding would not need to distinguish new stock from old stock because the mouldings would not deteriorate with time. A variation of the average-costing system is also used in continuous production systems – for example, where the company is producing petrol from crude oil.

- ✓ **Specific-identification inventory system:** This system actually tracks the value of each individual product in a company's inventory. For example, car dealers track the value of each car in their stock by using this method. The net income is calculated by subtracting the cost of goods sold that have been specifically identified.

✔ **Market inventory system:** This system sets an inventory value based on current market value. Companies whose inventory values can change numerous times, even throughout a day, usually use this valuation method. For example, dealers in precious metals, commodities, and publicly traded securities commonly use this method.

In most cases, companies use the FIFO, or average-costing inventory system. Specific-identification inventory is used only by companies that sell major items in which each item has a unique set of add-ons, such as cars or high-end computers. Therefore, each product being sold has a different cost of sale value. The market inventory system is used primarily by companies that sell marketable securities and precious metals.

These methods of valuing inventory may be used by companies in their internal reporting. Notice that all but the final method are attempting to measure the cost of producing inventory whereas the market inventory system method is based on the current market value of inventory.

When it comes to financial reporting, the accounting standard dealing with inventories IAS (International Accounting Standards) 2 states that inventories should be measured as the lower of cost and *net realisable value*. The accounting policies will tell you whether cost has been estimated using the FIFO, average-costing, or specific identification system. Net realisable value is the estimated selling price of the item of inventory less the estimated costs of completion and any costs necessary to make the sale. If net realisable value of any individual items of stock are below their cost then the notes to the accounts will disclose the aggregate amount of the write-down.

The way a company values its inventory can have a major impact on its bottom line. The reason is that the figure a company uses on its income statement for cost of sales depends on the costs it assigns to the inventory it sold during the period covered by that income statement. The inventory's value shown on the balance sheet is what's left over and still held by the company, so the *ending inventory's value* is the value of the goods still held by the company. This value is listed as a current asset on the balance sheet.

If you're a company outsider, you won't be able to get the details needed to calculate the value of the products left in inventory and will have to depend on the notional value on the balance sheet. In fact, many times, only the company insiders directly involved in inventory decision-making have access to cost details. Many companies consider actual inventory costs to be a trade secret, and they don't want their competitors to know the details. Nonetheless, understanding what's behind those numbers and how different inventory methods can impact the bottom line is important for understanding financial reports.

Tracking inventory

Inventory tracking methods can be a highly honed science for large corporations that involve extensive computer programming and management, or they can be as simple as taking a count of what's in stock. Companies use one of the following two systems to keep track of their goods on hand:

✔ **Periodic inventory tracking:** A company periodically counts inventory on hand to verify how many of the products are left on the shelves (if the company has retail outlets) and how many are left to be sold in the warehouse (or in cartons in the back of a store, if the company has retail outlets). Most companies that use a periodic inventory system do a physical count at least monthly and possibly as often as daily, depending on the company's sales volume.

✔ **Perpetual (or continuous) inventory system:** Using this system, a company gets an updated inventory count after each sale. When you get a receipt that lists a long string of numbers next to each product's name that you bought, the company most likely uses a perpetual inventory system. The long string of numbers is the tracking number assigned to the inventory in the computer system.

You've probably been the victim of a company's perpetual inventory system when you try to buy something at a store when the cash register is down. Many people have been in stores that couldn't make a sale because the cash register was down, and the store had no way to manually handle the sale.

If you're comparing two companies that use two different methods, you need to take that fact into consideration when doing the comparisons. You can find out in the notes to the financial statements which method a company is using. (We discuss inventory valuation methods in greater detail in Chapter 9.)

To calculate a company's cost of sales, you must know the value assigned to the *beginning inventory* (which is the same as the ending inventory for the previous period and is also the same as the inventory number you find on the balance sheet). The beginning inventory is the number that is used at the beginning of the next accounting period, so any purchases made during this accounting period is added on to the beginning inventory. Finally, you need to know the number for the amount of inventory left at the end of the accounting period, which is called the *ending inventory.* Using those figures, here's the formula for calculating the cost of sales:

1. **Find the value of the goods available for sale.**

   beginning inventory + purchases = goods available for sale

2. **Calculate the value of items sold.**

   goods available for sale − ending inventory = items sold

Applying Inventory Valuation Methods

To give you an idea of how inventory can impact the bottom line, we have created an inventory scenario to take you through the calculations for cost of sale value by using two key methods: FIFO and average costing.

In both cases, we use the same beginning inventory, purchases, and ending inventory for a one-month accounting period in March.

1. **100 (beginning inventory) + 500 (purchases) = 600 (goods available for sale)**

2. **600 (goods available for sale) – 100 (ending inventory) = 500 (items sold)**

Three inventory purchases were made during the month:

March 1	100 at £10
March 15	200 at £11
March 25	200 at £12

The beginning inventory value was 100 items at £9 each (assume, for simplicity in this illustration, that this is the same whichever system is being used).

FIFO

To calculate FIFO, you don't average costs. Instead, you look at the costs of the first units the company sold. With FIFO, the first units sold are the first units put on the shelves. Therefore, beginning inventory is sold first, then the first set of purchases, followed by the next set of purchases, and so on.

To find the costs of sales, add the beginning inventory to the purchases that took place during the reporting period. The remaining 100 units at £12 are the value of ending inventory. Here's the calculation:

Beginning inventory:	100 at £9	=	£900
March 1 purchase:	100 at £10	=	£1,000
March 15 purchase:	200 at £11	=	£2,200
March 25 purchase:	100 at £12	=	£1,200
Cost of sales		=	£5,300
Ending inventory:			
From March 25:	100 at £12	=	£1,200

In this example, the cost of sales includes the value of the beginning inventory plus the first two purchases on March 1 and 15 and part of the purchases on March 25. Those units remaining on the shelf are from the last purchase on March 25. The cost of goods sold is £5,300, and the value of the inventory on hand, or the ending inventory, is £1,200.

Average costing

Before you can use the average-costing inventory system, you need to calculate the average cost per unit.

100 at £9	= £900 (beginning inventory)

Plus purchases:

100 at £10	= £1,000 (March 1 purchase)
200 at £11	= £2,200 (March 15 purchase)
200 at £12	= £2,400 (March 25 purchase)
Cost of goods available for sale	= £6,500

Average cost per unit:

£6,500 (cost of goods available for sale) ÷ 600 (number of units) = £10.83 (average cost per unit)

After you know the average cost per unit, you can calculate the cost of sales and the ending inventory value pretty easily by using the average-costing inventory system:

Cost of sales	500 at £10.83 each	=	£5,417
Ending inventory	100 at £10.83 each	=	£1,083

So the value of cost sales using the average-costing method is £5,417. This is the figure you would see as the cost of sales line item on the income statement. The value of the inventory left on hand, or the ending inventory, is £1,083. This is the number you would see as the inventory item on the balance sheet.

Comparing inventory methods and financial statements

Looking at the results of each method side-by-side shows you the impact that the inventory valuation method has on the income statement:

Income Statement Line Item	Averaging	FIFO
Sales	£10,000	£10,000
Cost of sales	£5,417	£5,300
Gross profit	£4,583	£4,700

FIFO gives companies the lowest cost of goods sold and the highest net income, so companies that use this method know that their bottom lines look better to investors.

Results for the inventory number on the balance sheet also differ using these different methods:

	Averaging	FIFO
Ending inventory	£1,083	£1,200

Determining Inventory Turnover

The big question you should have for any company is how quickly is it selling its inventory and turning it into a profit. As long as that company turns over its inventory quickly, you probably won't find outdated products sitting on the shelves. But if the company's inventory moves slowly, you're more likely to find a possible problem in the valuation of its inventory.

You use a three-step process to find out how quickly product is moving out of the door.

Calculating inventory turnover

Here's the three-step formula for calculating a company's inventory turnover:

1. **Calculate the average inventory (the average number of units held in inventory).**

   beginning inventory + ending inventory ÷ 2 = average inventory

2. **Calculate the inventory turnover (the number of times inventory is completely sold out during the accounting period).**

   cost of goods sold ÷ average inventory = inventory turnover

3. **Calculate the number of days it takes for products to go through the inventory system, according to the accounting policies note to the financial statements.**

   365 ÷ inventory turnover = number of days to sell all inventory

In this calculation, you find out the number of days it took the company to sell all its inventory.

We use Tesco's and Marks and Spencer's 2007 income statements and balance sheets (see Appendix A) to show you how to calculate inventory turnover and the number of days it takes to sell that inventory. Both Tesco and Marks and Spencer use the lower of cost and market value inventory system to value their inventory, according to the accounting policy in their notes to the financial statements. Because they do this they cannot overstate the value of an item which for whatever reason has fallen below its cost price. This is particularly important in the garment industry where articles can go out of fashion and lose a lot of their original value. We can't tell which costing system is used but it is likely to be FIFO.

Here's the method to find out how quickly Tesco sells out all its inventory:

1. **Find the average inventory.**

   Use the inventory on hand February 25, 2006, as the beginning inventory, and use the inventory remaining on February 24, 2007, as the ending inventory.

   £1,464 (beginning inventory) + £1,931 (ending inventory) ÷ 2 = £1,698

2. **Calculate the inventory turnover.**

   You need the cost of sale figure on the 2007 income statement to calculate the inventory turnover.

   £39,401 (cost of sales) ÷ £1,698 (average inventory) = 23.2 (inventory turnover)

   This figure means that Tesco completely sold out its inventory 23.2 times during 2007.

3. **Find the number of days it takes for Tesco to sell out all its inventory.**

   365 (days) ÷ 23.2 (inventory turnover) = 15.7

Tesco took 15.7 days to sell out all its inventory. So every 15.7 days, Tesco turned over all its inventory. As an investor reading this report, you can assume that on average, Tesco sells all inventory on hand every 15.7 days. Remember, though, that won't be true for every item that Tesco sells. Popular items, such as vegetables, may sell out and new stock may be needed every day, whereas less popular items, such as digital radios, may sit on the shelf for several weeks or more. This calculation gives you an average for all types of products sold.

Here's the method to find out how quickly Marks and Spencer sells out all its inventory:

1. **Find the average inventory.**

   Use the inventory on hand March 31, 2006, as the beginning inventory, and use the inventory remaining on March 31, 2007, as the ending inventory.

   £374.30 (beginning inventory) + £416.30 (ending inventory) ÷ 2 = £395.30

2. **Calculate the inventory turnover.**

   To do so, use the cost of sales number on the 2007 income statement.

   £5,246.90 (cost of goods sold) ÷ £395.30 (average inventory) = 13.3 (inventory turnover)

   This figure means that Marks and Spencer completely sold out its inventory 13.3 times during 2007.

3. **Find the number of days it takes for Marks and Spencer to sell out all its inventory.**

   365 (days) ÷ 13.3 (inventory turnover) = 27.5

So Marks and Spencer sells all its inventory every 27.5 days. That figure is just about 12 days slower than Tesco's, which may look like a significant difference, but remember that Marks and Spencer product mix of food to other products is very different to Tesco's, which accounts for at least some of the difference.

What do the numbers mean?

Tesco takes 15.7 days and Marks and Spencer take 27.5 days to sell all their inventory (see preceding two sections), so they turn over their inventories approximately 23 and 13 times per year respectively. To judge how well both companies are doing, check the averages for the industry. You can do so online by obtaining a report from ICC Information Service using the Accounting Web Web site www.accountingweb.co.uk/icc.

Retailers, particularly efficient ones like these two companies, have very high inventory turnover ratios. To get a comparison with a company in a different industry, take Molins, a company in heavy engineering making factory plant and machinery. We would expect its inventory turnover to be very much lower than the retailers. It turns over its inventory only about 3 times in a year.

If the company you're evaluating has a slower inventory turnover than the standard for the industry, look for explanations in the managers' comments and the notes to the financial statements to find out why the company is performing worse than its competitors. If the rate is higher, look for explanations for that as well; don't get too excited until you know the reason why. The better numbers may be because of a one-time inventory change. It's useful to compare the inventory turnover trend from one year to the next as well as checking it against the industry average.

Investigating Tangible Fixed Assets Turnover

Next, you want to test how efficiently a company uses its fixed assets to generate sales, known as the *tangible fixed assets turnover*. *Tangible fixed assets* are assets that a company holds for business use for more than one year and that aren't likely to be converted to cash any time soon. Tangible fixed assets include items such as buildings, land, manufacturing plants, equipment, and furnishings. Using the tangible fixed assets ratio, you can determine how much per pound of sales is tied up in buying and maintaining these long-term assets versus how much is tied up in assets that are more quickly used up. If the economy goes sour and sales drop, reducing variable costs is much easier than reducing costs for maintaining fixed assets. The higher the tangible fixed assets turnover ratio, the more nimble a company can be when responding to economic slowdowns.

Calculating fixed assets turnover

The fixed assets turnover ratio formula is

sales ÷ tangible fixed assets = tangible fixed assets turnover ratio

We show you how to calculate this ratio by using the net sales figure of Marks and Spencer's and Tesco's income statements and the tangible fixed assets figures from their balance sheets (see Appendix A). For both companies, you have to add several line items together, such as buildings, tools, equipment, and so on. In the case of Tesco and Marks and Spencer you add property plant and equipment and investment property. Here are the calculations.

Tesco:

£42,641 (sales) ÷ £17,832 (tangible fixed assets) = 2.4 (tangible fixed assets turnover ratio)

Marks and Spencer:

£8,588.10 (sales) ÷ £4,069.60 (tangible fixed assets) = 2.1 (tangible fixed assets turnover ratio)

What do the numbers mean?

At first glance, Tesco seems to use its tangible fixed assets more efficiently. A higher fixed assets ratio usually means that a company has less money tied up in tangible fixed assets for each pound of sales revenue that it generates. If the ratio is declining, that can mean that the company is over-invested in fixed assets, such as plant and equipment. To improve its fixed assets turnover ratio, a company may need to close and sell some of its plants and equipment that it no longer needs. Obviously in the case of these two retailers they have a huge amount of money tied up in property – their stores – so we should not expect this ratio to be very high.

You can tell whether a company's fixed asset turnover ratio is increasing or decreasing by calculating the ratio for several years and comparing the results. The balance sheet includes two years' worth of data. So in this example, you can request the financial statements for 2005. Then you'd have the data for 2007 and 2006 on the 2007 balance sheet, and you'd have the data for 2005 and 2004 on the 2005 balance sheet.

To get a comparison with another industry, Molins, an engineering company, has a tangible fixed assets turnover of 4.2.

Tracking Total Asset Turnover

Finally, you can look at how well a company manages its assets overall by calculating its total asset turnover. Rather than just looking at inventories or fixed assets, the *total asset turnover* measures how efficiently a company uses all its assets.

Calculating total asset turnover

The formula for calculating total asset turnover is

sales ÷ total assets = total asset turnover

We use information from Marks and Spencer's and Tesco's income statements and balance sheets to show you how to calculate total asset turnover. You can find the sales figure at the top of the income statement and the total assets at the bottom of the assets section on the balance sheet (Sometimes companies do not show this figure and you will have to add non-current assets to current assets to get the total assets figure). Here are the calculations.

Tesco:

£42,641 (sales) ÷ £24,807 (total assets) = 1.7 (total asset turnover)

Marks and Spencer:

£8,588.10 (sales) ÷ £5,381.00 (total assets) = 1.6 (total asset turnover)

What do the numbers mean?

Both Marks and Spencer and Tesco have similar asset ratios, so their efficiency in using their total assets to generate revenue is about equal. Both companies only hold about 16 per cent of their assets in current assets, which is a reflection of the business they are in with customers paying cash and the retailers taking credit from their suppliers.

Molins, who have to give their customers credit, has more than half its total assets in current assets, giving them the ability to pay their short-term bills.

A higher asset turnover ratio means that a company is likely to have a higher return on its assets, which some investors believe can compensate if you see the company has a low profit ratio. By *compensate*, we mean that the higher return on assets could mean increased valuation for the company and, therefore, a higher share price.

In addition to looking at the asset turnover ratio, when determining stock value, you need to calculate the profit ratios and return on assets, which we show you how to calculate in Chapter 11. Aside from inventory turnover, another key asset to consider is accounts-receivable turnover, which we discuss in Chapter 16.

Chapter 16

Examining Cash Inflow and Outflow

• •

In This Chapter

▶ Finding out how fast customers pay

▶ Considering slow-paying customers

▶ Making sure companies pay bills quickly

▶ Digging into discount offers

• •

Is the money flowing? That's the million-dollar, and sometimes multimillion-dollar, question. Measuring how well a company manages its inflow and outflow of cash is crucial.

In this chapter, we review the key ratios for gauging cash flow and show you how to calculate them. In addition, we explore how companies use their internal financial reporting to monitor slow-paying customers and discuss whether paying bills early or on time is better and how you can test that issue.

Assessing Trade-Receivable Turnover and Average Collection Period

Sales are great, but if customers don't pay on time, the sales aren't worth as much to a business: late payers mean that companies have to borrow money to finance customer debt or miss out on opportunities for future investment because they don't have the cash the customers owe them. In fact, someone who doesn't pay at all for the products they take is no better for business than a thief. When you're assessing a company's future prospects, one of the best ways to judge how well it's managing its cash flow is to calculate the *trade-receivable turnover ratio* and from that the average collection period. When you calculate the trade receivable turnover ratio, you're testing how fast the customers are actually paying those bills.

A balance sheet lists customer credit accounts under the line item 'Trade and other receivables'. Any company that sells its goods on credit to customers must keep track of to whom it extended credit and whether or not those customers paid their bills in a reasonable time.

What you're trying to calculate here is the amount of time that customers take to pay normal bills issued in the normal course of business. You therefore have to find the 'Trade receivables' item in the notes to the accounts to separate them from other types of receivables – such as *prepayments* when a company has paid in advance for products or services that it will receive in the next year. Sometimes it's not so straightforward and when there's no actual line saying 'Trade receivables' you may have to study the note and eliminate items that are obviously not trade receivables to find the figure you're looking for.

Financial transactions involving credit-card sales aren't figured into accounts receivable but are handled like cash. The type of credit we're referring to here is *in-store credit* or *company credit,* which is when the bill the customer receives comes directly from the store or company where the customer purchased the item.

When a store or a company makes a sale on credit, it enters the purchase on the customer's credit account. At the end of each billing period, the store or company sends the customer a bill (often called an *invoice*) for the purchases that the customer made on credit. The customer usually has between 10 and 30 days from the billing date to pay the bill.

Calculating trade-receivable turnover

Here's the two-step formula for testing trade-receivable turnover:

1. Find the trade-receivable turnover ratio.

Here's how:

sales (or revenue) ÷ trade receivables = trade-receivables turnover ratio

If you work inside the company, an even better test is to use annual credit sales rather than sales as shown in the financial statements, because sales includes both cash and credit sales. But if you're an outsider reading the financial statements, you can't find out the credit sales number.

2. Find the average collection period (the time it takes customers to pay their bills).

Here's how:

365 days ÷ trade-receivables turnover ratio = average collection period

This ratio is very industry dependent. For example, if a computer company sells a complex product and has a problem with implementation, the customer may not pay their bill until the problem is solved. Such companies are bound to have much longer collection periods than the two retailers we are studying.

Think about the retail business. We cannot tell how much of their sales are on credit and how much in cash by reading the income statement; but we know that the vast amount of their customers will pay their bills in cash or its equivalent at the checkout. We should expect them, therefore to have a very short collection period. As a comparison we will also give the ratios for a company called Molins who sell machinery for making cigarettes and for packaging. This illustrates the difference between such a company and the retailers.

Here's how to test trade receivables turnover by using Marks and Spencer's and Tesco's 2007 income statements and balance sheets.

To find Tesco's turnover:

1. **Find Tesco's trade-receivables turnover ratio for 2007.**

   £42,641 (net sales) ÷ £771 (trade receivables) = 55

2. **Find the average credit collection period.**

   365 days ÷ 55 (trade-receivables turnover ratio) = 7 days

Tesco's customers, cash and credit, averaged about 7 days to pay their bills.

Comparing this data with the previous year's is a good idea to see whether the situation is getting better or worse. If you use the same process to calculate Tesco's 2006 average credit collection period, you find the answer is 6 days, meaning that the company took slightly longer in 2007 to collect than it did the year before. In order to understand the significance of this, look at what is happening with similar companies as well as within the industry. The longer credit collection period may be an internal company problem, or an industry-wide problem related to changes in the economic situation. In the case of Tesco, with its very short collection period, the difference is probably insignificant.

To find Marks and Spencer's turnover:

1. **Calculate Marks and Spencer's trade-receivables turnover ratio for 2007.**

   £8,588.10 (net sales) ÷ £67.90 (trade receivables) = 126

2. **Calculate the average sales credit period.**

   365 days ÷ 126 (trade-receivables turnover ratio) = 3 days

Finding the right credit policy

Setting the right trade-receivables policy can have a major impact on sales. For example, a company could require customers to pay within ten days of billing or it will close their accounts. That may be too strict, and customers could end up walking out of the store or stopping doing business with the company because they can't charge to an account. Another common credit policy that could be too strict would be one that requires too high a salary level to qualify, forcing too many customers to go elsewhere to buy the products they need.

Looking at the other side of the coin, a credit policy that is too loose may allow customers 60 days to pay their accounts. By the time the company realises that it has a non-paying customer, the customer could already have charged a large sum to the account. If the customer never pays the account, the company would have to write it off as a bad debt.

Marks and Spencer's trade receivables turned over more often (at an average of 3 days) than Tesco's (at an average of 7 days) in 2007.

Is that an improvement or step backward for Marks and Spencer? Using the 2006 numbers, you find that Marks and Spencer took 2 days to collect from its customers in 2006. That means that the company experienced a slight lengthening in its trade-receivables collection period.

Looking at heavy engineering company Molins, you find that its trade-receivables turnover ratio was 7 at about the same time giving it a collection period of 55 days. Most industries come somewhere within a range that has retailers at the fast end to engineering companies (who are bound to take longer) at the slow end.

What do the numbers mean?

The higher a trade-receivables turnover ratio is, the faster a company's customers are paying their bills. Usually, the trade-receivables collection is directly related to the credit policies set by the company. For example, a high turnover ratio may look very good, but that ratio may also mean that the company's credit policies are too strict, and it's losing sales because few customers qualify for credit. A low accounts-receivable turnover ratio usually means that a company's credit policies are too loose, and the company may not be doing a good job of collecting on its accounts.

The retail companies that we are examining are unlikely to have major levels of bad debt – although both need to make some provision for possible bad debts in their personal finance arms. If the amount of bad debts is material to the financial statements, then the amount written off will be disclosed in the notes to the accounts.

As an investor, if a company has a longer collection period than its competitors you may want to call their investor-relations department to find out about its longer trade-receivables collections period and what the company is doing to improve these numbers.

Taking a Close Look at Customer Accounts

If you're working inside a company and have responsibility for customer accounts, you get an internal financial report called the *accounts-receivable aging schedule (or aged debtors)*. This schedule summarises the customers with outstanding accounts, the amounts they have outstanding, and the number of days that their bills are outstanding. Each company designs its own report, so they don't have any required formats. Check out Table 16–1 to see an example of an accounts-receivable aging schedule.

Table 16–1:	Accounts-Receivable Aging Schedule for ABC Company, as of 31 March 2007				
Customer	**30–45 Days**	**46–60 Days**	**61–90 Days**	**Over 90 Days**	**Total**
DE Company	£100	£50	£0	£0	£150
FG Company	£200	£0	£0	£0	£200
HI Company	£200	£100	£100	£50	£450
JK Company	£300	£150	£50	£50	£550
Total	£800	£300	£150	£100	£1,350

After you get the aging schedule, you can quickly see which companies are significantly past the due date in their payments. Many firms begin cutting off customers whose accounts are more than 60 or 90 days past due date. Other firms cut off customers when they're more than 120 days past due date. No set accounting rule dictates when to cut off customers who haven't paid their bills; this decision depends on the internal control policies the company sets.

In the aging schedule example for ABC Company, the JK Company looks like its account needs some investigating. Although a company can carry past-due payments because of a dispute about a bill, after that dispute goes beyond 90 days, the company awaiting payment may put restrictions on the other company's future purchases until its account gets cleaned up. HI Company seems to be another slow-paying company that may need a call from the accounts-receivable manager or collections department.

Many times, a company salesperson makes the first contact with the slow paying customer. If the salesperson is unsuccessful, the company initiates more severe collection methods, with the highest level being an outside collection agency or court action. Companies with strong collection practices do a gentle reminder call when an account is more than 30 days late and push harder as the account is more and more past its due date.

When a company decides that it probably will never collect on an account, it writes off the account as a bad debt in the Bad Debt Account. Each company sets its own policies about how quickly it will write off a bad debt. A company usually reviews its accounts for possible write-offs at the end of each accounting period. We talk more about accounts receivable and their impact on cash flow in Chapter 17.

Finding the Accounts-Payable Turnover Ratio

A company's reputation for paying its bills is just as important as collecting from its own customers. If a company develops the reputation of being a slow payer, it can have a hard time buying on credit. The situation can get even more serious if a company is late paying its loans. In that case, a company can end up with increased interest rates while its credit rating becomes lower and lower. We discuss the importance of a good credit rating in Chapter 19.

You can test a company's bill-paying record with the accounts-payable turnover ratio. In addition, you can check how many days a company takes to pay its bills by using the days-in-accounts-payable ratio.

Calculating the ratio

The *accounts-payable turnover ratio* tests how quickly a company pays its bills. You calculate this ratio by dividing the cost of sales (you find this figure on the income statement) by the average accounts payable (you find the accounts-payable figures on the balance sheet). Using the average number rather than the closing figure on the balance sheet is a technique that some people use and we use it here for completeness.

Here's the formula for the accounts-payable turnover ratio:

cost of sales ÷ average accounts payable = accounts-payable turnover ratio

We use Tesco and Marks and Spencer's income statements and balance sheets for 2007 to compare their accounts-payable turnover ratios.

To calculate Tesco's ratio:

1. Find the average accounts payable.

£2,832 (2006 accounts payable) + £3,317 (2007 accounts payable) ÷ 2 = £3,074.5 (average accounts payable)

2. Calculate Tesco's accounts-payable turnover ratio.

£39,401 (cost of sales) ÷ £3,074 (average accounts payable) = 12.8

Tesco turns over its accounts payable 12.8 times per year.

To calculate Marks and Spencer's ratio:

1. Find the average accounts payable.

£242.60 (2006 accounts payable) + £259.70 (2007 accounts payable) ÷ 2 = £251.15 (average accounts payable)

2. Use that number to calculate Marks and Spencer accounts-payable turnover ratio.

£5,246.90 (cost of sales) ÷ £251.15 (average accounts payable) = 20.9

Marks and Spencer turns over its accounts payable 20.9 times per year, which is a good bit faster than Tesco.

What do the numbers mean?

The higher the accounts-payable turnover ratio, the shorter the time is between purchase and payment. If a company has a low turnover ratio, this may indicate that it has a cash-flow problem.

Each industry has its own set of ratios. The only way to accurately judge how a company is doing with paying its bills is to compare it with similar companies and the industry.

Determining the Number of Days in Accounts-Payable Ratio

The *number of days in accounts-payable ratio* lets you test the average length of time a company takes to pay its bills. If a company is taking longer to pay its bills each year, or if it pays its bills over a longer time period than other companies in its industry, it may be having a cash-flow problem. Also, if a company pays its bills quicker than other companies in the same industry, that could be a problem, too: they could hang on to the cash for longer and save themselves interest on their short-term loans. We could have used the same method of calculation here as we did for the average collection period, but again for completeness we are using a different technique that will give the same answer.

Calculating the ratio

Use the following formula to calculate the number of days in accounts payable:

average accounts payable ÷ cost of sales × 365 days = days in accounts payable

We can use Tesco's and Marks and Spencer's balance sheets and income statements to find the number of days in accounts-payable ratio. Fortunately, we don't have to calculate average accounts payable if you calculated the accounts-payable turnover ratio in the section 'Finding the Accounts-Payable Turnover Ratio' earlier in this chapter.

Tesco:

£3,074 (average accounts payable) ÷ £39,401 (cost of sales) × 365 = 28.5 days

Tesco takes about 28.5 days to pay its bills, or about 4 weeks, which is very different from the 7 days the company takes to collect from customers, as the accounts-receivable turnover ratio shows. Therefore, Tesco is receiving cash from its customers much faster than it's paying out cash to its suppliers. That is a healthy financial sign and an indication that, because of the nature of its business, there's no cash-flow problem. You could say that they are using their muscle to pass their cash-flow problems to their suppliers.

Marks and Spencer:

£251.20 (average accounts payable) ÷ £5,246.90 (cost of sales) × 365 = 17.5 days

Marks and Spencer takes about 17.5 days, or less than three weeks, to pay its bills. Marks and Spencer's accounts-receivable turnover ratio showed that its customers take slightly more than 3 days to pay their bills. Therefore again, Marks and Spencer gets cash in much more quickly than its suppliers get paid.

Consider Molins, an engineering company, at the other end of the spectrum. Molins takes 55 days on average to get its cash in, while it has to pay its suppliers within 41 days. This means that it will have to have spare cash at all times to make sure it can pay its bills.

What do the numbers mean?

If the number of days a company takes to pay its bills increases from year-to-year, it may be a red flag indicating a possible cash-flow problem. To know for certain what's happening, compare the company with similar companies and the industry averages.

Just like accounts receivable prepares an aging schedule for customer accounts, companies also prepare internal financial reports for accounts payable that show which companies they owe money to, the amount they owe, and the number of days for which they've owed that amount.

Deciding Whether Discount Offers Make Good Financial Sense

One common way that companies encourage their customers to pay early is to offer them a discount. When a discount is offered, a customer (in this case, the company that must pay the bill) may see a term such as '2/10 net 30' or '3/10 net 60' at the top of its bill. '2/10 net 30' means that the customer can take a 2 per cent discount if it pays the bill within 10 days; otherwise, it must pay the bill in full within 30 days. '3/10 net 60' means that if a customer pays the bill within 10 days, it can take a 3 per cent discount; otherwise, it can pay the bill in full within 60 days. Other terms are used to express the same idea. Frequently one company makes an agreement with another that covers all its purchases. The agreement states what their discount is and how quickly they must pay to get it. To encourage companies to take the discount the supplier often puts in big letters the amount they save by paying the invoice early.

Taking advantage of this discount saves the customers money, but if the customer doesn't have enough cash to take advantage of the discount, it needs to decide whether to use its credit line to do so. Comparing the interest saved by taking the discount with the interest a company must pay to borrow money to pay the bills early can help a company decide whether or not using credit to get the discount is a wise decision.

The formula for calculating the annual interest rate is

[(% discount) ÷ (100 − % discount)] × (365 ÷ number of days paid early) = annual interest rate

We calculate the interest rate based on the early-payment terms stated earlier.

For terms of 2/10 net 30

You first must calculate the number of days that the company would be paying the bill early. In this case, it's paying the bill in 10 days instead of 30, which means it's paying the bill 20 days earlier than the terms require. Now calculate the interest rate, using the annual interest-rate formula:

[2 (% discount) ÷ (100 − 2 (% discount) = 98)] × (365 ÷ 20 (number of days paid early)) = 37.24%

That percentage is much higher than the interest rate the company may have to pay if it needs to use a credit line to meet cash-flow requirements, so taking advantage of the discount makes sense. For example, if a company has a bill for £100,000 and takes advantage of a 2 per cent discount, it has to pay only £98,000, and it saves £2,000. Even if it must borrow the £98,000 at an annual rate of 10 per cent, which would cost about £537 for 20 days, it still saves money provided it can borrow the money to pay the bill within 10 days.

For terms of 3/10 net 60

First, find the number of days the company would be paying the bill early. In this case, it's paying the bill within 10 days, which means it's paying 50 days earlier than the terms require. Next, calculate the interest rate, using this formula:

[3 (% discount) ÷ (100 − 3 (% discount) = 97] × (365 ÷ 50 (number of days paid early)) = 22.58%

Paying 50 days earlier gives the company an annual interest rate of 22.58 per cent, which is likely to be higher than the interest rate it'd have to pay if it needed to use a credit line to meet cash-flow requirements. But the interest rate isn't nearly as good as the terms of 2/10 net 30. A company offered 3/10 net 60 terms will probably still choose to take the discount, as long as the cost of its credit lines carry an interest rate that's lower than that available with these terms and, of course, if it has a credit facility that allows it to do so.

What do the numbers mean?

For most companies, taking advantage of these discounts makes sense, as long as the annual interest rate calculated using this formula is higher than the one they must pay if they borrow money to pay the bill early. This becomes a big issue for companies, because unless their inventory turns over very rapidly, 10 days probably isn't enough time to sell all the inventory purchased before they must pay the bill early. Their cash wouldn't come from sales but, more likely, from borrowing.

If cash flow is tight, a company would have to borrow funds using its credit line to take advantage of the discount. For example, if the company buys £100,000 in goods to be sold at terms of 2/10 net 30, the company could save £2,000 by paying within 10 days. If the company hasn't sold all the goods, it would have to borrow up to £98,000 for 20 days, which wouldn't be necessary if it didn't try to take advantage of the discount. Assume that the annual interest on the credit line for the company is 9 per cent. Does it make sense to borrow the money?

A company would need to pay the additional interest on the amount borrowed only for 20 additional days (because that's the number of days the company must pay the bill early). Calculating the annual interest of 9 per cent of £98,000 equals £8,820, or £24 per day. Borrowing that money would cost an additional £480 (£24 times 20 days). So even though the company must borrow the money to pay the bill early, the £2,000 discount would still save the company £1,520 more than the £480 interest cost involved in borrowing the money.

Chapter 17

How Companies Keep the Cash Flowing

In This Chapter

▶ Slowing down bill paying

▶ Collecting accounts receivable more quickly

▶ Ordering less inventory

▶ Finding quick cash

M anagers sometimes face a shortage of cash to pay the bills and need to find ways to fix the problem. They can use a number of different strategies to get their hands on cash quickly when running a business.

In this chapter, we review the pros and cons of the possible fixes available when a manager finds a red flag about a company's cash flow.

Slowing Down Bill Payments

Short on cash? Well, maybe you can just let your bills slide. It may not be the most responsible policy, but sometimes doing so can get a company through a financial rough patch – as long as its suppliers are relatively patient. *Trade financing* is when businesses buy on credit and don't have to pay cash upon receipt of the goods. Often, these businesses must pay for those goods within 30, 60, or 90 days. When cash gets tight, one of the first strategies many small-business owners use – and even some large corporations – is to pay their bills more slowly and, sometimes very late, to make it through a cash crunch.

This practice is known as '*stretching accounts payable*' or '*living on your suppliers*'. Some companies use this strategy as long as their suppliers tolerate the late payments – in other words, until their suppliers threaten non-delivery of goods. The primary advantage of this plan is that the manager or business owner doesn't need to look for a way to borrow additional money to pay operating expenses. The big disadvantage is that companies can build bad reputations among their suppliers and are less likely to get trade financing in the future.

Paying bills early can be an even bigger advantage for companies than delaying payments for as long as possible. In Chapter 16, we talk about how much money companies can save by taking advantage of trade discounts rather than paying bills on time. Although slowing bill payment may be the easiest way to deal with a cash-flow problem, it's the option with the least advantages and the greatest potential for hurting business operations in the long term, especially when suppliers finally decide to stop providing the goods needed.

When reading a financial report, you can test to see whether a company may be choosing a bill-paying delay strategy by calculating its accounts-payable turnover ratio (refer to Chapter 16). If the turnover of accounts payable is slowing down from one year to the next, that may be a sign that the company has a cash-flow problem.

Collecting Accounts Receivables Faster

If a company owes more money than it has, clearly, it needs to bring in more money. A business whose cash is tight often brings in more money by speeding up the collection of its *accounts receivables* – money owed by customers who bought on credit or people who borrowed from the company. To collect the money, a company must make changes to its credit policies. A company can make these changes to one or more of five basic variables in its credit policy:

- ✔ **Credit period:** Companies can change the length of time they give their customers to pay for their purchases. A liberal credit period can give customers 60 or 90 days to pay, whereas a conservative credit period can allow as few as ten days.

- ✔ **Credit standards:** In times of trouble, a company can loosen the policies it uses to determine a customer's credit eligibility. For example, a company that requires customers to have an income level of at least £50,000 to get a £1,000 credit line may decide to allow customers to get the £1,000 credit line with an income of only £30,000. This policy change increases the credit-customer base and allows more people to buy on credit, thereby increasing sales; however, the change can also lead to more customers who'll have difficulty paying their bills.

✔ **Collection period:** Companies with strict collection policies can begin contacting slow payers or prohibiting them from making further purchases, even if their account is just a few days late. Other companies wait at least 60 days or longer before they follow up on late accounts. Shortening the credit period can get more cash in the door quickly, but this policy can also cause customers to buy fewer products or to move their business to another store or company.

✔ **Discounts:** Companies can encourage their customers to pay their bills earlier by using a discount programme. We discuss using discount programmes in greater detail in Chapter 16. For example, a company can offer customers a 2 per cent discount for paying their bills within 10 days of receiving the bill, but if the customers wait 30 days to pay their bills, the company expects the payment in full. Deciding to add or change a discount programme may speed up cash collections, but also lowers the profit margin on sales because these discounts bring in less revenue.

✔ **Fees and late payments:** Companies must decide whether or not they want to charge late fees or interest to customers who don't pay on time. Companies with a strict collection process charge a late fee one day after the due date of a bill and start adding interest for each day that the payment is late. Companies with a liberal collection policy don't charge late fees or add interest charges to late payers. For example, a company could charge a £25 late fee when a bill is paid ten days after it is due to encourage on-time payment. This strategy encourages slow payers to pay more quickly, but can also chase customers away if one of the company's competitors doesn't impose late fees or interest charges.

Before a company that's trying to speed up its incoming cash flow makes any changes to its credit policy, it must look at a number of financial variables to determine the long-term impact the change may have on its sales and profit margin. Stricter accounts-receivable policies are likely to irritate customers and increase staff workload, whereas looser policies may encourage more sales but result in more bad debt that a company has to write off.

Companies must carefully assess the potential cash-inflow change and potential staff costs, as well as the impact a policy change may have on customers before they change their credit policies. Though at first glance the change may look like a good idea for improving cash flow, its long-term impact may actually reduce sales or profits. Top executives must discuss with managers in sales, marketing, accounting, and finance the potential impact the changes in credit policy may have to fully assess the possible ramifications of the change. For instance, any change in credit policy increases the staff's workload. When a company eases its credit standards and increases the number of customers who can buy on credit, it needs more staff to manage its accounts receivable and keep track of all the new customer accounts. If a company decides to make its credit standards stricter and requires a more time-consuming credit check before establishing new customer accounts, the company has to hire more staff to do those credit checks or hire an outside contractor to do the checks. Either way, a stricter policy costs more money and may drive customers away.

TIP

You can test whether a company is having problems collecting from its customers by calculating its accounts-receivable turnover ratio. To find out how to calculate this ratio, turn to Chapter 16.

Borrowing on Receivables

Rather than delving into the complicated realm of credit-policy changes (see preceding section), many companies use *invoice factoring*. In this type of programme, a company sells its trade receivables, which include all accounts of customers who buy on credit, to an outside party – usually a bank or other financial institution – in an arrangement called 'factoring' to get immediate cash for its receivables. As the receivables come in from customers, the company repays the financial institution. Most companies retain the *servicing rights* of the receivables, which means that they continue to collect from customers and receive servicing fees for doing that collection. Factoring companies also take over the whole sales ledger and actively collect debts.

Two standard options for selling receivables are:

- **Selling the receivables for less than they are worth:** For example, a factoring arrangement's terms may be that the company gets 92 pence for each pound of receivables, which, in essence, is equivalent to an 8 per cent interest rate.

- **Paying interest as if the company had taken out a loan secured by a physical asset, such as a building:** For example, a company's credit terms for the factoring arrangement may set up an annual interest rate of 8 per cent. But for customers who pay their bills within 30 days, the amount of interest they actually pay on the accounts receivable loan is only $\frac{1}{12}$ of 8 per cent for the one month that they borrowed the money while waiting for a customer to pay.

In addition, companies usually have to pay upfront charges of 2–5 per cent to set up the programme.

The biggest advantage of using factoring is that a company has immediate access to cash. The biggest disadvantage is that the company ends up with less than the full value of the receivables when it collects from its customers because of discounts or any interest paid on those receivables.

You can find out whether or not a company uses invoice factoring by reading the notes to the financial statement. If a company does use this type of financing, information about the money it has borrowed on a short-term basis (called *short-term financing*) is included in the notes to the financial statements.

Reducing Inventory

Companies in a cash-flow crunch sometimes decide to reduce their on-hand inventory. Doing so certainly reduces the amount of cash that must be laid out to pay for that inventory, but can also result in lost sales if customers come in to buy a product and don't find it on the shelves. Then customers are more likely to go to a competitor than wait for the product to arrive.

Many companies use a *just-in-time inventory process*, which means the product shows up at a company's door just before it's needed. To set up this type of system, a company must know how many sales it normally makes over a period of time and how long it takes to get new products. Then the company calculates when it must order new products so it receives them just in time before the shelves become empty. This system reduces the inventory a company has to store in its warehouses and the cash payments it must make to suppliers for the products it purchases. When done correctly for a product that moves quickly off the shelves, the company may even sell the product and collect cash before it needs to pay the bills. This strategy certainly helps a company manage its cash flow and reduce the amount of cash it must borrow to pay for inventory.

The big disadvantage of using a just-in-time inventory system is that estimates are sometimes wrong. For example, a company decides when it needs to reorder and how much it needs to reorder based on historical sales data. If a product's popularity increases dramatically before a company can adjust its inventory-purchasing process, store shelves may be empty for days before new products arrive – just when the public is rushing to get the product. As a result, the company loses sales to a competitor who still has the product on its shelves. Any cash that customers would have paid for those goods that were not available is cash that's permanently lost to the company.

Other times, a just-in-time inventory system breaks down because a problem occurs in the supply chain. For example, if a customer orders a product from a company in Singapore, and a major storm shuts down the manufacturing plant for a week or more, product deliveries will be delayed. The company selling the product may be left with empty shelves because the inventory on hand ran out and the new inventory won't show up for a few weeks until the manufacturing plant can restore its operations and begin shipping products again. The result is a lot of cash lost to the company because customers are forced to buy the goods elsewhere.

Using the financial reports, you can test how quickly a company's inventory turns over by calculating the inventory turnover ratio (refer to Chapter 15). However, you won't be able to tell whether a company regularly runs out of products on its shelves by reading the financial reports. You can determine that issue only by periodically stopping by stores to find out.

Although reducing inventory does save the company the cash upfront that it must pay to buy that inventory, inventory reduction could actually result in a loss of sales and less cash in the long run if customers have to go elsewhere to find the products they want. Inventory reduction makes sense only when the company believes the product is sitting too long on the shelves, and there isn't enough customer interest in buying the product.

Getting Cash More Quickly

The most flexible way for a company to keep its cash moving is to have numerous options in place so it can borrow cash when needed or speed up cash receipts. Companies can choose among the following options to keep their cash flowing:

- **Credit cards:** Credit cards can be a great way for a company to conserve cash and pay bills. Banks offer companies a range of credit cards, debit cards, and other short-term cash options to help companies maintain cash flow. Banks can put controls on these cards to ensure that a company's employees don't abuse them.

- **Lines of credit:** Lines of credit allow companies to access cash as needed. The bank or financial institution sets a maximum amount of credit that the company can borrow and then gives the company cheques, or allows it to transfer cash into another current account, making it easy for the company to get cash when needed.

- **An unsecured line of credit:** This type of credit isn't backed by the company's assets, which means that if the company can't pay back the loan, the financial institution cannot seize its assets.

- **A secured line of credit:** This type of credit is backed by the company's assets, so the bank can foreclose and take possession of the asset that backs the line of credit if the company fails to pay back the loan.

- **Electronic bill payment:** Many companies allow customers to pay their bills online and send in bills by e-mail to speed up the cash-collection process. When they get money from customers more quickly, companies speed up their incoming cash flow.

✔ **Merchant services:** A company can get access to their customers' money much more quickly by using electronic payment systems when accepting credit and debit cards. Nearly all stores now use electronic payment systems rather than paper copies when accepting credit cards. Rather than waiting for paper transactions to yield cash – which sometimes occurs days later – companies can use electronic payment systems that can access cash within minutes.

✔ **Loan guarantee scheme:** In this arrangement the government provides a guarantee to the clearing banks that lend to small businesses. Specifically intended for medium-term finance, the scheme has a limit – currently 70 per cent of loans up to £100,000. The cost to the company is that it pays a premium for the guarantee of 1–2 per cent.

✔ **Leasing and hire purchase:** Both of these methods spread out the payments for an asset. A finance charge is made for the arrangement, the equivalent of interest, and this interest can be quite high if the asset is in demand – or reasonably low when the suppliers are looking for customers. Car manufacturers, for example, give very good terms for leasing their cars when the car market is sluggish.

Part V
The Many Ways Companies Answer to Stakeholders

'I think the directors are expecting
a stormy meeting.'

In this part . . .

No public company operates in a vacuum. Instead, every public company must answer to its shareholders and lenders as well as government overseers and financial analysts. On top of all that, auditors must certify that what a company reports is correct. All these parties play some role in why annual reports are presented in the way they are today. In this part, we discuss some of the key outside entities a company must answer to. We also take a look at the ways some companies play games with the numbers that they report.

Chapter 18

Finding Out How Companies Find Errors: The Auditing Process

● ●

In This Chapter

▶ Getting acquainted with audits

▶ Checking out the auditing process

▶ Discovering the role of generally accepted accounting principles

▶ Exploring the present condition and the future of auditing

● ●

Most readers of financial reports don't work for the company and, therefore, must depend on the truthfulness of the company's management in reporting its financial statements. Can you depend on the numbers you see?

The question is valid, especially considering the corporate scandals that have rocked the City since the collapse of Barings Bank in 1995. The Barings case, and other financial reporting scandals such as those at Enron, the Maxwell Group or Parmalat, have led investors to be wary about the numbers companies report in their financial reports. (To find out more about what happened at Barings, Enron, The Maxwell Group, and Parmalat see Chapter 22.)

In this chapter, we explore how third parties get involved to keep company records on the up-and-up.

Meeting Mr or Ms Auditor

Company outsiders can't be sure that the information that they see is an accurate reflection of a company's financial situation unless a disinterested third party reviews the company's operations and its financial statements and determines that the reports are free of fraud and misrepresentation. Called an *audit*, this process is crucial for verifying the accuracy of a company's financial reports.

All companies, other than those which satisfy the legal definition of small, are required to have their results checked by a third party, called an *auditor*, to be sure the reports truthfully portray the financial health of the company.

Under the Companies Act, an individual or firm is eligible for appointment as a statutory auditor if the individual or firm is a member of a recognised supervisory body and eligible for appointment under the rules of that body.

At present, the UK government has approved five bodies as recognised supervisory bodies. These are:

- Institute of Chartered Accountants in England and Wales (ICAEW)
- Institute of Chartered Accountants in Scotland (ICAS)
- Institute of Chartered Accountants in Ireland (ICAI)
- Association of Chartered Certified Accountants (ACCA)
- Association of Authorised Public Accountants (APA)

At the time of writing, all of the FTSE 100 companies – the biggest 100 companies in the country – are audited by one of the 'Big Four' firms of chartered accountants (PriceWaterhouseCoopers, KPMG, Ernst & Young, and Deloitte). This situation has arisen not because of any regulatory impediment which restricts other firms but simply as a result of the free choice of the companies concerned. There is ongoing discussion as to whether having all of the audits of this group of companies being undertaken by such a small number of audit firms is a good thing, but there is no obvious way to achieve greater diversification.

As suggested by the title 'registered supervisory body', the accountancy bodies must monitor the work of their members and discipline those who fall short. In addition, the auditors of listed companies are also subject to review by the Audit Inspection Unit (AIU). The AIU, which is part of the Professional Oversight Board (POB), was set up following the government's post-Enron review of the regulation of the UK accounting profession. The Unit commenced visits to firms of auditors in June 2004 and, not surprisingly, started with the Big Four. So far, the AIU have not identified any major problems in UK auditing and in their latest available report, published in June 2007, they state 'the AIU considers the quality of auditing in the UK to be fundamentally sound'.

It is essential that the auditors can express an independent view on the financial statements but auditors often provide other services to their clients such as tax planning and consulting. The Auditing Practices Board has developed a set of ethical standards which restrict what 'other services' auditors can provide to their audit clients. Where other services are permitted, the auditors must then consider how they can ensure their independence is not compromised and must discuss such issues with the audit client.

The Auditing Practices Board

The body charged with setting the rules for auditors in the UK is the Auditing Practices Board (APB). The APB is itself answerable to the Financial Reporting Council (FRC). The APB (and their predecessors) had been setting standards in the UK for many years but in 2005, they decided to adopt International Standards on Auditing (ISAs). The reason for this was that the European Union had stated a desire to unify auditing standards across the European Economic Area and the way that this was to be achieved was by adopting the International Standards set by the International Auditing and Assurance Standards Board (IAASB) based in New York.

The APB was so enthusiastic about this development that they stated that ISAs would be compulsory for UK audits from the audit of years ended on or after December 2005.

Two problems:

✔ First, the EU did not immediately go ahead with their plan and, at the time of writing, there is still no date by which the rest of Europe will follow the UK's lead.

✔ Second, when the APB reviewed the existing ISAs they discovered that, in some respects, the ISAs were not as good as the old UK auditing standards. Accordingly the APB set about upgrading the ISAs by adding in additional requirements taken from the old standards. To distinguish these amended documents from the original ISAs the standards in use in the UK are called International Standards on Auditing (UK and Ireland) or, in short ISA (UK&I).

As a result of these two problems, the UK is currently out of line with the rest of the world. This may well be fixed shortly because the IAASB is working on a revamp of their standards and presumably, when the upgrade has been completed, both the EU and the APB will be happy to converge on the revamped ISAs. It should be added, however, that this is not expected to be before 2010.

Despite this, there is still an uneasy feeling that auditors might use the audit as a way to identify other services they can sell to their clients. Immediately post-Enron, statistics showed that for every £1 that auditors earned from their listed clients, they earned £3 for other services. By 2006, that figure had improved to a ratio of £1:£1 – better, but still a cause for concern. In the future, auditors may possibly be banned from providing any non-audit services to audit clients.

Delving Into the Auditing Process

If you've worked in a business, you know how nervous some managers become when auditors show up at their door. An audit isn't a complete surprise to a business, however. Auditors sit down with top management and the audit committee to discuss the audit process and to schedule the audit for a time that's least disruptive to the business. For example, a retail company certainly doesn't want auditors checking out its stores during the end-of-year holiday rush.

Getting an audit when it's not required

Some partnerships or audit-exempt companies choose to pay for an audit, but they're not required to do so. They do it primarily because the banks or financial institutions that lend them money request it. A partnership may also choose to pay for an audit if several partners are involved in the business but only one of the partners runs the day-to-day operations. The partners who are not involved in the day-to-day activities may want to have the books audited by an independent outsider to be sure the active partner is accurately reporting the company's financial activities to them.

Before auditors show up at a business's door, they meet with key executives and board members who serve on the audit committee to discuss the scope and objectives of the audit. For example, an audit may include a complete review of the company's operations or it could just be an audit of one aspect of the operation, such as collections from customers. The objectives of a full audit are to express an opinion on the company's financial statements and that is the only sort of audit that we are concerned with in this book.

Even when a company has no desire to mislead investors and others, honest mistakes can happen. Sometimes errors occur because a company's accounting system is flawed or isn't capable of handling changing company conditions, especially when a company is growing rapidly. Other times, a company's accountants might present wrong numbers because of the difficulties involved in accounting estimates or because they don't have a good understanding of the latest accounting principles related to the presentation of some of the numbers.

Fraudulent financial reporting, on the other hand, results when management decides to deliberately distort the numbers to make the company's financial results look better than they actually are. Sometimes companies withhold negative information to avoid an investor backlash and a drop in share value. Companies often deceive without the knowledge of the auditors, but sometimes the auditors are persuaded to permit interpretations of accounting standards that others consider to be bending the rules rather than breaking them. Turn to Chapter 21 to get the dirt on fraudulent financial reporting.

Gathering knowledge of the business

The audit is based on a thorough understanding of the business and the industry in which the company operates. The auditor therefore builds up a detailed permanent file which contains the auditor's understanding of the client and its environment in regards to the following aspects:

✔ **Industry, regulatory, and other external factors, including the applicable financial reporting framework.**

✔ **Nature of the entity, including the entity's selection and application of accounting policies.**

✔ **Objectives and strategies and the related business risks that may result in a material misstatement of the financial statements.** Business risks may lead to problems in the financial statements.

✔ **Measurement and review of the entity's financial performance.** The auditor is interested in the internal measures that the company uses to monitor performance – often known as key performance indicators or KPIs – because the existence of KPIs may put pressure on the client's staff to manipulate the results in order to achieve financial targets.

✔ **Internal control including the information system and the control activities.** Control activities are the policies and procedures that help ensure that management directives are carried out; for example, making sure that necessary actions are taken to address risks that threaten the achievement of the entity's objectives.

Examples of specific control activities include those relating to the following:

- Authorisation such as the checking of expense claims or invoices.
- Performance reviews such as budgetary control or the reviews of amounts due from customers.
- Information processing controls over data entry.
- Physical controls such as password controls and locking valuable assets in the safe.
- Segregation of duties which ensures that the work of one individual is checked by another.

The auditor places a heavy emphasis on understanding and testing the company's controls. If controls are sound then the auditor is able to reduce the quantity of detailed audit work performed.

Planning

Armed with a thorough knowledge of the business, the auditor is now ready to plan the audit. This procedure involves a consideration of where errors are most likely to occur. The auditor describes this process as risk assessment.

The auditor also has a brainstorming meeting involving all of the members of the audit team when the issues of risk and fraud are considered. The auditor tries to identify where fraud or error could occur so that the work can be targeted appropriately.

Once all the knowledge has been gathered and risks assessed, the auditor designs procedures to respond to the risks. The auditor performs some work on all major areas of the accounts but the work is less in the areas considered to be at lower risk.

Performing fieldwork

Auditors perform *fieldwork* when they visit individual offices and locations operated by the company to determine whether the internal controls are actually being implemented properly. For example, if a company requires a certain type of coding when an order is charged to a customer's account and that coding is not being used consistently, some customers may be getting merchandise for which they're not billed.

In the field, auditors may watch a company's employees carry out tasks being reviewed to be sure that they're performing them correctly. However, observation may affect the employees' behaviour so auditors prefer to rely on documentary evidence. For example, if the company requires a manager's signature before a customer is given a refund, the auditor reviews company records of refunds randomly to be sure that signature process is being followed.

Although the top manager at a location probably knows when the auditors are due to arrive, the rest of the staff is usually surprised by their arrival. Any findings during the fieldwork become part of the draft report to management.

After the auditors review internal controls they test various financial transactions to be sure that the proper procedures are being followed. Auditors review records randomly to be sure the staff are completing transactions as specified by internal control procedures.

For example, when auditing the operations of a bank, the auditor wants to know if the bank's procedures for approving a loan are being followed correctly. Random files are probably checked for loans to be sure all needed approvals are in place. When visiting retail stores where refunds of a certain size must be approved by the store's general manager, auditors review the records of refunds to be certain that signature procedures are being followed. The various internal controls auditors decide to test are determined at the planning stage (see 'Planning' earlier in this chapter).

The type of fieldwork required depends on the type of business. Auditors for a bank visit offices in the corporate headquarters, as well as bank branches, to complete their fieldwork. Auditors for a corporation with retail stores do their fieldwork in the corporate headquarters, regional headquarters, and individual retail stores. As well as checking the operation of controls (compliance tests) the auditors also check the accuracy of the amounts in the financial statements (substantive tests). These substantive tests may involve checking that the amounts have been calculated in accordance with accounting standards – for example, that the value of inventory has been calculated using an acceptable method (go to Chapter 15 for more on calculating inventory values).

Substantive tests also involve a consideration of estimates and judgements made by the company's accountants. The company needs ways of estimating what proportion of customers will fail to pay their accounts or what proportion of goods will be returned for credit after the end of the financial year. The auditors check on the estimation methods and assumptions used by the company's management to see if the resulting amounts are reasonable.

As the auditors work in the field, they discuss any significant discrepancies with top management at the field locations. Usually auditors work with management to resolve any problems before they complete the audit report.

The auditors compile a written report to management which includes the issues identified during fieldwork. This report mainly consists of matters that will not be included in the audit report attached to the annual accounts.

Most companies work to fix problems internally and a by-product of the audit is that the auditors help their client to identify areas of weakness. Reports to management are not released publicly. However, if an issue was identified which indicated that the accounts were not true and fair then this would be reported in the audit report issued with the financial statements.

Creating an audit report

After the auditors complete their fieldwork, they finalise their *audit report*, which is attached to the published accounts.

The audit report follows a standard format in accordance with ISA (UK&I) 700. It usually has the following sections:

✔ **Introduction:** Identifies the elements of the financial statements on which the auditors are commenting. Note that the auditors' report never covers the narrative material such as the chairman's report.

✔ **Respective responsibilities of directors and auditors:** Usually includes a statement in which the auditors declare that their report has been prepared solely for the company's members (shareholders) and therefore the auditors do not accept any liability to any other person who might see the report.

✔ **Basis of audit opinion:** Includes a brief summary of what an audit involves. The wording includes phrases such as 'examination, on a test basis, of evidence relevant to the amounts and disclosures in the financial statements', and 'assessment of the significant estimates and judgements made by the directors', and 'whether the accounting policies are appropriate'. These phrases are intended to cover the auditors' backs in the event of later problems.

✔ **Opinion:** Contains three bullet points in the standard unmodified opinion. First, a statement that the financial statements give a true and fair view in accordance with the relevant accounting framework; second, a statement that the financial statements have been prepared in accordance with the Companies Act; and third a statement that the information given in the directors' report is consistent with the financial statements.

An audit report may be modified because the auditors wish to draw attention to a particular matter in the financial statements – this is not a qualified opinion. An audit report is qualified if the auditors disagree with the company's treatment of a problem area or if the auditors are unable to get sufficient information to support the audit opinion. We discuss these issues more in Chapter 5.

Filling the GAAP

The auditors' primary role is to make sure that a company's financial statements are presented fairly and accurately. As part of this, they must ensure that *Generally Accepted Accounting Principles* (GAAP) are followed.

GAAP principles help a company determine the amount of financial information it must disclose and help the company measure its assets, liabilities, revenues, expenses, and equity. That information makes up the financial statements, including the balance sheet (refer to Chapter 6), the income statement (also known as profit and loss statement, look at Chapter 7 for more), and the statement of cash flows (refer to Chapter 8). The GAAP principles list the way in which a company must report the financial information on each line item of the financial statements – these principles fill bookshelves in an accountant's office.

GAAP principles for an accountant are highly technical explanations of how the value of each asset, liability, or equity listed on the balance sheet is calculated. GAAP principles also provide technical detail on how to report revenue and expenses on each line item of the income statement.

Accounting standards: Four important qualities

The primary accounting-standard-setting body for listed companies in the UK is the International Accounting Standards Board (IASB). It's responsible for developing GAAP principles, as well as updating the GAAP principles already developed to reflect changes in the ways companies operate. These changes occur as new ways of doing business become commonplace in the business world.

To be precise, UK listed companies must prepare their group accounts using International Standards as approved by the European Union (EU). In theory, therefore, it is the European Union who is the standard setter. In practice, the EU generally endorses the IASB's standards and, so far, there has only been one standard where the EU has made a variation to the standards laid down by the IASB. This affects the treatment of certain sorts of financial instruments but should not concern you greatly in your reading of the accounts.

For UK companies that are not listed, the standard setting body is the UK Accounting Standards Board (ASB). There are a number of detailed differences between the standards set by the IASB and the standards set by the ASB. However, the ASB is working on converging with international methods and any remaining differences should be ironed out in the medium-term future (say five years or so).

The IASB specifies four qualitative characteristics that make the information provided in financial statements useful to users. These four characteristics form the basis for designing the technical GAAP requirements:

- ✔ **Understandability:** Financial information should be readily understandable by users. However, users are assumed to have a reasonable knowledge of business and economic activities and accounting and a willingness to study the information with reasonable diligence. Not that easy then!

- ✔ **Relevance:** To be useful, information must be relevant to the decision-making needs of users. Relevance of information is also affected by its nature and materiality. Information is material if its omission or misstatement could influence the economic decisions of users taken on the basis of the financial statements.

- ✔ **Reliability:** Information has the quality of reliability when it's free from material error and bias and can be depended upon by users to represent faithfully that which it purports to represent or could reasonably be expected to represent.

✔ **Comparability:** Users must be able to compare the financial statements of an entity through time in order to identify trends in its financial position and performance. Users must also be able to compare the financial statements of different entities. Hence the measurement and disclosure of financial information must be carried out in a consistent way throughout an entity and over time for that entity and in a consistent way for different entities. Since companies may adopt different accounting policies, those policies must be clearly disclosed so that different approaches can be identified.

Changing principles: More work for the IASB

GAAP principles aren't set in stone. As business needs and the way companies do business change, so must the principles. The various standard setters around the world have always addressed new issues as they arise and provided guidance.

But now, the driving force behind change is the desire for convergence. The EU has achieved convergence between the many various approaches used throughout Europe by the adoption of International Financial Reporting Standards (IFRS). This adoption has given the IASB standards a great boost and many other countries have followed the European lead. At the last count, over 90 countries were following IFRS.

The next big challenge is convergence with the US. The approach to accounting standards in the US is more detailed when compared with the UK and IASB approach which are more principles based. The standard setter in the US, the Financial Accounting Standards Board (FASB) has published well over 100 accounting standards compared with the IASB where the number stands at about 40.

The IASB and the FASB are now working together on a number of joint projects. Full convergence looks to be many years away but, at least, progress is being made.

Chapter 19

Checking Out the Analyst–Company Connection

. . . .

In This Chapter

▶ Getting to know the analysts

▶ Exploring the bond raters

▶ Understanding the stock ratings

▶ Talking to analysts

. . . .

A nalysts regularly get into the act not by talking companies through their operational issues but by developing rankings that reflect a company's value. The way analysts rate a company can have a major impact on that company's share price and its value to investors. This chapter reviews the types of analysts and the way a company feeds financial information to them.

Typecasting the Analysts

You may not realise that several different types of analysts master various domains of financial analysis. These analysts, many of whom have completed an MBA and/or a gruelling testing process to get a qualification from bodies such as the Securities and Investment Institute, serve different roles for different people:

✔ **For large investment groups (such as mutual or pension funds):** Determines whether a company's stock price accurately reflects that company's worth and whether the stock fills a particular niche that the group wants to fill in its overall portfolio management objectives.

✔ **For financial institutions:** Analyses a company's debt structure and determines whether the company is bringing in enough money to pay its bills so that the institution can decide whether to lend the company money and at what interest that loan should be made.

✔ **For brokerage houses:** Provides individual investors with analysis about the companies they're considering for their portfolio. Their reports are available to anyone who uses the brokerage house for stock transactions. Unless you have a very large portfolio and can pay the analyst, you won't have an analyst work specifically for you. That's why you need to read and analyse financial reports yourself.

✔ **For bond rating firms:** Reviews a company's debt structure, financial health, and bill-paying ability in order to rate the bonds issued by the companies.

Reports from bond-rating companies are especially helpful because they focus on any debt problems the company may be facing. You can then check out the financial reports yourself and find the red flags more easily.

Regardless of what type of analyst you're dealing with, the one thing you can be sure of as an individual investor is that analysts aren't working for you unless you're the one paying them for developing the information. Instead, they primarily gear their reports to the needs of those who do pay them.

The way analysts view a company can make or break the value of the company's stock. If a well-respected analyst writes a negative report after seeing the financial reports, the share price is guaranteed to drop at least temporarily. Red flags raised by analysts will help you find crucial details you should look for when reading a company's financial reports.

Although analysts can help you find problems, you must do the research and financial analysis yourself before you invest by reading financial reports from the company, as well as stories in the financial press. Remember, an analyst's primary concern is to serve the people or companies that pay him.

The following sections describe the different types of analysts.

Buy-side analysts

Buy-side analysts work primarily for large institutions and investment firms that manage mutual funds, pension funds, or other types of multimillion-pound private accounts. Buy-side analysts are responsible for analysing stocks that portfolio managers are considering for possible purchase and placement in various portfolios managed by their firms. In other words, buy-side analysts' bosses are major institutional buyers of stock. Some buy-side analysts work for mutual funds or pension funds directly; others work for independent analyst firms hired by the mutual funds or pension funds. You rarely see this type of analyst's research available on the public market, but much of the information does trickle out in the financial press through statements made by fund managers.

Buy-side analysts write reports that help portfolio managers determine whether the stock fits the firm's portfolio management strategy. Even a stock that most analysts would pan may get a positive report inside a buy-side analytical shop. For example, if the portfolio managers are looking for candidates for a value portfolio made up of stocks currently beaten down by the market but with good potential to rebound, buy-side analysts for this portfolio manager may recommend buying a share that has just lost half its value.

A portfolio manager is selecting a share to fill a particular niche he wants to fill in his fund portfolio. That might not be the best share to balance out what you need in your own portfolio. Managers of funds that focus on growth shares will be looking at companies that fill that niche. Managers of funds that focus on foreign shares will be looking for companies that fit that objective.

Find.co.uk is one of the leading portals that, amongst other things, rate mutual funds for individual investors. It's a good place to get ideas for possible additions to your share portfolio. On the Web site www.find.co.uk, you find, among other things, listings of funds set out in the order of their performance over five years. You also frequently find stories about which shares mutual fund managers are buying and why they're buying them. Of course, you can't just buy shares based on these stories. You need to read the financial reports yourself and do your own analysis of these reports.

Sell-side analysts

As an individual investor, you are most likely see reports from *sell-side analysts*. These analysts work for brokerage houses or other financial institutions that sell shares to individual investors. You get reports written by these analysts when you ask your broker for research on a particular stock.

You can't take everything you get from sell-side analysts as gospel. Their primary purpose is to help the company's salespeople make sales. As long as your interests match the interests of the broker and brokerage house, the sell-side analytical reports can be helpful. But as scandals that were exposed after the Internet and technology stock crash of 2000 have shown (see the sidebar 'Analysing the analysts'), conflicts of interest can exist between a brokerage house's need to make money by selling shares and an individual investor's need to make money by owning shares that go up in value.

Analysing the analysts

During the scandal-ridden technology crash of 2000, sell-side analysts working for brokerage houses were caught between the needs of their firms' investment banking division (which sells new public offering of shares or bonds and arranges mergers and acquisitions) to help sell the new offerings handled by that division and the needs of their firms' individual investors, who were clients of the salespeople. The investment banking side won, and individual investors got ripped off.

By writing glowing reports about the shares or bonds involved in potential or current investment banking deals, sell-side analysts helped pull in new investment banking clients and kept existing clients happy. While the brokerage houses made millions on investment banking deals, individual investors lost big chunks of their portfolios buying the recommended stocks that later went sour. Many of the stocks recommended by the sell-side analysts dropped dramatically in value after the market crash of 2000, leaving investors with

ruined portfolios filled with worthless shares. Overall, investors lost billions.

New York State Attorney General Eliot Spitzer helped expose this entire mess by unearthing e-mails from superstar analysts like Henry Blodget of Merrill Lynch, who wrote great reports about stocks being sold by his investment banking divisions while privately calling these stocks 'dogs', 'junk', and 'toast'. Spitzer charged that Blodget's recommendations helped bring in $115 million in investment banking fees for Merrill Lynch. Blodget got rich, too. He took home about $12 million in compensation, according to Spitzer's findings.

Merrill Lynch wasn't the only company exposed during Spitzer's investigation. Other firms caught in his net included Morgan Stanley Dean Witter & Co., and Credit Suisse First Boston. In fact, most brokerage houses on both sides of the pond that have an investment banking division got caught up in the scandal.

Many brokerage houses were more concerned about making money by selling shares than they were about helping investors put together share portfolios that met their goals and taking into consideration the amount of risk they wanted to take. Many investors lost 50 per cent or more of the money they had invested in shares during the 1990s and early 2000s before the stock market crashed. They were not well served by the analysts, who should have been accurately reporting the risks of investing in many of the companies whose financial reports they analysed for investors.

You must take the responsibility yourself to read and analyse reports. You can't depend on an analyst unless you pay that analyst out of your own pocket to do the analysis.

TECHNICAL STUFF

General principles of regulation

Brokers and bankers are regulated by the Financial Services Authority. Similar to the Security Exchange Commission in the US, the FSA holds its members to strict codes of practice. Unlike in the US, these regulations are not necessarily built into the law. But if you deal with an organisation that is regulated by the FSA you should find that it adheres to the following general principles as well as a whole raft of detailed requirements:

✔ **Integrity:** A firm must conduct its business with integrity.

✔ **Skill care and diligence:** A firm must conduct its business with due skill, care, and diligence.

✔ **Management and control:** A firm must take reasonable care to organise and control its affairs responsibly and effectively with adequate risk management systems.

✔ **Financial prudence:** A firm must maintain adequate financial resources.

✔ **Market conduct:** A firm must observe proper standards of market conduct.

✔ **Customers' interests:** A firm must pay due regard to the interests of its customers and treat them fairly.

✔ **Communication with clients:** A firm must pay due regard to the information needs of its clients, and communicate information to them in a way which is clear, fair, and not misleading.

✔ **Conflicts of interest:** A firm must manage conflicts of interest fairly, both between itself and between a customer and another client.

✔ **Customer: relationships of trust:** A firm must take reasonable care to ensure the suitability of its advice and discretionary decisions for any customer who is entitled to rely upon its judgement.

✔ **Clients' assets:** A firm must arrange adequate protection for clients' assets when it is responsible for them.

✔ **Relations with regulators:** A firm must deal with its regulators in an open and co-operative way, and must disclose to the FSA appropriately anything relating to the firm of which the FSA would reasonably expect notice.

Brokerage companies used to avoid scandals and conflicts of interest by protecting themselves with what's called a *Chinese wall*. Analysts kept their work separate from the investment banking division (which sells new public offerings of stocks or bonds and arranges mergers and acquisitions), and their remuneration wasn't dependent on what business they helped to bring in. At some point in the past 20 years, this wall broke down, and sell-side analysts became partners with the investment banking side to help the firm make money. If a company won new investment banking business, it rewarded analysts with fees or commissions.

As an investor, you can quickly determine whether there's a conflict between your interests and the financial interests of the brokerage house or analyst when you see the new disclosures required in any transaction that you undertake. Read the small print. You can also look at the brokerage house's historical ratings for a company's shares and see how successful it has been in accurately reporting the share's value in the past. The City generally is sensitive to accusations of ripping off the 'little people' and therefore you should take action and complain if you ever think that a firm you are dealing with has infringed any of these guidelines.

When you read a sell-side analyst's report and see that the brokerage firm gets fees for investment banking services from the company that's the subject of the report, realise that the brokerage firm makes more money from its investment banking business than it does from you. Take what you find to be useful from the report, but be sure to do your own additional research.

Independent analysts

You may wonder if you can depend on any analysts out there. Well, the answer is yes and no. Certainly, some independent analyst groups – those that are *not* paid by a brokerage house or other financial institution but provide reports for a fee paid by people who want them – report on companies as well. The problem is that independent analyst groups work for people who can afford to pay them, meaning that you must have a portfolio of at least half a million pounds or you must be able to pay a large annual fee. Few individual investors meet the criteria to access the confidential reports of independent analysts because they can't afford to pay the price to access them.

Many independent analysts do sell the reports through financial Web sites for a per-report fee to individuals who are researching a specific company. Your general rule about independent analysts' reports should be to take what information you find useful, but be sure to do additional research on your own. The report you buy from the independent analyst on a particular company is one that was developed for one of the analyst's clients and not specifically for you.

After reading about analysts, you may think you don't have a chance to get good information from any analyst. Your best place to find research that isn't tainted by the investment banking business of your brokerage firm is to visit the Web sites of major investment research firms like Dun and Bradstreet (www.dnb.co.uk) and Standard & Poor's (www.standardandpoors.co.uk). You have to pay fees to access their confidential services, but they're much more reasonable than those of an independent analyst whom you might hire as an individual and can be as low as £100 per year, depending on what information you need.

Bond analysts

Bond analysts are most concerned about the liquidity of a company and the company's ability to make its interest payments, repay its debt principal, and pay its bills.

Bond analysts evaluate financial reports, management quality, the competitive environment, and overall economic conditions, but they do so with a cautious eye. If bond analysts make a mistake, they're likely to err on the side of caution. Many people believe bond analysts actually provide the best source of objective company research available to individual investors. Most of these bond analysts work for independent bond rating agencies, as we describe in the next section.

When you're looking to buy shares, pay attention to the warnings of bond analysts. You certainly don't want to invest in a company that can't meet its financial obligations and may go bankrupt. Use bond analysts' red flags to help you find the critical information when you read and analyse financial reports yourself.

Regarding Bond Rating Agencies

Bond ratings have a great impact on a company's operations and the cost of funding its operations. The quality rating of a company's bonds determines how much interest the company will have to offer to pay in order to sell the bonds on the public bond market. Bonds that are rated with a higher quality rating are considered less risky, so the interest rates that must be paid to attract individuals or companies that will buy those bonds can be lower. Bonds with the lowest ratings, which are also known as *junk bonds*, require companies that issue these bonds to pay much higher interest rates to attract individuals or companies that will buy those bonds.

Bonds are a type of debt for a company. The individual or company that buys a bond is lending money to the company that it expects to get back. The company must pay interest on the money that it is borrowing from these bondholders.

Building bond rating's big guns

Standard and Poor's is one of the premiere bond-rating firms. The company's founder, Henry Varnum Poor, built his financial information company on the 'investor's right to know'. His first attempt at providing this type of financial information can be found in his 1860 book, *History of Railroads and Canals of the United States,* where he included financial information about the railroad industry. Today, Standard & Poor's is a leader in independent credit ratings, risk evaluation, and investment research. It has the largest cadre of credit (bond and other debts) analysts in the world, totalling 1,250 around the globe.

John Moody started his rating service in 1909 and was the first to rate public market securities. He adopted a letter-rating system from the mercantile exchange and credit-rating system that had been used since the late 1800s. By 1924, Moody's ratings covered nearly 100 per cent of the US bond market. It is now a global company servicing most countries in Europe. To this day, Moody's prides itself on ratings based on public information and is written by independent analysts who don't answer to the requests of bond issuers.

You should be familiar with the three key rating agencies, all based in the US but all with subsidiaries in the UK and other European countries where you can find out what bond analysts think:

- ✔ **Standard & Poor's:** You've probably heard of Standard & Poor's because of its S&P 500, which is a collection of 500 stocks that form the basis for a *stock market index* (a portfolio of stocks for which a change in price is carefully watched) in the US. The equivalent in the UK is the FTSE 100, a list of the biggest 100 companies listed on the London Stock Exchange. From time to time the FTSE 100 is revised adding some companies and taking others off. Many funds base their portfolios on this index, which is seen as one of the best indicators of stock market performance. When a company is added to the list, its share price usually goes up; when it's taken off the list, its share price usually drops. You can find the list on the company's Web site at www.ft.com. The credit rating agency Standard & Poor's is at www.standardandpoors.com.

- ✔ **Moody's Investor Service:** Moody's specialises in credit ratings, research, and risk analysis, tracking more than $30 trillion of debt issued in the US domestic market as well as debt issued in the international markets. In addition to its credit rating services, Moody's publishes investor-oriented credit research, which you can access at www.moodys.com and navigate to the UK data.

✔ **Fitch Ratings:** The youngest of the three major bond-rating services is Fitch Ratings (www.fitchratings.com). John Knowles Fitch founded Fitch Publishing Company in 1913. The company started as a publisher of financial statistics. In 1924, Fitch introduced the credit-rating scales that are very familiar today: 'AAA' to 'D'. Fitch is best known for its research in the area of complex credit deals and is thought to provide more rigorous surveillance than other rating agencies on such deals.

The UK also has many other bond rating and investor advice companies but they tend to be smaller and more specialised than the big three. The big three are so well established in the UK that, at the date of writing, they are the only bodies recognised by the Financial Services Authority as External Credit Assessment Institutions for the purpose of assessing risk when calculating capital resources of investment firms.

Each bond-rating company has its own alphabetical coding for rating bonds and other types of credit issues, such as commercial paper (which are shorter-term debt issues than bonds).

Table 19–1 shows how companies' bond ratings compare.

Table 19–1	Bond Ratings		
Bond Quality	*Moody's*	*Standard & Poor's*	*Fitch*
Best quality	Aaa	AAA	AAA
High quality	Aa	AA	AA
Upper medium grade	A	A	A
Medium grade	Baa	BBB	BBB
Speculative	Ba	BB	BB
Highly speculative	B	B	B
High default risk	Caa or Ca	CCC or CC	CCC, CC, or C
In default	N/A	D	DDD, DD, or D

Any company bonds rated in the 'highly speculative' category or lower are considered to be junk bonds. Companies in the 'best quality' category have the lowest interest rates, and interest rates go up as companies' ratings drop. A key job of any company's executive team is to feed bond analysts critical financial data to keep a company's ratings high. Financial reports are one major component of that information.

Standard & Poor's (S&P) makes its bond ratings publicly available with links on its Web site home page. You can search for information about any company's debt ratings.

Whenever a change occurs in the ratings, the rating services issue an extensive explanation about why the company's ratings have changed. The press releases issued by the rating companies explaining these changes can be an excellent source of information if you're looking for opinions on the numbers you see in the financial reports. You can find these press releases on the bond rating companies' Web sites, as well as in news links on financial Web sites.

Delving Into Share Rating

Share rating is a much different game than bond rating. Although bond raters err on the side of caution, share raters, who for general public consumption are primarily sell-side analysts, seem to err on the side of optimism. You rarely find a share with a *sell rating* (a recommendation to sell the stock). In fact, when analysts recommend a *hold rating* (which is intended to mean you should hold the share, but probably not buy more) experienced investors understand it to mean sell.

Just as with bond ratings, each firm, including stockbrokers, has its own vocabulary when rating shares. A *strong buy* from one firm may be called a *buy* in another firm and may be on the *recommended* list in a third firm. You can never know which company is right, but after following a firm's share ratings for a while, you can understand how their systems work and how accurate they are compared with what actually happens to the price on the stock market. We don't put much faith in the share analyst rating system, and you shouldn't, either.

Because various companies' rankings may differ dramatically, you need to check out ratings from several different firms and research what each firm means by its ratings. A share that's rated as a 'market outperformer' may sound pretty good. But in reality, it may not be a good investment, which may become clear when you compare rankings of other firms and find that they consider the company a 'neutral' or 'hold' stock.

As you start doing independent research on a company after reading its financial reports, take every thing you read with a grain of salt. Collect all the information you can and then do your own analysis of the information you gather. In Part III of this book, we show you how to analyse the numbers in financial reports.

Looking at How Companies Talk to Analysts

Companies not only send out financial reports to analysts, but they also talk with analysts regularly about their reports. Sometimes you have access to what is said by reading analysts' responses to briefings or reading press releases.

Analyst briefings

Each time a company releases a new financial report, it usually schedules an analyst and press briefing to discuss the results. Usually, these briefings include the chairman, chief executive officer (CEO), and chief financial officer (CFO), as well as other top managers.

The briefings usually start with a statement from one or more of the company representatives and then are opened to those listening for questions. In most cases, only some analysts and sometimes the financial press are allowed to ask questions. Their reports on these briefings can be quite useful as the analysts and journalists should have probed for the companies' weaknesses and then written them up.

In the US private investors can attend some of these briefings, or analyst calls, in person. The biggest advantage of listening to these briefings is that analysts ask questions of the executives that help you focus on the areas of concern in the financial reports. Turn to Chapter 20 to find out a little more about analyst briefings in the US.

Press releases

Companies often feed information to analysts through press releases. Luckily, individual investors can easily access these press releases on financial Web sites and the companies' own sites. But remember that press releases are always going to be only what the company wants you to know. Learn to read between the lines and ask questions of the investor relations department for the company releasing the information if something concerns you.

The financial journalists' comments on the press releases, which are written after the press release is issued, are probably a more important source of information. Companies put out a lot more press releases than there are stories printed in the paper about those releases. In fact, most press releases end up in the wastepaper basket, and you never see them in the newspaper because a financial reporter determines the information isn't worth a story.

You can easily track press releases online. A good Web site for following not only a company's press releases, but also any stories mentioning the company, is www.FT.com. You can find out about any recent press coverage for a company by searching the Web site using the company's name or multi-letter abbreviation for the company's shares. You can find links to recent press coverage and press releases by typing press releases and the name of the company into the search box. If you want to go further back in history, most companies post at least three years' worth of press releases in the press section of their Web sites.

Road shows

Companies use road shows to introduce new securities issues, such as initial stock or bond offerings. Road shows are presentations by the company and its investment bankers to the analyst community and other major investors in the hope of building interest in the new public offering. As an individual investor, you're unlikely to be able to attend these shows unless you're a major investor.

Chapter 20

How Companies Soothe the Shareholders

In This Chapter

▶ Attending annual shareholder meetings
▶ Continuing to invest by using company incentive programmes
▶ Using company communications on the Web

*H*appy shareholders don't necessarily mean a happy company, but they're a good start. Although a company collects most of the money generated from share transactions at the time when the share is first sold to the public during an initial or secondary public offering, shareholders still hold a bit of power over management. Angry shareholders showed what their wrath could do when their lack of support for Disney CEO Michael Eisner helped oust him from the chairmanship of the board in 2004. In the UK, investors in Spirent voted against the board in favour of a takeover by Sherborne Investors, causing the ousting of the main board executives.

Sending out half-yearly and annual reports aren't the only strategies companies use to keep their shareholders informed and happy. Other activities include annual general meetings, extraordinary meetings, Web site services, e-mails, share-investment plans, and individual investor contact. In this chapter, we review the steps that companies take to inform their investors of operations and to respond to any investor concerns.

Knowing What to Expect from an Annual General Meeting

A company must, at the very least, hold an *annual general meeting* for its shareholders. These events are often gala affairs that are more like a carefully orchestrated pep rally than a place where you can get solid information. The company's top officers make presentations highlighting what they want you to know and put on a show that closely resembles what you can find in the glossy portion of an annual report.

The big advantage of being at the company's annual general meeting is that you can ask questions, which you can't do if you just read the financial reports at home. Prepare yourself before the meeting by reading the recent financial reports, as well as annual reports for the past couple of years, so you're fully armed with detail about what has gone on in the past. Make a list of questions that you want answered by the company's executives so you're ready to ask them when they open up the floor for questions.

If you're a shareholder, the company notifies you about the date and location of the meeting. Note that if shareholders are unhappy with the corporation's board or its executives, annual general meetings can turn into major shouting matches when the floor is opened to questions and comments. In addition to asking questions, shareholders vote on any open issues.

Almost every annual general meeting includes the election of at least some members of the board of directors. Most companies stagger the election of board members over a number of years so that the entire board doesn't change in one year.

Other issues that involve major changes to the way the company does business are also voted on. For example, if the company plans a major change in executive remuneration, it's voted on at the annual general meeting. In the past shareholders rarely interfered with boardroom pay but there have been a number of shareholder revolts against some very large compensation packages that directors were proposing to pay each other.

Sometimes, shareholders add their own issues to the agenda. For example, environmentalists who own shares in the company may seek a shareholder vote on how a company gets rid of its waste (to ensure that controls to protect the environment are in place) or how a company develops land it owns near a wildlife preserve (to be sure wildlife is protected during and after construction).

Innovative companies see annual general meetings as a way to communicate effectively with their investor base. The problem for many companies is that most shareholders don't show up. But the Internet can help reach shareholders who don't attend. Some companies place all their meeting materials on a Web site, and some companies also webcast the meeting itself and archive it for shareholders who aren't able to watch it on the Web site when the meeting takes place. HBOS is a good example of this.

Culling Information from the Annual General Meeting

Today, investors get information not only by reading press releases or newspapers, but also by attending annual general meetings. (See the preceding section 'Knowing What to Expect from an Annual General Meeting' for more information on these meetings.) Special events – such as a change in company leadership or the purchase of another company – can also prompt companies to set up extraordinary general meetings. By listening at these meetings, you usually get more details about whatever issues are being discussed.

The company's chief executive officer (CEO), chairman, and chief financial officer (CFO) typically participate. They usually start by discussing the recently released financial reports or by explaining the impact that any special event has on the company; then they usually open the meeting to questions.

The question-and-answer part of the meeting is often the most revealing. During this portion of the meeting, you can judge how confident senior managers are about the financial information that they're reporting. Questions from the audience usually elicit information that press releases or the annual or half-yearly reports haven't revealed. Analysts and big institutional investors rarely ask the questions since they can talk to directors on a different platform; you can learn a lot by listening to conversations between directors and investors.

Listen closely to how the company's senior managers answer questions. Often during this question-and-answer period, management answers many questions that you may have. If not, don't hesitate to write or call the investor relations department of the company to get an answer to a specific question you may have about the financial report or the special event discussed during a meeting.

The language participants use at such a meeting is different from the language you use every day. Familiarise yourself with the most commonly used terms before attending your first meeting. We list most of the key terms and abbreviations used during the meetings in Part III of this book, where we discuss analysing the numbers. Get comfortable with terms like *earnings per share* (EPS), *EPS growth, net income, cash,* and *cash equivalents.*

If you hear a term you don't understand, write it down, and research it after the meeting. Then the next time you go to one, you'll have a better understanding of what's being discussed.

Listening between the lines

Pay attention to how the executives handle the meeting and to the words they use. When management is pleased with the results, you usually hear very upbeat terms, and they talk about how positive things look for the future of the company. When management is disappointed with the numbers, they're more apologetic, and the mood of the meeting is more low-key. Rather than talk about a rosy future, they'll probably explain ways in which they can improve the disappointing results.

You'll most likely need to listen to more than one meeting held by a particular company before you start picking up the nuances and moods of the executives. Try attending as many meetings of those companies whose shares you own as you can. Whether a shareholder or not you can listen to a recording of it after it occurs. Many companies post recordings of their annual general meetings on their Web sites, just like they post press releases.

Take the time to read the financial reports before the meeting so you're at least familiar with the key points that management will discuss during the meeting. After you've attended a meeting and read the press reports about a particular company, you'll find that the information management discusses will become much clearer to you.

Here are a few areas you'll want to pay attention to:

✔ **Earnings expectations:** All meetings about a company's financial results include information about whether or not a company has met its own earnings projections or the projections of financial analysts. If a company misses its own earnings projections, the mood of the meeting will be downbeat, and the share price is likely to drop dramatically after the meeting if it has not already done so in advance of the meeting.

That doesn't mean you must sell the shares you own, if you happen to be a shareholder. In fact, if you're at the meeting because you think you'd like to buy more shares, you might want to do so after the share price is driven down by the bad news. The key for you as a shareholder is to analyse what is being said and whether you think the company does have a good chance of turning around the bad news. Good news, on the other hand, can drive the share price higher. Be careful not to jump on the bandwagon right after major good news is announced. Usually, the share price will fall back down to a more realistic price once the initial rush to buy is completed.

✔ **Revenue growth:** Listen for information about the company's revenue growth and whether it has kept pace with its earnings growth. During an economic slowdown, watching revenue growth becomes very important, because a company can play with the numbers to make them look better. In fact, some companies practise what is called 'window dressing' (using accounting tricks to make a company's financial statements look better) to make sure their earnings meet expectations. Earnings growth is easier to manipulate than revenue, so earnings usually become part of that window dressing. Growth in revenue is the key to continued earnings growth in the future. We talk more in Chapter 22 about how a company can manipulate its results.

If you hear numerous questions about revenue-growth figures, such questions may be a sign that shareholders suspect a problem with the numbers or are very disappointed with the results. When you hear shareholders' questions about revenue or any other issues over and over again, take a closer look at these numbers yourself. Do further analysis and research before you decide to buy or sell the company's stock.

You may find judging the mood of the shareholders or the company executives hard when you go to your first meeting, but as you research more and more about the same company, you'll be able to judge more easily the mood of meetings, press releases, and other types of information flow.

You can judge whether or not the executives are confident in their reporting by how quickly they answer questions. When executives are comfortable and confident in the numbers that they're reporting, they answer questions quickly, without rustling through papers. If they're very cautious with their answers and are constantly taking time to look through their papers, you can be sure they're not comfortable with the report and must carefully check themselves before answering the questions. Sometimes, they may take a long time to answer a simple question. If company executives seem unsure or respond slowly, take this as a red flag that you need to do a lot more homework before making any decisions about buying more shares or selling the shares of that company.

Looking towards the future

Listen to the vision that the company's executives portray for the future. Does the vision they present inspire you, or do you think the executives didn't present a clear vision for the company's future and how they plan to get there? If you find the executives uninspiring, there's a good chance that they're not doing a good job of inspiring their employees either. If you see a downward trend in the company, the lack of inspiration may be one of the reasons for that trend. When company executives lack inspiration for the company's future, you have good reason to stay away from investing in that company.

Keeping employees happy is important for the future of any company. During meetings, you can judge whether or not employees are satisfied by listening for information about the success or failure the company is having attracting new employees or retaining existing ones. If the company reports a problem with either of these two things, trouble may be on the horizon. High employee turnover is bad for the growth of any company. And if a company has trouble finding and recruiting qualified employees, that, too, is a bad sign for the future.

Don't ever plan to buy or sell shares based only on what you hear during meetings or read from material the company sends you or puts on its Web site. Use them as one more way to gather information about a share that you're thinking of buying or for tracking shares that you already own.

Checking Out How the Board Runs the Company

Corporate governance is the way a board of directors conducts its own business and oversees a corporation's operations. Ultimately, the board of directors is liable for every decision that the company makes, but in reality, only major shifts in the way the company operates make it to the board for decision. Most day-to-day decisions are made by the company's executives and managers: Shareholders need to know about the major decisions that are taken up to the board. For example, if the executives recommend that the company take on a new product line that would involve a large investment of cash, the board would be consulted for this decision.

CEOs get better rises

From the summer of 2005 to the summer of 2006 average CEO remuneration packages increased by 28 per cent. This compares with inflation running at 2.8 per cent. This increase is also well above average wage increases across the whole economy which stood at 4 per cent. Despite this the chairman of one FTSE 100 company simply brushed aside concerns over soaring directors' pay saying that annual rises in excess of inflation are 'simply a fact of corporate life'.

Executive pay has become a significant issue as a result of this and other statistics. Indeed shareholders revolted over the pay package that GlaxoSmithKline proposed for its senior executives. Another primary concern is when the company underperforms and the CEO is forced to resign but walks away with massive payments received under their contractual arrangements.

For these and other reasons shareholders owe it to themselves, and each other, to take an interest and, if possible, attend companies' annual general meetings.

The shareholder landscape changed dramatically after the corporate scandals of the 2000s exposed severe corporate governance problems, beginning with the collapse of Enron. Today, shareholder groups, many led by institutional investors such as pension plans and mutual funds that own large blocks of shares in various companies, closely watch the following four major issues in the companies in which they own shares.

- ✔ **Composition of the board of directors:** Shareholder groups monitor the make-up of the board, how board members are chosen, and how many members serving on the board are truly independent – meaning that they're not directly involved in the day-to-day operations of the company. Outsiders prefer that a majority of the members of the board of directors are non-executive directors – that is, they're not involved in the day-to-day operations of the company. They are committed to the long-term success of the company but not if it tries to take short cuts on, for example, health and safety. They also look for unnecessary risks and any skirting around legal considerations.

- ✔ **Remuneration packages for board members and CEOs:** These details are on public record now in the annual report. In addition, shareholders must approve of, or be notified of, any major benefits or compensation offered to the company's executives, such as *share-option plans* (offers to buy company stock at prices below market value). Shareholders complain bitterly if they believe executives are receiving excessive remuneration.

✔ **Takeover defences and protections:** In some cases, board members place defences against the possibility of a takeover of the company. For example, Comcast unsuccessfully attempted a hostile takeover of Disney during the famous battle between shareholders, led by Roy Disney, who was attempting to oust Eisner. Sometimes these defences help protect shareholders from a corporate raider that wants to buy the company and sell off the pieces, which can leave shareholders with shares worth very little. Other times, these defences prevent the takeover by some other company that may benefit the shareholders but not the current management team and board of directors (especially if the leadership ranks would change under the new owners, and they could lose their jobs). Shareholder groups watch whatever takeover defences or protection are put into place by the board to be sure the best interests of the shareholders are being protected, not just the best interests of the directors and the management team.

✔ **Audits:** A primary responsibility of the board of directors is to review the audits of the company's books and be certain that they're being done properly by both the internal and the external auditors. Good corporate governance requires that independent board members make up audit committees. Prior to the Enron scandal, many audit committees (even if they existed) weren't independently run, which allowed company insiders to control not only how the money was spent, but also how the money was being recorded in the company's books and how the financial results were reported to outsiders. This insidious practice allowed top executives to more easily hide any misdeeds or misuse of funds. (For more on audits, refer to Chapter 18.)

Speaking Out at Meetings: Proxy Votes

Shareholders can voice their opinions during any type of meeting called by the board of directors to address a specific issue. At these meetings, shareholders cast weighted votes based on the number of shares they hold. These weighted votes are called *proxy votes*. If board members aren't responsive to shareholder concerns on any of the issues in the list in the preceding section 'Checking Out How the Board Runs the Company', they might find themselves defending a major challenge at the annual general meeting.

Prior to the Enron scandal, a shareholder rarely brought forth an issue for the rest of the shareholders to vote on; usually, the company's board of directors controlled what the shareholders voted on. If a shareholder issue even made it to the point of being voted on by the other shareholders, it rarely had a chance of passing. Today, shareholders are more successful at getting issues on the agenda to be voted on at an annual general meeting; sometimes, they win the proxy vote, and sometimes, they lose.

Hewlett-Packard's costly clash

Walter Hewlett, son of one of the co-founders of Hewlett-Packard, led one of the most costly battles with a CEO and a board of directors when he tried to stop a merger with Compaq. Hewlett lost the fight with the CEO and the board of directors when the final vote of the shareholders ended in approving the merger.

Hewlett reported that he spent $32 million on his attempt to stop the merger. Financial analysts speculated that Hewlett-Packard's board of directors, led by CEO Carly Fiorina, spent at least twice that amount on advertising in the major media markets where most of Hewlett-Packard's shareholders lived, plus on other actions, to defend its merger decision.

In addition to the costly advertising, Hewlett-Packard's board racked up about $70 million in expenses to defend its merger decision, including an estimated $3 million to individually call its shareholders and another $25 million in mailings to its shareholders. Hewlett-Packard also paid $33.5 million to investment banker Goldman Sachs, which handled the merger deal. Analysts guesstimate that Hewlett-Packard's total cost for this fiasco was $100 to $125 million, and a good portion of that money was necessary only because of the shareholder battle.

A proxy fight can cost a corporation millions of pounds no matter who wins; the preparation and mailing of the opposing arguments costs money and some of these battles go on for months and even years.

Moving away from battling it out

Since the success of a number of shareholder fights, companies have been finding ways to negotiate with unhappy shareholders rather than fight it out in a proxy vote.

To avoid a costly proxy fight, boards of directors negotiate with unhappy shareholders, normally large institutional investors, by meeting with them quietly behind closed doors and discussing the issues upon which they disagree, with the hope that they can find a solution that both sides can accept. If the shareholders and the board of directors fail to find common ground, a proxy fight is likely. Knowing that a proxy fight can cost millions, more corporations are wising up to the fact that they should listen to their shareholders.

Major leaders of proxy fights are large institutional shareholders, along with the help of pension funds and some mutual funds. These large institutional investors hold large blocks of shares in their pension or mutual-fund portfolios, so they have a lot to lose if a company doesn't do what they believe it should do.

Many times, the issues include the way in which the board of directors operates and how many independent directors will serve on the board and its various committees. The committee these groups are most concerned about is the audit committee. Shareholder groups want the audit committee to be made up primarily of independent board members to be sure that the audits are done in their best interests and not the best interests of the company insiders.

Sorting through reports and proxy votes

Sending out reports on an annual and biannual basis is the primary way a corporation informs its shareholders about its performance. Usually, the corporation sends the annual report before the annual general meeting along with information on the votes that will take place at the meeting. Proxy information is a critical part of the annual report package sent to investors. Voting by proxy is the primary way shareholders get to voice their position on board decisions.

The communication includes information about proxy votes, along with the board of directors' position on any issues that will be presented at the annual general meeting. If the board brings an issue to the shareholders for a vote, the board explains the issue and its position. If a group other than the board brings the issue to the shareholders, the board states the issue and discusses why it's in favour of, or opposed to, the issue. In most cases, the board opposes issues brought by outside sources.

The group bringing the issue to the shareholders, or opposing an issue that the board decided to bring to the shareholders, is also likely to send out its position to the shareholders. In fact, Walter Hewlett spent about $15 million mailing information to Hewlett-Packard shareholders in an attempt to stop the merger with Compaq, which we discuss in the sidebar 'Hewlett-Packard's costly clash'.

Catching Up on Corporate Actions

Corporations must report special events to their shareholders as soon as the event can *materially impact* (affect the profits or losses of a company) the results of the company. The most common special events might include:

- **Acquisitions:** Before a company can finalise plans to acquire another company, it must report those plans to its shareholders.

- **Class-action lawsuits:** If a company is the defendant in a class-action lawsuit that can have a material impact on its results in the future, the company must report the lawsuit and discuss its potential impact with company shareholders.

✔ **Mergers:** If two companies plan on merging, the companies' management must not only inform their shareholders but also ask their shareholders to vote on the merger. If the shareholders in either company vote against the merger, the deal will probably be cancelled. Sometimes companies may revise the deal and attempt a second shareholder vote.

✔ **Dividends:** Whenever the board decides to pay dividends, it has to report that information to the shareholders. Of course, dividends are one of the few things that boards enjoy reporting, so they usually make a very public announcement about it to shareholders.

✔ **Bonus issue:** A *bonus issue* or *share split* is when the board decides to make one share worth more than one share. For example, a bonus issue may be two shares for one, which means that each shareholder gets two shares for each share that they hold. Usually a company announces a bonus issue when it believes the price of its share is too high for the market. So a share that sells for £10 before a two-for-one share split will sell for £5 a share after the split.

In short, a company must give its shareholders the low-down on anything that materially impacts the value of the company.

Buying shares carries risk

As a client of a stockbroker you can use what is known as an execution only service. This is the cheapest way of using stockbrokers since they merely process the transaction you request, and have no part in advising you which shares you should buy or sell.

Alternatively you can ask the stockbroker for its advisory service and they will make recommendations for you to follow or reject. They do this, of course, for a fee.

Another possibility is to choose to have the stockbroker run the whole portfolio and then you have no part in the decision making process at all. This tends to be the most expensive way of operating.

If you decide to deal through Independent Financial Advisors, choose them carefully. Make sure they have experience of people who are seeking the same kind of advice as you are: it's an extremely difficult choice and personal recommendation from a friend or family member may be the best way to go. Make sure also that they go through the proper procedures before selling you a product. Once again you can agree that they should advise you and make recommendations or merely show you their products. To do this they need to do an extensive fact find to understand the detail of your financial position and needs. Don't forget that in all circumstances the IFAs have to make a living, by you paying them a fee or by taking commissions on the products they sell you from the insurance company or other provider. This potential commission gives them an unhealthy bias towards recommending those products that make them the most money.

Staying Up-to-Date Using Company Web Sites

The Internet provides an excellent way for companies to stay in touch with their investors. Companies can include an unlimited number of pages on Web sites that investors can access whenever it's convenient for them. Because investors can print multiple copies of the information provided online for free, the company doesn't have to worry about the expenses of providing thousands of pages of information to its investors.

In addition to basic information – such as company headquarters, addresses, phone numbers, and key executives – many companies post their company's history, market share, vision and mission statements, credit ratings, and share dividend history. In addition, many companies post all the information from their annual general meetings and financial reports, as well as press releases and key executives' speeches. So the Internet is a handy tool that gives investors greater access to company activities and helps the company keep its investors better informed – which improves the company's long-term relations with its investors.

After reading the information provided, investors who have a question can find information about who to contact and how to contact the company by phone, Internet chat room, or e-mail. On many company Web sites, investors can also order paper copies of previous annual and biannual reports that are up to five years old.

Chapter 21

Keeping Score When Companies Play Games with Numbers

In This Chapter

▶ Discovering the methods of creative accounting

▶ Finding massaged company earnings

▶ Recognising beefed-up revenues

▶ Spotting expense-cutting strategies

▶ Detecting cash-flow games

Companies cooking the books – and we don't mean throwing them in a raging fire in disgust – fuelled a game of hide-and-seek among company outsiders that resulted in billion-dollar losses for investors over the past few years. In some cases, company insiders used numerous tactics to deceive their shareholders and pad their own pockets.

Throughout most of this book, we concentrate on reading financial reports that accurately portray the financial status of a company, but unfortunately that isn't always the case. The pressure companies face to meet the expectations of the City drive many companies to play with their numbers. When expectations aren't met, the company's share price is beaten down, which lowers the market value of the company. Sometimes this game to meet expectations goes beyond legal methods to fraud and deception.

In this chapter, we review the primary tools that companies use to hide their financial problems and to deceive the public and the government.

Getting to the Bottom of Creative Accounting

Enron, once the world's largest energy trader, now lives in infamy as the host of one of the world's largest accounting scandals. After the company declared bankruptcy in 2001, Congress enacted legislation to correct the flaws in the US financial reporting system and protect investors and consumers from misleading accounting practices. But corporate lobbyists are powerful, and no doubt it won't be long before Congress deems the new laws 'too burdensome' for companies and weakens them by passing new legislation.

In the meantime, the public's faith in corporate financial accounting has taken a nosedive, in large part because of the glut of 'creative accounting' that came to light in the US during the late 1990s. Companies that practise creative accounting deviate from generally accepted accounting principles. The financial reports they issue use loopholes in financial laws in ways that are, at the very least, misleading, and in some cases illegal, to gain an advantage for the company over the users of those financial reports.

In the UK, the problem of creative accounting had been recognised for many years before the Enron scandal broke. In 1992, Terry Smith wrote a book called *Accounting for Growth* (Century Business) which revealed many of the methods that companies used to massage their figures. His book became an action plan for the UK Accounting Standards Board and over the next ten years or so many of the opportunities for creative accounting were blocked.

Ironically, UK-listed companies are now governed by International Financial Reporting Standards, and these standards don't deal with creative accounting dodges as thoroughly as the UK standards.

One of the problems with the Enron accounts was that they did not include off-balance sheet financing vehicles. This term is used to describe the situation where a company transfers liabilities to other companies or business entities which they own or influence. In the UK, such situations would be dealt with by requiring the consolidation of the other entities into the main company. There was no equivalent requirement under the rules laid down by the US standards setters – the Financial Accounting Standards Board (FASB) and so, in this respect at least, Enron were not breaking any accounting rules. In the UK, this problem had been dealt with in the Financial Reporting Standard *FRS 5: Reporting the substance of transactions* which was published way back in 1994 by the Accounting Standards Board (ASB).

For more details about Enron see Chapter 22.

Defining the scope of the problem

In the hundreds of cases where companies *restated their earnings* (that is, when companies changed the numbers they originally reported to the general public to correct 'accounting errors'), company insiders had used creative accounting techniques to cook the books. And when trying to unearth the accounting problem, you have to be creative yourself.

In these scandals, some company insiders used corporate accounts for personal purposes, such as buying expensive cars or numerous houses and taking luxury trips – all at the expense of shareholders. Rather than using profits to grow the company and increase the value of the shares for the people who own them, these insiders lined their own pockets.

How did they get away with that? Well, most board members were closely tied to the corporate chiefs, which meant that no one was really watching the honey pot – or the hands going into it. In some cases, these close ties were members of the same family who wouldn't question their father or brother. In other cases, the board members were close friends and didn't want to question a buddy. You can find more details about these scandals in Chapter 22.

Company insiders use different techniques to cook the books. In some cases, earnings are *managed,* meaning that companies use legitimate accounting methods in aggressive ways to get the bottom-line results that they need. Other companies present revenues that are pure fiction. Still others toy with how they handle their capital financing, while some companies overvalue assets or undervalue liabilities. Those who want to deceive company outsiders can use a variety of these tactics.

Following recipes for cooked books

Former Securities and Exchange Commission (SEC) chairman Arthur Levitt groups these creative techniques – which he calls 'accounting hocus-pocus' – into the following five categories.

✓ **Big-bath charges:** Company insiders use this technique to clean up their balance sheet by giving it a 'big bath', meaning that they wash away past financial problems. When earnings take a big hit, some executives hope that the City will look beyond a one-time loss and focus on future earnings.

A common time to use this practice is when the company decides to restructure some parts of its business – for example, when two divisions of a company merge or a single division is split into two. During the restructuring process, executives can clean up any problems in previous reporting. This cleaning process may include hiding past financial reporting problems. The accounting problems washed off the books can be deliberate or non-deliberate accounting errors made during previous reporting periods.

The big-bath is often used when the former management have resigned because the new management can blame all of the problems on the previous board.

✔ **Creative acquisition accounting:** Levitt also calls this category 'merger magic' because it includes the technique in which companies use acquisitions to hide their problems. It's particularly useful when the acquisition is merely a share exchange, rather than a cash exchange. By setting a stock price for an acquisition that fits what a company needs to hide, a lot of past accounting problems can disappear like magic because the higher stock price can cover up problems, such as previous losses that were not accurately reported.

Usually, company insiders can erase the problems in a popular write-off called *in-process research and development*, which is a one-time charge mentioned in the notes to the financial statements detailing an acquisition. Getting rid of problems with this charge removes any future earnings drag, and future earnings statements look better.

✔ **Miscellaneous cookie-jar reserves:** Companies that use liabilities rather than revenue to hide problems do so by using what Levitt calls 'cookie jars'. When using this technique, company insiders make unrealistic assumptions about company liabilities. In a good year, a company assumes that its sales returns will be much higher than they have been historically. These higher assumptions are 'banked' as a liability, which means they're added to an accrual account that can be adjusted in a later year (for more on accrual accounting refer to Chapter 4). When a company has a bad year and needs to manage its earnings, it can massage those earnings by reducing the actual sales returns, using some of the banked sales returns from the cookie jar.

The cookie jar is often used as part of a big-bath, described earlier in this list. The company anticipates future costs and includes them in the current year's balance sheet as liabilities. Automatically, this means they get charged against the current year's profit (or, usually, they increase the current year's loss) rather than future profit. Because the current year's results are already appalling, the hope is that nobody notices the extra charges slipped through in the current year. And again, if it can all be blamed on the old board of directors then so much the better!

✔ **Materiality:** In accounting, the generally accepted principle is to report only financial matters that are likely to have a material effect on the company's earnings. Whether an item has a material effect on a company's bottom line is purely a judgement call made by company executives and the auditors. For example, a £1 million loss in inventory may have a material effect on a company's bottom line if the company's total profits are

£10 million. But that same million-pound loss for a company that reports multibillion-pound earnings may not be considered material because that loss has less impact on the company's bottom line.

Companies that play the materiality game set a percentage ceiling under which errors don't matter because they're not material. For example, the multibillion-pound company may decide that as long as errors reflect less than 5 per cent of any department's revenues, the error isn't material to the company's results. But those little errors can add up when spread carefully across a company's financial reports. Sometimes small errors can help the company make up for the penny or two loss per share that might miss the City's expectations and cause the share price to drop. Any time a company misses expectations – even by pennies – the share price takes a drop, and the company's overall value on the market may also fall by millions of pounds.

✔ **Revenue recognition:** Companies using this technique boost their earnings by manipulating the way they count sales. For example, these companies recognise a sale before it's complete or count something as sold even though the customer still has options to terminate, void, or delay the sale. We give a lot of examples of this in the next section.

We discuss how company insiders use these various techniques, but too often, you don't find out about the deception until someone inside the company decides to blow the whistle or the company goes into administration or liquidation.

Unearthing the Games Played with Earnings

All companies manage earnings to a certain extent because they want their bottom lines to look as good as possible, and they use whatever accounting method gets them there. For example, a company can improve its earnings by using different methods for valuing assets and costs – the accounting policies and methods that a company uses can have a great impact on its bottom line (flip to Chapter 6 for more on valuing assets).

In accrual accounting, revenue is recognised when it's earned (when payment for the product or service is due), and expenses are recognised when they are incurred (when the purchase is complete even if cash has not yet been paid). Go to Chapter 4 for more details. Cash doesn't have to change hands for revenue to be earned or expenses incurred. The key is whether the revenue is actually earned and the expenses are actually incurred, or whether a company is reporting them prematurely or fictitiously.

The Generally Accepted Accounting Principles (GAAP) that govern reporting practices are pretty flexible (refer to Chapter 18 for more on GAAP). Managing earnings becomes abusive when it involves using tricks that actually distort a company's true financial picture to present the desired view to outsiders. And the games that companies play along those lines are numerous. The only limit to these games is the creativity of those who manage the company's finances.

Companies usually play with numbers that impact revenue recognition or expense recognition. That's really the bottom line for any company: the amount of revenue that a company took in or the amount of expenses that it paid out in order to generate that revenue. All the other numbers that a company reports are simply setting out the details of how their final revenue and expense figures were arrived at.

Reading between the revenue lines

In this section, we cover the gamut of revenue recognition games, from slight misrepresentations to gross exaggerations. Unfortunately, many of these problems are difficult for readers who are company outsiders to find. Still, if you're an investor, you need to be familiar with the terms we discuss in this section so you can understand news reports about problems that may exist inside a company.

In the UK, the manipulation of revenue is known as *aggressive earnings management* and auditors are charged under International Standards on Auditing to presume that there is a significant risk of fraud in the area of revenue recognition.

Goods ordered but not shipped

In some cases, a company considers goods that have been ordered but not yet shipped to be part of its revenue earned. In the long term, this system can create not only an accounting nightmare, but also a nightmare for managers throughout the company. Orders can get severely backlogged and, ultimately, the company may have a lot of problems satisfying its customers.

This practice can have a big impact on a company's bottom line. Accrual accounting is specifically designed to match revenue with expenses each accounting period. As more and more goods build up that are ordered but not shipped, financial reports overstate the company's revenue and understate expenses until the deception is exposed. Eventually, the company will have to admit its game-playing and restate its net income, which is likely to result in a profit reduction or possibly even a loss.

Executives and managers just delay the inevitable when they practise this game. Some do it to maintain their bonuses as long as possible. Others do it because they don't want to face the reality of the company's financial position. And I'm sure there are many more excuses companies make when the game is finally exposed.

A variation on this theme is the bill-and-hold transaction where the supplier is asked to delay the despatch of the goods. See 'Bill-and-hold transactions' later in this section.

Goods shipped but not ordered

Some companies get even more aggressive with their deception, counting goods that they've shipped but that customers haven't ordered yet. Companies that use this technique commonly ship items for inspection or demonstration purposes in the hope that customers will buy the product. This tactic can help a company meet its revenue for the upcoming reporting period – the company counts these unordered goods as sales, even though the products haven't really been sold. However, during the next period, when customers who received the goods decide not to purchase and return the merchandise, the company must subtract these sales from its revenue.

As the problem snowballs, a company has to ship more and more orders without actually having the sales to meet its revenue expectations. Each month the company has to reverse a greater percentage of its revenue, and as a result, the company has to make up the shortfall by shipping an even greater number of units without actual orders. Eventually, the company won't be able to keep up the deceptive practices and will have to correct its financial statements, lowering the amount it reported as revenue and reducing its net income. This financial correction will probably send shockwaves through the stock market, and the share price will drop dramatically.

Extended reporting period

Some companies try to meet revenue expectations by keeping their books open for a few days – or even a few weeks – into the next reporting period in order to generate last-minutes sales. This tactic eventually creates major financial reporting problems for the company because it has been taking the sales from what should have been reported as income during the next reporting period. Eventually, the company has to reveal its deceptive practices because it has to leave its books open longer and longer each period to meet the next period's expectations.

Pure fiction

The most outrageous acts are the ones that involve reporting purely fictional sales. How do companies do this? Well, they recognise revenue for sales that were never ordered and never shipped. Company insiders fill financial records with false order, billing, and shipping information. Eventually, the lack of actual cash forces the company to reveal its games, and the company will probably go bankrupt.

Channel stuffing

Channel stuffing is a way for companies to get more products out of their manufacturing warehouses and onto distributors' and retailers' shelves. The most common method is to offer distributors large discounts so that they stock up on products. Distributors buy more product than they expect to sell because they can get it so much cheaper. Then distributors sell the product to their customers; however, several months or even a year may pass before they sell all the products.

Although this strategy is a legitimate type of revenue, it will come back to haunt the company in later accounting periods, when distributors have so much product on their shelves that they don't need to order more. At some point in the future, new orders drop, which means fewer sales and a drop in revenue reported on the income statement. Less revenue translates to lower net income, which is seen as a bad sign by the City, and the share price takes a dive.

Side letters

Sometimes companies make agreements with their regular customers outside the actual documentation used for the corporate reporting of revenue. This agreement is called a *side letter*. The side letter involves the company and customer changing terms behind the scenes, such as allowing more liberal rights of return or rights to cancel orders at any time that can, essentially, kill the sale. Sometimes these agreements go as far as excusing the customer from paying for the goods.

In all cases, the side-letter terms eventually result in turning revenue that was recognised on a previous income statement into a non-sale, by the return of goods or possibly, the treatment of the goods as 'on consignment' (see the following section 'Rights of return'). This practice makes revenue from these sales look better initially, but the revenue is later subtracted when the goods are returned.

Rights of return

Giving customers liberal return rights is another way of getting customers to order goods, even when they're not sure if they'll be able to resell them. By offering distributors or retailers terms that allow them to order goods for resale that they can return as much as 12 months later if they don't sell, the sales, in essence, aren't really sales and shouldn't be recognised as revenue on a company's financial report. Rights of return are offered to most customers, but when payment for goods depends on the need for the distributor or retailer to first resell the goods, the recognition of that revenue is questionable. Again, it may be more appropriate to treat such 'sales' as goods on consignment.

Goods on consignment actually remain the property of the original seller until the retailer sells them on to a third party. In this case, the goods continue to be included in the inventory of the original seller. They are included at cost and therefore the revenue is not recognised and no profit is taken until the goods are sold on to the eventual customer.

Related-party revenue

Related-party revenue comes from a company selling goods to another entity in which the seller controls the management of operating policies. For example, if the parent company of a tissue manufacturer sells the raw materials needed for manufacturing that tissue to its subsidiary, the parent company can't count that sale of raw materials as revenue. Whenever one party to the transaction can control or significantly influence the decision of the entity that wants to buy the goods, a company can't recognise the sale as revenue.

In the preceding group situation, the parent company would recognise the revenue from the sale in its own accounts (a credit) and the subsidiary would recognise the costs (a debit). On consolidation, when the results of all the group companies are added together, this credit and debit would cancel out. The problem would arise if the subsidiary still held the raw material in stock at the end of the financial year (or indeed if the raw material had been used in producing finished goods which were still in stock). In this case, any profit made when the parent sold the goods to the subsidiary would need to be reversed in the group accounts.

Bill-and-hold transactions

Sometimes a buyer places an order but asks the company to hold onto the goods until it has room in its store or warehouse. So the company has sold the goods but hasn't shipped them yet. This sale is called a *bill-and-hold transaction.*

In IAS 18: *Revenue*, the International Accounting Standards Board (IASB) has a set of criteria that a company must meet in order for it to recognise revenue for items it hasn't shipped yet. These include

- ✔ It is probable that the delivery will be made.
- ✔ The item is on hand, identified, and ready for delivery to the buyer at the time the sale is recognised.
- ✔ The buyer specifically acknowledges the deferred delivery instructions.
- ✔ The usual payment terms apply.

Upfront service fees

Companies that collect upfront service fees for services that they provide over a long period of time, such as 12, 24, 36, or 60 months, must be careful about how they recognise this revenue. If a company collects fees to service equipment upfront, these fees can't be counted as revenue when the money is collected. The IASB requires that such companies recognise their revenue over time as the fees are earned. Companies that recognise this type of revenue all at once are prematurely recognising revenue.

A supplier may deliver an IT packaged solution which includes hardware (guaranteed for twelve months), software, maintenance (for three years), training and technical support (for a period of 24 months). A single fee is quoted to the customer but the supplier needs to break this fee into its constituent parts in order to decide how the revenue on each part should be recognised.

Rendering of services

More generally, an agreement to provide services often stretches for a period which covers the year-end of the provider of those services. It might be thought that revenue should not be recognised until the service is complete but that is not what the IASB think. In IAS 18, they say that when the outcome of a transaction involving the rendering of services can be estimated reliably, the revenue associated with the transaction should be recognised by reference to the stage of completion of the transaction at the balance sheet date.

A major change in UK accounting occurred in 2005 when the Urgent Issues Task Force (UITF, a subcommittee of the Accounting Standards Board) released their Abstract 40 entitled *Revenue recognition and service contracts: Mitigating its effect*, the document made it clear that the principles of accounting for service contracts extended to short-term contracts in progress. For example, consider a kitchen fitter with a year-end of 31 December 2007. At that date they are part of the way through installing a kitchen for a customer for whom they have quoted a fee of £20,000. The fee of £20,000 was broken down as to £12,000 for materials and £8,000 for labour. At 31 December they have provided 75 per cent of the material for the job and completed half of the work. Abstract 40 requires them to recognise revenue of £13,000 (that is 75 per cent of £12,000 plus 50 per cent of £8,000) in their accounts for the year-ended 31 December 2007. Prior to the publication of Abstract 40, the kitchen fitter would not have recognised any revenue until the job was finished.

Detecting creative revenue accounting

With so many tricks up so many corporate sleeves, you may feel that you're at the mercy of the tricksters. You can get to the bottom of many of the common creative accounting tactics described in the preceding sections by carefully reading and analysing the financial reports, but you'll have to play detective and crunch some numbers.

Reviewing revenue recognition policies

The financial report section called 'notes to the financial statements' is a good source for finding out at what point a company actually recognises a sale as revenue. Some companies recognise revenue before they deliver the product or before they perform the service. If you come across this scenario, try to find details in the notes to the financial statements that indicate how the company really earned its revenue. If you can't, call the company's investor relations department to clarify the company's revenue-recognition policies, and be sure that you understand why it may be justified in recognising revenue before delivery or performance has been completed.

When a company indicates in the notes to the financial statements that it recognises revenue at the time of delivery or performance, that timing may seem perfect to you, but you must look further to see if there are other policies that might negate a sale. Dig deeper into the revenue-recognition section of the notes to find out what the company's rights-of-return policy is and how it determines pricing. (See the section 'Rights of return,' earlier in this chapter.) Some companies may allow a price adjustment or have a liberal return policy that may cancel out the sale.

Take note if you find that the company recently changed its revenue-recognition policies. Just the fact that the company is changing those policies can be a red flag. This change may have come about because the company is having difficulty meeting the expectations of the City. The company may decide to recognise revenue earlier in the sales process, which could mean that more of this revenue reported on the income statement may have to be subtracted in later reporting periods. Scour the revenue-recognition section of the financial report until you understand how the change impacted the company's revenue recognition. You may want to review the annual reports from the past few years to compare the old revenue policies with the new ones.

Evaluating revenue results

Reported revenue results for the current period don't tell the whole financial story. You need to review the revenue results for the past five half-years (at least) or past three years to see whether any inexplicable swings in seasonal activity exist. For example, extremely high numbers for retail outlets in the last part of the year (October to December) aren't unusual. Many retailers make about 40 per cent of their profits during that quarter due to holiday sales.

Be sure that you understand the fluctuations in revenue for the company you're investigating and how its results compare with those of similar companies and the industry as a whole. If you see major shifts in revenue results that normal seasonal differences can't explain, an alarm should go off in your head. Take the time to further investigate the reason for these differences by reading reports by analysts who cover the company, and by calling the company's investor relations office. Large shifts in revenue can be a sign of revenue management.

Monitoring trade receivables

Trade receivables track customers who buy on credit. You want to be sure that customers are paying promptly for their purchases, so watch the trend in trade receivables closely. In Chapter 16, we show you how to calculate trade-receivables turnover. Compare the *turnover ratio,* which measures how quickly customers pay their bills, for at least the past five periods to see whether a change in trend has occurred. If you notice that customers are taking longer to pay their bills, it can be a sign that the company has trouble collecting money, but it can also indicate aggressive earnings management. Either way, this should raise a red flag for you as a financial report reader.

While you're investigating, check the percentage rate of change for trade receivables versus the percentage rate of change for net revenue over the same period. For example, if the balance in trade receivables increases by 10 per cent and net revenues increase by 25 per cent, that may be a sign of game-playing. Normally, these two accounts increase and decrease by similar percentages year to year unless the company offers its customers a significant change in credit policies. If you see significant differences between these two accounts, it may be another sign of aggressive earnings management.

Check to see if the changes you're seeing match trends for similar companies or the industry as a whole. If not, ask investor relations people to explain what's behind the differences. If you don't like the answers or can't get answers that make sense to you, don't buy the stock or consider selling the stock you already have.

Assessing physical capacity

Evaluating *physical capacity,* the number of facilities the company has and the amount of product the company can manufacture, is another way to judge whether or not the company is accurately reporting revenue. You need to find out if the company truly has the physical capacity to generate the revenue that it's reporting. You do so by comparing the following ratios:

- **Revenue per employee (revenue ÷ number of employees):** If the annual report doesn't mention the number of employees, you can call investor relations or find it in a company profile on one of the financial Web sites, such as www.find.co.uk or uk.finance.yahoo.com.

- **Revenue per pound value of property, plant, and equipment (revenue ÷ pound value of property, plant, and equipment):** You can find the pound value of property, plant, and equipment on the financial report's balance sheet.

> ✔ **Revenue per pound value of total assets (revenue ÷ pound value of total assets):** You can find the number for total assets on the financial report's balance sheet or you may need to add together the figures for current assets and non-current assets.

> ✔ **Revenue per square foot of retail or rental space, if appropriate (revenue ÷ square foot of retail space):** You can find details about retail or rental space in the managers' discussion and analysis or the notes to the financial statement sections of the annual report or in the profile on a financial Web site.

Compare these ratios for the past five periods and also compare the ratios to ones of similar companies and ones for the industry as a whole. If you see major differences from accounting period to accounting period or between similar companies, it may be a sign of a problem. For example, if revenue per employee is much higher, or if revenue per dollar value of property, plant, or equipment far exceeds that of similar companies or that of previous periods, this may be a sign of aggressive earnings management.

Exploring Exploitations of Expenses

If a company is playing games with its expenses, the most likely place you'll find evidence is in its capitalisation or its amortisation polices. You can find details about these policies in the notes to the financial statements. For further explanation of amortisation, refer to Chapter 4.

Companies that want their bottom lines to look better may shift the way that they report depreciation and amortisation, which are the tools they use to account for an asset's use and to show the decreasing value of that asset. To make their net incomes look better, companies can play games with the amounts they write off. They do so by writing off less than they should and lowering expenses.

In addition to depreciation and amortisation schedules, a company can play games with expenses when reporting some types of advertising, research and development costs, patents and licences, asset impairments, and restructuring charges. In some cases, companies can *capitalise* (spread out) their expenses over a number of months, quarters, or years. Spreading out expenses can certainly improve a company's bottom line because the expenses will be lower in the first year they are incurred, and lower expenses mean more net income.

So the key question is whether a company is spreading its expenses out properly or whether it's improperly managing its bottom line. You can find details in the accounting-policies section in the annual report. We point out the key policies to review in this chapter, but if the company is playing games, detecting anything out of the ordinary is difficult to do by using the annual reports. You'll have to depend on reports in the financial press to see if problems are detected or exposed by a whistle-blower.

Advertising expenses

Companies report most advertising expenses in the accounting period when they were incurred; however, for some types of advertising, companies can spread the expense out over a number of periods.

The primary type of advertising costs that companies sometimes spread out over a number of periods is direct-response advertising. *Direct-response advertising* is mailed directly to the consumer. For example, when a company sends out an annual catalogue, it might spread out the costs for that direct-mail over the year, as long as the company can show that it receives orders from that catalogue throughout the year.

To find out a company's policy on advertising expenses, look in the notes to the financial statements. The best accounting policy is to write off all advertising expenditure as it is incurred since the company does not control the future possible income.

Research and development costs

Companies are supposed to charge most research and development costs in the profit and loss account of the current period being reported on in the financial statements. Sometimes companies try to stretch out those expenses over a number of periods so the reduction in net income won't be necessary all in the same year. If fewer expenses are subtracted from revenues, net income will be higher, which makes the company look more profitable. However, some development expenditure must be carried forward as an asset so that the costs of development are matched with the future expected revenues from the new products. The IASB have set out detailed rules in IAS 38 for when R&D expenditure should be expensed and when it should be carried forward as an asset.

To see how the company expenses its research and development, read the notes to the financial statements. If you're uncertain about the accounting policies that the notes present, don't hesitate to call investor relations and ask questions until you understand what you're reading.

Patents and licences

Understanding the accounting for patents and licences can be difficult. Usually, the expenses a company incurs during the research and development phase – before it receives a patent or licence – must be written off in the year when they occurred (unless they satisfy the rules mentioned above for development costs), and they cannot be capitalised (written off over a number of years). But a company *can* capitalise some expenses, such as those it incurs to register or defend a patent. A company can also capitalise a patent or licence it purchased as an asset at the purchase price. Companies like to capitalise a patent or licence because such a large purchase can significantly reduce their net income, so most prefer to write it off over several years, if they can, to reduce the hit.

All patents and licences that a company purchased are included as assets on the balance sheet. In addition, the balance sheet includes the costs of registering patents or licences for products developed in-house. The value of these patents and licences is amortised over the time period for which they're *economically viable* (meaning for as long as the company benefits from owning that patent or licence).

Companies can play games with the value of patents and licences, as well as with the time periods for which they'll be considered economically viable. To see what a company says about its patent and licence accounting policies, read the notes to the financial statements. Compare its policies with those of similar companies to see whether they appear reasonable or whether the company may be overstating its value or capitalising its expenses in a way that differs from their competitors. For example, if Company A makes widgets and says the patent for its type of widgets is good for ten years, and Company B makes a different kind of widget and says its patent is economically viable for 20 years, you probably want to call investor relations and find out why Company B believes it has an economically viable widget for so much longer than its competitor.

Asset impairment

Tangible assets depreciate based on set schedules, but not all intangible assets face a rigid amortisation schedule. For example, goodwill is an intangible asset that may not be amortised each year. This item on the balance sheet has long had potential for creative accounting practitioners. Today, most companies have goodwill on their balance sheets because many large public companies are formed by buying smaller companies.

There are two ways that goodwill can arise but in either case the value of goodwill is based on the amount of money or shares that are paid for an acquisition over and above what the net tangible assets are worth.

Where a company acquires an unincorporated business then the goodwill is quite simply the difference between the amount paid (in cash or shares) and the value of the net assets acquired. The goodwill arises naturally as a result of the double-entry bookkeeping system. Notice that the business acquired ceases to exist as a separate entity.

The second way that goodwill arises is when consolidated accounts are prepared. In this situation, the acquiring company has bought the shares in another company and the cost of those shares is shown in the acquiring company's balance sheet. The two companies continue in separate existence and their accounting records are kept separately. At the end of each year each separate company prepares their own financial statements and these are then combined to prepare consolidated accounts. In the consolidation process, goodwill arises as the difference between the cost of the acquisition in the acquirer's balance sheet and the cost of shares and net assets acquired in the subsidiary's balance sheet.

In the past, companies amortised goodwill over its expected useful life by writing off part of its value each year. Today, a company must prove that the value of its goodwill has been impaired (worth less than it was in a previous year) before it can write it off. The IASB requires in IFRS 3 that companies test goodwill to see if there is any impairment to its value before they write off any value.

The value of goodwill is tested based on a number of factors, including:

- ✔ Competition and the ability of those competitors to negatively affect the profitability of the business that a company acquired.
- ✔ The current or expected future levels of industry consolidation.
- ✔ The impact that potential or expected changes in technology may have on profitability.
- ✔ Legislative action that results in an uncertain or changing regulatory environment.
- ✔ Loss of future revenue if certain key employees of the acquisition company aren't retained.
- ✔ The rate of customer turnover, or how fast old customers leave and new customers arrive.
- ✔ The mobility of customers and employees.

If you see that a company has written off goodwill or any other asset under the rules of impairment, look for an explanation about how the company calculated that impairment in its notes to the financial statements. If you don't understand the explanation, ask the investor relations office questions.

Restructuring charges

Restructuring charges is one of the primary ways that companies can hide all sorts of accounting games. A company can *restructure* itself by combining divisions, having one division split off into two or more, or dismantling an entire division. Any major change in the way that a company manufactures or sells its products usually entails restructuring.

Whenever a company indicates restructuring charges on its financial statements, carefully scour the notes to the financial statements for reasons behind those charges and the method the company has used to calculate the amount that it has written off. Find out what costs the company allocated to the restructure, and carefully read the details for those costs. The restructuring method is a great way for a company to get rid of losses in one-time charges and clean out the books. (See the section 'Big-bath charges', earlier in this chapter.) Luckily, restructuring charges are a red flag that analysts watch closely for and, if considered appropriate, a company's accounts could be referred to the Financial Reporting Review Panel for further consideration.

In the notes to the financial statements, you usually find a note specifically detailing the restructuring and its impact on the financial statements. You may also find mentions of restructuring charges or plans in the management's discussion and analysis section of the financial report. When a company restructures it can incur costs for many items such as asset impairment, lease termination, plant and other closures, redundancy pay, benefits, relocation, and retraining. All these areas give creative accountants a lot of room to fiddle with the numbers.

The company must specify costs not only for the current period, but also costs for all future years in which the company anticipates additional costs, and any related write-offs in periods prior to the one being reported. Analysts watch these charges very closely to try and identify any loopholes that allow companies to charge recurring operating expenses to their restructuring – something which companies may do to improve the appearance to outsiders of the earnings results from company operations.

Finding Funny Business in Assets and Liabilities

Overvaluing assets or undervaluing liabilities can give a distorted view of a company's earning power and financial position. These practices can have a devastating impact when the company must finally admit to its game-playing.

Recognising overstated assets

Overstated assets make the company look financially healthier to annual report readers than it truly is. A company may report that it has more cash due than it really does or that it holds more inventory than is actually on its shelves. A company may also report that the value of its inventory is greater than it really is.

Trade receivables

The trade-receivables section of the financial report is the place where you may find an indication of premature or fictitious revenue recognition. One way a company can overstate its trade receivables is to post sales to customers who return the items early the following month without paying for them. The value of those goods reduces the trade receivables during the next accounting period, but the deception makes the current period look like more revenues were received than should actually have been counted because the sales are premature or fictitious.

That's not the only way that a company can overvalue its trade receivables. Another account attached to trade receivables is the provision for doubtful debts. At the end of each accounting period, a company identifies past-due accounts that probably won't get paid. The company adds the value of these past-due accounts to the provision for doubtful debts, which reduces the value of trade receivables.

A company that wants to play with its numbers and indicate that its financial position is actually better than it appears reduces the amount it sets aside for doubtful debts. Gradually, the number of days the company takes to collect on its trade receivables goes up as more and more late- or non-payers are left in trade receivables. As the number of days collecting on its trade receivables goes up, the amount of cash the company takes in from customers who are paying off their purchases bought on credit slows down.

 You can test the trend for trade receivables by using formulas we explain in Chapter 16. Test the trend by calculating days in trade receivables for the past three to five periods. If you see the number of days in trade receivables gradually rising, that's a sign of a problem, and may represent an attempt to recognise revenue prematurely or fictitiously. But it may also represent a problem of credit policies that are too liberal. We discuss that issue in greater detail in Chapter 16.

Inventory

There are five different inventory valuation methods, and each one yields a different net income for the company (go to Chapter 15 for more on this). Inventory policy isn't the only way a company can shift the value of its inventory on the balance sheet. Other common methods used include

- ✔ **Overstating physical count:** Although this is absolute fraud, companies take this route to improve the appearance of their balance sheets. Sometimes they alter the actual count of their inventory; other times, they don't subtract the decrease in inventory from the physical count. Companies may also leave damaged goods in the inventory count, even though they have no value.

- ✔ **Increasing reported valuation:** Some companies don't even bother messing with their inventory counts. A simple journal entry increasing a company's inventory valuation and decreasing its costs of goods sold can improve appearances on both the balance sheet and the income statement. The assets side of the balance sheet looks better and the net income figure improves, too – which ultimately raises retained earnings to hide the existence of the journal entry and keep the balance sheet in balance.

- ✔ **Delaying an inventory write-down:** Company management periodically writes down the value of their inventory when they determine that the products are obsolete or slow-moving. Because the decision to write down inventory is purely up to management, during a rough year, a company may delay writing down inventory to make its numbers look better.

 Any time you suspect that inventory may be the object of financial game-playing, you can test your theory by calculating the number of days inventory sits around the company. We show you how to test the number of days inventory sits around in Chapter 15. Look for trends by running the numbers for the past three years. If you see that the number of days that inventory sits around gradually increases, definitely suspect a problem. The problem may not be creative accounting. It may be a sign of other problems, such as reduced consumer interest in the product or a bad economic market. The only way you'll find out is to ask your questions to the company's investor relations department.

Undeveloped land

Land never depreciates. But shareholders don't have any details about where the land that a company owns is located, so they can never truly assess the value of undeveloped land on a balance sheet. This fact allows a lot of room for creative accounting and leaves the financial reader in the dark when it comes to finding this problem. Unfortunately, in a sketchy situation like this one, all you can do is wait for a whistle-blower to expose it.

Of course, the opposite problem might arise. The company might own a very valuable piece of land but the reader of the financial statements has no idea of this fact because the land is included at its original cost and it was bought many years ago.

Unusual assets

As is the case with undeveloped land (see preceding section), financial reports don't usually detail all of the assets that the company might own. For example, the company might have bought paintings or sculptures to brighten up the office. If you do see such assets mentioned in the financial statements then, unless you're looking at the financial statements of an art gallery, be wary. This sort of item shouldn't be a major asset for most companies that aren't in the art business.

If you see a non-art business with a significant level of assets tied up in art-work, ask investor relations why the company's spending so much money on art. Frankly, a company that ties up its money in art rather than using it to grow the business is not one we'd want to own stock in.

Looking for undervalued liabilities

Undervaluing liabilities can certainly make a company look healthier to financial report readers, but this deception is likely to lead a company down the path to bankruptcy. Games played by misstating liabilities frequently involve large numbers and hide significant money problems.

Accounts payable

An increase in accounts payable is usually directly related to the fact that a company is delaying payments for inventory or services. To test for a problem, you need to calculate the accounts-payable ratio, which we show you how to do in Chapter 16. If you find a trend indicating that the number of days a company takes to pay its accounts payable is steadily increasing, test the number of days in inventory, as we show you in Chapter 15.

If a company fails both tests, investigate further. Even though a company may not be playing games with its numbers, take these signs as an indication of a worsening problem. With the trends you're noticing, definitely call investor relations and ask for explanations about why the company has been paying its bills more slowly or why the inventory has been sitting on the shelves for longer periods of time.

If investor relations don't answer the questions to your satisfaction, don't buy the stock. If you already do own the stock, you might want to consider selling it if you believe the company is hiding the truth.

Accrued expenses payable

Any expenses that a company hasn't paid by the end of an accounting period are *accrued* (posted to the accounts before cash is paid out) in the current period, so these expenses can be matched to current period earnings. This amount is added to the liability side of the balance sheet.

Unpaid expenses can include just about any expense for which the company gets a bill and has a number of days to pay, such as

- ✔ Administrative expenses
- ✔ Insurance
- ✔ Salaries
- ✔ Selling costs
- ✔ Utilities

If the bill arrives during the last week before a company closes its books, the company most likely accrues it rather than pay it. Most companies cut off paying bills several days before they close their books so the staff can concentrate on closing the books for the period.

If a company needs to improve its net income, it can manage its numbers by not accruing bills and instead paying them in the next accounting period. The problem with this strategy is that the next accounting period has more expenses charged to it than the company actually incurred during that accounting period. The expenses are higher, and therefore, the net income is lower in the next reporting period.

You can test for this particular game by watching the trend for accrued expenses payable. Check to see whether accrued expenses payable is going up or down from accounting period to accounting period. Usually, accrued expenses payable stay pretty level from year to year. If you see a steady decline, the company may be doing some creative accounting, or maybe the company's expenses decrease is simply due to discontinued operations or other changes. If you see a declining trend, look deeper into the numbers to see whether you can find an explanation. If not, call investor relations to find out why the trend for accrued payables shifts from accounting period to accounting period.

Provisions

Provisions are liabilities of uncertain timing or amount. A company should only accrue for a provision when an obligation has arisen as a result of an event which occurred before the balance sheet date and if payment is likely to be needed to settle this obligation. For example, if a company is involved in a lawsuit that it is likely to lose then a provision should be made for the best estimate of the amount required to settle the case.

Note that a company must determine three factors before it can include a provision in its balance sheet:

- ✔ The obligation must have arisen as a result of an event which occurred before the balance sheet date.
- ✔ The company deems that it's probable that it will need to settle the obligation.
- ✔ The company can reasonably estimate the costs that will be incurred.

If a company has not determined these three issues, you'll probably find a note about the potential liability (which is known as a *contingent liability*) in the notes to the financial statements. Read the notes about contingencies, and research further any items that you think the company may not be fully disclosing. You do so by reading analysts' reports on the company or by calling the investor relations department to ask questions about any issues mentioned in the notes to the financial statements.

Pay down liabilities

Another way that the companies that were involved in the scandals of the past few years played with their numbers was by indicating that they paid down their liabilities when they actually didn't. To make their balance sheets look better, companies transferred debt to another entity owned by the company, its directors, or its executives to hide the company's true financial status.

You probably won't have any way of knowing if this is happening until a company insider decides to expose the practice or other problems catch up with them.

Playing Detective with Cash Flow

The statement of cash flows (refer to Chapter 8) is derived primarily from information found on a company's income statement and balance sheet. You usually don't find massaged numbers on this statement because it's based primarily on the numbers that have already been shown on the balance sheet and income statement. But you may find that the presentation of the numbers hides cash-flow problems.

Discontinued operations

Discontinued operations occur when a company sells part of its business or shuts down some of its activities, such as closing a manufacturing plant or putting an end to a product line. Many companies that discontinue operations show the impact it has on their cash in a separate line item of the financial report. Companies that are having cash-flow problems with continuing operations may not separate these results on their cash-flow statements. Because the accounting rules don't require a separate line item, this strategy is a convenient way to hide the problem from investors – who don't do a good job of reading the small print in the notes to the financial statements anyway.

If discontinued operations have an impact on a company's income statement, you'll see a line item there because there areadditional revenues or additional expenses related to the shutdown. You can find greater detail about those discontinued operations in the notes to the financial statements. Any time you see mention of discontinued operations in the income statement, or in the notes to the financial statements, be sure that you also see a separate line item in the statement of cash flows. If you don't, use the information you glean from the income statement and the notes to the financial statements to calculate the cash flow from operations.

To calculate the *cash flow from operations* (cash received from the day-to-day operations of the business, usually from sales), subtract any cash generated from discontinued operations (which you find noted on the income statement) from the net income reported on the statement of cash flows. When looking at a company's profitability from the cash perspective, you want to consider only cash generated by ongoing operations.

When you take on the role of detective, you may uncover a cash-flow problem that the financial wizards carefully concealed because the rules allow such a misleading presentation. In Chapter 17, we show you numerous calculations for testing a company's cash flow. Be sure to do those calculations using the cash flow from ongoing operations having first removed income from discontinued operations.

Corporation tax paid

Just like with discontinued operations, the amount of corporation tax that a company pays can distort its operating cash flow. The reason is that in some situations, companies pay taxes as a one-time occurrence, such as taxes on the net gain or loss from the sale of a major asset. The income taxes a company pays for these one-time occurrences shouldn't be included in your calculations related to operating cash flow.

TIP

Seeking information on questionable reporting

If you want to find more information about companies that may be playing games with their numbers, a good place to turn is the reports of the Financial Reporting Review Panel (FRRP) which can be accessed via the Web site of the Financial Reporting Council www.frc.org.uk. You can access the reports via the press releases issued by the FRRP.

The reports of the FRRP give an outline of the issues and identify how the company must correct their current reporting practices. So far, all cases investigated by the FRRP have been settled by negotiation with the companies concerned and there has been no need to resort to court action.

By reviewing the sections on investing or financing activities in the statement of cash flows, you can find any adjustments that you may need to calculate the operating cash flow. Here are two key adjustments you need to make to find the actual net cash from operations (the amount of cash generated from the company's day-to-day operations):

- ✔ **Gains from sales of investments or fixed assets:** If a company gains from the sale of investments or fixed assets (for example, buildings, factories, vehicles, or anything else the company owns that can't be quickly converted to cash) that weren't part of operations, you should exclude the taxes paid on these gains Taxes paid on one-time gains distort the true cash flow from operations.

- ✔ **Losses from sales of investments or fixed assets:** If a company loses from the sale of investments or fixed assets, the tax savings a company gets from the loss increases its cash flow. You need to subtract these tax savings from the net cash so your operating cash flow accurately reflects the cash available from operations.

Part VI
The Part of Tens

'I think this company's in serious
trouble - this isn't dress-down Friday
- today's only Wednesday.'

In this part . . .

Here you find quick information about some juicy topics. We tell you about financial reporting scandals that shook the world, give you ten indications that a company may be falling on hard times, and list great places for you to turn when you want more information about the goings-on in the financial world.

Chapter 22

Ten Financial Crises That Rocked the World

In This Chapter

▶ Taking a look at foul play

▶ Learning from the misfortunes of others

▶ Finding fallout from faulty accounting

Sometimes, our financial system goes wrong. In these circumstances, it is very tempting to look around for somebody to blame. If we have suffered loss then we deserve to be compensated – or do we?

Some people think that accountancy is a form of advanced arithmetic. As such, the accounts should be an exact representation of the real world position of the company concerned. But accountancy is not an exact science. The records of the past (the bookkeeping) should be a true reflection of the facts, but there are many subjective judgements which need to be made in order to arrive at the financial statements.

In this chapter, we report on situations where things went wrong. Some arose because of the criminal behaviour of the individuals concerned. In other situations people suffered a loss that wasn't caused by dishonesty – or even incompetence. What links these stories together is that they all provide us with an opportunity to avoid repeating the mistakes made in previous crises.

Enron: Be Cautious of Explosive Growth

Enron (once the world's largest energy trader) has practically become synonymous with 'corporate scandal'. Sure, some major scandals occurred before Enron, but the downfall of this company in 2001 rattled the markets with the massive scope of the misdealing that came to light. By how much Enron misstated its earnings is still an open question, but Enron definitely overstated its profits and hid debts totalling billions of dollars by improperly using *off-the-books* (not shown on their financial statements) partnerships to give investors a false impression about its financial position. Arguably the number could be as high as $20 billion.

Enron's misdeeds didn't stop with only misleading investors; company insiders also misled the Texas power market and the California energy market and bribed foreign governments to win contracts abroad. Enron's lead in the energy-trading scandals exposed the manipulation of the energy market by other key energy companies, including CMS Energy, Duke Energy, Dynegy, and Reliant Energy.

The Enron scandal also took down one of the big five accounting firms, Arthur Andersen, although their convictions for fraud were reversed on appeal. Enron declared bankruptcy at the end of 2001 facing about $100 billion in claims and liabilities from shareholders, bondholders, and other creditors.

Some executives pleaded guilty to felony charges. A federal jury in Houston indicted two of Enron's former chief executives, Kenneth L Lay and Jeffrey Skilling, on charges of fraud and insider trading in 2004. Lay was found guilty but died before sentence while Skilling received a jail sentence of 24 years. Former Enron finance chief, Andrew S Fastow, who allegedly pocketed $60 million in company money without the board's knowledge, pleaded guilty and co-operated with the investigation. He was sentenced to six years in prison on one count of conspiracy to commit wire fraud and one count of conspiracy to commit securities fraud.

Today the company is much smaller and is operating under the supervision of a bankruptcy court. Its primary business focuses on the transportation of natural gas.

When you look at the explosive growth of a company – particularly one growing in an established industry by mergers and acquisitions – try to understand how they're doing it. If the way they're operating is really opaque, then maybe avoid them. But it's hard to ignore spectacular growth, so invest – but remember such growth never goes on for ever so don't forget to take some profits from time to time.

Adelphia and Hollinger: Be Wary of Lavish Lifestyles

Adelphia (a broadcasting and cable TV company) came to a crisis because of its greedy top executives: John Rigas, founder of the company, and his son, Timothy Rigas. The Rigases used the corporation as their personal piggy bank, stealing $100 million from the company that they used for luxurious personal residences, trips, and other items.

In 2004, John and Timothy Rigas were found guilty of concealing $2.3 billion in loans, which were hidden in small companies left off Adelphia's books. The Securities and Exchange Commission (SEC) charged that in addition to hiding debt, Adelphia inflated earnings to meet Wall Street expectations between at least 1998 and March 2002; falsified statistics about the company's operations; and concealed blatant self-dealing by the Rigas family, which founded and controlled Adelphia.

Two other executives from Adelphia were arrested in 2002 after the scandal broke. Michael Rigas, another son of John Rigas, and Michael Mulcahey, the company's former director of internal reporting, were both found not guilty.

Conrad Black famously followed the Rigas example, robbing Hollinger International of millions of dollars to fund a lavish lifestyle. It was said that he used the company as though it were his own and did not belong to the company's shareholders. His appeal against the jury's verdict was rejected and he was sentenced to six-and-a-half years in prison on 10 December 2007.

Take care when thinking of buying the shares in a company whose senior managers' lifestyles are lavish and highly publicised in newspapers and magazines.

WorldCom/MCI: If It Looks too Good to Be True . . .

WorldCom (a telephone company) overstated its cash flow by improperly booking $11 billion in company revenues. The company was first to announce that it needed to restate its financial reports in March 2002, but it wasn't clear which financial statements the company needed to restate, or why.

Bernard Ebbers, WorldCom's founder, was given $400 million in off-the-books loans by the company. Criminal fraud charges were filed against Ebbers and former Chief Financial Officer (CFO) Scott Sullivan. Sullivan pleaded guilty to three criminal charges related to the fraud as part of a deal to co-operate with prosecutors in their case against Ebbers. Ebbers was found guilty of fraud in 2005 and given a prison sentence of 25 years and Scott Sullivan five years.

Investor groups filed a class-action case against WorldCom's former directors, former executives, 18 banks, and former outside auditor Arthur Andersen. A few of these plaintiffs settled out of court in 2004; the settlement included a $50 million payment by some former WorldCom directors and a $2.65 billion settlement by Citigroup, a bank that had promoted WorldCom's stocks and bonds as good investments, even though it had concerns about WorldCom's rocky financial position.

Other banks involved in the class action refused to settle at that time, insisting that the banks could not determine which financial statements were false and how the company misstated them. However, as time passed, all remaining investment banks have settled – and probably at higher figures than could have been achieved earlier. The class action is now believed to have raised over $6 billion.

WorldCom filed for bankruptcy protection in 2002. The company emerged from bankruptcy as MCI in 2004, which is the name of a company it bought along the way to building its kingdom. As part of the bankruptcy settlement among the company, the courts, and the creditors the company's debt was reduced by 85 per cent to $5.8 billion, still leaving many creditors with little or nothing. Shareholders also were left with nothing, and their shares were worthless after the company emerged from bankruptcy. In turn, MCI was acquired in 2005 by Verizon Communications Inc, which thus became the biggest telecoms company in the US at the time.

If it looks too good to be true it probably is.

Parmalat: Keep It Simple

Parmalat is a good example of just how complicated these situations can be. Everybody knows that some sort of wrongdoing has occurred because 11 people were found guilty in June 2005 for their part in the collapse of the company. But these 11 are those who received reduced sentences (of up to two and a half years) in return for co-operating with the prosecution.

At the time of writing, Calisto Tanzi, the founder of the company, is on trial with others, including external auditors, for market rigging, providing false accounting information and misleading Italy's stock-market regulator. Tanzi has also been indicted along with about 20 others for fraudulent bankruptcy and criminal association. In addition, five major international banks are due to stand trial for alleged market manipulation. So something big happened – but what?

This much is clear. Parmalat started as a small food company in northern Italy in the 1960s but had grown over the next 40 years to be a major international supplier of dairy products. Their problems came to public notice in 2003 when they had difficulty making a bond payment of 150 million euros. This made no sense since, according to the accounts, Parmalat had very healthy balances of cash on hand. The company then admitted that an amount of 3.9 billion euros, which it thought it had in the bank, did not in fact exist. It later emerged that the auditors had sought confirmation of this bank balance from the Bank of America, had received confirmation of the balance on the bank's headed paper, but the bank said later that the letter was forged. People inside the company as well as outside had been taken in by this device.

As the problems escalated, it emerged that the group actually owed over 14 billion euros in debt – more than double the amounts booked on the balance sheet. Investigators allege that Parmalat borrowed money from banks, justifying the loans through fictitious sales. The loans were then moved to other companies which were not included in the consolidated accounts.

There are allegations of double-billing (charging for the same sale twice) and suggestions that the true position was that the company had been suffering substantial losses throughout the 1990s, but we will probably never know, let alone understand, what really happened.

Look for companies who keep their financial activities open and simply stated.

Independent Insurance: Unreliable Info, Higher Risk

At Southwark Crown Court three former directors of Independent Insurance were found guilty of conspiracy to defraud. The charge was that between 1 January 1997 and 17 June 2001, contrary to common law, they conspired together and with others to defraud directors, employees, auditors, actuaries, reinsurers, shareholders, policy holders, creditors and others who had a legitimate interest in knowing the financial condition of Independent Insurance Company Limited and the Independent Insurance Group Plc by misleading them about the true extent of the liabilities of the said companies.

The 'indie trial' which resulted in the handing down of sentences of seven, four, and three years on the three directors, is a useful case study for readers of this book. In simple terms, it has been reported that Independent Insurance received claims from its customers that were not entered into its accounting system. Consequently nobody, not even the company's own directors, knew how large its liabilities were. It was this lack of information that led to the demise of the company. Faced with losses which could not be quantified, and unable to go ahead with a planned rights issue, the company ceased to trade in 2001. Whether there was indeed fraud does not change the important learning point from the indie trial. The directors cannot manage a company without reliable information. If the directors do not have reliable information, then potential investors have even less chance of making reasoned decisions. An investor must look at the reputations of the top people and make a judgement – although it is always easier to judge these things with the benefit of hindsight!

Some of the firm's 500,000 private and corporate policyholders have been given a total of £357 million from the Financial Services Authority's compensation scheme since the collapse; but this is a slow process and resulted in financial difficulties for many people who thought they were insured by a reputable company.

Versailles: Don't Follow the Money-Go-Round

Versailles Trade Finance Ltd (VTFL) was set up in 1991 to provide bridging, or temporary finance for small businesses. The big banks often neglect this area and Carl Cushnie, the founder of the company, claimed to have come up with a new risk-free way to lend to small businesses. It was akin to factoring, selling your accounts receivable at a discount in order to get cash in now, but worked as follows: A client of VTFL wished to sell goods to a customer. Instead the goods were sold to VTFL at a discount (VTFL's commission) and VTFL then sold them on to the final customer at full price. VTFL would pay the client 80 per cent of the value within 7 days of the sale. The balance, less interest and commission would be passed on when VTFL was paid by the customer.

Money was raised from banks and other backers to finance VTFL. Money was also raised from wealthy individuals (known as 'Traders') to finance another group company called Versailles Traders Ltd. The group grew rapidly. It was floated as Versailles Group plc in 1995 and, at its height, the company was valued by the market at £630 million.

However, most of the activity in the company involved transactions with other group companies as money was passed around the group. False documents and management accounts were given to the auditors to hide the fraud. The Serious Fraud Office (SFO) has given a restatement of turnover figures for the years from 1991 to 1999. Out of reported turnover in that period of over £680 million, less than £90 million was genuine.

The company collapsed following a DTI investigation in 1999 owing £70 million to the banks. The Traders had lost £23 million. Cushnie and his Finance Director, Frederick Clough, were both sent to jail for six years.

Barings Bank: Security, Accuracy, and Incompetence

Nick Leeson, a so-called rogue trader, worked for Barings Bank in Singapore as a trader in futures and options. He was regarded as a star because of the profits he was generating from arbitrage trading activities that were, on the face of it, reasonably risk free. He had in fact set up an internal account number 88888 in which to conceal the actual massive losses his activities were incurring. Between 1992 and 1995 the losses reached £830 million – enough to bring the bank down.

The Bank of England in its report concluded as follows:

- ✔ The losses were incurred by reason of unauthorised and concealed trading activities.
- ✔ The true position was not noticed earlier by reason of a serious failure of controls and managerial confusion within Barings.
- ✔ The true position had not been detected prior to the collapse by the external auditors, supervisors, or regulators of Barings.

So there it is again: The crucial importance of secure systems offering managers and directors an accurate picture of the organisation's financial affairs in time for them to realise what is going on in the physical world by studying the resulting numbers. The fascinating aspect of the case was to see how easily the guardians of the shareholders, the highly experienced external auditors, could be outwitted by a relatively junior trader. Okay, some incompetence existed, but remember that security and accuracy of information is not easy to achieve.

Equitable Life: Spread Your Pension Bets

The story of Equitable Life seems like a financial scandal at first but when looked at dispassionately the story is one of bad luck as much as anything – with a bit of bad judgement thrown in.

The impact of what went wrong was that many pensioners had a far smaller pension than they were expecting after saving in the long term with Equitable Life. (Equitable Life started business in 1762, so they were no spring chickens at the game when it all went wrong.)

In the 1950s Equitable Life started offering Guaranteed Annuity Rates (GARs) to its savers. This safeguarded its pensioners from some of the volatility of stock and money markets by offering a fixed rate of annuity when it came to cashing in their pensions. At the start pensioners probably got a little less than they would have got if they had taken normal market risk. However, high inflation in the seventies, when Equitable were still offering guaranteed annuities, was followed 20 years later by the low inflation and low interest rates of the nineties. This meant that Equitable Life could not possibly pay the guaranteed rates without damaging enormously its other pensioners. They tried to get out of the contracts but the courts would not let them.

So there was a compromise and everyone, those with and without GAR's, got less pension than they were expecting. So bad luck or bad judgement, but no scandal surely. What we learn from this is not to put our pension savings in one pot: Spread it around a number of providers.

Robert Maxwell: Unfit to Lead

The sheer complexity of corporate and financial life does give those people who will stop at nothing the opportunity to damage other people by their unscrupulous and criminal dealings. Maxwell is a good example of this.

In 1969 a financial scandal cost Maxwell his political career and the control of his business. Despite the fact that a DTI report following these events had dubbed the man 'unfit' to run a public company, Maxwell, plainly it should be noted an extraordinary and charismatic man, bought back his company and clawed his way back into running a large media corporation using a huge amount of debt to finance his dealings. That finance became strained until it looked as though he would have problems meeting interest and repayment obligations. Simply put he then used his companies' pension funds to buy shares in his own companies; this propped up the share price and he used these shares as collateral for further loans.

So this tale is different from the ones where tycoons put their company's money into their own pockets – this time Maxwell was using the complex nature of cross-shareholdings and so on to prevent normal market forces from hindering what he aspired to achieve. In the end the result is the same, the companies went bust and the pension pot was empty.

They have of course, tightened up the rules on pensions but there are some observers who think that it could still happen again. Perhaps the message from this one is that if a man has been reported unfit to run a company and his empire looks too good to be true, we should use those clues to avoid those shares like the plague.

Northern Rock: Financial Problems Without Wrongdoing

Northern Rock provided the UK with its first bank run for more than a hundred years. Queues formed outside the branches of the Northern Rock as depositors sought to remove their savings. No doubt, when the dust settles, there will be demands for heads to roll. Probably the Northern Rock name will cease to exist having been gobbled up by a bigger rival. But has anyone actually done anything wrong? There is no suggestion that the financial statements do not reflect the true position of the company. The balance of trade receivables shown in the financial statement will already take account of the expected losses on bad debts. The problem is not with financial reporting but with the very nature of business itself.

Taking a broad look at potential investments

The stories we have told in this chapter have concentrated heavily, perhaps too heavily, on fraud. Fraud makes the headlines and the stories are always interesting, but through cases such as Equitable Life, Northern Rock and underfunded pensions, we have tried to demonstrate that financial crises can arise through a change in market conditions or even a change in the way that information is reported.

To return to the main themes of this book, when you invest in a company, you must obtain the financial statements. You would be very unfortunate indeed if the statements were tainted by deliberate fraud but remember that accountancy requires

the directors to make a lot of subjective decisions so read the accounting policies very carefully.

But you must go beyond the financial statements and examine the business review (this may be called the Operating and Financial Review) and any other statements made by management. This is where you find the details of the business strategy. Try to decide what could go wrong with the strategy. Remember that, if the company is earning high returns then they may well be taking higher risks. If you invest in such a company, then it might give you good returns but, equally, there is no point in complaining if the downside occurs and you are the loser.

Northern Rock depended for its cash liquidity on borrowing short-term money from other banks for short periods instead of the normal model of having a high level of depositors' long-term savings. When the US had its own crisis caused by banks lending sums of money to people who were not very good credit risks this rolled out into a world wide credit crunch. Banks were simply loathe to lend money into the short term wholesale, that is other banks, market. This gave Northern Rock massive liquidity problems that were only solved when the Bank of England became a lender of last resort and lent the bank billions of pounds. The Bank of England also stopped the run by guaranteeing depositors savings.

Northern Rock's business plan – previously seen as entrepreneurial – is now seen as too risky. Therefore, the market has reacted and shares are marked down. The company has the same assets and liabilities as before but now the market thinks it is worth a fraction of what it was at the start of the crisis. What the Northern Rock case illustrates is that it is difficult to run a big business when the decisions you make today can come back to haunt you in five, ten, or even twenty years time – if you doubt the truth of this, then ask Equitable Life. (See the section 'Equitable Life: Spread Your Pension Bets', earlier in this chapter.)

To move to a different issue, financial reporting itself is full of difficulties. For example, a few years ago, it was revealed that company pension funds were massively underfunded. This had been brought to light, we were told, by a new method of accounting for pension liabilities which had just been introduced by the UK Accounting Standards Board. The problem was that very few people (other than actuaries) understood what the figures actually meant. For example, a deficit of £10 billion sounds like a lot of money but the new rules had been introduced immediately after the dot.com crash and a large part of the deficit would disappear as the stock market recovered. What sounded like a financial scandal when the news broke turned out to have no evidence of wrongdoing.

Chapter 23

Ten Signs That a Company's in Trouble

In This Chapter

▶ Pondering money problems

▶ Finding reporting foibles

▶ Identifying inventory unease

*I*f you don't recognise traffic signs, driving is going to be pretty hairy. By the same token, if you don't recognise a company's danger signs by reading the financial reports, your investment decisions may not be the best ones.

Many companies put out glossy financial reports with the most graphically pleasing sections providing only the news about the company that its managers want you to read. Don't be fooled. Take the time to read the pages in smaller print and the ones without the fancy graphics, because these pages are where you find the most important financial news about the company. The following are key signs of trouble that you may find within these pages.

Lower Liquidity

Liquidity is the ability of a company to quickly convert assets to cash so it can pay its bills and meet other debt obligations, such as a mortgage payment on a bill or a payment due to bond investors. The most liquid asset a company holds is its cash in a current or savings account. Other good sources are cash equivalents, which include holdings that a company can quickly convert to cash, such as marketable securities, certificates of deposits, or other types of investments that can sell quickly and be turned into cash.

Other assets take longer to turn into cash, but they can be more liquid than long-term assets such as a building or equipment. Take, for instance, trade receivables. Trade receivables can often be liquid holdings for a company as long as its customers are paying their bills on time. If customers are paying late, the company will find that its trade receivables are 'less liquid', meaning that it takes longer for the company to collect that cash. We show you how to test a company's trade receivables management in Chapter 16.

Another sign of trouble may be inventory. If a company's inventory continues to build, a company may have less and less cash on hand as it ties up more money in the products it's trying to sell. We show you how to test a company's inventory management in Chapter 15, and how to test a company's overall liquidity in Chapter 12.

Low Cash Flow

If you don't have cash, you can't pay your bills. The same is true for companies. You need to know how well a company manages its cash, and you can't do that just by looking at the balance sheet and income statement. Neither of these statements reports what's actually happening with cash.

The only way you can check out a company's cash situation is by using the cash-flow statement. We show you numerous ways to test a company's cash flow in Chapter 13. If you find that a company can't meet its cash obligations after doing the calculations in Chapter 13, or is close to reaching that point, this situation is a clear sign of trouble.

Disappearing Profit Margins

Everyone wants to know how much money a company makes – in other words, its profits. If you find a company's profit dropping year to year, that's a clear sign of trouble.

Companies must report their profit results for the current year, in addition to the previous year, on their income statements, one of the three key financial statements that are part of the financial reports. (Refer to Chapter 7 for more information about income statements.) When investigating a company's viability, looking at the past five years or more – if you can get the data – is a good idea. Luckily, finding a company's historical profit data is easy. Most companies post some previous years reports on their Web sites.

Any time you notice that a company's profit margins have fallen from year to year, take it as a clear sign that the company is in trouble. Research further to find out why, but definitely don't invest in a company with falling profit margins unless you get good, solid information about an expected turnaround and how the company plans to pull that off. To find out more about how to test whether or not a company is making a profit, turn to Chapter 11.

Revenue Game-Playing

A day rarely goes by when you don't see a story about company bigwigs who've played with their company's revenue results. Although the number of companies being exposed for revenue problems has certainly fallen since the height of the scandals set off by the fall of Enron in 2001, a steady stream of reporting about the games that companies play with their revenue continues.

Problems can include managing earnings so that results look better than they are and actually creating a fictional story about earnings. We talk more about how companies play games with their revenue numbers in Chapter 21.

The Financial Reporting Review Panel (FRRP) performs some proactive monitoring of company financial statements. They announce each year the business sectors that they will examine in the coming year. In addition, they respond to complaints or tip-offs. If the FRRP begins an investigation, you are unlikely to know about it until the FRRP, or the company, issue a press release.

The initial stages of an investigation usually involve private enquiries between the FRRP and the company. The issues concerning the FRRP may well be resolved without any publicity. Alternatively, at the end of an investigation, having reached agreement with the company concerned, the FRRP issue a press release giving an outline of the problem and the agreed solution. Often the agreed solution is to use a different approach to measurement or disclosure in the following year's financial statements. Only rarely has the FRRP insisted that a company reissues a previous set of accounts.

Too Much Debt

Borrowing too much money to continue operations or to finance new activities can be a major red flag that indicates future problems for a company, especially if interest rates start rising. Debt can overburden a company and make it hard for a company to meet its obligations, eventually landing the company in bankruptcy.

You can test a company's debt situation by using the ratios in Chapter 12. Compare a company's debt ratios with those of others in the same industry to judge whether or not the company is in worse shape than its competitors. These ratios are calculated based on numbers presented in the balance sheet and income statement.

Unrealistic Values for Assets and Liabilities

Some companies can make themselves look financially healthier by overvaluing their assets or undervaluing their liabilities:

- *Overvalued assets* can make a company appear as if its holdings are worth more than they are. For instance, if customers aren't paying their bills, but the trade-receivables item isn't properly adjusted to show the likely bad debt, the trade and other-receivables item will be higher than it should be.

- *Undervalued liabilities* can make a company look as though it owes less than it actually does. An instance of this would be when debts are moved off the balance sheet to another subsidiary to hide the debt. Concealing debts in this way is just one of the things Enron, and other scandal-ridden companies, did to hide their problems.

If a company has hidden its problems well to offset the overvaluing of assets or the undervaluing of debt, equity is probably overstated as well.

If you suspect a company of either possibility, it's a clear sign of trouble ahead. You should certainly begin to suspect a problem if you see stories in the newspapers about the company's auditors or the Serious Fraud Office raising questions regarding a company's financial statements. You may be able to spot them sooner by using the techniques we discuss in Chapter 22.

A Change in Accounting Methods

Accounting rules are clearly set in the Generally Accepted Accounting Principles (GAAP) developed by the International Accounting Standards Board (IASB). You can find details about the GAAP at the IASB's Web site (www.iasb.org).

Sometimes a company can file a report that's perfectly acceptable by GAAP standards, but it may hide a potential problem by changing its accounting methods. For example, all companies must account for their inventory by using one of four possible methods. Changing from one method to another can have a great impact on the bottom line. To find out whether this kind of change has occurred, read the fine print in the financial notes.

We talk more about accounting methods in Chapter 4 and delve even deeper into inventory-control methods in Chapter 15.

Questionable Mergers and Acquisitions

Mergers and acquisitions can be both good news and bad news. Usually, you won't know whether a merger or acquisition will actually be good for a company's bottom line until years later. So be careful about buying into the fray when you see stories about the possibility of a merger or acquisition. If you don't already own shares, stay away until the dust settles and you get a clear view of how the merger or acquisition impacts the companies involved. If you do own shares, closely follow all the reports by the financial press and the financial analysts. You are, as a shareholder, able to vote for or against the merger or acquisition if it involves the exchange of shares.

You can get to know the issues by reading what the company sends out when it seeks your vote. Follow the stories in the financial press. Read reports from analysts about the merger or acquisition.

For example, just ask Time Warner workers what they think about their company's merger with AOL; I'm sure you'll hear many words of disgust, most not printable. Many of these employees held large chunks of shares in their retirement portfolios, which have lost most of their value. Time Warner shares dropped from a market value of $52.56 per share in January 2001, when the merger was approved by the US government, to $15.11 per share in September 2003, when the Time Warner board decided to drop AOL from its name, acknowledging the failure of the merger that was valued at $112 billion when it happened in 2000.

You don't see much about mergers and acquisitions in the three key financial statements – income statement, balance sheet, and statement of cash flows; they rarely take up more than a line item. The key place to find out about the impact of mergers and acquisitions is in the notes to the financial statements, which we talk more about in Chapter 9.

We can't tell you how to read the tea leaves and work out whether a merger or acquisition will ultimately be a good idea, but we can warn you to stay away if you don't already own shares. If you're a shareholder who eventually has to vote on the merger or acquisition before it can be approved, read everything you can get your hands on that discusses the financial impact for the company related to the merger or acquisition.

Slow Inventory Turnover

One way to see whether a company is slowing down is to look at its *inventory turnover* (how quickly the inventory the company holds is sold). As a product's lifespan nears its end, moving that product off the shelf tends to be harder and harder.

When you see a company's inventory turnover slowing down, it may indicate a long-term or short-term problem. Economic conditions, such as a recession – which isn't company specific – may be the cause of a short-term problem. A long-term problem may be a product line that isn't kept up to date, so customers are looking to other companies or products to meet their needs. We show you how to pick up on inventory-turnover problems in Chapter 15 by using numbers from the income statement and the balance sheet.

Slow-Paying Customers

Companies report their sales when the initial transaction occurs, even if the customer hasn't yet paid cash for the product. When a customer pays with a credit card issued by a bank or other financial institution, the company considers it cash. Only credit issued to the customer directly by the company selling the product is not reported as cash received. The reason is that the customer won't have to pay cash until the company that issued the credit bills him. For example, if you have an account at Staples that you charge your office supplies on, Staples won't get cash for those supplies until you pay your monthly statement. If, instead, you bought those same supplies using a Visa or MasterCard, the credit-card company would deposit cash into Staples' account and then work to collect the cash from you.

Companies track non-cash sales to customers whom they have given credit to directly in an account called trade receivables, and customers are billed for payments.

But not all customers pay their bills on time. If you see a company's trade receivables numbers continuing to rise, it may be a sign that customers are slowing down their payments, and eventually, the company may face a cash-flow problem. Go to Chapter 16 to find out how to detect trade-receivables problems.

Chapter 24

Ten Top-Notch Online Resources

In This Chapter

▶ Finding financial reports

▶ Looking for analysis and advice

▶ Keeping up-to-date on investing and business news

*T*he Internet has made accessing financial reports – and getting to the bottom of the numbers – easier than ever. You can instantaneously find a wealth of financial report information (often for free!) on the Web. Here are ten of our favourite sites.

Companies House

If you go to Companies House (www.companieshouse.gov.uk) you can find financial reports and other details of companies. By entering the company's name or registration number you can access a certain amount of free information, such as the company's registered office (where documents can be served) and the nature of its business.

Companies House also tells you the date of the last annual return and the latest year for which accounts have been filed. The due date for the next filing of annual return and accounts will also be shown. If you wish to access information about the company's members, directors, or the financial statements themselves then this has to be paid for – the annual return and the accounts can be obtained online for the princely sum of £1 each.

Remember that companies which obey the legal definition of a small company are entitled to file abbreviated accounts which contain very little information. The page containing the free information will tell you if the accounts are abbreviated by saying 'Total exemption small' after the date of the last accounts.

IASB

The International Accounting Standards Board (IASB) develops the Generally Accepted Accounting Principles (GAAP) that govern financial report presentation and contents. You can access the current rules and read about new rules under consideration at IASB's Web site, www.iasb.org. The IASB's magazine *Update* can be accessed free online and this tells you about the progress being made on current projects. Unfortunately, the accounting standards themselves are only available on payment of a fee.

In Chapter 18 we talk more about the role of IASB and how it develops the GAAP rules.

 UK listed companies must follow International standards in the preparation of their group accounts. Other UK companies follow the standards of the UK Accounting Standards Board. Their Web site can be accessed via www.frc. org.uk – the Web site of the Financial Reporting Council. The FRC Web site can also be used to access reports of the Financial Reporting Review Panel and the Web site of the Auditing Practices Board.

Yahoo! Finance UK

Although Yahoo! Finance (uk.finance.yahoo.com) may not be the most sophisticated financial Web site, it excels as one of the easiest sites to use for accessing basic financial statistics for all companies that are publicly traded. All you need to know is the company's stock symbol to access the information for free, and if you don't know the symbol, you can search by the company name.

After you access the main page for a company, you find its current trading statistics and any news headlines of articles that mention the company. On the left-hand side of the page, you find links for historical prices, basic charts, technical analysis, message boards discussing the company, a company profile, information on director dealings in the shares, analyst opinions and estimates, and broker reports (some you don't have to pay for, but others send you to Web sites of companies that do charge for the reports). You can also link through the annual reports button to the company's latest annual report.

Standard & Poor's

When you hear the initials S&P (Standard & Poor's), you probably think of the S&P 500, which is a select group of US *large-capitalisation stocks* (stocks for companies that have a market value greater than $10 billion) whose prices are monitored daily and used as one gauge of how well the US stock market is doing. However, S&P's primary financial role is rating the credit worthiness of a company's bonds that are offered for sale.

You can access credit ratings for each company and industry statistics at S&P's Web site (www2.standardandpoors.com).You can also find recent press reports of any changes to a company's credit rating for free after you register on the site (registration is also free). You can search for press reports by company and by industry, but you can't access full S&P reports for free.

 You can find some S&P information, charged for on their site, at no charge at *Business Week's* investing Web site (www.businessweek.com/investor/), after you click through to Europe.

Biz/ed

Biz/ed says that it is a Web site for students and educators in business studies, economics, accounting, leisure, sport, recreation and travel and tourism. Our interest in it is that it provides online training in a wide range of accounting topics. Go to www.bized.co.uk. In the Quick Jump box at the top left-hand corner of the home page, select 'Accounting' from the drop down menu where it says 'Choose subject' and click 'Go to Resources'. This will take you to a wealth of useful learning material.

In particular, clicking on 'Financial Accounting' and then 'Financial Ratio Analysis' leads you to explanations and worked illustrations of many of the ratios discussed in this book. Some industry ratios are also available.

Financial Times

The *Financial Times* is the UK's premier business newspaper. You can find it on the Internet at www.ft.com/home/uk. The Web site includes recent articles from the paper updated for the Web site. Using the navigation menu on the left-hand side you can look at an archive of articles on everything from markets to companies to personal finance. On the Web site `ft.ar.wilink.com` you can get easy access to company annual reports. Most are available to be downloaded, or they can be sent to you by post if you want to feel the glossiness – or absence of glossiness – of the actual report.

Accounting Web: ICC

ICC have provided industry ratios for many years. Originally, they published an annual volume giving industry averages for many of the key accounting ratios. Now, the information is available online via `www.accountingweb.co.uk/icc`. A lot of the basic information is also available from Companies House (see the first section of this chapter), but ICC also provide packages of data such as five years accounts. Obviously, this sort of information is not available free of charge. As part of their 'Overview report' (cost £14) they provide a company and industry comparison which is a ratio and percentage based table of company performance against industry sector. This information includes industry quartiles for business ratios.

Find

As well as links into investor information on companies and click-throughs to other providers of specialist information, `www.find.co.uk` also provides a pretty comprehensive personal finance service including background information as well as specific product profiles. For example if you click through to pensions you can get everything you need from a beginner's guide to understanding the risks and returns of pensions.

Be careful, most of the sites that Find connects to are the sites of companies selling products, but it's a good source if you are educating yourself in personal finance or, for example, thinking of choosing companies to put into your own pension scheme.

Department of Business, Enterprise and Regulatory Reform

Formerly the Department of Trade and Industry (DTI), the Department of Business, Enterprise and Regulatory Reform's site (`www.berr.gov.uk`) offers a range of interesting business-related topics. For example, the link to the Business Link Web site gives practical advice on what to do if you are planning on setting up in business yourself.

The main interest in this Web site for readers of this book is the information provided about the implementation of the new Companies Act via the 'Better Business Framework' tab. If, on the other hand, you want copies of legislation then the relevant Web site is the Office of Public Sector Information at www.opsi.gov.uk where all recent UK legislation can be downloaded without charge.

Reuters

You can access current business news for free at Reuters' Web site (www.reuters.co.uk). Reuters offers sector and industry analysis, as well as a number of good tools for stock investors. You can also access company and research reports from many brokerage companies. Some of these reports are free, and others require payment.

Part VII
Appendixes

'DO YOU MIND?!!'

In this part . . .

In Appendix A, we show you sample financial reports from two major retail companies, Tesco and Marks and Spencer. We also give you some of the key ratios you can use to interpret the results. In Appendix B, we provide a glossary to help you wind your merry way through the world of financial reporting.

Appendix A
Financial Statements

....

*Y*ou can read all day about financial statements, but until you take a peek at the real thing, you don't have a complete understanding of what they show, how they're set up, and what you can expect to find. On the pages that follow, we show you examples of reports from two companies, Tesco and Marks and Spencer. Both companies are in the retail industry, which makes comparing them that much more valuable.

You're likely to notice a lot of similarities and some striking differences. For example, companies differ in where they give out information that is not covered by the rules and regulations. Some will choose to put a particular item in the statements, whilst others could choose to put the same item in the notes to the accounts.

Not every company presents the information on its financial statements in the same way, but every company has to follow the reporting guidelines set out by the International Accounts Standard Board (see Chapter 19) and must provide the information according to generally accepted accounting principles (GAAP: See Chapter 18). So no matter how the information makes its way onto the page, it must be complete and accurate. (And if it isn't, the reporting company may end up in a heck of a scandal.)

It is also very useful to make comparisons between the company last year and the company the year before. In the second part of this Appendix we have given a summary of all the figures and ratios you are going to learn how to identify in the course of the book.

Tesco plc Group income statement Year ended 24 February 2007

	notes	2007 £m	2006 £m
Continuing operations			
Revenue (sales excluding VAT)	2	42,641	39,454
Cost of sales		(39,401)	(36,426)
Pensions adjustment – Finance Act 2006	23	258	–
Impairment of the Gerrards Cross site		(35)	–
Gross profit		3,463	3,028
Administrative expenses		(907)	(825)
Profit arising on property-related items	2/3	92	99
Operating profit	2	2,648	2,280
Share of post-tax profits of joint ventures and associates			
(including £47m of property-related items (2005/06–£nil))	13	106	80
Profit on sale of investments in associates	13	25	–
Finance income	5	90	114
Finance costs	5	(216)	(241)
Profit before tax	3	2,653	2,235
Taxation	6	(772)	(649)
Profit for the year from continuing operations		1,881	1,576
Discontinued operation			
Profit/(loss) for the year from discontinued operation	7	18	(10)
Profit for the year		1,899	1,576
Attributable to:			
Equity holders of the parent		1,982	1,570
Minority interests		7	6
		1,899	1,576
Earnings per share from continuing and discontinued operations			
Basic	9	23.84p	20.07p
Diluted	9	23.54p	19.76p
Earnings per share from continuing operations			
Basic	9	23.61p	20.20p
Diluted	9	23.31p	19.92p

Tesco plc Group balance sheet 24 February 2007

	notes	2007 £m	2006 £m
Non-current assets			
Goodwill and other intangible assets	10	2,045	1,525
Property, plant and equipment	11	16,976	15,882
Investment property	12	856	745
Investments in joint ventures and associates	13	314	476
Other Investments	14	8	4
Deferred tax assets	6	32	12
		20,231	18,644
Current assets			
Inventories	15	1,931	1,464
Trade aid other receivables	16	1,079	892
Derivative financial instruments	20	108	70
Current tax assets		8	–
Cash and cash equivalents	17	1,042	1,325
		4,168	3,751
Non-current assets classified as held for sale and assets of the disposal group	2	408	168
		4,576	3,919
Current liabilities			
Trade and other payables	16	(6,046)	(5,083)
Financial liabilities			
– Borrowings	19	(1,554)	(1,646)
– Derivative financial instruments and other liabilities	20	(87)	(239)
Current tax liabilities		(461)	(462)
Provisions	21	(4)	(2)
		(8,152)	(7,432)
Liabilities directly associated with the disposal group	7	–	(86)
		(8,152)	(7,518)
Net current liabilities		(3,576)	(3,599)
Non-current liabilities			
Financial liabilities			
– Borrowings	19	(4,146)	(3,742)
– Derivative financial instruments and other liabilities	20	(399)	(294)
Post-employment benefit obligations	23	(950)	(1,211)
Other non-current liabilities	18	(29)	(29)
Deferred tax liabilities	6	(535)	(320)
Provisions	21	(25)	(5)
		(6,084)	(5,601)
Net assets		10,571	9,444
Equity			
Share capital	24/25	397	395
Share premium account	25	4,376	3,988
Other reserves	25	40	40
Retailed earnings	25	5,693	4,957
Equity attributable to equity holders of the parent		10,506	9,380
Minority interests	25	65	64
Total equity		10,571	9,444

Sir Terence Leahy
Andrew Higginson
Directors

Tesco plc Group cash flow statement Year ended 24 February 2007

	notes	2007 £m	2006 £m
Cash flows from operating activities			
Cash generated from operations	28	3,532	3,412
Interest paid		(376)	(364)
Corporation tax paid		(545)	(429)
Net cash from operating activities		2,611	2,619
Cash flows from investing activities			
Acquisition of subsidiaries, net of cash acquired		(325)	(54)
Proceeds from sale of subsidiary, net of cash disposed		22	–
Proceeds from sale of joint ventures and associates		41	–
Purchase of property, plant and equipment and investment property		(2,852)	(2,561)
Proceeds from sale of property, plant and equipment		809	664
Purchase of intangible assets		(174)	(139)
Net increase in loans to joint ventures		(21)	(16)
Invested in joint ventures and associates		(49)	(34)
Dividends received		124	82
Interest received		82	96
Net cash used in investing activities		(2,343)	(1,962)
Cash flows from financing activities			
Proceeds from issue of ordinary share capital		156	123
Net increase in/(repayments of) borrowings		184	(109)
New finance leases		99	–
Repayment of obligations under finance leases		(15)	(6)
Dividends paid		(467)	(441)
Own shares purchased		(490)	(59)
Net cash used in financing activities		(533)	(492)
Net (decrease)/increase in cash and cash equivalents		(265)	165
Cash and cash equivalents at beginning of year		1,325	1,146
Effect of foreign exchange rate changes		(18)	16
Cash and cash equivalents at end of year		1,042	1,327
Less cash held in disposal group		–	(2)
Cash and cash equivalents not held in disposal group	17	1,042	1,325

* Results for the year ended 25 February 2006 include 52 weeks for the UK and the Republic of Ireland and 14 months for the majority of the remaining International businesses.

Marks and Spencer plc Consolidated income statement

	notes	52 weeks ended 31 March 2007 £m	52 weeks ended 1 April 2006 £m
Revenue – continuing operations	2.3	8,586.1	7,797.7
Operating profit – continuing operations	2.3	1,045.9	850.1
Finance income	5	33.8	30.5
Finance costs	5	(143.0)	(134.9)
Analysed between:			
Before exceptional finance costs	5	(112.6)	(134.9)
Exceptional finance costs		(30.4)	–
Profit on ordinary activities before taxation – continuing operations	4	936.7	745.7
Analysed between:			
Before property disposals and exceptional items		965.2	751.4
Profit/(loss) on property disposals	3	1.9	(5.7)
Exceptional finance costs	5	(30.4)	–
Income tax expense	6	(277.5)	(225.1)
Profit on ordinary activities after taxation – continuing operations		659.2	520.6
Profit from discontinued operation	7A	0.7	2.5
Profit for the year attributable to shareholders		658.9	523.1
Basic earnings per share	8A	39.1p	31.4p
Diluted earnings per share	8B	38.5p	31.1p
Basic earnings per share from continuing operations	8A	39.1p	31.3p
Diluted earnings per share from continuing operations	8B	38.5p	31.0p

Marks and Spencer plc Consolidated balance sheet

	notes	As at 31 March 2007 £m	As at 1 April 2006 (restated) £m
ASSETS			
Non-current assets			
Intangible assets	13	194.1	163.5
Property plant and equipment	14	4,044.5	3,575.8
Investment property	15	25.1	38.5
Investment in joint venture	16	9.3	9.0
Other financial assets	17	3.0	3.3
Trade and other receivables	18	247.0	242.8
Deferred tax assets	25	11.6	83.9
		4,534.6	4,116.8
Current assets			
Inventories		416.3	374.3
Other financial assets	17	50.9	48.8
Trade and other receivables	18	196.7	210.5
Derivative financial instruments	23	2.4	76.4
Cash and cash equivalents	19	180.1	362.6
Assets of discontinued operation		–	69.5
		846.4	1,142.1
Total assets		5,381.0	5,258.9
LIABILITIES			
Current liabilities			
Trade and other payables	20	1,043.9	867.8
Derivative financial instruments	23	8.3	8.0
Borrowings and other financial liabilities	21	461.0	1,052.8
Current tax liabilities		87.3	58.7
Provisions	24	5.7	9.2
Liabilities of discontinued operation		–	20.5
		1,8062	2,017.0
Non-current Liabilities			
Borrowings and other financial liabilities	21	1,234.5	1.133.8
Partnership liability to the Marks & Spencer UK Pension Scheme	22	496.9	–
Retirement benefit deficit	11	283.3	794.9
Trade and other payables	20	87.6	74.8
Derivative financial instruments	23	0.2	9.5
Provisions	24	16.8	19.1
Deterred tax liabilities	25	7.3	6.1
		2,126.6	2,038.2
Total liabilities		3,732.8	4,055.2
Net assets		1,648.2	1,203.7
EQUITY			
Called up share capital – equity	26.27	424.9	420.6
Share premium account	27	202.9	162.3
Capital redemption reserve	27	2,168.5	2,113.8
Hedging reserve	27	(4.4)	(8.0)
Other reserve	27	(6,542.2)	(6,542.2)
Retained earnings	27	5,397.1	5,057.2
Total shareholders' equity		1,646.8	1,203.7
Minority interest in equity		1.4	–
Total equity		1,648.2	1.203.7

Approved by the Board
21 May 2007
Stuart Rose, Chief Executive
Ian Dyson, Group Finance Director

Marks and Spencer plc cash flow statement

	notes	52 weeks ended 31 March 2007 £m	52 weeks ended 1 April 2006 £m
Cash flows from operating activities			
Cash generated from operations – continuing	29A	1.442.6	1,183.6
Cash generated from operations – discontinued	29B	0.7	13.9
Tax paid		(150.8)	(101.5)
Net cash inflow from operating activities		1,292.5	1,096.0
Cash flows from investing activities			
Disposal of subsidiary, net of cash disposed		48.8	
Capital expenditure and financial investment	29C	(712.0)	(266.3)
Interest received		13.2	12.9
Net cash outflow from Investing activities		(650.8)	(253.4)
Cash flows from financing activities			
Interest paid		(123.4)	(142.8)
Exceptional interest paid		(21.6)	–
Other debt financing	29D	(479.2)	(420.0)
Equity dividends paid		(260.6)	(204.1)
Other equity financing	29E	9.2	55.8
Net cash outflow from financing activities		(875.6)	(711.1)
Net cash (outflow)/inflow from activities		(233.9)	131.5
Effects of exchange rate changes		(1.5)	1.6
Opening net cash		282.4	149.3
Closing net cash	30A	47.0	282.4

Table A–1	Profitability and Market Value			
	Tesco		Marks and Spencer	
EPS	2007	2006	2007	2006
Basic	23.84	20.07	39.1	31.4
Diluted	23.54	19.79	38.5	31.1
P/E ratio	June 2007		June 2007	
Share price	457.75		674	
Diluted EPS	23.54		38.5	
	19.4		17.5	

Table A–1 *(continued)*

	Tesco		Marks and Spencer	
Yield	**Apr-07**		**Apr-07**	
Dividend per share	8.91		15.5	
Share price	457.75		674	
	1.9%		**2.3%**	
Dividend cover	**2007**	**2006**	**2007**	**2006**
Diluted EPS	23.54	19.79	38.5	31.1
Dividend per share	8.91	7.8	15.5	12.3
	2.64	**2.54**	**2.48**	**2.53**
Return on sales (ROS)	**2007**	**2006**	**2007**	**2006**
Profit before tax	2,653	2,235	936.7	745.7
Sales	42,641	39,454	8,588.1	7,797.7
	6.22%	**5.66%**	**10.91%**	**9.56%**
Return on assets (ROA)	**2007**	**2006**	**2007**	**2006**
Profit for year	1,899	1,576	659.9	523.1
Total assets	24,807	22,563	5,381.0	5,258.9
	7.66%	**6.98%**	**12.26%**	**9.95%**
Return on equity (ROE)	**2007**	**2006**	**2007**	**2006**
Profit for year	1,899	1,576	659.9	523.1
Shareholders equity	10,571	9,444	1,648.2	1,203.7
	17.96%	**16.69%**	**40.04%**	**43.46%**

	Tesco		Marks and Spencer	
Gross margin (GM)	**2007**	**2006**	**2007**	**2006**
Gross profit	3,463	3,028	3,341.2	2,985.6
Sales	42,641	39,454	8,588.1	7,797.7
	8.12%	**7.67%**	**38.90%**	**38.29%**
Operating margin (OM)	**2007**	**2006**	**2007**	**2006**
Operating profit	2,648	2,280	1,045.9	850.1
Sales	42,641	39,454	8,588.1	7,797.7
	6.21%	**5.78%**	**12.18%**	**10.90%**
Net profit margin (PM)	**2007**	**2006**	**2007**	**2006**
Profit for the year	1,899	1,576	659.9	523.1
Sales	42,641	39,454	8,588.1	7,797.7
	4.45%	**3.99%**	**7.68%**	**6.71%**

Table A–2: Liquidity

	Tesco		Marks and Spencer	
	2007	**2006**	**2007**	**2006**
Current ratio				
Current assets	4,576	3,919	846.4	1,142.1
Current liabilities	8,152	7,518	1,606.2	2,017.0
	0.56	**0.52**	**0.53**	**0.57**
Quick assets				
Current asset	4,576	3,919	846.4	1,142.1
Inventory	1,931	1,464	416.3	374.3
	2,645	**2,455**	**430.1**	**767.8**

(continued)

Table A–2 *(continued)*

	Tesco		Marks and Spencer	
Quick ratio				
Quick assets	2,645	2,455	430.1	767.8
Current liabilities	8,152	7,518	1,606.2	2,017.0
	0.32	**0.33**	**0.27**	**0.38**
Income gearing				
Interest paid	376	364	145.0	142.8
Operating profit	2,648	2,280	1,045.9	850.1
	0.14	0.16	0.14	0.17
Total liabilities				
Non-current liabilities	6,084	5,601	2,126.6	2,038.2
Current liabilitities	8,152	7,518	1,606.2	2,017.0
	14,236	**13,119**	**3,732.8**	**4,055.2**
	2007	**2006**	**2007**	**2006**
Debt to equity				
Total liabilities	14,236	13,119	3,732.8	4,055.2
Equity	10,571	9,444	1,648.2	1,203.7
	1.35	**1.39**	**2.26**	**3.37**
Total debt				
Short-term borrowing	1,554	1,646	461.0	1,052.8
Long term debt	4,146	3,398	1,234.5	1,133.8
Current portion of long term debt	0	344		
	5,700	**5,388**	**1,695.5**	**2,186.6**

	Tesco	Marks and Spencer		
Total capital				
Total debt	5,700	5,388	1,695.5	2,186.6
Equity	10,571	9,444	1,648.2	1,203.7
	16,271	**14,832**	**3,343.7**	**3,390.3**
Debt to capital ratio				
Debt	5,700	5,388	1,695.5	2,186.6
Total capital	16,271	14,832	3,343.7	3,390.3
	0.35	**0.36**	**0.51**	**0.64**

Table A–3 — Cash Flow

	Tesco		Marks and Spencer	
Free cash flow	**2007**	**2006**	**2007**	**2006**
Cash flow provided by operating activities	3,532	3,412	1,442.6	1,183.6
Net cash used in investing activities	2,343	1,962	650.8	253.4
Dividends paid	467	441	260.6	204.1
Interest paid	376	364	145.0	142.8
Tax paid	545	429	150.8	101.5
	−199	**216**	**235.4**	**481.8**
Cash on sales	**2007**	**2006**	**2007**	**2006**
Cash flow provided by operating activities	3,532	3,412	1,442.6	1,183.6
Sales	42,641	39,454	8,588.1	7,797.7
	8.3%	**8.6%**	**16.8%**	**15.2%**

(continued)

Table A–3 *(continued)*

	Tesco		Marks and Spencer	
	2007		**2007**	
Average current liabilities				
Last year current liabilities	8,152	7,518	1,606.2	2,017.0
Previous year current liabilities	7,518	5,680	2,017.0	1,237.4
	7,835	**6,599**	**1,811.6**	**1,627.2**
Current cash debt coverage ratio				
Cashflow provided by operating activities	3,532	3,412	1,442.6	1,183.6
Average current liabilities	7,835	6,599	1,811.6	1,627.2
	0.45	**0.52**	**0.80**	**0.73**
Average total liabilities	**2007**	**2006**	**2007**	**2006**
Last year total liabilties	14,236	13,119	3,732.8	4,055.2
Previous year total liabilties	13,119	11,501	4,055.2	3,958.1
	13,678	**12,310**	**3,894.0**	**4,006.7**
Cash debt coverage ratio				
Cash flow provided by operating activities	3,532	3,412	1,442.6	1,183.6
Average total liabilities	13,678	12,310	3,894.0	4,006.7
	0.26	**0.28**	**0.37**	**0.30**
Cash requirement				
Net cash used in investing activities	2,343	1,962	650.8	253.4
Cash dividends paid	467	441	260.6	204.1

	Tesco	Marks and Spencer		
Interest paid	376	364	145.0	142.8
Tax paid	545	429	150.8	101.5
	3,731	**3,196**	**1,207.2**	**701.8**
Cash flow coverage ratio				
Cash flow provided by operating activities	3,532	3,412	1,442.6	1,183.6
Cash requirement	3,731	3,196	1,207.2	701.8
	0.95	**1.07**	**1.19**	**1.69**

Table A–4	Turnover and Assets			
	Tesco	Marks and Spencer		
	2007	**2006**	**2007**	**2006**
Average inventory				
Beginning Inventory	1,464	1,309	374.3	338.9
Ending Inventory	1,931	1,464	416.3	374.3
	1,698	**1,387**	**395.3**	**356.6**
Inventory turnover				
Cost of sales	39401	36426	5246.9	4812.1
Average inventory	1,698	1,387	395.3	356.6
	23.2	**26.3**	**13.3**	**13.5**
Number of days to sell inventory				
Days in year	365	365	365	365
Inventory turnover	23.2	26.3	13.3	13.5
	15.7	**13.9**	**27.5**	**27.0**

(continued)

Table A–4 *(continued)*

	Tesco		Marks and Spencer	
	2007	2006	2007	2006
Fixed assets				
Property pant and equipment	16,976.0	15,882.0	4,044.5	3,575.8
Investment property	856.0	745.0	25.1	38.5
	17,832	**16,627**	**4069.6**	**3614.3**
Fixed assets turnover ratio				
Sales	42,641	39,454	8588.1	7797.7
Fixed assets	17,832	16,627	4069.6	3614.3
	2.4	**2.4**	**2.1**	**2.2**
	Tesco		Marks and Spencer	
	2007	2006	2007	2006
Total asset turnover				
Sales	42,641	39,454	8,588.1	7,798
Total assets	24,807	22,563	5,381.0	5,258.9
	1.7	**1.7**	**1.6**	**1.5**

Table A–5   Inflow and Outflow of Cash

	Tesco		Marks and Spencer	
	2007	2006	2007	2006
Trade receivable t/o ratio				
Net sales	42,641	39,454	8,588.1	7,797.7
Trade receivables	771	648	67.9	42.0
	55	**61**	**126**	**186**

Average collection period in days

Days in year	365	365	365	365
Trade receivable t/o ratio	55	61	126	186
	7	**6**	**3**	**2**

Average accounts payable

Trade payables 2006/2005	2,832.0	2,819.0	242.6	195.30
Trade payables 2007/2006	3,317.0	2,832.0	259.7	242.6
	3,074.5	**2,825.5**	**251.2**	**219.0**
	2007	**2006**	**2007**	**2006**

Accounts payable turnover ratio

Cost of sales	39,401	36,426	5,246.9	4,812.1
Average accounts payable	3,074.5	2,825.5	251.2	218.95
	12.8	**12.9**	**20.9**	**22.0**

Average payment period – days

Average accounts payable	3,074.5	2,825.5	251.2	219.0
Cost of sales	39,401	36,426	5,247	4,812
	28.5	**28.3**	**17.5**	**16.6**

Appendix B

Glossary

● ●

accounts payable: An account that tracks the money a company owes to its suppliers, contractors, and others who provide goods and services to the company.

accounts receivable: An account that tracks individual customer accounts listing money that customers owe the company for products or services they've purchased. Also known as trade receivables or trade debtors.

accrual accounting: An accounting method in which a company records revenues and expenses when the actual transaction is completed rather than when cash is received or paid out.

accrued liabilities: The expenses a company has incurred but not yet paid for at the time the company closes its accounting books for the period to prepare its financial statements.

aggressive earnings management: A technique that uses legitimate accounting methods in aggressive ways to get the bottom-line results that a company needs.

amortise: To reduce the value of an intangible asset by a certain percentage each year to show that it's being used up.

arm's length transaction: A transaction that involves a buyer and a seller who can act independently of each other and have no financial relationship with each other.

assets: Things a company owns, such as buildings, inventory, tools, equipment, vehicles, copyrights, patents, furniture, and any other items it needs to run the business.

audit: The process by which a registered auditor verifies that a company's financial statements have met the requirements of the generally accepted accounting principles. In the UK, this is expressed as a 'true and fair view'.

auditors' report: A letter from the auditors stating that a company's financial statements show a true and fair view (or setting out any modifications to that opinion); a company includes this letter in its annual report.

balance sheet: The financial statement that gives you a snapshot of the assets, liabilities, and shareholders' equity as of a particular date.

buy-side analysts: Professionals who analyse the financial results of companies for large institutions and investment firms that manage mutual funds, pension funds, or other types of multi-million-dollar private accounts.

capital expenditures: Money a company spends to buy or upgrade major assets, such as buildings and factories.

capital gains: The profits a company makes when it sells an asset for more than it originally paid for that asset.

cash-basis accounting: An accounting method in which companies record expenses and revenues in their financial accounts when cash actually changes hands, rather than when the transaction is completed.

cash-equivalent accounts: Asset accounts that a company can easily convert to cash, including current accounts, savings accounts, and other holdings.

cash flow: The amount of money that moves into and out of a business.

cash flow from operations: Cash a company receives from the day-to-day operations of the business, usually from sales of products or services.

chart of accounts: A listing of all a company's open accounts that the accounting department can use to record transactions.

consolidated financial statement: A report that combines the assets, liabilities, revenues, and expenses of a parent company with that of any companies that it owns.

contingent liabilities: Possible financial obligations that arise from past events and whose existence will be confirmed only by the occurrence or non-occurrence of one or more uncertain future events not wholly within the control of the reporting entity. A company should report a contingent liability except when it determines that the possibility of a payment being required is remote.

convertibles: Shares promised to a lender who owns bonds that can be converted to stock.

corporate governance: The way a board of directors conducts its own business and oversees a corporation's operations.

cost of goods sold: See cost of sales.

cost of sales: A line item on the income statement that summarises any costs directly related to selling a company's products. Also known as cost of goods sold.

current assets: Things a company owns that will be used up or converted into cash in the next 12 months.

current liabilities: Amounts that a company owes in the next 12 months.

depreciate: Reduce the value of a tangible asset by a certain percentage each year to show that the asset is being used up (aging).

discontinued operations: Business activities that a company halted, such as the closing of a factory.

dividends: The portion of a company's profits that it pays out to investors according to the number of shares that the investor holds.

double-entry bookkeeping: An accounting method that requires a company to record every transaction using debits and credits to show both sides of the transaction.

durable goods: Goods that last for more than one year.

earnings per share: The amount of net income that a company makes per share available on the market.

EBITDA: An acronym for *earnings before interest, taxes, depreciation, and amortisation*, which may be shown as a line item on the income statement.

equity: The residual interest in the assets of the entity after deducting all of its liabilities. This used to be known as shareholders' funds.

expenses: Any costs not directly related to generating revenues. Expenses fall into four categories: operating, interest, depreciation/amortisation, and taxes.

fair value: The amount for which an asset could be exchanged, or a liability settled, between knowledgeable, willing parties in an arm's length transaction.

financial statements: A company's reports of its financial transactions over various periods, such as monthly, quarterly, or annually. The three key statements are the balance sheet, income statement, and statement of cash flows.

fixed assets: See non-current assets.

fixed costs: Those expenses which do not vary with the level of output such as rent or management salaries.

fraudulent financial reporting: A deliberate attempt by a company to distort its financial statements to make its financial results look better than they actually are.

generally accepted accounting practice (GAAP): Rules for financial reporting that are either embodied in accounting standards or have grown up as accepted practice.

going-concern: The assumption that the company will continue in operation for the foreseeable future without the intention or necessity to discontinue or significantly scale-down its level of operations.

goodwill account: An account that appears on the balance sheet when a company has bought another company for more than the actual value of its assets minus its liabilities. Goodwill includes things such as customer loyalty, exceptional workforce, and a great location.

gross margin: A calculation of one type of profit based solely on sales and the cost of producing those sales.

gross profit: The revenue earned minus any direct costs of generating that revenue, such as costs related to the purchase or production of goods before any expenses including operating, taxes, interest, depreciation, and amortisation.

income statement: A report that shows a company's revenues and expenses over a set period of time; an income statement is also known as a *profit and loss account* or P&L.

initial public offering (IPO): The first time a company's stock is offered for sale on a public stock market.

insolvent: No longer able to pay bills and other obligations.

in-store credit: Money lent directly by a company to its customers for purchases of that company's products or services.

intangible assets: Anything a company owns that isn't physical, such as patents, copyrights, trademarks, and goodwill.

intellectual property: Works, products, or marketing identities for which a company owns the exclusive rights, such as copyrights, patents, and trademarks.

interest expenses: Charges that must be paid on borrowed money, usually a percentage of the debt.

internal financial report: Summary of a company's financial results that is distributed only inside the company.

International Accounting Standards Board (IASB): A body that establishes the standards of financial accounting and reporting which must be followed by all European listed companies.

liabilities: Money a company owes to its creditors, for amounts such as loans, bonds, and unpaid bills.

liquidity: A company's ability to quickly turn an asset into cash.

limited company: Separate legal entity formed for the purpose of operating a business and to limit the owners' liability for actions the company takes.

long-term assets: See non-current assets.

long-term debt or liabilities: See non-current liabilities.

majority interest: The position a company has when it owns more than 50 per cent of another company's voting shares.

managing earnings: See aggressive earnings management.

marketable securities: Holdings that companies can easily convert to cash, such as shares and bonds.

material changes: Changes that may have a significant financial impact on a company's earnings.

material misstatement: An error that significantly impacts a company's financial position.

net assets: The value of things owned by a company after the company has subtracted all liabilities from its total assets. This will be equal to the value of equity.

net business income: Business income or profit after a company has subtracted all its business expenses.

net marketable value: The book value of investments, adjusted for any gains or losses.

net profit: A company's bottom line, which shows how much money the company earned after it deducts all its expenses.

net sales or net revenue: Sales a company made minus any adjustments to those sales.

non-current assets: Assets that a company will use for more than a 12-month period, such as buildings, land, and equipment.

non-current liabilities: Financial obligations that a company must pay more than 12 months in the future, such as mortgages on buildings.

non-operating income: Income from a source that isn't part of a company's normal revenue-generating activities.

notes to the financial statements: The section in the annual report that offers additional detail about the numbers provided in those statements.

operating cash flow: Cash generated by company operations to produce and sell company products.

operating expense: Any expense that goes into operating a business but isn't directly involved in producing or creating the product – for example, advertising, subscriptions, or equipment rental.

operating lease: Rental agreement for equipment that offers no ownership provisions.

operating margin or profit: A company's earnings after it has subtracted all costs and expenses directly related to the core business of the company – its sales of product or services.

operating period: A specific length of time, which may be a day, month, quarter, or year, for which financial results are determined.

ordinary shares: A portion of a company bought by investors, who are given the right to vote on board membership and other issues taken to the shareholders for a vote.

parent company: A company that controls one or more other companies that it has bought in order to build the company.

partnership: A business that is owned by more than one person and is not incorporated.

physical capacity: The number of facilities a company has and the amount of product the company can manufacture.

Preference share: A type of share that usually gives its owners no voting power in the company's operations. Dividends are usually fixed and, although they are not guaranteed, they must be paid before any dividend can be paid to ordinary shareholders.

profit: The amount of money the company earned after paying all expenses.

Profit and loss account (P&L): See income statement.

provision: A liability of uncertain timing or amount. A company should recognise a provision in the financial statements when it is more likely than not that a payment will be required to settle the obligation.

proxies: Paper ballots sent to shareholders so they can vote on critical issues that will impact the company's operations, such as members of the board of directors and executive remuneration.

receivership: An arrangement in which a company can avoid liquidating itself and, instead, work with a court-appointed trustee to restructure its debt and thus avoid bankruptcy.

recognise: To record a revenue, expense, asset or liability in a company's books.

related-party: A party can be related to an entity in a number of ways including where they are members of the same group of companies, where the party is a director or key manager of the entity or where the party is a close family member of a director or key manager of the entity. Two parties are also related if they are subject to common control.

related-party transaction: A transfer of resources, services or obligations between related parties, regardless of whether a price is charged. Related party transactions are disclosed in financial statements because of the possibility that they may be carried out at a value that is not a fair value.

restate earnings: To correct 'accounting errors' by changing the numbers originally reported to the general public.

restructure: To reorganise business operations by means such as combining divisions, splitting divisions, dismantling an entire division, or closing manufacturing plants.

retained earnings: Profit that a company doesn't pay to shareholders over the years accumulates in the retained earnings account.

revenue: Payments a company receives for its products or services.

royalties: Payments a company makes for the use of intellectual property owned by another company or individual.

secondary public offerings: The sale of additional shares to the general public by a company that already has its shares quoted on the public stock market.

secured debt: Money borrowed on the basis of collateral, which is usually a major asset such as a building.

securities: Shares and bonds sold on the public financial markets.

shareholders' funds: See equity.

share-option plan: An offer a company gives to employees and board members to buy the company's shares at prices below market value.

short-term borrowings or debt: Lines of credit or other debt that a company must repay within the next 12-month period.

side letters: The agreements a company makes with its regular customers outside the actual documentation it uses in a formal contract to purchase or sell the goods.

sole proprietorship: A business that was started and owned by an individual and that is not incorporated.

solvency: A company's ability to pay all its outstanding bills and other debts.

statement of cash flows: One of the key financial statements; reports a company's performance over time, focusing on how cash flowed through the business.

share incentives: Shares that a company offers as part of an employee remuneration package.

tangible asset: Any asset that you can touch, such as cash, inventory, equipment, or buildings.

tax liability account: An account that tracks tax payments that a company has made or must still make.

trade debtors: See trade receivables.

trade receivables: An account that tracks individual customer accounts listing money that customers owe the company for products or services they've purchased. Also known as trade debtors or accounts receivable.

trading securities: Securities that a company buys as a short-term investment until the company decides how to use the money for its operations or growth.

turnover: Revenue received from sales.

unrealised losses or gains: Changes in the value of a holding that hasn't sold yet but has a market value that has increased or decreased since the time it was bought.

variable costs: Costs that change based on the level of output, such as raw materials or employee overtime.

venture capitalist: A person who invests in start-up businesses, providing the necessary cash in exchange for some portion of company ownership.

volume discount: A reduced rate received by a business that agrees to buy a large number of the manufacturer's product.

wholly owned subsidiary: A company whose shares are purchased in full by another company.

working capital: A company's current assets minus its current liabilities; this figure measures the liquid assets a company has at its disposal to continue building its business.

Index

• A •

abbreviated accounts, 11, 325
accounting. *See also* Chart of Accounts
  accounting method changes, 322–323
  accrual method, 44–46, 100, 111, 349
  amortisation, 48–50
  cash-basis, 43–46, 350
  computerised, 50
  creative, 284–287, 292–295
  debits and credits, 47–48
  depreciation, 48–50
  double-entry bookkeeping, 14, 46–47, 351
  GAAP principles for, 257–258
  ICC Information Service Web site, 328
  income statement, 47
  online training Web site, 327
  policies, notes, 127–130, 153
Accounting for Growth (Smith), 284
accounting policies
  changes in, 71, 144–145
  depreciation, 127–128
  expenses, 127, 129–130
  notes to financial statements,
    127–130, 153
  revenue, 127–129
Accounting Standards Board (ASB)
  consolidation requirements, 284
  merger accounting dealt with, 148
  non-listed companies using, 257
  operating and financial report rules, 15
  pension fund regulations, 140
  reporting the substance of transactions,
    284
  responsibilities, 17
  standards for OFR, 65
  Web site, 326
accounts. *See* Chart of Accounts

accounts payable
  described, 54, 349
  increase in, 302
  number of days in accounts-payable
    ratio, 234–235
  statement of cash flows, 117–118
  stretching, 240
  trade and other payables, 89
  turnover ratio, 232–233
accounts receivable (trade receivables)
  aging schedule, 231–232
  borrowing on, 242–243
  collections, speeding up, 240–242
  current assets, 86–87
  defined, 52, 86, 349, 357
  managing, 241–242
  monitoring, 294
  operations, 117
  overvalued, 144, 300
  selling, 131
  turnover ratio, 227–231
accrual accounting
  described, 44, 46, 349
  expenses, 287
  revenue, 100, 287
  statement of cash flows, 111
accrued expenses payable, 302–303
accrued liabilities, 89, 349
accrued payroll taxes, 54
accumulated amortisation, 49
accumulated depreciation, 52, 84
acquisitions
  methods of, 150–151
  notes to financial statements,
    137–138, 154
  questionable, 286, 323
  special events report, 280
actuary, 139
Adelphia and Hollinger scandal, 310–311
administrative expenses, income
    statement, 105

advertising expense, reporting policy, 130, 296

advertising and promotion, income statement, 105

aggressive earnings management, 285, 288, 294, 349

aging schedule (or aged debtor), accounts receivable, 231–232

AIM (Alternative Investment Market), 12, 33

AIU (Audit Inspection Unit), 17, 250

allowances, 102

amortisation
  accounting policies, 127
  described, 48–50, 349
  expenses, 57
  fraudulant reporting, 295
  income statement, 106
  intangible assets, 48–50, 349

analysts
  bond, 265
  buy-side, 260–261
  communicating with, 269–270
  financial reports used by, 11
  independent, 264–265
  roles of, 259–260
  sell-side, 261–264

angel (private investor), 29

annual general meeting, shareholders, 272–276

annual report. *See also* balance sheet; income statement; statement of cash flows
  auditor's report, 16, 62, 69–73
  chairman's statement, 15, 62
  copies of, obtaining, 97
  Corporate Governance Report, 63
  corporate message, 64
  directors' report and directors' remuneration report, 62
  executives and board of directors listed in, 64
  financial highlights, 74–75
  financial statements for, 16, 62–63, 73–74
  hiding negative information, 13, 62–63, 75
  Marks and Spencer, 125
  mission statement, 15
  notes to financial statements, 63, 75
  Operating and Financial Review (OFR) section, 15, 64–69
  overview, 15–16, 61–63
  private company filing, 39
  proxy information, 280
  statements to shareholders, 63
  Tesco, 125
  Web site resources, 328

APB (Auditing Practices Board), 70, 250–251, 326

Apple Computer (company), 35

arm's length transaction, 349

artwork, as asset, 302

ASB (Accounting Standards Board)
  consolidation requirements, 284
  merger accounting dealt with, 148
  non-listed companies using, 257
  operating and financial report rules, 15
  pension fund regulations, 140
  reporting the substance of transactions, 284
  responsibilities, 17
  standards for OFR, 65
  Web site, 326

assets. *See also* intangible assets; inventory (or stock); tangible assets
  accounts, 51–53
  balance sheet, 82–88
  current, 85–88, 180
  defined, 10, 349
  depreciation policy, 128
  double-entry bookkeeping, 47
  hidden, 83
  impairment of, 66, 297
  Marks and Spencer, 345–346
  net, 81, 353
  non-current, 82–85
  notes to financial statements, 127
  overvalued, 144, 299–302, 322
  patents and licenses purchased, 297
  return on assets (ROA), 172–173, 174, 340
  Tesco, 345–346
  total asset turnover, 225–226
  unusual, 302

associates, 84–85, 148
Audit Inspection Unit (AIU), 17, 250
Auditing Practices Board (APB), 70,
    250–251, 326
auditor's report. *See also* audits
  board of directors' review, 278
  creating, 255–256
  described, 16, 350
  modified, 70–73
  private companies, 31
  significant uncertainties found, 72
  standard (unmodified), 69–70
audits. *See also* auditor's report
  audit-exempt companies obtaining, 252
  auditors, 73, 250–251
  board of directors' review, 278
  changing auditors, 73
  described, 12, 249, 349
  fees, 38
  GAAP principles for, 256–258
  problems found by auditor, 71
  process for, 251–256
  public and private companies, 12
average-costing inventory system, 86,
    216–217, 219, 220

• *B* •

bad debt, 230–232
balance sheet
  accrued expenses payable, 302–303
  assets, 82–88
  big-bath charges, 285–286
  capital, 93
  consolidated, 338
  date of, 78–79
  described, 16, 350
  equity, 91–94
  formats for, 80–82
  goodwill account, 297–298
  intangible assets, 50
  inventory valuation's effect on, 221
  liabilities, 88–90
  Marks and Spencer, 84, 338
  numbers rounded off in, 79
  overview, 77–78
  private companies, 31

Tesco, 84, 335
  trade and other receivables, 228
bank overdraft, 131
bankers, investment, 34, 40–41
Barings Bank scandal, 314–315
Barrow, Colin (*Understanding Business
    Accounting For Dummies*), 88
basic earnings per share, 110
best efforts agreement, 41
big-bath charges, balance sheet, 285–286
bill payments
  bill-and-hold transaction, 289, 291
  discounts for early payments,
    235–237, 241
  electronic, 244, 245
  slowing down, 235, 239–240
  trade-receivable turnover, 228–231
  turnover ratio, calculating, 232–235
Biz/ed (Web site), 327
Blodget, Henry (Merrill Lynch analyst), 262
board of directors
  audit reviews, 278
  composition of, 277
  elections, 272
  forming, 22
  governance of, 276–278
  listed in annual report, 64
  remuneration packages for, 277
  Sarbanes-Oxley Act requirements, 38
  shareholders monitoring, 277–278
  takeover defences and protections, 278
bond analysts, 265
bonds
  defined, 91
  junk, 265
  long-term, 131
  payable (debentures), 54
  rating agencies, 260, 265–268
bonus issue/share split, 281
bookkeeping
  double-entry, 14, 46–47, 351
  general ledger, 51
borrowings
  on accounts receivable, 242–243
  long-term, 89–90, 131–134
  short-term, 89, 131, 356

Branson, Richard (businessman), 28
brokerage houses, 260–264
budget
  bottom-up approach, 206
  categories, common, 209–211
  committee, 206–207, 210–211
  disputes, resolving, 207
  expectations, 205
  goal setting, 207–209
  internal financial report, 211–213
  master budget, 210
  monthly budget reports, 211–213
  sales forecast, 207–208
  top-down approach, 206
buildings, 52
business segment breakdowns, notes, 140–142
business types. *See also* partnerships; private companies; public (listed) companies
  private limited companies, 22–24
  public limited companies (PLCs), 12, 22–24, 27, 40
  sole traders, 19–20, 356
  unlisted companies, 37, 127, 257
Business Week Web site, 327
buyout methods, 108, 150–151
buy-side analysts, 260–261, 350

• C •

capital
  balance sheet, 93
  capital gains, 168, 350
  defined, 93
  equity, 93
  expenditure, 119, 350
  improvements, 112
  negative working capital, 181
  resources, annual report, 68
  working, 357
capitalised expenses, 297
capitalised leases, 83–84, 135
cash. *See also* cash flow; statement of cash flows
  in bank, 53
  budget, 210
  on deposit, 53

equivalents, statement of cash flows, 123–124, 190, 350
petty cash (cash on hand), 53
public companies, 36
from selling shares, 35
sources of, 29
tracking, 87–88
cash flow. *See also* statement of cash flows
  accounts payable turnover, 232–235
  accounts receivable turnover, 227–231
  bill payments, slowing down, 235, 239–240
  cash return on sales ratio, 192–193
  cash-debt coverage ratio, 196–198
  cash-flow coverage ratio, 198–201
  current cash-debt coverage ratio, 194–198
  described, 10, 14, 350
  discontinued operations, 123, 143, 155, 304–305, 351
  discounts, 235–237, 241
  free, 190–192
  internal reports, 14
  low cash flow problems, 320
  Marks and Spencer, 343–345
  negative, 196, 198
  problems, hiding, 304–305
  public versus private companies, 36
  quick cash, 244–245
  reducing inventory, 243–244
  Tesco, 343–345
cash-basis accounting, 43–44, 45–46, 350
centralised account system, 87
chairman's statement, annual report, 62
channel stuffing, 290
Chart of Accounts
  asset accounts, 51–53
  defined, 350
  equity accounts, 54–55
  expense accounts, 56–57
  liability accounts, 53–54
  overview, 50–51
  revenue accounts, 55–56
Chinese wall, 263
collection period, 228, 241
collections, accounts receivable, 240–242
Combined Code on Corporate Governance, 37–39

commitments and contingencies, 143
companies. *See also* business types
  nonlisted, 37, 127, 257
  ranking with ROA (return on assets),
    172–173
  takeover defences and protections, 278
  Web site resources, 282
Companies Act, 31, 250, 329
Companies House
  abbreviated accounts filed at, 11
  about, 325
  financial reports from, 23–24, 97
  medium and large-size private companies
    filing with, 12
  rules for filing with, 17
  Web site, 13, 325
competitors, 11, 29, 36, 208
computerised systems, 47, 50
consolidated financial statement. *See also*
    financial statements
  accounts, 148
  defined, 350
  key transactions, 152
  Marks and Spencer, 149
  methods of buying up companies,
    150–151
  notes to, 153–155
  overview, 147–149
  reading, 151–153
  Tesco, 149
contingent liabilities, 350
control activities, 68, 253–254
convertibles, 110, 350
cookie-jar reserves, 286
copyrights, 53, 82
corporate governance, 276–278, 351
Corporate Governance Report, 63
corporate message, annual report, 64
corporation tax paid, 305–306
cost of sales. *See also* sales
  cost of sales number, 215
  defined, 351
  described, 56, 96, 103–104
  finding, 219
  income statement, 96, 103–104
costs
  control problems, 68
  defined, 10

fixed, 352
  public companies, 36
  variable, 357
creative accounting
  detecting, 292–295
  hiding financial problems with, 284–287
credit
  cards, 54, 181, 228, 244
  in-store, 352
  lines of, 244
  policy for customers, 230, 240–242
  ratings, Web site, 327
  standards, 240
credit period, 240
credits and debits, double-entry
    accounting, 47–48
currency exchange, statement of cash
    flows, 123
current assets
  accounts, 52–53
  accounts receivable, 86–87
  cash, 87–88
  defined, 52, 85, 351
  inventory (or stock), 52, 85–86
  investments, 87
  other, 88
current cash-debt coverage ratio, 194–198
current liabilities
  accounts, 54
  accrued liabilities, 89, 349
  current tax payable, 89
  described, 88–89, 351
  provisions, 89
  short-term borrowings, 89, 131, 356
current ratio, 180–181, 341
customers
  accounts-receivable aging schedule (or
    aged debtor), 231–232
  balance sheet, 228
  credit policy for, 240–242
  discounts for early payments,
    235–237, 241
  electronic bill payment, 244, 245
  invoicing, 228
  largest, 141
  side letters, 290
  slow-paying, 227, 232, 241, 324

• D •

debentures (bonds payable), 54
debits and credits, double-entry
    accounting, 47–48
debt
  bad debt, 230–232
  bonds, 265
  cash-debt coverage ratio, 196–198
  current cash-debt coverage ratio, 194–198
  current ratio, 180–181, 341
  debt to equity, 342
  debt to shareholders' equity, 184–186
  debt-to-capital ratio, 186–188, 342
  doubtful, 67, 300
  excess, 321–322
  funding, 172
  long-term (non-current liabilities), 90, 354
  Marks and Spencer, 342
  new, 122
  paying off, 122
  secured, 356
  short-term, 356
  Tesco, 342
defined contribution plan, 139
Department of Business, Enterprise and
    Regulatory Reform, 328–329
Department of Trade and Industry
    (DTI), 328
depreciation
  accumulated, 52, 84
  calculating, 48–49
  defined, 351
  expenses, 57, 116
  fraudulant reporting, 295
  motor vehicles, 48–49
  notes to financial statement, 127–128
  property, 83
  statement of cash flows, 116
  taxes and, 107
diluted earnings per share (EPS), 110, 164
direct method, statement of cash flows,
    113–115
directors
  annual report, 15, 62
  report, 31, 75
  responsibilities, 16
Directors' Remuneration Report, 62,
    67, 136

disclosure, public versus private
    companies, 36
discontinued operations
  defined, 351
  hiding negative information, 304–305
  notes to financial statements, 143, 155
  statement of cash flows, 123
discounts
  accounts receivable, 241
  benefits of, 240
  for early payments, 235–237, 241
  purchase discounts, 56
  sales, 56, 101–103
  volume discounts, sales, 102, 357
discretionary cash, 190–192
distribution expenses, income statement,
    105
distribution systems, 68
dividends
  consolidated financial statements, 152
  defined, 351
  dividend cover, 167–169, 340
  dividend yield, 166–167, 340
  high yields, 169
  paying, 91, 121
  per share, 110
  preference shares, 92
  shareholders, 91
  shareholders informed on, 281
double-entry bookkeeping, 14, 46–47, 351
doubtful debts, annual report, 67, 300
drawing account, 94
Dun and Bradstreet Web site, 264
durable goods, 351

• E •

earnings
  aggressive earnings management, 285,
    288, 349
  expectations, 274–275
  fraudulant reporting, 287–295
  restating, 285, 356
earnings per share (EPS)
  calculating, 110, 160, 164–166
  defined, 351
  diluted, 110, 164
  Marks and Spencer, 162
  Tesco, 162

EBIT (earnings before interest and
   taxes), 58
EBITDA (earnings before interest, taxes,
   depreciation, or amortisation), 58,
   107–108, 351
economic conditions, sales forecast, 208
Eisner, Michael (Disney CEO), 271
electronic bill payment, 244–245
emphasis of matter paragraph, 72
employees. *See also* pensions
   financial reports needed by, 10
   participation in budgeting process, 206
   retirement benefits, notes, 138–140
   share incentives, 67
   turnover, 276
Enron scandal, 38, 277–278, 284, 309
environmental concerns, 142–43, 272
environmental and product liabilities,
   annual report, 66
EPS (earnings per share)
   calculating, 110, 160, 164–166
   defined, 351
   diluted, 110, 164
   Marks and Spencer, 162
   Tesco, 162
equipment lease, 135
Equitable Life scandal, 315
equity
   balance sheet, 91–94
   capital, 93
   Chart of Accounts, 54–55
   debt to equity, 342
   defined, 10, 54, 78, 91, 351
   double-entry bookkeeping, 47
   drawing, 94
   other reserves, 93
   owner's, 54, 91
   retained earnings, 55, 93, 356
   return on equity (ROE), 173–174
   share capital, 91–93
European Union (EU), 148, 251, 257–258
events, significant, 39, 142–143
execution only service, 281
executives
   annual report of, 15
   budget set by, 206
   financial reports for, 10

listed in annual report, 64
   remuneration packages, 272, 277
   reporting at annual meeting, 275–276
expenses
   accounts, 56–57
   accrual accounting, 287
   accrued expenses payable, 302–303
   capitalised, 297
   defined, 56, 105, 351
   fraudulant reporting, 295–299
   income statement, 96, 105–107
   interest, 57, 353
   notes to financial statement, 129–130
Exxon (oil company), 142

• F •

fair value, 351
FASB (Financial Accounting Standards
   Board), 258, 284
fees
   accounts receivable, 241
   audit, 38
   financial advisors, 281
   legal, 38, 279
   management, 152
   upfront service fee, 292
fictional sales, 289–290
FIFO (first in, first out) inventory system,
   85, 216–217, 219–220, 221
finance expense, income statement, 106
finance income, income statement, 106
finance leases, 135
Financial Accounting Standards Board
   (FASB), 258, 284
financial advisors, choosing, 281
financial highlights, annual report, 15,
   74–75
Financial Reporting Council (FRC), 16–17,
   37, 39, 306, 326
Financial Reporting Review Panel (FRRP),
   17, 306, 326
Financial Reporting Standard for Small
   Entities (FRSSE), 32, 127
Financial Reporting Standard (FRS),
   139, 284

financial reports. *See also* annual report;
  financial statements; fraudulent
  financial reporting
  abbreviated, 11, 325
  comparing, 128, 130, 258
  copies of, obtaining, 97
  documentation for, 38
  extended reporting period, 289
  external, 11–13
  GAAP standards for, 257–258
  internal, 13–14, 211–213
  limited companies, 23–24
  online resources, 13, 126, 325–329
  overview, 9–11
  partnerships, 21, 24
  public limited companies (PLCs),
    12, 23–24
  reading before shareholders meeting, 274
  Sarbanes-Oxley Act requirements, 38
  small companies, 127
  sole trader, not required for, 20
  'window dressing', 275
Financial Services Authority (FSA), 263
financial statements. *See also* financial
  reports; *specific types of statement*
  annual report, 62, 73–74
  described, 16, 352
  overview, 73–74, 333
  private companies, 30–32
  public (listed) companies, 37–39
  rules and regulations for filing, 17
Financial Times (UK newspaper), 163,
    327–328
Find.co.uk, 261, 328
first in, first out (FIFO) inventory system,
    85, 216–217, 219–220, 221
fiscal year, operating on, 79
Fitch Ratings (bond-rating service), 267
fixed assets. *See* long-term assets; non-
    current assets
fixed costs, 352
foreign currency exchange, statement of
    cash flows, 123
fraudulent financial reporting. *See also* red
    flags; scandals
  assets and liabilities misrepresented,
    299–304

cash flow problems, 304–306
  creative accounting, 284–287, 292–295
  debt excess, 321–322
  described, 252, 352
  exploiting expenses, 295–299
  fictional sales, 289–290
  hiding negative information, annual
    report, 13, 62–63, 75
  mergers and acquisitions, questionable,
    323
  revenue recognition games, 288–295, 321
  Web site resource, 306
FRC (Financial Reporting Council), 16–17,
    37, 39, 306, 326
freight charges, cost of sales, 56
FRRP (Financial Reporting Review Panel),
    17, 306, 326
FRS (Financial Reporting Standard),
    139, 284
FSA (Financial Services Authority), 263
FTSE 100 companies, 250, 266
furniture and fittings, long-term asset,
    52, 83
future, looking towards, 276

• *G* •

gains, unrealised, 87, 357
general ledger, bookkeeping practices, 51
Generally Accepted Accounting Principles
    (GAAP)
  accrual accounting required by, 44
  audit principles, 256–258
  current rules, accessing, 326
  defined, 352
  standards for financial reports, 17,
    257–258
GlaxoSmithKline (company), 142, 277
going-concern, 72, 352
golden share, 91
goods on consignment, 291
goodwill
  acquisitions, 137
  balance sheet, 297–298
  defined, 53, 82, 154, 352
  notes to financial statements, 154
gross margin, 175, 341, 352
gross profit, 57, 98, 104–105, 352

• H •

Her Majesty's Revenue and Customs (HMRC), 20–21
Hewlett, Walter (businessman), 279–280
Hewlett-Packard company, 279
highlights, financial, 74–75
hire purchase contract, 135
hold rating, shares, 268

• I •

IAS (International Accounting Standards), 83, 96, 217, 291, 292
IASB (International Accounting Standards Board)
  about, 326, 353
  accounting standards set by, 257–258
  direct method format preferred by, 113
  merger accounting banned by, 148
  Update magazine, 326
  Web site, 326
ICC Information Service Web site, 223, 328
IFRS (International Financial Reporting Standards), 96, 258, 284
income gearing, 183–184, 342
income statement
  annual report, 95
  consolidated, 337
  cost of sales, 96, 103–104
  described, 16, 47, 74, 352
  earnings per share, 110
  expenses, 96, 105–107
  formats for, 97–99
  gross profit, 98, 104–105, 352
  inventory valuation's effect on, 220–221
  Marks and Spencer, 337
  net income, 128, 173, 215
  net profit or loss, 109
  non-operating income or expense, 108–109
  overview, 96–97
  profit or loss, 96, 107–109
  revenue accounts, 55–56
  Tesco, 334
  year end date, 97
incorporating, 22

independent analysts, 264–265
Independent Insurance scandal, 313
indirect method, statement of cash flows, 114–115
industry competition data, sales forecast, 208
industry economic conditions, sales forecast, 208
information technology, 38
initial public offering (IPO), 35, 37, 352
in-process research and development, 286
insider dealing, 39
insolvency, 352
institutional shareholders, 279
in-store credit, 352
intangible assets. *See also* goodwill
  amortisation, 48–50, 349
  defined, 82, 353
  intellectual property, 53, 353
  net book value, 50
interest
  ability to pay, 183–184
  consolidated financial statements, 152
  expenses, 57–58, 353
  interest rate risk, 130, 133–134
  rate, calculating, 236
  receivables sold, 242
internal financial reports
  accounts-receivable aging schedule, 231–232
  cash flow, 14
  defined, 353
  monthly budget reports, 211–213
  overview, 13–14
  red flags system, 211–212
  uses for, 213
  year-to-date section, 211
International Accounting Standards Board (IASB)
  about, 326, 353
  accounting standards set by, 257–258
  direct method format preferred by, 113
  merger accounting banned by, 148
  Update magazine, 326
  Web site, 326
International Accounting Standards (IAS), 83, 96, 217, 291–292

International Financial Reporting
  Standards (IFRS), 96, 258, 284
International Standards on Auditing (ISA),
  70, 251, 255–256
Internet stock crash (2000), 37, 262
inventory (or stock)
  average-costing system, 86, 216–217,
    219–220
  beginning, 218
  cost of sales, finding, 219
  current asset, 85–86
  described, 52
  ending, 217–218
  filing requirements, 217
  financial statement comparisons, 220–221
  first in, first out (FIFO), 85, 216–217,
    219–220, 221
  internal reports, 14
  just-in-time inventory process, 243
  large-capitalisation, 327
  last in, first out (LIFO), 86, 216–217
  market inventory system, 217, 222
  overstated valuation, 300–301
  reducing, 243–244
  specific-identification system, 86, 216–217
  statement of cash flows, 117
  tangible fixed assets turnover, 224–225
  total asset turnover, 225–226
  tracking methods, 218
  turnover, calculating, 221–224
  turnover, slow, 324
  valuation methods, 215–221
investment bankers, 34, 40–41
investment groups, 259
investment research firms, major, 264–265
investments. *See also* shares
  associates and joint ventures, 84–85
  Business Week Web site, 327
  current assets, 87
  gains from sales of, 306
  industry statistics Web site, 164
  joint ventures, 85, 148
  loss from selling, 306
  researching, 164
  statement of cash flows, 112, 115, 119–120
  subsidiaries, 152
  value investing, 164
investors, 11, 29, 67, 166

invoice factoring, 242–243
IPO (initial public offering), 35, 37, 352
ISA (International Standards on Auditing),
  70, 251, 255–256

Jobs, Steve (founder of Apple
  Computer), 35
John Lewis Partnership (company), 33
joint ventures, 85, 148
junk bonds, 265
just-in-time inventory process, 243

key performance indicators (KPIs), 75, 253

labour, direct labour budget, 210
land, 52, 301
large-capitalisation stocks, 327
large-size companies, 12, 206
last in, first out (LIFO) inventory system,
  86, 216, 217
lawsuits, 72, 142–144, 280
leases
  capitalised, 83–84
  finance, 135
  leasehold improvements, 52
  notes to financial statements, 134–135
  operating, 135
  property, 83
leasing and hire purchase, 245
legal fees, 38, 279
leverage, 185–186
leveraged buyout, 108
Levitt, Arthur (Securities and Exchange
  Commission chairman), 285
Lewis, John Spedan (businessman), 33
liabilities. *See also* non-current liabilities
  balance sheet, 88–90
  Chart of Accounts, 53–54
  contingent, 350
  current, 54, 88–89, 180
  deferred tax liabilities, 90, 107
  defined, 10, 353

double-entry bookkeeping, 47
long-term, 54, 90
Marks and Spencer, 342
net current assets, 81, 89
provisions, 303–304
Tesco, 342
transferring, 284, 304
undervalued, 144, 302–304
unrealistic values, 286, 322
licenses, 297
LIFO (last in, first out), 86, 216–217
limited companies
defined, 353
financial reports, 23–24
limited liability partnership (LLP), 24–25
private limited companies, 22–24, 40
public limited companies (PLCs), 12,
22–24, 27, 40
setting up, 22–23
taxes, 23
lines of credit, for quick cash, 244
liquidations, notes to financial statement,
155
liquidity
annual report, 69
current ratio, 180–181, 341
debt to shareholders' equity, 184–186
debt-to-capital ratio, 186–188, 342
defined, 36, 353
income gearing ratio, 183–184, 342
lower liquidity problems, 319–320
Marks and Spencer, 341–343
public versus private companies, 36–37
quick ratio, 181–183
Tesco, 341–343
listed companies. *See* public (listed)
companies
LLP (limited liability partnership), 24–25
loans
calling, 188
guarantee scheme, 245
lease obligations, 134–135
notes to financial statements, 130–135
par value of, 133
payable, 54
London Stock Exchange – Alternative
Investment Market (AIM), 12, 33
London Stock Exchange – Main Market, 33,
41–42

long-term assets, tangible, 52, 82–83. *See
also* non-current assets
long-term borrowings
current portion, 89
described, 90
Marks and Spencer, 133–134
notes to financial statements, 131–134
Tesco, 132–134
long-term debt or liabilities. *See* non-
current liabilities
long-term liabilities, 54, 90, 196. *See also*
pensions
long-term notes or bonds, 131
loss
defined, 10
income statement, 96, 98, 107–109
unrealised, 87, 357

• *M* •

majority interest, share acquisition,
150, 353
management fees, subsidiary paying, 152
managers, 10, 13–14
manufacturing and operational details, 141
manufacturing capacity, 68
margins
gross, 175, 341, 352
net profit, 177–178, 193, 341
operating, 176–177, 341, 354
profit margin, disappearing, 320–321
market inventory system, 217, 222
market research, sales forecast, 208
market share data, sales forecast, 208
market value/share price, 163–164
marketing expenses, income statement,
105
markets for trading shares. *See* stock
exchange
Marks and Spencer (retail company)
annual report, 189
consolidated balance sheet, 338
consolidated income statement, 337
inflow and outflow of cash, 346–347
liquidity, 341–343
profitability and market value, 339–341
statement of cash flows, 124, 339
turnover and assets, 345–346
Web site, 125, 189

material changes, 12, 353
material misstatement, 70, 353
materiality, 286–287
materials, direct materials budget, 210
Medium Term Note (MTN), 131–133
medium-sized companies, 12, 31–32
merchant services, 245
merger accounting, 147–148
mergers
  benefits of, 147
  notes to financial statements, 137–138,
    154
  questionable, 323
  shareholders role in, 281
Merrill Lynch (investment firm), 262
Microsoft (software company), 164, 208
minority interest, share acquisition,
  150–151
mission statement, annual report, 15
Model Code, 39
Molins (heavy engineering company)
  inventory turnover, 223
  number of days in accounts-payable
    ratio, 235
  tangible fixed assets turnover, 225
  total asset turnover, 226
  trade-receivable turnover, 230
monthly budget reports, 211–213
Moody's Investor Service (bond rating
  agency), 266–267
motor vehicles, 48–49, 52
mutual funds, rating, 261

• *N* •

National Insurance Contributions
  (NICs), 20
net assets, 81, 353
net book value, 50
net cash, 306
net current assets, 81, 89
net income, 173, 215, 295, 354
net marketable value, 354
net profit, 58, 109, 193, 354
net profit margin, 177–178, 193, 341
net realisable value, 217
net sales or net revenue, 294, 354
NICs (National Insurance Contributions), 20

Nomad (nominated advisor), 33
non-current assets
  accumulated depreciation, 84
  capitalised leases, 83–84
  defined, 354
  furniture and fixtures, 83
  gains from sales of, 306
  investments, 84–85
  losses from sales of, 306
  property, plant, and equipment, 82–83
  turnover, 224–225
non-current liabilities
  deferred tax liabilities, 90
  defined, 354
  long-term borrowings, 89–90, 131–134
  post employee benefit obligations, 90
nonlisted companies, 37, 127, 257
non-operating expense, 108–109
non-operating income, 108–109, 177, 354
Northern Rock scandal, 316–318
notes to financial statements
  accounting policies, 127–130
  accounts receivable (trade receivables),
    228
  borrowings, 130–134
  business segment breakdowns, 140–142
  consolidated financial statements,
    153–155
  deciphering, 126–127
  described, 63, 354
  events, significant, 142–143
  importance of, 75, 125–126
  in-process research and development, 286
  lease obligations, 134–135
  for listed vs. unlisted companies, 127
  mergers and acquisitions, 137–138
  pension and retirement benefits, 138–140
  private companies, 31
  red flags, 143–145
  restructuring charges, 299
  revenue-recognition policies, 293
  share-based payments, 136–137
  subsidiaries, associates and joint
    ventures, 148
number of days in accounts-payable ratio,
  234–235
numbers, rounding off, 79

• O •

off-balance sheet financing vehicles, 284
Office of Public Sector Information Web
  site, 329
Operating and Financial Review (OFR)
  annual report, 15, 64–69
  business performance, 141
  described, 62
  interest rate risk management, 133
operating margin, 176–177, 341, 354
operations
  accounts payable, 117–118
  accounts receivable (trade receivables),
    117
  annual report, 67–68
  cash flow, 112–113, 116–119
  depreciation, 116
  described, 106, 354
  discontinued, 123, 143
  efficiency of, 169
  expenses, 57
  inventory, 117
  notes to consolidated financial
    statements, 155
  operating cash flow, 165, 354
  operating lease, 135, 354
  operating period, 354
  operating profit, 58, 98, 354
  research and development, 68
orders, unfilled and backlogs, sales
  forecast, 208
ordinary (or equity) shareholders, 91
ordinary shares, 354
owner diversification, advantage of, 35
owner's equity or capital, 54, 91

• P •

P&L (profit and loss account). *See* income
  statement
parent company, 355
Parmalat scandal, 312–313
partnerships
  described, 21, 355
  financial reports, 21
  getting an audit when it's not required, 252
  limited liability partnership (LLP), 24–25

multiple, 33
taxes, 21
patents, 82, 106, 297
payables. *See* accounts payable
payroll taxes, 45, 54
P/E (price/earnings) ratio
  average, 163
  calculating, 161–163, 166
  current, 161
  described, 160
  forward, 161
  historic, 161, 164
  market value/share price, 163–164
  Marks and Spencer, 162–163, 339
  Microsoft, 164
  negative, 160
  projected, 161
  Tesco, 162–163, 339
  variations, 164–166
pensions
  accounting policies, 127
  analysts role in, 259
  notes to financial statements, 138–140
  post employee benefit obligations, 90
  red flags, 145
  safety of, 140
  valuations, 66
periodic inventory tracking, 218
perpetual (or continuous) inventory
  system, 218
personal finance Web site, 328
petty cash (cash on hand), 53
physical capacity, 68, 294–295, 355
plant and equipment, 52, 83, 135
Plus Markets Group (PMG) PLUS, 12, 34
Poor, Varnum (Standard & Poor's founder),
  266
portfolio manager, 261
preference share, 55, 355
preference shareholders, 91–93
prepayments, 228
press releases, 268–270
price/earnings (P/E) ratio. *See* P/E
  (price/earnings) ratio
pricing policy, sales forecast, 208
private companies
  advantages of, 27–29
  audit needed for, 12
  disadvantages of, 29–30

private companies *(continued)*
  filing financial statements, 30–32
  going public, 39–42
  large-size, 12
  limited, 22–24, 40
  medium-sized, 12, 31–32
  small, 11–12, 32, 325
private investor (angel), 29
Pro forma EPS, 165
product development expense, reporting, 129
product improvements, 68
profit. *See also* P/E (price/earnings) ratio
  capital gains, 168, 350
  defined, 10, 355
  earnings per share, calculating, 110, 160
  gross, 57, 98, 104–105, 107, 352
  income statement, 98
  net profit, 58, 109, 193, 354
  net profit margin, 177–178, 193, 341, 341
  non-operating income, 108–109
  operating, 58, 98, 107
  profit margin, disappearing, 320–321
  before taxation, 170
profit and loss account (P&L). *See* income statement
property, plant, and equipment, 82–83, 93
prospectus, 40–41
provisions, 89, 303–304, 355
proxies, 278–280, 355
public companies, nonlisted, 37
public limited companies (PLCs). *See also* public (listed) companies
  described, 12, 22, 27
  financial reports, 12, 23–24
  private limited company becoming, 40
  selling shares, 27
  taxes, 23
public (listed) companies. *See also* public limited companies (PLCs)
  advantages of, 35–36
  consolidated accounts, requirements for, 148
  disadvantages of, 35–37
  filing financial reports, 12–13, 34, 37–39
  financial statistics for, locating, 326
  listing with Main Market, 41–42

listing with US stock exchange, 38
markets for trading shares, 33–34
notes to financial statements, 127
private company becoming, 39–42
purchase discounts, cost of sales, 56
purchases, cost of sales, 56

• *Q* •

qualified opinion, modified auditor's report, 72–73
quick cash flow, 244–245
quick ratio, 181–183, 342

• *R* •

rating agencies, 260, 265–268
ratings
  bonds, 265–268
  credit, 327
  shares, 268
receivership, 355
recognition, 287, 355. *See also* revenue recognition
red flags. *See also* fraudulent financial reporting
  accounting method changes, 322–323
  accounting policy changes, 144–145
  assets and liabilities unrealistic, 144, 322
  assets written off as impaired, 298
  auditor's, 69
  bill payments slowing down, 235, 239–240
  bond analysts', 265
  changing auditors, 73
  executives unsure response at annual meeting, 275
  finding, 143–145
  internal reports use of, 211–212
  lawsuits, 143–144
  low cash flow problems, 320
  low dividend cover, 168
  lower liquidity, 319–320
  negative P/E (price/earnings) ratios, 160
  negative working capital, 181
  net revenue or net sales increase, 294
  in notes to financial statements, 143–145
  pension obligation difficulties, 145

press reporting on, 144
profit margins disappearing, 320–321
restructuring charges, 299
revenue-recognition policy changes, 293
significant events, 142–143
slow inventory turnover, 324
slow-paying customers, 324
related-party, 291, 355
remuneration packages, 62, 67, 136, 277
rendering of services, 292
reported EPS, 165
research and development, 68, 106,
    286, 296
restate earnings, 285, 356
restructuring
    charges, annual report, 66, 299
    defined, 62, 356
    hiding financial problems during,
        285–286, 299
    notes to financial statements, 143
retained earnings, 55, 93, 356
retirement benefits, notes, 138–140
return on assets (ROA), 172–174, 340
return on equity (ROE), 173–174, 340
return on sales (ROS), 169–171, 340
returns, 102–103, 290–291
Reuters' Web site, 329
revaluation reserve, 93
revenue
    accounts, 55–56
    accrual accounting, 100, 287
    aggressive earnings management, 285,
        288, 349
    creative accounting, detecting, 292–295
    defined, 100–101, 356
    games played with, 287–295, 321
    gross profit, 57, 98, 104–105, 107, 352
    growth, 275
    income statement, 96, 99–105
    net revenue or net sales, 354
    notes to financial statements, 127–129
    ratios, 295
revenue recognition
    defined, 355
    evaluating revenue results, 293–294

game-playing, 287–295
notes to financial statements, 128–129
Operating and Financial Review (OPR),
    65–66
policies, reviewing, 293
revenue defined, 100–101
ROA (return on assets), 172–174, 340
road shows, 270
Robert Maxwell scandal, 316
royalties, 106, 356

• S •

sales. *See also* cost of sales
    budget, 209–210
    cash return on sales ratio, 192–193
    collectibility policy, 129
    consolidated financial statements, 152
    on credit, 228
    debits and credits effect on, 47–48
    described, 10, 55
    discounts, 56, 101–103, 357
    fictional, 289–290
    forecast, developing, 207–208
    goods ordered but not shipped, 288–289
    net sales or net revenue, 354
    parent company buying from
        subsidiaries, 152
    purchase discounts, cost of sales, 56
    recognised as revenue, 100–101
    return on sales (ROS), 169–171, 340
    returns and allowances, 56, 102–103, 129
    Sales Ledger, 51
    volume discounts, 102, 357
S&P (Standard & Poor's), 264, 266–268, 327
Sarbanes-Oxley Act, 38
scandals. *See also* fraudulent financial
        reporting
    about, 17
    Adelphia and Hollinger, 310–311
    Barings Bank, 314–315
    brokerage houses' role in, 261–263
    corporate governance problems, 277
    Enron, 38, 277–278, 284, 309
    Equitable Life, 315
    executive remuneration packages, 67

scandals *(continued)*
  Independent Insurance, 313
  Northern Rock, 316–318
  Parmalat, 312–313
  Robert Maxwell, 316
  technology crash of 2000, 37, 262
  Versailles Trade Finance Ltd (VTFL), 314
  WorldCom/MCI, 311–312
secondary public offerings, 356
secured debt, 356
securities, 353, 356–357
sell rating, shares, 268
sell-side analysts, 261–264
service contracts, 292
share capital, 55, 91–93
share-based payment, 67, 128, 136–137
shareholders
  annual report statements, 63, 280
  biannual reports, 280
  debt to shareholders' equity, 184–186
  dividends, 91, 166
  general meeting, annual, 272–276
  influence of, 271
  institutional, 279
  monitoring the board of directors, 277–278
  negotiating with, 279–280
  ordinary (or equity) shareholders, 91
  preference shareholders, 91–93
  shareholders' equity, 172–173
  special events reports, 280–281
  voting by proxy, 278–280, 355
  Web site services, 273, 282
shares. *See also* stock exchange
  acquisitions, 150–151, 154
  bonus issue/share split, 281
  buying back, 121
  execution only service, 281
  hold rating, 268
  incentives, 67, 357
  issuing, 120
  ordinary shares, 354
  prices, 40, 161
  ratings, 261, 268
  risks of buying, 281
  sell rating, 268

share premium, 55, 93
share-option plan, 277, 356
  Web site, 161
short-term borrowings, 89, 131, 356
short-term debt, 356
side letters, 290, 356
small companies
  budgeting process, 206
  described, 32, 127
  exception from cash-flow statement, 31
  financial reporting requirements, 32, 127
  investment property of, 83
  merger accounting, permission to use, 148
  notes to financial statements, 127
  private, 11–12, 32, 325
Smith, Terry *(Accounting for Growth)*, 284
sole trader, 19–20, 356
solvency, 189–192, 356
special events reports, shareholders,
    280–281
special line items, statement of cash flows,
    122–123
specific-identification inventory system,
    86, 216–217
Spitzer, Eliot (Attorney General), 262
Standard & Poor's (S&P), 264, 266,
    267–268, 327
statement of cash flows. *See also* cash flow
  accrual accounting, 111
  annual report, 16
  cash and cash equivalents, 123–124,
    190, 350
  described, 16, 74, 111–112, 189, 356
  financing activities, 112, 115, 120–122
  foreign currency exchange, 123
  formats for, 113–116
  inventory, 117
  investment activities, 112, 115, 119–120
  Marks and Spencer, 339
  operating activities, 112–113, 116–119, 350
  private companies, 31
  problems with cash flow, hiding, 304–306
  special line items, 122–123
  Tesco, 336
  UK standards, 113

statements to shareholders, annual report, 63
stock. *See* inventory (or stock)
stock exchange. *See also* shareholders; shares
  Alternative Investment Market (AIM), 12, 33
  choosing, 41
  Main Market, 33, 41–42
  Plus Markets Group (PMG) PLUS, 12, 34
  requirements for listing on, 41
  US stock market, 38, 327
stock market index, 266
stockbroker, using, 281
stock-costing systems, 86
subsidiary
  bought through share acquisition, 150–151
  consolidated financial statements, 152
  defined, 148
  minority interest in, 151
  tax requirements, 148–149
  wholly-owned, 150, 357

• *T* •

takeover defences and protections, 278
tangible assets
  current, 52–53
  defined, 48, 51, 357
  depreciated, 48, 351
  fixed assets turnover, 224–225
  long-term, 52, 82–83
taxes
  accounting policies, 128
  corporation, 148, 305–306
  current tax payable, 89
  deferred tax liabilities, 90, 107
  expense account, 57
  investments or fixed assets, 306
  limited companies, 23
  limited liability partnership (LLP), 24
  National Insurance Contributions (NICs), 20
  overview, 106–107
  partnerships, 21, 24
  payable, 89
  payroll, 45, 54
  public limited companies (PLCs), 23
  sole trader, 20
  tax liability account, 45, 357
  taxation receivable, 88
  Value Added Tax (VAT), 20, 54
technology crash of 2000, 37, 262
Tesco (retail company)
  annual report, 125, 189
  balance sheet, 84, 335
  cash flow, 343–345
  income statement, 334
  inflow and outflow of cash, 346–347
  liquidity, 341–343
  profitability and market value, 339–341
  statement of cash flows, 124, 336
  turnover and assets, 345–346
  Web site, 125, 189
total asset turnover, 225–226
total capital, 342
Tracy, John A (*Understanding Business Accounting For Dummies*), 88
trade creditors. *See* accounts payable
trade debtors. *See* accounts receivable (trade receivables)
trade financing, 239
trade receivables. *See* accounts receivable (trade receivables)
trade sanctions, 141
trademarks, 82
Transparency Directive, 39
turnover
  accounts payable, 232–233
  accounts receivable (trade receivables), 227, 228–231
  defined, 357
  employee, 276
  inventory, 221–224
  Marks and Spencer, 345–346
  revenue received from sales, 357
  tangible fixed assets, 224–225
  Tesco, 345–346
  total asset, 225–226
Tyco scandal, 38
types of business. *See* business types

• U •

UK Listing Authority (UKLA), 41
Understanding Business Accounting For Dummies (Tracy and Barrow), 88
underwriting guarantee, 40
undeveloped land, 301
unincorporated businesses, 94
unrealised losses or gains, 87, 357
Update magazine, 326
Urgent Issues Task Force (UITF), 292
US stock market, 38, 327
utilities, 91, 169

• V •

Valdez oil spill, 142
valuation methods, 127, 215–221
Value Added Tax (VAT), 20, 54
value investing, 164
variable costs, 357
venture capitalist, 29, 92, 357
Versailles Trade Finance Ltd (VTFL) scandal, 314
vesting conditions, 136
Virgin Group (private company), 28
volume discounts, sales, 102, 357

• W •

Web sites
  Accounting Standards Board (ASB), 326
  Biz/ed, 327
  Business Week, 327
  Companies House, 13, 23, 325
  Department of Business, Enterprise and Regulatory Reform, 328–329
  Dun and Bradstreet, 264
  financial, 294
  Financial Reporting Council (FRC), 306, 326
  Financial Reporting Review Panel (FRRP), 306
  financial reports, 13, 97, 126
  Financial Times, 327–328
  Find.co.uk, 261, 328
  Fitch Ratings, 267
  FTSE 100 companies, 266
  Her Majesty's Revenue and Customs (HMRC), 21
  ICC Information Service, 223
  industry statistics, 164
  International Accounting Standards Board (IASB), 326
  investment research firms, 264–265
  Marks and Spencer, 125
  Moody's Investor Service, 266
  mutual funds, rating, 261
  Office of Public Sector Information, 329
  press releases, 269, 270
  Reuters, 329
  share prices, 161
  Standard & Poor's (S&P), 264, 266, 327
  Tesco, 125
  Yahoo! Finance UK, 161, 326
'window dressing' financial reports, 275
working capital, 181, 357
WorldCom/MCI scandal, 311–312
Wozniak, Steve (founder of Apple Computer), 35

• Y •

Yahoo! Finance UK Web site, 161, 326

FOR DUMMIES®

Do Anything. Just Add Dummies

UK editions

SELF HELP

978-0-470-51291-3

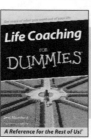
978-0-470-03135-3

978-0-470-51501-3

BUSINESS

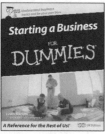
978-0-7645-7018-6

978-0-7645-7056-8

978-0-7645-7026-1

PERSONAL FINANCE

978-0-7645-7023-0

978-0-470-51510-5

978-0-470-05815-2

Answering Tough Interview
Questions For Dummies
(978-0-470-01903-0)

Being the Best Man
For Dummies
(978-0-470-02657-1)

British History
For Dummies
(978-0-470-03536-8)

Buying a Home on a Budget
For Dummies
(978-0-7645-7035-3)

Buying a Property in Spain
For Dummies
(978-0-470-51235-77)

Buying & Selling a Home For
Dummies
(978-0-7645-7027-8)

Buying a Property in Eastern
Europe For Dummies
(978-0-7645-7047-6)

Cognitive Behavioural Therapy
For Dummies
(978-0-470-01838-5)

Cricket For Dummies
(978-0-470-03454-5)

CVs For Dummies
(978-0-7645-7017-9)

Detox For Dummies
(978-0-470-01908-5)

Diabetes For Dummies
(978-0-470-05810-7)

Divorce For Dummies
(978-0-7645-7030-8)

DJing For Dummies
(978-0-470-03275-6)

eBay.co.uk For Dummies
(978-0-7645-7059-9)

Economics For Dummies
(978-0-470-05795-7)

English Grammar For Dummies
(978-0-470-05752-0)

Gardening For Dummies
(978-0-470-01843-9)

Genealogy Online
For Dummies
(978-0-7645-7061-2)

Green Living For Dummies
(978-0-470-06038-4)

Hypnotherapy For Dummies
(978-0-470-01930-6)

Neuro-linguistic Programming
For Dummies
(978-0-7645-7028-5)

Parenting For Dummies
(978-0-470-02714-1)

Pregnancy For Dummies
(978-0-7645-7042-1)

Renting out your Property
For Dummies
(978-0-470-02921-3)

Retiring Wealthy For Dummies
(978-0-470-02632-8)

Self Build and Renovation
For Dummies
(978-0-470-02586-4)

Selling For Dummies
(978-0-470-51259-3)

Sorting Out Your Finances
For Dummies
(978-0-7645-7039-1)

Starting a Business on
eBay.co.uk For Dummies
(978-0-470-02666-3)

Starting and Running an Online
Business For Dummies
(978-0-470-05768-1)

The Romans For Dummies
(978-0-470-03077-6)

UK Law and Your Rights
For Dummies
(978-0-470-02796-7)

Writing a Novel & Getting
Published For Dummies
(978-0-470-05910-4)

Available wherever books are sold. For more information or to order direct go to www.wiley.com or call 0800 243407 (Non UK call +44 1243 843296)

FOR DUMMIES®

Do Anything. Just Add Dummies

HOBBIES

978-0-7645-5232-8

978-0-7645-5395-0

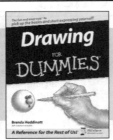

978-0-7645-5476-6

Also available:

Art For Dummies
(978-0-7645-5104-8)

Aromatherapy For Dummies
(978-0-7645-5171-0)

Bridge For Dummies
(978-0-471-92426-5)

Card Games For Dummies
(978-0-7645-9910-1)

Chess For Dummies
(978-0-7645-8404-6)

Improving Your Memory
For Dummies
(978-0-7645-5435-3)

Massage For Dummies
(978-0-7645-5172-7)

Meditation For Dummies
(978-0-471-77774-8)

Photography For Dummies
(978-0-7645-4116-2)

Quilting For Dummies
(978-0-7645-9799-2)

EDUCATION

978-0-7645-5434-6

978-0-7645-5581-7

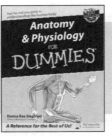

978-0-7645-5422-3

Also available:

Algebra For Dummies
(978-0-7645-5325-7)

Astronomy For Dummies
(978-0-7645-8465-7)

Buddhism For Dummies
(978-0-7645-5359-2)

Calculus For Dummies
(978-0-7645-2498-1)

Cooking Basics For Dummies
(978-0-7645-7206-7)

Forensics For Dummies
(978-0-7645-5580-0)

Islam For Dummies
(978-0-7645-5503-9)

Philosophy For Dummies
(978-0-7645-5153-6)

Religion For Dummies
(978-0-7645-5264-9)

Trigonometry For Dummies
(978-0-7645-6903-6)

PETS

978-0-470-03717-1

978-0-7645-8418-3

978-0-7645-5275-5

Also available:

Labrador Retrievers
For Dummies
(978-0-7645-5281-6)

Aquariums For Dummies
(978-0-7645-5156-7)

Birds For Dummies
(978-0-7645-5139-0)

Dogs For Dummies
(978-0-7645-5274-8)

Ferrets For Dummies
(978-0-7645-5259-5)

Golden Retrievers
For Dummies
(978-0-7645-5267-0)

Horses For Dummies
(978-0-7645-9797-8)

Jack Russell Terriers
For Dummies
(978-0-7645-5268-7)

Puppies Raising & Training
Diary For Dummies
(978-0-7645-0876-9)

FOR DUMMIES®

The easy way to get more done and have more fun

LANGUAGES

978-0-7645-5193-2

978-0-7645-5193-2

978-0-7645-5196-3

Also available:

Chinese For Dummies
(978-0-471-78897-3)

Chinese Phrases
For Dummies
(978-0-7645-8477-0)

French Phrases For Dummies
(978-0-7645-7202-9)

German For Dummies
(978-0-7645-5195-6)

Italian Phrases For Dummies
(978-0-7645-7203-6)

Japanese For Dummies
(978-0-7645-5429-2)

Latin For Dummies
(978-0-7645-5431-5)

Spanish Phrases
For Dummies
(978-0-7645-7204-3)

Spanish Verbs For Dummies
(978-0-471-76872-2)

Hebrew For Dummies
(978-0-7645-5489-6)

MUSIC AND FILM

978-0-7645-9904-0

978-0-7645-2476-9

978-0-7645-5105-5

Also available:

Bass Guitar For Dummies
(978-0-7645-2487-5)

Blues For Dummies
(978-0-7645-5080-5)

Classical Music For Dummies
(978-0-7645-5009-6)

Drums For Dummies
(978-0-471-79411-0)

Jazz For Dummies
(978-0-471-76844-9)

Opera For Dummies
(978-0-7645-5010-2)

Rock Guitar For Dummies
(978-0-7645-5356-1)

Screenwriting For Dummies
(978-0-7645-5486-5)

Songwriting For Dummies
(978-0-7645-5404-9)

Singing For Dummies
(978-0-7645-2475-2)

HEALTH, SPORTS & FITNESS

978-0-7645-7851-9

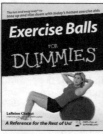

978-0-7645-5623-4

978-0-7645-4233-6

Also available:

Controlling Cholesterol
For Dummies
(978-0-7645-5440-7)

Diabetes For Dummies
(978-0-470-05810-7)

High Blood Pressure
For Dummies
(978-0-7645-5424-7)

Martial Arts For Dummies
(978-0-7645-5358-5)

Menopause FD
(978-0-470-061008)

Pilates For Dummies
(978-0-7645-5397-4)

Weight Training
For Dummies
(978-0-471-76845-6)

Yoga For Dummies
(978-0-7645-5117-8)

FOR DUMMIES®

Helping you expand your horizons and achieve your potential

INTERNET

978-0-470-12174-0

978-0-471-97998-2

978-0-470-08030-6

Also available:

Blogging For Dummies
For Dummies, 2nd Edition
(978-0-470-23017-6)

Building a Web Site For
Dummies, 3rd Edition
(978-0-470-14928-7)

Creating Web Pages
All-in-One Desk Reference
For Dummies, 3rd Edition
(978-0-470-09629-1)

eBay.co.uk
For Dummies
(978-0-7645-7059-9)

Video Blogging FD
(978-0-471-97177-1)

Web Analysis For Dummies
(978-0-470-09824-0)

Web Design For Dummies,
2nd Edition
(978-0-471-78117-2)

DIGITAL MEDIA

978-0-7645-9802-9

978-0-470-17474-6

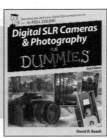

978-0-470-14927-0

Also available:

BlackBerry For Dummies,
2nd Edition
(978-0-470-18079-2)

Digital Photography
All-In-One Desk Reference
For Dummies
(978-0-470-03743-0)

Digital Photo Projects
For Dummies
(978-0-470-12101-6)

iPhone For Dummies
(978-0-470-17469-2)

Photoshop CS3 For Dummies
(978-0-470-11193-2)

Podcasting
For Dummies
(978-0-471-74898-4)

COMPUTER BASICS

978-0-470-13728-4

978-0-470-05432-1

978-0-471-74941-7

Also available:

Macs For Dummies,
9th Edition
(978-0-470-04849-8)

Office 2007 All-in-One Desk
Reference For Dummies
(978-0-471-78279-7)

PCs All-in-One Desk
Reference For Dummies,
4th Edition
(978-0-470-22338-3)

Upgrading & Fixing PCs
For Dummies, 7th Edition
(978-0-470-12102-3)

Windows XP For Dummies,
2nd Edition
(978-0-7645-7326-2)
